Revolutionaries to Race Leaders

Revolutionaries to Race Leaders

Black Power and the Making of African American Politics

CEDRIC JOHNSON

UNIVERSITY OF MINNESOTA PRESS

Minneapolis · London

An earlier version of chapter 4 was previously published as "From Popular Anti-Imperialism to Sectarianism: The African Liberation Support Committee and Black Power Radicals," *New Political Science* 25, no. 4 (December 2003); reprinted with permission from Taylor & Francis.

Published by the University of Minnesota Press
111 Third Avenue South, Suite 290
Minneapolis, MN 55401-2520
http://www.upress.umn.edu

Library of Congress Cataloging-in-Publication Data

Johnson, Cedric, 1971–
   Revolutionaries to race leaders : Black power and the making of African American politics / Cedric Johnson.
        p.   cm.
   Includes bibliographical references and index.
   ISBN 978-0-8166-4477-3 (hc : alk. paper)—ISBN 978-0-8166-4478-0 (pb : alk. paper)—ISBN-10: 0-8166-4477-2 (hc)—ISBN-10: 0-8166-4478-0 (pb)
   1. African Americans—Politics and government—20th century.   2. Black power—United States—History—20th century.   3. Radicalism—United States—History—20th century.   4. African American leadership—History—20th century. 5. African American   political   activists—History—20th   century.   6. African   American intellectuals—History—20th century.   7. Revolutionaries—United States—History—20th century.   8. United States—Race relations—Political aspects—History—20th century.   I. Title.
   E185.615.J59 2007
   322.4089'96073—dc22   2007008264

Printed in the United States of America on acid-free paper

The University of Minnesota is an equal-opportunity educator and employer.

For Lietha Davis and Morris Davis Jr.

Contents

Acknowledgments

This project began as a dissertation at the University of Maryland. I was blessed with an incredibly talented, supportive dissertation committee. Sincerest thanks go to my dissertation chair, Ronald W. Walters, who adamantly supported this project from our earliest conversations. My research benefited immeasurably from his rich, extensive personal history with the civil rights movement and post-segregation black politics. The late Linda Faye Williams shaped this project and my thinking on race and American politics in profound ways. I hope this book would have made her proud. I seriously doubt that I would have completed my graduate studies without the constant support and wisdom of Ollie Johnson. I am also thankful to Clarence Stone, whose graduate course on power, leadership, and social change convinced me that there was room within the discipline of political science to do work that was historically nuanced and politically relevant. Sincerest thanks go to Elsa Barkley-Brown, who shared her many personal experiences and keen insights regarding the National Black Independent Political Party. During my time in College Park, I was blessed with the friendship and community of some incredibly creative and smart people. I am forever grateful to Wendy Smooth, Yusifu Bangura, Tamelyn Tucker-Worgs, Donn Worgs, Adolphus Belk Jr., Tom Ricker, Erika Gordon, Guy E. DeWeever, Avis Jones-DeWeever, Guichard Cadet, Kweku Nuamah, Sekou Franklin, Bernard Moore, Delgreco Wilson, Phyllis Jeffers, Michelle Miller, Reggie Tynes, Ester Carr, Levita Mondie, and Farah Cherry.

At various stages, this research benefited from the insights and assistance of archivists and staff at Howard University's Moorland-Spingarn Research Center, the University of Maryland's McKeldin Library, the University of Rochester's Rush Rhees Library, Hobart and William Smith Colleges' Warren Hunting Smith Library, and Preston Wilcox of AFRAM Associates in Harlem. Paulette Pierce, Yolanda Robinson, Lewis Randolph, and Albert Green graciously opened their homes and private archives to an eager graduate student. I am also indebted to the dozens of movement activists who shared their time and experiences with me in formal and impromptu interviews. During the formative stages of this project, Terry Joiner provided exceptional transcription services and moral support.

This work would not have been possible without the generous financial assistance of many institutions, including the James MacGregor Burns Academy of Leadership and the Committee on Africa and the Americas at the University of Maryland and, most recently, the Office of the Provost at Hobart and William Smith Colleges. I am grateful for the support and advice of my students and colleagues in Hobart and William Smith Colleges' political science department

I am thankful for my year as a postdoctoral fellow at the University of Rochester's Frederick Douglass Institute for African American Studies. The Douglass Institute's Works-in-Progress Seminar provided me with an excellent place to workshop many of these chapters. Fredrick Harris, Valeria Sinclair-Chapman, Jim Johnson, John Michael, Larry Hudson, Cilas Kemedijo, and Dior Konate all provided encouragement, insight, and a stimulating environment. Extra special thanks go to Jesse Moore, who was always willing and able to offer a close reading of my work and generous feedback and to Ghislaine Radegonde-Eison, whose South-of-France hospitality and good conversation made a Southern boy feel at home.

Early drafts of these chapters were presented at various conferences, including the Controlling Bodies, Controlling Spaces (CTRL) conference at McGill University and the Remaking Revolution conference at Hobart and William Smith Colleges. I shared with Benita Roth, Michael West, and William G. Martin an incredibly stimulating and memorable fall afternoon during the Tri-Campus Workshop on Contentious Politics at Binghamton University's Fernand Braudel Center for the Study of Economies, Historical Systems, and Civilizations. I thank all of the participants in these and other forums whose thoughtful questions, barbs, and praise forced me to refine my arguments and stretch in ways I never anticipated.

So many friends, comrades, and acquaintances have given me inspiration and encouragement over the years: Brad Darjean, Duwarn Porter, Eric Chatman, the late Quinn Dickerson, David Canton, Roxana Walker-Canton, Cameron Barron, the late Lisa Y. Sullivan, Phil Davis, Marcus Watts, Zachary Williams, Father Albert J. MacKnight, Reggie Tynes, Craig Rimmerman, Dunbar Moodie, Betty Bayer, Chris Gunn, Thelma Pinto, George Joseph, the late Deborah Tall, David Weiss, Anna Creadick, Jodi Dean, David Ost, Paul Passavant, Lee Quinby, Donna Albro, Kanate Dahouda, Geoffrey Whitehall, Iva Deutchman, DeWayne Lucas, Sherrow Pinder, Lars Toender, Nick Ruth, Robert Andolina, Nic Sammond, Millery Polyne, Niambi Carter, Anthea Butler, Jewel Prestage, William E. Nelson, Ronald Terchek, Ike Okafor Newsum, Dorith Grant-Wisdom, Ernest Wilson, Peniel Joseph, Errol Henderson, Grace Lee Boggs, Willie Legette, and Moriba Karamoko. Our time spent in classrooms, conferences, bar rooms, and cyberspace has made me a better thinker and ultimately a better person. Rochester's labor and progressive activist community has been a constant source of inspiration and grounding. I am especially thankful for the friendship and example of Vincent Serravallo, Jon Garlock, Linda Donahue, Marilyn Anderson, Bill McCoy, Susan Taylor-Brown, Jim Schmidt, Denise Young, Renan Selgado, Mike Roberts, Joseph Hill, Nate Brown, John Vasko, Jason Crane, Franlee Frank, and J. Bediaku Manin.

Stephen Ward, Ollie Johnson, Adolph Reed Jr., Roderick Sias, and Kevin Dunn all took time out of their hectic schedules to read all or part of this manuscript. I truly appreciate their wisdom, bare knuckled criticism, and most of all, their friendship. When this project was first contracted with the University of Minnesota Press, I had the good fortune of working with Carrie Mullen. I am thankful for her early guidance and enthusiasm for this project. Pieter Martin took the book through its final stages with grace and professionalism. I am thankful for his humor, patience, and encouragement during the home stretch. Thanks as well to the editorial assistants who helped to move this project along, Andrea Patch and Jason Weidemann. I am also thankful for the copyediting work of Dennis Troutman and Laura Westlund. I would also like to thank Alex Willingham and Jerry Watts, who served as outside reviewers for my initial prospectus. Your generous comments were just the right dose of critical feedback, honesty, and encouragement needed to christen this project.

My family has been a constant source of inspiration, unconditional love, and support. My mother, Ethel Davis Johnson, helped to finance much of my graduate education and this project through low-interest loans and grants-in-aid. More important, her lifetime commitment to education and social justice helped to plant the seeds of this project some time ago. I am thankful to my sister, Cherida Gary, her husband, LaShawn, and their children, Nigel and Niyah, for providing me with a summer retreat on Detroit's Westside. Thanks to my father, Wadsworth Johnson, for his love, support, and advice. His definition of the golden rule—that is, "the man with the gold makes the rule"—still informs most of what I have to say about American history and politics. My extended family in South Louisiana made it difficult for me to leave the state and even tougher to stay away. Many gracious thanks to Elizabeth White, Kim Sam, Gustavia Payne, Kenneth Davis, Fred Payne, Desmond Payne, Ron Payne, Angie Payne, Charles White, Brittini White, Michelle Scott, and Duane Scott. I also thank my mother-in-law, Deborah Wilson, my niece and nephew, Devin and Alexis Wilson, and my grandmother-in-law, Dovie Hall, for their constant encouragement and love.

I hope that my children, Kimathi, Cabral, and Zora, know that their love, presence, and laughter are as vital to me as air and water. Thank you for reminding me how precious life truly is. My partner Sekile might as well be a coauthor for this book. When we first met at Ohio State University, she somehow endured my early ramblings about Black Power and African American politics. For more than a decade she has continuously supported me through my bouts of bad faith, writing slumps, and fits of self-importance. In turn, I have been continuously awed by her intellect, courage, and humanity.

My maternal grandmother Lietha Davis and my uncle Morris Davis Jr. did not live to see the completion of this book. Their critical spirit fills these pages, nonetheless. Even as they pushed me to avoid a life of toil, both constantly reminded me of the limitations of individualistic success and the basic ethical problem of durable inequality in a land of affluence. I am indebted to my grandmother for my ability to make a good roux and for instilling in me the value of community.

Having spent most of her life under Jim Crow apartheid, she supported my education in every possible way. I will miss our early morning coffee conversations, her mother wit, and sweet manner. My uncle was a brick mason, a rolling stone, and a consummate hell-raiser. My mother's baby brother was more than my uncle—he was my surrogate big brother, roommate, teacher of the ways of the world, and ultimately my muse. With much love and gratitude, this book is for them.

Abbreviations

6PAC	Sixth Pan-African Congress
ALDCC	African Liberation Day Coordinating Committee
ALSC	African Liberation Support Committee
ANC	African National Congress
BPP	Black Panther Party for Self-Defense
BWC	Black Workers Congress
CFUN	Committee for a Unified Newark
CPUSA	Communist Party of the United States of America
CAP	Congress of African Peoples
CORE	Congress of Racial Equality
CBC	Congressional Black Caucus
EXCO	Executive Council of the National Black Political Assembly
FRELIMO	Frente de Libertação de Moçambique (Mozambique Front of Liberation)
GOAL	Group of Advanced Leadership
IBW	Institute of the Black World
IFCO	Interreligious Foundation for Community Organization
MXLU	Malcolm X Liberation University
MPLA	Movimento Popular de Libertação de Angola (The People's Movement of Angolan Liberation)
NOI	Nation of Islam

NAACP	National Association for the Advancement of Colored People
NBIPP	National Black Independent Political Party
NBPA	National Black Political Assembly
NBPC	National Black Political Council
NCPP	National Committee for a People's Politics
NPOC	National Party Organizing Committee
OAAU	Organization of Afro-American Unity
PAC	Pan African Congress
PAIGC	Partido Africano de Independêcia da Guiné e Cabo Verde (African Party for the Independence of Guinea-Bissau and Cape Verde)
SWP	Socialist Workers Party
SWAPO	South West Africa People's Organization
SNCC	Student NonViolent Coordinating Committee
SOBU	Student Organization of Black Unity
UNITA	União Nacional para a Independêcia Total de Angola (National Union for the Total Independence of Angola)
YOBU	Youth Organization of Black Unity
ZANU	Zimbabwe African National Union
ZAPU	Zimbabwe African Peoples Union

Note on Usage

Throughout this book, I use the terms "black" and "African American" interchangeably. I do not capitalize "black" or "white" when they are used as racial descriptors. Such racial markers are not transhistorical, nor are they rooted in some biological essence. Instead, my usage reflects the view that racial identity is the product of historically unique power configurations and material conditions. This view contradicts the literary practice common to much Black Power radicalism, where racial descriptors are capitalized to denote a distinctive, coherent political community and assert an affirmative racial identity. When quoting historical texts, I maintain current usage of the author and preserve the tendency to capitalize racial descriptors that was popular during the Black Power era. Given that this period was one of considerable redefinition with respect to identity among African Americans, the reader will encounter "Negro," "black," and "Black" as well as "Afro-American," "Afrikan," and "African American." I hope my presentation of these different naming practices creates a sense of historical debate and contingency over racial identity.

Introduction
All Power to the People?

The Negro movement represents an *indirect* challenge to
the capitalist status quo not because it is programmatically
anti-capitalist, but because full integration of the Negro in
all levels of American society *is not possible within the present
framework of the American system.*
—*Harold Cruse*

Everybody knows that all the people don't have liberties.
All the people don't have freedom. All the people don't have
justice and all the people don't have power so that means
none of us do. Take this country and change it. Turn it
upside down and put the last first and the first last. Not only
for black people, but for all people.
—*Kathleen Neal Cleaver*

In early June 1966, James Meredith began his March Against
Fear, a 220-mile hike down Highway 51 from Memphis, Tennessee, to
Jackson, Mississippi. This route would take the lone marcher through
some of the most doggedly segregationist counties in the South.
An activist who integrated the University of Mississippi in 1962,
Meredith hoped that this courageous act against one of the last bastions of Jim Crow segregation would inspire others to take progressive
action. On the second day of the march, however, he was shot in an
ambush. Following his shooting, Meredith's procession was taken up
by a mix of activists, including the more moderate, clergy-based wing

of the civil rights movement as personified by Martin Luther King Jr. as well as the Southern Christian Leadership Conference (SCLC) and the younger, more militant cadre of the Congress of Racial Equality (CORE) and the Student Nonviolent Coordinating Committee (SNCC). Although Meredith's injuries were not life threatening, the hegemony of liberal integrationism within the civil rights movement was not so fortunate. The march quickly became the setting where smoldering tensions over strategies and aims ignited.

Along the march route, organizers stopped in towns for momentary respite and public rallies to stimulate voter registration among local blacks. At a stop in Greenwood, SNCC activist Stokely Carmichael was arrested after protesting police orders that prohibited marchers from erecting tents on a local school ground. After he was released on bond, an agitated Carmichael told a rally of some six hundred people that "[t]his is the twenty-seventh time I have been arrested. I ain't going to jail no more." Carmichael then said that because black people had been demanding freedom for years and received little in return, "[w]hat we gonna start saying now is 'Black Power.' "[1] With that speech, Carmichael captured much of the frustration and impatience many activists felt toward the stalled project of liberal integration. More importantly, the phrase Black Power effectively reoriented the terms of black public debate from the task of attaining equal constitutional protection, which framed local struggles against desegregation since the landmark 1954 *Brown* decision, toward the actual seizure of state power.

The demand for Black Power was rooted in the New Nationalist militancy of the late fifties and early sixties. This more northern, metropolitan political tendency developed alongside the southern desegregation campaigns and was stimulated by the anticolonial, 1955 Bandung Conference. Although Malcolm X would become the most iconic figure to emerge from this subculture, other signposts included *Liberator* magazine, the early writings of Harold Cruse and James Boggs, the 1963 Grassroots Leadership Conference in Detroit, and organizations such as On Guard, the Group of Advanced Leadership, the Provisional Committee for Free Africa, the Freedom Now Party, and the San Francisco Bay Area, Afro-American Association. The New Nationalists' sharp criticisms of liberal integration, calls for black self-determination, and anticolonial politics prefigured the tone and aims of Black Power radicalism. In contrast to the New Nationalist militancy of the late fifties and early sixties, many Black Power radicals would take firm stances against interracialism and make more assertive demands for black political autonomy.

Carmichael helped to popularize the Black Power slogan, but others, most notably Richard Wright, predated his usage.[2] The slogan, "Black Power for black people" had been used by SNCC cadre during their Alabama campaigns in 1965. Willie Ricks, a seasoned SNCC activist and adamant black nationalist, promoted the concept in his speeches before the Meredith March. According to historian Clayborne Carson, Ricks was "the first to sense the impact that could be achieved by publicly combining a racial term that previously held negative connotations with a goal that always had been beyond the reach of black people as a group."[3] In a contested election, Carmichael became SNCC chairman in May 1965. SNCC members had initially reelected Alabama native and future Georgia Congressman John Lewis, but pressure from those who desired a more militant representative led to Lewis's resignation and replacement by Carmichael.

Carmichael's election only a few short months after Malcolm X's assassination reflected a deeper ideological shift in SNCC from interracialism and nonviolent direct action toward the politics of racial self-assertion. Born in Port of Spain, Trinidad, and reared in New York City, Carmichael had been a key player in founding the Lowndes County Freedom Organization, an independent political party formed among rural black Alabamans in 1964, which adopted the image of a black panther as its official party symbol. As historian Charles Payne notes, "The shift from the religious Alabaman [Lewis] to the brasher, more eloquent New Yorker also symbolized a shift in the organization's self-presentation."[4] Elevation of Carmichael as a media spokesperson following the Meredith March also marked a departure from the participatory democratic thrust of the southern campaigns toward a leadership-centered politics. Activists within SNCC were growing frustrated with interracial liberalism. In response, many embraced more nationalistic approaches and called for the expulsion of whites from the organization.[5] Carmichael's speech in

Greenwood, the escalating racial militancy that ensued, and the firestorm of media coverage and condemnation it generated among the civil rights establishment effectively christened the Black Power movement. NAACP head Roy Wilkins condemned militant expressions of Black Power as "a reverse Mississippi, a reverse Hitler, a reverse Ku Klux Klan."[6] Major newspapers ran stories equating Black Power with black domination. Such stories stoked the fears of many whites already anxious following major urban rebellions in Harlem and Rochester, New York, in 1964 and the Watts section of Los Angeles in 1965. Whereas mainstream news pundits and moderate civil rights leaders tended to portray Black Power as a dangerous distraction from the goal of liberal integration, the new politics of racial self-assertion attained considerable popularity within black public life during the decade following the Meredith March.

The Black Power movement might best be understood as a historical debate over the character and address of post–Jim Crow race advancement projects rather than the projection of some common political will. The Black Power years were marked by a radical artistic renaissance, fierce political organizing, and vigorous ideological debate. The period was characterized by a vibrant black public sphere composed of a diverse array of bookstores; alternative magazines and underground newspapers; radio and television programs; small local publishing houses; and scores of political organizations, independent schools, study groups, and university-based black/Africana studies departments and research centers. Many activists rallied around the ideal of indigenous control—the seizure of those institutions and resources within black communities. Still, the Black Power movement contained much ideological and regional variation.

Some more moderate renditions of black power sought institutional access as a penultimate goal rather than as a strategy. More radical activists called for the rejection of Western aesthetic standards, solidarity with oppressed peoples in the Third World, and, in some corners, anticapitalist revolution. The period saw the birth of cultural nationalist organizations such as the Black Arts Repertory Theater/ School, Us Organization, Committee for a Unified Newark, Student Organization of Black Unity (later renamed Youth Organization of Black Unity), and Ahidiana; revolutionary black left organizations such as the Black Panther Party for Self-Defense, the Third World Women's Alliance, the League of Revolutionary Black Workers, and the Black Workers Congress; black united front formations such as the Congress of African Peoples, the African Liberation Support Committee (ALSC), and the National Black Political Assembly; mainstream political organizations such as the Congressional Black Caucus and the National Conference of Black Mayors; and politically committed, professional associations such as the National Conference of Black Political Scientists and the National Association of Black Social Workers, among others.[7] This book contributes to the growing body of work on Black Power radicalism by offering a critical interpretation of the conservative political dynamics of this movement and its legacies for contemporary African American politics.

In a most basic sense, this book explores the creation story of post-segregation African American politics. At its core, this study calls into question those modes of political engagement that have become hegemonic within black public life since the late sixties. The evolution of Black Power as a form of ethnic politics limited the parameters of black public action to the formal political world. Insurgent demands for black indigenous control converged with liberal reform initiatives to produce a moderate black political regime and incorporate radical dissent into conventional political channels. In what follows, I examine the winding historical path from the defiant calls for systemic transformation and radical self-governance during the civil rights and Black Power movements toward the consolidation of a more conservative politics predicated on elite entreaty, racial self-help, and incremental social reforms. This book critiques the historical retreat from democratic popular struggles within African American political life and ultimately calls for the renewal of political antagonism.

Although I approach postsegregation African American politics with the "bottom-up" political sensibility of autonomist Marxism and the new labor history, this study focuses deliberately on the middle ground between the powerful and the wider citizenry. I examine that tier of activists, intellectuals, and politicians who at various turns were swept up into the whirlwind of popular opposition alongside workers, students, and the poor and who, ultimately, helped to restore popular consent for America's liberal democratic capitalist system. This account of the historical shift from radical protest to systemic politics seeks to highlight competing social visions and paths not taken.

Black Self-Governance: Radical and Conservative

The New Nationalist militancy of the late fifties and early sixties and the demand for Black Power were powerful antidotes to Cold War liberalism. Black nationalist discourse captured the historical statelessness of African Americans under slavery, debt peonage, and Jim Crow segregation. The Black Power slogan was radical in its allusions to genuine self-determination by African Americans and the achievement of direct democracy in spheres of productive activity beyond formal democratic institutions. The epigrams that announce this introduction capture the most democratic edges of sixties black radicalism. In the aftermath of the 1963 March on Washington, former Communist Party member and black nationalist intellectual Harold Cruse concluded that liberal reform was not enough to achieve social justice. The full integration of African Americans was, he argued, "not possible within the present framework of the American system." Although major civil rights reforms enacted by the Johnson administration ensured basic citizenship rights, such changes did not overturn the power alignments and racist cultural assumptions that governed everyday life. Likewise, although desegregation ensured greater consumer choice, the fundamental property relations that reproduced inequality were left intact. For many Black Power radicals, such as the Black Panther Party's Kathleen N. Cleaver, revolutionary transformation was needed to achieve true democracy. Through social struggle, activists might achieve a kind of secular redistribution of power, wealth, and freedom, which would, to paraphrase the Gospel of St. Matthew, "put the last first and the first last."

The slogan "All Power to the People," like its political kin "Black Power," spoke simultaneously of the possibility of universal democracy and the historical reality of inequality and exclusion. Though the former phrase is most often associated with the Black Panther Party for Self-Defense, it was adopted and taken up by other black radicals and antiwar activists. In many respects, the desire for more meaningful political power and more genuine democratic existence conveyed in these slogans embodies the most radical promise of the sixties writ large. Much of the ambiguity inherent in these slogans is rooted in the contradictory meaning of "people" in European languages. As Italian philosopher Giorgio Agamben notes, this term always names "the constitutive political subject as well as the class that is excluded—de facto, if not de jure—from politics."[8] Agamben continues:

> What we call people was actually not a unitary subject but rather a dialectical oscillation between two opposite poles: on the one hand, the *People* as a whole and as an integral body politic and on the other hand, the *people* as a subset and as a fragmentary multiplicity of needy and excluded bodies; on the one hand, an inclusive concept that pretends to be without reminder while on the other hand, an exclusive concept known to afford no hope; at one pole, the total state of the sovereign and integrated citizens and at the other pole, the banishment—either court of miracles or camp—of the wretched, the oppressed and the vanquished

This book explores manifestations of this "dialectical oscillation" within black power discourse between "the People" as a potential universal democratic subject and "the people" as the object of governance. Whereas the phrase "Black Power" conjured up the possibility of a revolutionary reckoning in American society, the actual conversion of movement activism into an elite-driven, black ethnic politics from the late sixties onward negated that radical promise.

Essentially, this is a study of the achievement of ideological consent rather than an account of co-optation. Instead of focusing on the incorporation of black political elites, I examine the assimilation of ruling ideas within postsegregation black political culture. Through an examination of key intellectual figures such as Cruse and Amiri Baraka and umbrella organizations such as the 1972 National Black Political Convention, ALSC, the National Black Political Assembly, and the National Black Independent Political Party (NBIPP), this book attempts to expose certain internal contradictions of Black

Power radicalism. In these specific cases, I illustrate how Black Power politics was shaped by prevailing discourses on power, race/ethnicity, and governance and, in turn, how African American activists, intellectuals, artists, and politicians altered the American political landscape.

The pacification of radical dissent resulted from the interplay of Black Power political demands and social management dynamics under late capitalism. Though less dramatic than those instances of state repression of Black Power radicals, softer forms of social management were more pervasive and lasting in their effects. The development of African American politics during the Black Power era was shaped by those technologies of citizenship, promoted through major civil rights reforms. Technologies of citizenship are defined by Barbara Cruikshank as "discourses, programs and other tactics aimed at making individuals politically active and capable of self-government."[9] She adds that these technologies are "modes of constituting and regulating citizens: that is, strategies for governing the very subjects whose problems they seek to redress—the powerless, the apathetic or those at risk."[10] Political elites, the intelligentsia, and community activists formed a crucial linchpin in the success of this social management strategy. In the wake of civil rights mobilization and urban riots, a wide range of governmental initiatives—including War on Poverty thrusts such as the Community Action Program, Legal Services, Volunteers in Service to America (VISTA), Head Start and Job Corps, as well as the 1966 Demonstration Cities legislation (Model Cities)—mobilized certain sectors of local black communities around a moderate form of political subjectivity that was amenable to system preservation.

The Johnson administration's War on Poverty initiatives served to recruit future black officials and facilitate their socialization into the world of public administration.[11] The 1964 Economic Opportunity Act (EOA) mandated that local community action programs designed to combat poverty elicit the "maximum feasible participation" of the urban poor "so as to best stimulate and take full advantage of capabilities for self-advancement and assure that those programs and projects are otherwise meaningful to and widely utilized by their intended beneficiaries."[12] Although EOA-derived community action programs were roundly criticized by various political camps that questioned their capacity to reduce poverty, the long-term political impact of these programs on black civic culture was significant. In 1969, former Johnson aide Daniel Patrick Moynihan predicted that

> Very possibly, the most important long run impact of the community action programs of the 1960s will prove to have been the formation of an urban Negro leadership echelon at just the time when the Negro masses and other minorities were verging toward extensive commitments to urban politics. Tammany at its best (or worse) would have envied the political apprenticeship provided the neighborhood coordinators of the antipoverty program.[13]

In his assessment of the War on Poverty and black leadership development, Peter Eisinger contends that "community action agencies provided highly visible settings in which people traditionally excluded from responsible public positions could gain political and administrative experience as well as public reputations."[14] Such state maneuvers were intended to corral dissident forces and stave off the so-called "crisis of governability."[15]

Notions of Black Power that conformed to prevailing ideas about ethnic pluralism gained ground in the years after the Meredith March.[16] The wave of racial fear and mainstream denunciation that followed the initial cry for Black Power gave their writings an air of controversy, but at its core, Carmichael and Charles V. Hamilton's 1967 book *Black Power: The Politics of Liberation in America* was essentially a reassertion of conventional ethnic group politics.[17] The authors contend that "[b]efore a group can enter the open society, it must first close ranks" and that "group solidarity is necessary before a group can operate effectively from a bargaining position of strength in a pluralistic society."[18] Referring to the history of white ethnics, Carmichael and Hamilton conclude that the ethnic paradigm is "a central fact of the American political system." Their discussion of pervasive, institutional racism and the futility of interracial coalition politics further legitimized the view that ethnic politics is the only viable alternative available to African Americans. In a rhetorical strategy central to much Black Power discourse, the authors allude to the back-drop of urban rebellion and potential for more devastating insurrection in the future as leverage for reformist demands.[19] This formulation of postsegregation black ethnic politics is reflected in much of the *New Black Politics* literature, which preoccupied scores of social scientists from the Black Power movement onward.[20]

During the seventies and eighties, the New Black Politics scholarship analyzed black political integration. This literature sheds light on various technical dimensions of black political incorporation, including electoral politics, party competition, bureaucratic administration, presidential politics, and policy-making at the municipal, state, and national level.[21] Such works are generally foregrounded in Black Power notions of politics that treat racial affinity and political interests as synonyms. Much of this work has operated from the assumption that black politicos are "fulfilling the legacy of Black Power" to use Ronald Walters' formative assessment.[22] In a similar vein, Martin Kilson confidently concluded that the new black political elite's proletarian origins would ensure "a certain perception of and empathy with the special material and psychological needs of the black lower strata and, thus, perhaps a capacity to articulate these needs in a manner reasonably satisfactory to wide segments of the lower strata."[23] In his recent defense of black political unity, Tommie Shelby speaks of the "seemingly involuntary readiness of most blacks to act individually and collectively to protect black people from harm and injustice."[24] Such writing most often assumes some coherent, transhistorical black interests in advance. These arguments tend to flatten class contradictions within the black population and minimize the presence of transracial organizations and forms of political community, for example, neighborhood associations, local political parties, unions. Consequentially, the inherently contentious nature of endogenous black politics—its color caste, ideological, class, gender, institutional, regional, and other dynamics—is ignored. As Adolph Reed Jr. notes, many scholars treat the black population as a "corporate political entity" and project the rhetoric and programs of black political elites as those of African Americans writ large.[25] In what follows, I approach black political life in a more discerning fashion. Indeed, the various organizations and political tendencies I examine make it difficult to hold onto claims of normative black interests. Instead, the African American population should be seen at any given historical moment as an ensemble of shifting and contradictory constituencies. I also attempt to illuminate the presence of class projects within the various agendas; organizational forms; and strategies proposed by activists, intellectuals, and politicos of divergent ideological camps. I try to unpack notions of race unity and race leadership, which are sedimented and naturalized within postsegregation black public discourse.

Robert C. Smith's pathbreaking analysis of black political integration stands out for his willingness to confront the limitations of systemic politics. He does not treat the shift from "protest to politics" as a "natural evolution," as Bayard Rustin claimed in his celebrated 1965 *Commentary* essay. Instead, in his 1996 book, *We Have No Leaders*, Smith offers a damning assessment of black political elites' departures from the egalitarian demands and disruptive tactics of the fifties and the sixties.[26] Although he is certainly sensitive to the different meanings that political integration carried for the black poor and working class and critical of the strategic choices made by contemporary black leaders, he does not offer a sustained, critical challenge to the leadership category itself. Smith appears to accept the idea that black politicos and civil rights leaders are the legitimate arbiters of African American political interests. Proceeding from the assumptions of ethnic pluralism, Smith contends that elected officials, leaders of major civil rights organizations, and clergy need to be more responsive to the most impoverished and marginalized segments of the black population.[27]

I have no quarrel with the basic ethical stance on democratic accountability implied in such criticisms of mainstream liberal black leadership. Contrary to this popular line of argument, however, this study does not merely call for a more accountable black leadership. I am more sympathetic to Frances Fox Piven and Richard Cloward's legendary defense of movement politics as the most effective means available to marginalized, poor, and working-class people to realize their historical will, but I am also well aware that social movements involve a diverse orchestra of social forces that includes progressive elites and powerful institutions as well as ordinary people. As the postwar southern desegregation campaigns clearly illustrated, middle-class leaders have—at certain historical junctures—been central to the development of popular, democratic movements. The object of critique in this work is not social status, but rather the complex of ideology that justifies material and political inequalities. The following chapters retrace and critique the acclimation of African American political life from demands for revolution and genuine self-governance toward systemic politics.

Part I, "Black Power and African American Politics," explores the ideological origins of Black Power radicalism within the New Nationalist subculture of the late fifties and early sixties. Chapters 1 and 2 examine Black Power militancy's convergence with ethnic pluralism through the activism and writings of Cruse and Amiri Baraka (LeRoi Jones). I chose these two figures because their individual stories reflect so much of the wider historical dynamics. In other words, Cruse and Baraka—like other individuals and organizations addressed here—are treated as holographic figures, luminaries whose individual achievements only make sense against the interference of larger historical developments. Cruse's fearless, critical intellectual work challenged Cold War American liberal and Marxist left orthodoxies and asserted the need for black autonomy and the importance of cultural politics in the age of mass communication. Baraka, on the other hand, shaped black political culture during the period through his artistry and efforts to operationalize Black Power via the construction of local and national political institutions. By retracing the political development of these two figures, I attempt to accomplish a few things.

First, I illuminate the context of pre–Black Power African American radicalism and contend that before 1965 such militant tendencies within and beyond the civil rights movement were more socially flexible and, more importantly, were directed at the transformation of cultural norms *and* political-economy. Second, I explore how ethnic pluralist assumptions about political activity were promoted within African American life around the mid-sixties. Third, I offer a critique of the vanguardism inherent in both men's writing and activism. Cruse and Baraka came to articulate an approach to political action that privileged elite brokerage. Although I laud the staunch ethico-political commitment implied in their embrace of vanguard politics and their willingness to "take the lead," this political orientation ultimately led away from the development of viable, popular opposition and served to legitimate the emerging regime of race-relations management. To the extent that I focus on the sources of radical decline, this study is written against the grain of the prevailing vindicationist trend in the literature on Black Power radicalism.

The Good Sixties, the Bad Sixties, and the Ends of History

The memory of Black Power and sixties radicalism has undoubtedly taken a beating at the hands of pop cultural interlocutors, neoconservatives, and liberal revisionists. In a perceptive analysis of how the culture industry capitalized on Black Power militancy, Cedric J. Robinson argues that blaxploitation cinema was, in fact, a corrupted cinema which degraded black actors and writers and subjected audiences to "a mockery of the aspirations of Black liberationists."[28] This consumer niche evolved in response to period debates over revolutionary black aesthetics, the opening up of public leisure space following the death of Jim Crow, and the gradual expansion of the black consumer public during the seventies. Local struggles in Newark; Oakland; Houston; Atlanta; Cairo, Illinois; and elsewhere provided the inspiration and raw material for blaxploitation cinema. Some films engaged in the direct copycatting of Black Power personalities such as the Angela Davis–look-alike heroines played most notably by Pam Grier (*Foxy Brown*, 1974; *Friday Foster*, 1974; and *Sheba, Baby*, 1975) and Rosalind Cash (*The Omega Man*, 1971, and *Melinda*, 1972) but also by Tamara Dobson (*Cleopatra Jones*, 1973) and Teresa Graves (*Get Christy Love*, 1975). As Robinson notes, blaxploitation cinema transmutated revolutionary politics into simplistic plot narratives that most often culminated in acts of revenge against a white crime boss. Other mainstream representations of Black Power radicalism range from comical renditions to veiled ideological assaults. In many of these portrayals, black radicals are painted as charlatans and criminals. Such popular representations of Black Power have endured well beyond the blaxploitation era.

Much pop cultural imagery of Black Power radicalism reinforces the conservative characterization of radicalism as the folly of youth.

Criticism of racist historiography, capitalism, imperialism, and other subjects of radical ire were repackaged as boyish curiosity and adolescent defiance in the character of Michael Evans on Norman Lear's hit situation comedy *Good Times*. Likewise, Lamont Sanford's short-lived embrace of the name "Kalunda" and a pseudo-African lifestyle on the 1970s' television show *Sanford and Son* satirized Black Power cultural politics as a passing, superficial phase. Additionally, the more subtle, yet equally damaging, "angry black" stereotype has become a routine fixture in African American–directed and produced films. As a prominent trope in U.S. mass media, the "angry black" invalidates discontent as a legitimate human expression while reducing politicized race consciousness to emotionalism. "Kalinga," the hypocritical militant in Keenan Ivory Wayan's *I'm Gonna Get You Sucka* (1988), and the radical minstrelsy of Chris Rock's "Nat X," on the late-night television show *Saturday Night Live,* are more contemporary descendants of this trend. The bold analysis of the U.S. racial order inherent in much Black Power rhetoric has been reinvented as racial paranoia in contemporary popular discourse. Those who criticize racial domination or white privilege provide comic relief as political misfits—relics of a bygone era. Other films reinvented Black Power to fit neoconservative politics.

Tom Hanks's hugely successful 1994 film *Forrest Gump* followed the life of a clueless but virtuous baby boomer as he rambles through some of the most significant political events of the postwar era. As Jennifer Hyland Wang notes, through its revision of sixties political history, the film abetted the Republican Revolution's war against the memory of sixties counterculture and campaign for congressional dominance.[29] Perhaps the film's neoconservative revisionist project is best summed up in the line where Hanks's affable protagonist relies on mother wit to make sense of a complicated world: "My momma always said you got to put the past behind you before you can move on."[30] With respect to American racial politics during the sixties, the film juxtaposes two archetypal black characters: Bubba, Forrest's best friend who dies in his arms in Vietnam; and a band of snarling, heavily armed, roguish Panthers. As Thomas Byers notes, "the good Black man is the soft spoken, apolitical friend to whites who dies for America; the bad ones are the violent loudmouths who refuse to do this, and whose opposition is coded as criminality."[31]

never heard this take b4!

Spike Lee's 1992 biopic *Malcolm X* and Melvin and Mario Van Peebles's 1995 film *Panther* offered a more sympathetic, but no less problematic, reminiscence of Black Power.[32] Although such films helped incite greater public discussion about sixties black radicalism, both films drew sharp criticism from some historians and Black Power veterans. In their focus on telegenic figures, each of these films endorses a powerful but problematic faith in social change through messianic politics. Most importantly, each film offered only tangential appreciation of either the historical Black Panther Party or Malcolm X's engagement with left democratic politics, with Van Peebles and Lee choosing instead to highlight notions of racial uplift and personal rehabilitation emergent from sixties radicalism that resonated with the neoconservative tenor of the Clinton era. Such unflattering pop representations of Black Power are buttressed by a broader stream of reactionary intellectual appraisals of sixties opposition.[33]

The racial hysteria and scapegoating that followed the sixties urban rebellions and demands for Black Power found respectable expression in the neoconservative rhetoric which gained popularity during the late seventies. Pop social theory of the Reagan era featured articulate whining about the "destructive" character of sixties radicalism and the loss of traditional American values. These texts merely inscribed in an academic language the fears and reactions to sixties counterculture, expressed decades earlier by the pioneers of the New Right. Best sellers such as Robert Bork's *Slouching Towards Gomorrah* and Allan Bloom's *The Closing of the American Mind* hoisted up an idyllic portrait of the postwar years as the golden age of modern American civilization—a world populated by God-fearing families; hardworking fathers; nurturing, domesticated mothers; disciplined, respectful children; and close-knit, homogenous neighborhoods, all held together by strong civic virtue and deep patriotic fervor. In the eyes of conservative pundits, the sixties were a time of libidinal excess and bacchanalian disrespect for authority. To say the least, these Reaganite impressions of postwar American history more closely resembled fifties sitcoms than social reality. The fifties were no lost social paradise. Rather, many of the problems that conservatives attribute to urban decline, liberal media, and the sexual revolution— teen pregnancy, marital infidelity, domestic violence, child abuse, property crime, and poverty—were present in the post–World War II period.[34]

The resurgence of public and academic interest in Black Power during the early nineties was framed and shaped by the end of the Cold War and these ongoing neoconservative efforts to bury the memory of sixties radicalism via the "culture wars." With the collapse of the Soviet Union and the dramatic student protests for liberal democratic reform in China's Tiananmen Square, neoconservative thinkers such as Francis Fukuyama prematurely announced the "end of history" and the final defeat of anticapitalist social struggles.[35] Contemporary intellectual efforts to recover Black Power radicalism have been provoked and influenced by decades of slander of the sixties and its legacies. Neoconservatives' diligent mischaracterizations of the origins, depth, and substance of sixties radicalism and the egalitarian visions it promoted served both to demonize left intellectuals, blacks, the poor, women, and youth—typically encoded as "special interests" in conservative parlance since the Reagan era—and to amass greater public support for the punitive social policy, fiscal conservatism, and privatization, central to the New Right's agenda. Much of the writing on Black Power that emerged during the late nineties attempts to vindicate sixties radical politics against its various critics and misrepresentations.

Many contend that their works aim to dispel the "good/bad sixties" dichotomy, which contrasts the heroic, nonviolent demonstrations against Jim Crow that flourished between the 1954 *Brown* decision and the 1965 Watts uprising, with the downward spiral of identity politics, open advocacy of armed rebellion, and sectarianism that followed the turn to Black Power.[36] This interpretative tendency is often attributed to the writings of New Left activists, such as Students for a Democratic Society veterans Todd Gitlin and Tom Hayden.[37] Under the good sixties/bad sixties narrative, Black Power is presented as "the 'evil twin' that wrecked civil rights," according to historian Peniel Joseph.[38] In his study of the New Communist Movement of the seventies, Max Elbaum contends that the bad sixties narrative

bolsters complacency masked by maturity by underestimating how profoundly periods of intense conflict can alter people's conception of what is possible and desirable. And it leads to the shortsighted politics of declaring out-of-bounds by definition any project that takes seriously the possibility of building a strong radical movement anchored in antiracism and solidarity with the Third World.[39]

In a comparable fashion, Nikhil Pal Singh contends that the bad sixties narrative implies that "meaningful social struggles must necessarily aspire to some form of hegemonic address."[40] The reparative works of Joseph, Elbaum, Singh, and others offer important counternarratives to the popular and conservative reinventions of Black Power noted above.

Efforts to rebut the good/bad sixties narrative have yielded much more fine-grained accounts of sixties and seventies black radicalism. Collectively, this body of scholarship has created a much more nuanced understanding of this movement's geographic, political, and ideological parameters. Given the mainstream smearing of Black Power radicalism, the efforts of historians to "set the record straight," dispel faulty historical accounts, and celebrate the neglected achievements of radical activists are understandable and, up to a point, warranted. Although I am certainly sympathetic to the political motivations behind the valorization of Black Power radicalism, uncritical celebration carries its own negative rewards.

The neoconservative ideological campaign to bury the memory of sixties black radicalism has had the effect of stalling the development of a critical orientation in the reparative literature on Black Power. Much of the focus on Gitlin's criticisms of identity politics has overshadowed his perceptive work on sixties radicalism and mass media. Consequentially, some of Gitlin's detractors have reduced him to a detestable caricature of New Left politics. Likewise, the charge of Eurocentric bias in good/bad sixties narratives is often underwritten by territorial knowledge claims and, ironically, silences those black and female critics *within* Black Power organizations and, more generally, black public life. Many activists publicly decried the retreats from purposive political action to ideological education, from participatory democratic formats to cults of personality, and from interracialism to ethnic politics. Ruby Doris Robinson, Martin Luther King Jr., Phil

Hutchings, Gwendolyn Patton, Julius Hobson, Rustin, and many others spoke out against prevailing orthodoxies within Black Power discourse. In the following chapters, I attempt to shed light on the lively internal debates that characterized the era. Such critical voices problematize any effort to vindicate sixties and seventies black radicalism against the "white left."

Although right-wing intellectuals have attempted to discredit sixties radicalism, with some exceptions, progressive and radical intellectuals on both sides of the veil have only begun to grapple with the sundry contradictions of the Black Power movement. The contemporary tendency to shrink from critical analysis of Black Power radicalism is especially ironic since this political movement emerged from energetic and often rowdy debates over the nature of racial inequality and the strategic aims and organizational forms that might effectively guide black political struggles. Some historians have minimized the need to wrestle with questions of failure. Robin Kelley writes that "too often our standards for evaluating social movements pivot around whether or not they 'succeeded' in realizing their visions rather than on the merits or power of the visions themselves."[41] In a similar vein, Joseph characterizes the critical literature on Black Power as being overly invested in the "archeology of failure."[42] I agree that there is need to leaven good sixties/bad sixties narratives with explorations of how social struggles evolved into the seventies and eighties. In fact, Chapter 5 of this book explores the National Black Political Assembly and NBIPP, two organizations that attempted to carve out a space for an autonomous black politics during the Carter and Reagan years. Even if we acknowledge the fact of movement successes and continuity, the reality of diminishing influence and popular resonance among radical forces remains. Black political activism during the closing decades of the twentieth century was not comparable to that of the civil rights and Black Power eras, in scope, amplitude, and actual political impact. The social fluidity, disruptive politics, and idealism that characterized the civil rights and black radical political tendencies of the fifties and the sixties dissipated as movement energies were channeled toward conventional pluralist politics.

This fact of movement decline and, to a point, failure must be addressed for its scholarly and political ramifications. From a basic scholarly standpoint, I do not see how our knowledge of sixties social struggles and their legacies for African American culture and politics can advance without subjecting that period's many personalities, organizations, and events to generous critical appraisal. And while this study does not pretend that sixties radicalism can be adapted slavishly to contemporary times, the prospects for developing viable opposition hinge on how well intellectuals and activists understand the historical processes that created our current political conditions. This book explores the Black Power movement as part of a historical cycle of struggle that achieved certain advances only to produce new contradictions.

This interpretation of the Black Power movement and its impact on the development of African American politics after segregation is guided by W. E. B. Du Bois' preparatory remarks for readers of *Black Reconstruction in America* (1935), his incomparable history of America's first experiment in racial democracy.[43] Writing at the height of Jim Crow segregation, Du Bois warned that he did not pen this history for those who regarded African Americans as "a distinctly inferior creation," incapable of self-governance. Therefore, he avoids draining his intellectual energy defending the basic fact of black humanity. The black social struggles of the sixties and seventies should be approached with the same attitude. That is to say, such history should be written as though African Americans were "ordinary human beings" capable of the same graft, heroism, tyranny, altruism, failures, and triumphs as all others. This study moves beyond those treatments that either demonize or vindicate black radical politics.

Whereas Part I explores the intellectual and social foundations of contemporary black ethnic politics, Part II, "Racial Technocrats, Democratic Struggles," examines the increasing organizational and strategic capitulation of radical forces to the terms of the liberal democratic political order. I examine a range of united front formations, which emerged from Black Power organizing. Given their cadre format and the thousands of activists, politicians, and citizens they engaged, these organizations represent ideal cases for comprehending the possibilities and limitations represented in Black Power politics. Chapter 3 revisits the historic 1972 National Black Political Convention held in Gary, Indiana. This event is often recalled as the pinnacle of Black Power activism and as an event that stimulated a wave of local black electoral mobilization during the seventies. In Chapter 3, I challenge the flawed assumption that racial unity is a prerequisite to addressing contemporary racial inequality. Although the 1972 Gary convention possessed the mystique of movement-styled politics, this event was an attempt to bureaucratize racial unity and, therefore, represented a departure from popular mobilization. Moreover, organizers operated from the problematic view that discernable differences of ideology among blacks were incidental to a presumably more fundamental, common racial interest.

Chapters 4 and 5 explore ALSC, the National Black Political Assembly, and NBIPP. I argue that these organizations partially conformed to a technocratic style of politics that gained ground among blacks during the seventies. These organizations helped to preserve a set of radical democratic ideals through their programmatic statements, but each eventually abandoned movement building for a form of elite politics. Chapter 4 critically examines the popular mobilizations conducted by ALSC activists and the organization's ultimate descent into sectarianism. Through the African Liberation Day mobilizations of the early seventies, ALSC activists sought to assist democratic struggles against Portuguese colonialism and white-settler rule in Southern Africa. ALSC activists crafted a popular anti-imperialism that drew support from blacks throughout the United States, Canada, and the Caribbean. Chapter 4 also identifies the sources of ALSC's demise and develops the claim that the conversion of many activists from nationalism to Marxist–Leninism stemmed from certain limitations of race-first politics. This turn to "scientific socialism" was progressive as it encouraged more critical perspectives of capital. However, inasmuch as radical activists fetishized Marxism, they departed from the intellectual and political spirit of materialist critique. Some radicals became convinced that doctrinaire ideology—and not historically discrete public issues—should serve as the basis for political work. This was an essentially flawed and counterproductive strategy. The mid-seventies' Marxist–Nationalist debate marked a tragic retreat from the powerful issue-driven alliances of the African Liberation Day mobilizations.

Chapter 5 examines the history of the National Black Assembly and its offshoot, NBIPP. Despite the heroic efforts of many activists, the Assembly and NBIPP fell short of developing effective political strategies that might mobilize broad constituencies and advance progressive politics. Generally, both the Assembly and NBIPP preserved the core progressive ideals that characterized much of Black Power radicalism. Likewise, each organization made commendable efforts to reform gender inequality within its ranks and forge a more cosmopolitan radical politics. However, the strategic choices and organizational priorities that characterized the Assembly during the late seventies suggest that even the radical cadre accepted the strategic turn from "protest to politics" and abandoned popular struggle as a means to pursue social justice ends. Although these organizations maintained a progressive face, activists adhered to a muted form of elite politics that privileged conventional political activities over the mobilization of constituencies outside radical circles.

In conclusion, I argue that black ethnic politics has run its course as an effective means to confront inequality. As well, I argue that the aims and forms of contemporary black public life must become more radically democratic. My closing arguments run counter to those who defend the strategic value of black identity politics. Given the presence of so many forces arrayed against the egalitarian legacies of the civil rights movement, it is not surprising that the "circle the wagons" sentiment would be in vogue in black public debate at the start of the twenty-first century. Nonetheless, American racial politics have become logarithmically more complex in the past four decades. The style of identity politics that grew out of the Black Power movement has not kept pace with such changes. Class inequality within the African American population has sharpened. Fresh waves of immigration, most notably from Mexico and Central America, have altered the color and dialect of American neighborhoods and workplaces. As well, in the post–September 11 world, anxieties over terrorism and economic insecurity have spawned new forms of xenophobia among native-born Americans—blacks and whites alike. Race certainly still matters, but not in the old Jim Crow ways. Consequentially, struggles *agree or no?*

against contemporary inequalities cannot be won primarily through race-first politics. This mode of political action may still retain a certain emotive power for its proponents, but it is inadequate as an antidote to hierarchy and exploitation. Instead, I argue for the instigation of popular, democratic struggles that are shaped by the everyday concerns and interests of working people and seek to transcend the culture and institutions of neoliberal capitalism.

PART I

BLACK POWER AND AFRICAN AMERICAN POLITICS

The "Negro Revolution" and Cold War America

Revolutionary Politics and Racial Conservatism in the Work of Harold Cruse

Labor cannot emancipate itself in the white skin where in the black it is branded.
—*Karl Marx, Das Kapital*

Hence we have the most unprecedented situation yet seen in the Western World—a Marxist movement with a time honored social theory which does not work out in life with a mass following, and a viable Negro movement of masses in movement which is stymied because it has no social theory or program to take it further.
—*Harold Cruse, "Marxism and the Negro"*

In his 1968 *New York Review of Books* essay on Harold Cruse's *The Crisis of the Negro Intellectual* and a handful of other relevant books on Black Power, Christopher Lasch asserted that "When all the manifestoes and polemics of the Sixties are forgotten, this book will survive as a monument of historical analysis—a notable contribution to understanding the American past."[1] Lasch was only partially right. Cruse's work had a profound impact on African American public debate during the sixties and beyond, but not as a "monument of historical analysis." Instead, his highly polemical reading of twentieth-century

African American political and intellectual development and defense of black cultural nationalist politics inspired heated debate and intense reconsiderations of liberal and revolutionary left politics. This was very much his desired effect. Cruse was well aware of the wages of radical criticism, styling himself as "a critical kamikaze fighter on the cultural front."[2] Moreover, he described his 1967 landmark work *The Crisis of the Negro Intellectual* as "premeditatively controversial." Once the smoke had cleared following its initial publication, Cruse confessed, "I quite naturally anticipated that I would be in for some rather heated counterattack from even certain Blacks (and whites) who were not mentioned in my protracted polemic. . . . I reiterate—this critical assault on Black social, political and cultural thought was premeditated. It was my conviction that Black social thought of all varieties was in dire need of some ultra-radical overhauling if it was to meet the comprehensive test imposed by the Sixties."[3] In March 2005, Cruse died quietly of heart failure at an assisted living home in Ann Arbor, Michigan. His popularity within African American public life had long since faded, but his critical spirit continued to haunt African American political thought and practice.[4] This chapter approaches Cruse's intellectual corpus and, in particular, his most well-known work, *The Crisis of the Negro Intellectual,* as an ideological cornerstone of postsegregation black politics.

The first part of this chapter situates Cruse's intellectual project within the context of post–World War II challenges to certain Marxist orthodoxies. Essentially, I contend that Cruse's writings during the sixties should be read as central to the evolution of the New Left despite his efforts to disassociate from the "black New Left" in *The Crisis of the Negro Intellectual*. Like Herbert Marcuse, James Boggs, and many others during the sixties, Cruse attempted to rethink conventional notions of radical subjectivity inherited from Old Left officialdom. Assessing the political climate of the postwar era, Cruse concluded that industrial workers were no longer the central protagonists of historical revolution. Instead, he privileged the role of colonized peoples—with blacks as America's domestic colony—in social transformation. Here I also explore Cruse's discussions of cultural revolution and his claims regarding the vanguard role of black intellectuals in light of the political decline of the mass worker.

The concluding sections take issue with certain core features of Cruse's radical theory. I engage more recent critics of Cruse who identify a pattern of increasing conservatism between Cruse's formative political essays with *Liberator* magazine and the publication of *The Crisis of the Negro Intellectual*. While I agree with the generic trajectory these authors identify and the unfortunate coziness Cruse's later writings find within the Cold War milieu, I challenge their equation of his theory with a variant of American exceptionalism. His abandonment of the colonial analogy most likely stemmed from his characteristic suspicion of "foreign ideologies" and revolutionary templates. At times, this interpretive tendency takes on nativist hues in his work, but ultimately it derives from his residual Marxist sensibilities. In their efforts to identify his shift away from left internationalism, such critics may miss Cruse's faith in materialist critique.

Although *The Crisis of the Negro Intellectual* and other influential essays such as "Revolutionary Nationalism and the Afro-American" became canonical texts within the seventies black nationalist discourse and were often deployed to justify anti-left politics, at its core Cruse's writings remained engaged with the Marxist tradition in meaningful ways. His intellectual style was no doubt influenced by Karl Marx's insistence on "ruthless criticism of everything existing." Marx asserted that such criticism "must not be afraid of its own conclusions, nor of conflict with the powers that be."[5] Despite his anti-communism, the ghost of Cruse's Marxist past reemerges in both his approach to the study of American life and culture and, perhaps more importantly, in his incomplete attempts to think through the possibility of developing a transformative left politics unique to American soil. Although latter-day critics most often dismiss the Marxist tradition as "totalizing" social theory, Marx's actual writings reflected a keen sensitivity to the uniqueness of local conditions.

In what follows, I attempt to disentangle the progressive critique of *society as it exists* that shapes Cruse's most delicious insights about American society from the conservative logic that informs his turn to black cultural nationalism. The promise of Cruse's social criticism was ultimately undermined by a racialized notion of culture that stood outside of political economy. His efforts to vindicate black cultural authenticity negated his critique of the ideological and material dimensions of African American life. At various moments, Cruse perceptively identified key class antagonisms among African Americans only to minimize their political import through the articulation of a cultural nationalist politics, which reduces such internal, organic dissension into a fictive political singularity. His turn to black nationalism/ethnic pluralism was an unfortunate development and might be understood in retrospect as a strategic concession emerging from his fatalistic view of postwar American politics. Cruse tabled the prospect for an American popular movement toward socialism and, instead, promoted a racially assertive, elite pragmatism. His politics fell prey to his own defeatist reading of black political development and that of American democratic struggles more generally.

Harold Cruse, the Cold War, and the Crisis of the American Left

Although Cruse is most readily remembered as a progenitor of black/Africana studies, his strident cultural nationalist politics have perhaps undermined substantial acknowledgment of his wider contributions to American political thinking. Cruse's intellectual project emerges within and against Marxist theory. He was not alone in his struggles with orthodox Marxism. Cruse's project evolved with the historical grain of the New Left and Cold War efforts to rethink class formation and the strategies and organizational forms that might support a viable transformative left politics. Like the writings of Betty Friedan, C. Wright Mills, Marcuse, Grace Lee, James Boggs, and many other American leftist contemporaries, Cruse's writings during the late fifties and sixties should be understood as an effort to reinvent American radicalism in light of the rise of Stalinism, the spread of Cold War social conformity in the United States, the emergence of the southern civil rights movement and Bandung era anticolonial struggles abroad, and the apparent failure of revolutionary formulae articulated by American left intellectuals during the prewar period.[6] At the heart of this crisis was the foundational stature of the mass worker within the Marxist tradition.

The revolutionary potential of the American mass worker was dashed by the advent of the consumer society. The Taylorization of work and regimentation of mass production in Europe and North America at the close of the nineteenth century helped to break the power of craft labor and yet simultaneously created a dangerous new situation for capital. The new social and economic conditions accompanying Fordism—spatial concentration of production, rapid urbanization, deskilling, and the accelerated pace of work under mechanized assembly lines—stimulated increased worker solidarity and the evolution of new tactics and forms of organization. Worker rebellion took the form of wildcat strikes, walkouts, factory takeovers, and work slowdowns. Such militancy precipitated the institutionalization of capital–labor conflicts and the advent of more comprehensive social management schema via the coordination of corporate interests and state planning. In an effort to curtail the disruptions caused by radical labor activism, the architects of the Keynesian welfare state increasingly supplemented the factory wage with a range of social amenities—public schools, housing subsidies, health insurance, pensions, unemployment insurance, and welfare assistance.

The evolution of the social wage was double-edged. At one level, these reforms were the progressive culmination of hard-fought social struggles among workers, the unemployed, and the Progressive era reformers. Yet from the vantage point of capital, the social wage promised to resolve problems of overproduction that precipitated the 1929 stock market crash and the Depression by increasing working-class purchasing power. According to President Franklin Roosevelt, the principal objective of the 1933 National Industrial Recovery Act was "to restore our rich domestic market by raising its vast consuming capacity."[7] The social Keynesian regime elaborated under New Deal legislation ultimately helped to incorporate and preempt the most disruptive potential of proletarian struggles.[8] Although the 1935 Wagner Act (the National Labor Relations Act) extended juridical recognition to labor, the 1947 Taft-Hartley Act (or Labor Relations Management Act) effectively undermined the kind of interwar radical trade unionism that threatened business as usual. As historian Nelson Lichtenstein concludes, the advent of industrial democracy "would engender that most precious commodity in the workaday world: informed and willing consent."[9] In addition to administrative promotion of consensual order, increased use of "labor-saving" technologies in manufacturing also served to tame the power of the mass worker through the threat of obsolescence.[10]

The "Red hunts" initiated by the FBI under J. Edgar Hoover and the investigations conducted by the Un-American Activities Committee of the House of Representatives rankled and severed the most radical elements from the American labor movement and banished the revolutionary aspirations of the Old Left from the realm of acceptable public debate.[11] The FBI was created in the aftermath of the 1917 Russian Revolution and during a period of robust union organizing throughout the United States. Between 1918 and 1921, U.S. Attorney General Alexander Palmer and his understudy Hoover arrested and deported thousands of socialists, communists, and radical labor activists during the "Palmer Raids." With the onset of the Cold War, efforts to root out communist sympathizers intensified. Although Republican Senator Joe McCarthy is most readily associated with the anti-communist crusades of the post–World War II years, many liberal, Democratic party politicians and trade union bureaucrats supported these efforts to discredit and marginalize radical alternatives. Congressional labor reforms, automation, the intensification of union-busting measures and red-baiting did not resolve class contradictions. Capital–labor conflicts only endured under new politico-economic arrangements and social terms. Nonetheless, the political abeyance of the mass worker initiated intense reconsiderations of his centrality in conventional left political theory. Cruse's intellectual formation coincides with these developments.

Cruse once characterized himself as "a carry-over from the World War II generation that came of maturity in the 1940s."[12] He was born in Petersburg, Virginia, on 8 March 1916. By his own account, his upbringing was "never stable" and he was the product of "the broken family syndrome." Cruse spent his childhood migrating back and forth between New York City and his southern birthplace, thus setting in motion his peripatetic lifestyle. At the age of 25, Cruse joined the "citizen's army" in 1941 and was stationed in the British Isles, Northern Africa, and Italy during World War II as part of the all-black 48th Quartermaster Regiment.

When Cruse fully embraced Marxist politics is not altogether clear from his scattered biographical reflections. He had encountered radical leftists during his teenage years in Harlem. Cruse recalled the vibrant intellectual culture of those years: "We used to have those debates in the YMCA, there were Communists debating, pro-black nationalists debating, anti-Communists debating, pro-Communists debating, NAACPers, the whole spectrum of critical opinion was being aired. So in those days—I use to tell people—anybody that couldn't argue Marx or Engels was considered a goddamn dummy."[13] His wartime tour of Europe led to interesting exchanges with Italian communists, which apparently intensified his appreciation of Marxism and shaped his decision to join the Communist party when he returned to civilian life in 1945.

His problems with the party centered primarily around his assertive position on cultural affairs and what he saw as the failure of party bureaucrats to deal effectively with the American racial question. After the war, Cruse entered into Communist Party politics and would remain an active member until 1952. During these years, he served as "the librarian and part-time reviewer" for the cultural department of the *Daily Worker*.[14] His turbulent relationship with the Communist Party pushed him toward a more critical posture regarding left orthodoxy and his original rethinking of Marxist ideas. As Cruse recalled, "Life circumstances, my creative psychology, plus the vagaries of the publishing field have made me a social critic almost against my will."[15] He thought that the war transformed the world in ways that rendered prewar social theory ineffective and time bound: "World War II shattered a world irrevocably. But people who thought as I did were called upon in 1945 to treat the postwar era with intellectual and critical tools more applicable to the vanished world of the thirties—a world we had never had time to understand as we lived it."[16] This passage captures a central thread running through Cruse's postwar intellectual work—basically, the view that social theory within American left circles had not kept pace with changing conditions. By his own account, Cruse felt that he was a casualty of Old Left orthodoxy:

> I could not function in the Left as a creative writer and critic
> with my own convictions concerning the "black experience" . . .
> my very first efforts at critical writing were published in a

Communist journal. It was the Communists' response to these articles that quickly convinced me of the gulf between their views and mine on critical and creative approaches to the black experience.[17]

During the intervening years between his departure from the Communist Party and the publication of *The Crisis of the Negro Intellectual*, Cruse lived for a time as a Greenwich Village bohemian, spending his days writing and doing odd jobs.[18] Apparently, Cruse wrote at least three plays during this period, *Furlough to the Cradle*, *Headline Hetty* (a musical), and *Irma Tazewell: A Maid's Dilemma* and also began working on a novel. After encountering difficulty having his plays staged, Cruse discovered avenues for publishing his political essays and became increasingly involved in anticolonial politics. In July 1960, he took part in an historic tour of revolutionary Cuba organized by Richard Gibson and the Fair Play for Cuba Committee.[19] Subsequently, Cruse became active in such proto–Black Power organizations as On Guard, the Freedom Now party, and the Black Arts Repertory Theater/School (BARTS) in Harlem. These activities and his political essays published in *Présence Africaine* and *Liberator* magazines served as workshops for Cruse's evolving critiques of the Old Left and black politics.

Cruse's efforts to critique and transcend Old Left orthodoxies found their most sustained manifestation in *The Crisis of the Negro Intellectual*. This work is an eclectic and wide-ranging volume that integrates biography, political theory, and cultural criticism. Cruse's style of presentation is closer to that of a storyteller than a social scientist. He spins off a number of impressionistic vignettes that, taken together, form a broad argument. His method of argument is rooted in the culture and idiosyncrasies of early-twentieth-century intellectual life—the golden age of the soapbox, pamphlet, and bullhorn. Historian William Jelani Cobb identifies Cruse and other figures such as Hubert Henry Harrison, Malcolm X, and John Henrik Clarke as part of the Harlem autodidact tradition. Contrasting this tendency with the intellectual style and preoccupations of late 1990s academe, Cobb asserts that Cruse "concerned himself with real, three-dimensional issues of power, organization, culture and progress—in contrast to the deconstructive word games that characterize much of the current discourse."[20] Although Cobb is correct in locating Cruse's style in pre–World War II black intellectual life, the characteristics he confines to Harlem's self-taught intellectuals were part of broader tendencies in American political culture during the formative stages of Fordism. The predominance of print media, the valuation of oral argument and encyclopedic recall of world history and current events, and multidisciplinary education were characteristic features of American activist-intellectual subcultures during an age that predated the hegemony of television and the growth of technocracy.

Cruse's masterwork was penned during a period of significant transition for the civil rights movement. In early 1965, he signed a contract to produce two books with William Morrow publishing company—the first of these would be *The Crisis of the Negro Intellectual* and the second would be a collection of earlier essays, *Rebellion or Revolution?*[21] This first major work spoke of the impasse over civil rights that followed the public relations triumph of the 1963 March on Washington and subsequent passage of major civil rights reforms. The eruption of black urban rebellions in Harlem and Rochester in 1964, Watts in 1965, and dozens of other cities through the end of the decade created an internal crisis of purpose and direction for the movement. Cruse rehearses what he perceives were the failures of the Old Left in the hopes that civil rights and Black Power activists did not repeat the same theoretical and tactical mistakes.

Cruse called for the development of a black nationalist politics that was "geared organically to the native American Revolutionary dynamic."[22] His personal disappointments—his unsuccessful career as a playwright and his serial rejection from Manhattan-based left journals—provide some insight into his motivations and help to explain his chosen targets of criticism. Cruse lambasted his black intellectual contemporaries—Cyril Briggs, Claude McKay, Otto Huiswood, James E. Jackson, and others—for toeing the Communist Party line uncritically and adopting foreign ideas to uniquely American problems. Essentially, he asserted that black intellectuals had failed to develop a radical philosophy of their own—instead, they looked beyond the immediate material and cultural realities of African

American life to adopt interpretations, strategies, and tactics from other places and other times uncritically. Cruse argued:

> Association with white [M]arxists warps the social perception of left-wing Negro Intellectuals to the extent that they fail to see the factors of their own dynamic. Over the past forty-five years many of the best Negro minds have been in, through, and out of the Marxist Left. Their creative and social perceptions have been considerably dulled in the process and their collective, cumulative failures over the decades have contributed to the contemporary poverty and insolvency of Negro Intellectuals as a class.[23]

In Cruse's estimation, such blind adoption heightened the dependency of black intellectuals and insured their ineffectiveness and underdevelopment. His core arguments in *The Crisis of the Negro Intellectual* rested on a conceptual dichotomy between nationalism and integrationism whereby the former is posed as the dominant but "rejected strain" of black social and political consciousness. Consequentially, integration was deemed inauthentic and politically futile. Cruse's formulation neglects the manifold ways that black nationalism draws on dominant narratives.[24] Despite the traditional view of subaltern nationalism as fundamentally separate from mainstream culture, Wilson J. Moses writes, "Black nationalism assumes the shape of its container and undergoes transformations in accordance with changing intellectual fashions in the white world."[25] Cruse also overstates black nationalism's historical prevalence as *the* mass ideology of African Americans. Racial stratification does not necessarily give rise to a coherent nationalistic politics. Stratification engenders different desires, forms of consciousness, and modes of politics that cannot be understood exclusively as nationalistic. *The Crisis of the Negro Intellectual* is fraught with other interpretative problems.

Cruse's scathing depiction of white Communist Party officials' paternalism and their unsatisfactory handling of racial matters has been criticized by a number of authors who offer a more sympathetic, nuanced view of black communists and the party's programmatic efforts.[26] Cruse's bold brush strokes create a portrait of black participation in the party as one long, sad song of "manipulation, disillusionment, and betrayal," to use Mark Naison's characterization.[27]

unilaterally true?

Surely, Cruse's diatribe against black left intellectuals leaves little room for the presence of those who engaged Marxism critically or openly disagreed with party officialdom. Moreover, throughout *The Crisis of the Negro Intellectual,* Cruse seems more content with scapegoating black left intellectuals than with devising a sustained critique of the broader problems of stale social theory, sagging popular resonance, and bureaucratic politics that mired the American left at midcentury. Keeping in mind the factual inconsistencies and overgeneralizations operative in Cruse's account, his bold insights regarding the dilemmas that the racial order posed for American left radicals are still valuable and outline an enduring challenge facing the development of a populist left politics.

Cruse never completely rejected the possibility of anticapitalist revolution in American society, but he did not think that orthodox Marxism as expressed in the Communist party's platforms and programmatic efforts was capable of facilitating such a transformation. Cruse asserted that the development of radical left politics was still plausible despite the cycle of protest, systemic recognition, and neutralization of the radical left under the New Deal: "All of this would seem to suggest that the American social system is immune to the trials of social revolution. But this is far from true, as any modern economist knows; for social revolution as such does not necessarily correspond to any preconceived formulas extracted from some foreign revolution of decades past. Each new social revolution is unique. There have been a variety of social revolutions but there will be still others."[28] For Cruse, the source of the crisis in western Marxism lay in the October 1917 Russian revolution whose agrarian context problematized certain theoretical predictions regarding proletarian revolution commonly attributed to Marx—even though his writings on these matters were fragmentary and contradictory.[29] Cruse noted that "every social revolution that has taken place since the Russian revolution has developed out of industrially backward, agrarian, semi-colonial or colonial conditions," while the white working classes in the advanced industrial countries had become "more and more conservative, procapitalist and *pro-imperialist.*"[30] Despite Cruse's tendency to overstate the political bankruptcy of organized labor and white workers, his comments illuminate an important set of challenges posed by the institutionalization of capital–labor conflicts.

Cruse charged that white radicals had not come to terms with this growing conservatism of white workers nor had they fully appreciated the coincidental rise of the southern civil rights movement and its revolutionary potential.

Like his treatment of black participation in the Communist Party, his analysis of the southern civil rights movement was troublesome and inconsistent. Cruse treats the "Negro movement" and labor as if these entities were mutually exclusive. Much of his narrative in *The Crisis of the Negro Intellectual* reinscribed the working class as exclusively white, waged, industrial, and male. Likewise, he acknowledged the decidedly cosmopolitan character of the civil rights movement at certain moments, only to characterize it as a black movement at others. Nonetheless, in Cruse's estimation, the struggle against desegregation had displaced the white working class as the "de facto radical force" in American society.[31] In more specific terms, Cruse argued: "The revolutionary initiative has passed to the colonial world, and in the United States is passing to the Negro, while Western Marxists theorize, temporize and debate. . . . What is true of the colonial world is also true of the Negro in the United States. Here, the Negro is the leading revolutionary force, independent and ahead of the Marxists in the development of a movement towards social change."[32]

Cruse's efforts to rethink left social theory and his assignment of vanguard status to colonial peoples were inspired by world historical events of the late fifties and early sixties. The very same year that the U.S. Supreme Court overturned *Plessy v. Ferguson*'s "separate but equal" precedent in the landmark *Brown* decision, the Viet Minh defeated the French military in the battle of Dien Bien Phu.[33] This victory ended eighty years of French colonial rule and brought the communists to power in Northern Vietnam. Halfway around the globe, the Kenyan Land and Freedom Army—or the "Mau Mau" as they became known in the Western press—waged war against the British.[34] As well, in April 1955, representatives of twenty-nine Asian and African nations converged in Bandung, Indonesia, to oppose colonialism and chart plans for increased cooperation among those who Richard Wright termed "the underdogs of the human race."[35] Such political stirrings in the colonies fired the imaginations of many intellectuals living in the West. The image of the armed peasant in revolt against Western military forces created the sense among many U.S.-based intellectuals that the tables were turning and the age of colonial empire was nearing its end. Although they each approached the problem of American class politics from different political tendencies and idioms within the left, writers such as Trinidadian Marxist C. L. R. James, Chrysler autoworker and grassroots intellectual James Boggs, and Frankfurt School exile Marcuse came to similar conclusions as Cruse regarding the revolutionary potential of American blacks.

In his 1948 essay "The Revolutionary Answer to the Negro Problem in the USA," James wrote:

> Let us not forget that in the Negro people, there sleep and are now awakening passions of a violence exceeding, perhaps, as far as these things can be compared, anything among the tremendous forces that capitalism created . . . their social force may not be able to compare with the social force of a corresponding number of organised workers, the hatred of bourgeois society and the readiness to destroy it when the opportunity should present itself, rests among them to a degree greater than in any other section of the population in the United States.[36]

James saw the black struggle as possessing an independent "vitality and validity of its own" and contested the view that their struggle for civil rights should be subordinated to the working class or subsumed under trade unions or left parties. He saw the southern civil rights struggle as a potential catalyst for more far-reaching proletarian struggles. His view diverged from Cruse in one crucial respect, however. Although James acknowledged the autonomy and influence of the civil rights movement, he maintained that the struggle against capital was fundamental. James's analytical attention to new social forces—blacks, women, intellectuals—predated Cruse's arguments by a decade. James's arguments and those of Boggs developed within the fertile intellectual milieu of the Johnson–Forest Tendency.

A small group of radical intellectuals in Detroit, the Johnson–Forest Tendency began working within the Trotskyist Workers Party in 1941 and later rejoined the Socialist Workers Party in 1947.[37] The group took its name from C. L. R. James, who used the pseudonym, J. R. Johnson, and Russian-born intellectual Raya Dunyevskaya, who published under the name Freddie Forest. They were joined by Chinese American activist-intellectual Grace Lee (aka Ria Stone in party circles). She was a Bryn Mawr–trained Philosophy Ph.D. who later married James Boggs after he joined the group. Other members of the Johnson–Forest Tendency included autoworkers Martin Glaberman and Johnny Zupan. Collectively and individually, the tendency produced a range of groundbreaking theoretical books and pamphlets on worker self-activity, critiques of the Leninist party, and the degradation of communism under Stalinist Bureaucracy, including *The American Worker* (1947), *State Capitalism and World Revolution* (1950), and *Facing Reality* (1958). Boggs's participation in the Johnson–Forest Tendency helped to shape his thinking on revolutionary Marxism and propelled him beyond the strictures of midcentury left orthodoxy. James and Grace Lee Boggs's proto-Black Power sentiments grated with the sensibilities of Glaberman and C. L. R. James around 1962 with the Boggses setting out on their own path.

Although he and Cruse allegedly clashed over the draft program of the Freedom Now Party, James Boggs offered a critique of the Old Left and the significance of the southern civil rights movement to left politics that developed in concert with Cruse's arguments.[38] Like Cruse, Boggs begins his analysis by acknowledging the growing conservatism of American factory workers. Both men were bothered by the failure of pre–World War II Marxist orthodoxies to keep pace with new political and economic conditions. Like Cruse, Boggs sought to grasp the unique features of postwar American society. His 1963 book *The American Revolution: Pages from a Black Worker's Notebook* reflects this desire to create homegrown revolution. This task would inform his and Grace Lee Boggs's intellectual project from the sixties onward. In a few especially perceptive passages, he notes the deleterious effects of automation and cybernetic command on the American working class and black workers in particular. Boggs argued that the pressures of automation shifted the class consciousness of workers from "hostility to the class enemy outside" toward "focus on antagonisms, struggles and conflicts among the workers themselves."[39] As a consequence of these technological forces, Boggs argued that the American working class was no longer a "homogeneous segregated bloc." Because work was becoming increasingly unnecessary under new productive technologies, old tactics, slogans, and aims were also becoming obsolete. He concluded that the "poverty-caused misery of the American masses has by no means been eliminated" but "it is so dispersed and scattered among various elements of the population that it does not constitute a fundamental and unifying issue to mobilize the masses of people in struggle."[40]

Under this state of affairs where consumption, automation, and the labor–management accord had undermined the insurgent potential of many factory workers, Boggs turned to the most marginal strata of workers as the leading edge of progressive change. Boggs wrote: "American Marxists have tended to fall into the trap of thinking of the Negroes as Negroes, i.e. in race terms, when in fact the Negroes have been and are today the most oppressed and submerged sections of the workers, on whom has fallen most sharply the burden of unemployment due to automation . . . The strength of the Negro cause and its power to shake up the social structure of the nation comes from the fact that in the Negro struggle all the questions of human rights and human relationships are posed. At the same time the American Negroes are most conscious of, and best able to time their actions in relation to, the crises and weaknesses of American capitalism, both at home and abroad."[41] German émigré Marcuse developed similar conclusions.

In *One Dimensional Man*, a work that influenced New Left student activism in a manner comparable to Cruse's sway over Black Power radicalism, Marcuse surveyed the stifling conformity of the American populace in the postwar years and attempted to explain the sources of mass quiescence. He concluded that the industrial working class was no longer the walking contradiction to capital that Marx witnessed and in the book's waning pages, he looked toward black Americans, inhabitants of the Third World, the unemployed, and the dispossessed as the new protagonists in social transformation. Marcuse wrote:

underneath the [American] conservative popular base is the substratum of the outcasts and outsiders, the exploited and persecuted of other races and other colors, the unemployed and the unemployable. They exist outside the democratic process; their life is the most immediate and most real need for ending intolerable conditions and institutions. Thus their opposition is revolutionary even if their consciousness is not . . . When they get together and go out into the streets, without arms, without protection, in order to ask for the most primitive civil rights, they know that they face dogs, stones, and bombs, jail, concentration camps, even death . . . The fact that they start refusing to play the game marks the beginning of the end of a period.[42]

Other writers from the period such as Frantz Fanon, Albert Memmi, and, to a lesser extent, Jean-Paul Sartre recognized the emerging political significance of colonized people, minorities, and other groups in ways that transcended the conventionally defined proletariat.[43]

Inasmuch as these authors attempt to name the revolutionary subject, they are burdened by similar conceptual problems. Namely, such assertions of black vanguardism shared a tendency to downplay the ideological and political diversity among "the wretched of the earth" and overinvest in the revolutionary potential of subaltern minorities and colonized peoples at the expense of other social forces.[44] Within a decade, these bold declarations of the black vanguard were rendered obsolete by the global, polyphonic eruption of social struggles against war, technocracy, and inequality, and the consequential patterns of counterinsurgency and reaction that subdued New Left social movements and, channeled antiracist and anticolonial struggles into regimes of race-relations management and neocolonial sovereignty. Nonetheless, taken together these writers identify a significant historical transition during the Cold War—the appearance of new political subjects and their threat to the established imperial order. Alongside these struggles for civil rights and national liberation, second-wave feminism, antiwar activism, student movements, and environmentalism would also encourage a critical revision of established modes of left political thinking and organizing and pose a more expansive political challenge to the ruling classes in the industrial West. Although some more recent theorists, particularly those associated with the new social movement literature, treat the emergence of these identity-based movements as a sign of the diminishing significance of class, their appearance did not signify the end of class antagonisms.[45] Cruse was especially prescient on these matters.

In defending his 1962 essay "Revolutionary Nationalism and the Afro-American" against criticism from reviewer Richard Greenleaf, Cruse called for the enlargement of conventional notions of class struggle to account for its increasingly global dimensions. He wrote: "The 'class struggle' is now supra-national—a struggle between Western nations and the colonial and semi-colonial world. It is a struggle between blocs and developing blocs—Common Market *vs.* Africa; U.S. *vs.* Latin America; U.S.S.R. and China *vs.* the West. In other words, it is a struggle between the 'have' and 'have-not' peoples, the world of super-developed capitalism vs. the underdeveloped world."[46] The coincidental insurgence of civil rights and anticolonial struggles did not in fact mean the supercession of class struggle. Even though certain identitarian tendencies descended into isolationism and political resignation, these popular movements transformed and deepened the struggle against capital's excesses and enabled the formation of new political alliances—e.g. the wages for housework movement; consumer identity campaigns that fostered stronger federal regulation of product safety standards; the emergence of black radical labor organizations like Dodge Revolutionary Union Movement, Ford Revolutionary Union Movement and their umbrella, the League of Revolutionary Black Workers in Detroit; heightened organizing among single mothers and the unemployed into welfare rights and poor people's organizations throughout the United States; and the development of political solidarity among students, workers, and immigrants during the May 1968 general strike in Paris and the equally wide-ranging constituencies drawn together via anti–Vietnam War mobilizations. Such international political developments simply rendered the most dogmatic readings of Marxism obsolete; demanded fresh, critical reassessments of inherited social theory; and necessitated a more thorough-going interrogation of productive relations and the historical nature of class composition—in effect, a return to the core truth of materialist critique, not its rejection. As Cruse himself noted, "the failure of the social revolution to materialize in the advanced capitalist countries does not at all invalidate Marx's dialectical method. What does become invalid is the subsequent application of the dialectical method by the followers of Marx in the twentieth century. We say this because if we accept the premise of dialectics then we accept the view that everything in social life is constantly changing, coming into existence, and passing away. But if this dialectical premise is 'truth,' why then is it assumed that everything in society is subject to the processes of change *except the historical role of the working class in advanced capitalist nations?* [emphasis mine]"[47]

What was required according to Cruse was the development of an indigenous American radical social theory—one that accounted for the emergence of "new forms of social consciousness" and the historical recomposition of social forces.[48] Through his engagement with the organized left, Cruse concluded that the Communist Party, the Trotskyites, and other left factions had failed at this task. Moreover, black intellectuals working in the orbit of these organizations were especially at fault. For Cruse, the distinctive social position of African Americans as a domestic colony placed them at the vanguard of the U.S. struggle. Since black radical activists had failed to fully appreciate this social reality, in Cruse's estimation they could not generate a reflexive social theory that transcended the limitations of left officialdom. Hence, he concluded, "It evidently never occurred to Negro revolutionaries that there was no one in America who possessed the remotest potential for Americanizing Marxism but themselves."[49] Although he was harshly critical of civil rights leaders' focus on liberal integration and suspicious of militant posturing around violent self-defense, Cruse ultimately saw the civil rights struggle as a potential opening for more far-reaching social transformations.

Despite common allusions to the "Negro revolution" circulating in movement circles and the mainstream press, Cruse thought that the civil rights struggle had not reached its potential as a genuinely revolutionary force. Although he was sympathetic to the Cuban revolution and speculated on its cathartic value for domestic black social struggles, he feared that younger militants' romanticism of guerilla warfare clouded their analysis of the American social context.[50] On these matters, he wrote: "People who call the Negro protest movement a black revolution do not really understand their own system, for a real revolution in their country would involve a social dynamic of many common parts. Such a revolution would have very little in common with the foreign revolutions they have read about. It would amount to a massive social transformation of a kind unheard of before, and the elements for it already exist within the society either actively or latently."[51] This passage illuminates Cruse's continuing engagement with Marxism even as he rejects political alliance with the organized left. He does not rule out the possibility of fundamental democratic transformation of U.S. politico-economic order but rejects stock formulae of revolutionary politics. Instead, Cruse reasserts the need for radical activists to comprehend the unique historical features of their national/local situation. As well, he alludes to "the future in the present"—the ingredients of a freer mode of existence that reside in the contemporary society waiting to be brought fully into being through social struggles.

In his efforts to comprehend the distinctive features of postwar American society and outline new routes toward radical social trans-formation, Cruse turned to the cultural sphere. He saw the develop-ment of mass communication technologies as a watershed that "drastically altered the classic character of capitalism as described by Karl Marx."[52] Cruse was especially attuned to the expanding political importance of the culture industry in postwar America. Ernest Kaiser, in his formative review of *The Crisis of the Negro Intellectual*, identifies media theorist Marshall McLuhan as an unacknowledged source of Cruse's arguments regarding cultural revolution.[53] Cruse defined cultural revolution as "an ideological and organizational approach to American social change by revolutionizing the adminis-tration, the organization, the functioning and the social purpose of the entire American apparatus of cultural communication and plac-ing it under public ownership." This focus on culture is perceptive inasmuch as it reveals Cruse's sensitivity to the enlarged place of communicative technologies in the development of consensus and the administration of the social order. As well, Cruse's writings on cultural revolution reveal an incredibly optimistic view of mass media and its emancipatory potential, which contrast sharply with the dystopian premonitions penned by Max Horkheimer, Theodor Adorno, and more recent leftist critics of mass media.[54] Cruse was alert to the negative consequences of corporate-controlled media, but he was equally sensitive to the democratic possibilities presented by new technologies. He noted "if the growth of capitalism creates its opposite—the working class—then it is possible to say that the growth of mass communications media coincided with the appearance of an opposing class-force of radical creative intellectuals."[55] Hence, high tech communications do not insure capital's hegemony, but rather these new arrangements may very well sow the seeds of opposition by opening horizontal routes of communication and making hardware and techniques more widely available. [56]

Cruse increasingly saw the cultural sphere—and not the factory or the state—as the primary battleground in the struggle to create a freer, more democratic society. He concluded that since "the alliance of white capital and labor obviates any challenge to the economic status quo where the production of basic commodities takes place, the Negro movement must challenge free enterprise *at its weakest link in the production chain, where no tangible commodities are produced.* This becomes the 'economic' aspect of the Negro movement [emphasis mine]." Cruse saw the culture industry as the Achilles heel of capitalism. The immaterial nature of this industry, he surmised, made it less susceptible to the kinds of interdependencies between labor and capital that facilitated the taming of interwar labor militancy under a new regime of contract negotiations and automated production. Knowledge workers or creative intellectuals were more akin to the pre-Fordist craft worker in that they possessed a high level of skill and productive autonomy that could not be as readily appropriated by capital.

Cruse's cultural turn is significant. Although his characterizations of black culture often retreated to problematic notions of racial authenticity that read the complexity out of black and American cultural development, Cruse thought that the storied contributions of blacks to American culture placed black creative intellectuals in a unique, privileged position. As he argued, "the Afro-American cultural ingredient in music, dance and theatrical forms . . . has been the basis for whatever culturally new and unique that has come out of America."[57] What was needed was the seizure of those media that might allow blacks to popularize a more democratic, open view of American history and society. Obviously, Cruse, like other radical intellectuals during the postwar era, realized that political organization was not enough, but that the struggle against inequality required positional warfare aimed at the promotion of more democratic values and ways of being. The backlash against civil rights reforms that transpired during the sixties and broke ground for the rise of the New Right illustrated that state reforms alone would not deliver racial equality. Instead, deeper, more wide-reaching changes in public perceptions of race, social mobility, and the common good were required as well. In these respects, Cruse's basic insistence on a left political theory that addressed cultural affairs has proved to be one of his most prophetic insights. Unfortunately, Cruse increasingly scorned the kind of broad-based social movement that might have actualized the democratic ownership of mass media he desired. Having discarded popular mobilization, his calls for cultural revolution amounted to a mere politics of cultural recognition within established state-market arrangements. The concluding section of this chapter critiques these conservative elements of his work.

From Materialist Critique to Racial Conservatism: Cruse's Ethnic Pluralism

Cruse was among the first to contemplate the "internal colony" or "domestic colony" as a framework for interpreting black American oppression. This construct's antecedents might be traced to the 1928 Sixth World Congress of the Communist International and the adoption of "self-determination for the black belt" of the U.S. South as the party's official line on the American race question, a policy shift that was no doubt propelled by the popularity of Garveyite nationalism.[58] Ironically, the colonial analogy recedes in importance in *The Crisis of the Negro Intellectual* at the very moment when other writers such as Stokely Carmichael, Robert Allen, and Eldridge Cleaver were popularizing its usage among Black Power radicals.[59]

Cruse employs the colonial analogy in his highly influential 1962 essay, "Revolutionary Nationalism and the Afro-American," which appeared in *Studies on the Left*. This essay was widely read among black radicals and is worth quoting at length:

From the very beginning, the American Negro has existed as a colonial being. His enslavement coincided with the colonial expansion of European powers and was nothing more or less than a condition of domestic colonialism. Instead of the United States establishing a colonial empire in Africa, it brought the colonial system home and installed it in the Southern states. When the Civil War broke up the slave system and the Negro was emancipated, he gained only partial freedom. Emancipation elevated him only to the position of a semi-dependent man, not to that of an equal or independent being . . . The only factor which differentiates the Negro's status from that of a pure colonial status is that his position is maintained in the "home" country in close proximity to the dominant racial group.[60]

Nikhil Pal Singh discerns a theoretical shift in Cruse's work from this emphasis on domestic colonialism and anticolonial politics in his formative political essays to an affection for the mainstream social science notion of ethnic pluralism in *The Crisis of the Negro Intellectual*. Perceptively, Singh situates this interpretive turn against the backdrop of the sixties ethnic revival led by writers such as Milton Gordon, Robert Dahl, Daniel Patrick Moynihan, and Nathan Glazer.[61] This apparent shift away from the colonial analogy toward ethnic politics is unsettling for Singh and others like Penny Von Eschen who celebrate the internationalist perspective of Cruse's writings from the early sixties and the postwar anticolonialism of W. E. B. DuBois, Paul Robeson, and the Council on African Affairs, among others. "In his bid to secure an authoritative claim upon the public discussion of 'race' in the United States," Singh asserts "Cruse not only distorted the historical record of black radicalism (including his own) but he also misread the real political tenor of ethnicity arguments."[62]

In a cornerstone chapter of *The Crisis of the Negro Intellectual* titled "The Individual and the Open Society," Cruse offered an important critique of American liberalism that contrasted its universalistic ideal of natural right with the historically exclusionary nature of national sovereignty. Essentially, he argued that there are no individual rights in any concrete sense outside of actual groups that protect and defend such rights through activism and the effective exercise of power. Here, Cruse claimed that power in American society is organized around ethnic blocs with Anglo-Saxon Protestants, white Catholics, and white Jews as the most dominant of these groups. He asserted the primacy of group power within American politics:

> On the face of it, this dilemma rests on the fact that America which idealizes the rights of the individual above everything else, is in reality, a nation dominated by the social power of groups, classes, in-groups and cliques—both ethnic and religious. The individual in America has few rights that are not backed up by the political, economic and social power of one group or another. Hence the individual Negro has, proportionately, very few rights indeed because his ethnic group (whether or not he actually identifies with it) has very little political, economic or social power (beyond moral grounds) to wield. Thus it can be seen that those Negroes and there are many of them, who have accepted the full essence of the Great American Ideal of individualism, are in serious trouble trying to function in America.[63]

Cruse's discussion of ethnic blocs meshes nicely with the ethnic revival in mainstream social science and provides a compelling justification for Black Power demands for self-determination and indigenous control. His discussion captures the tenuous nature of liberal individualism and the power of ethnic and religious affinities in American politics. His formulation, however, inherits the ethnic paradigm's many weaknesses.

First, Cruse gives us a highly selective reading of the history of white ethnic assimilation in the United States. White ethnic mobility in the twentieth century was not achieved exclusively through ethnic solidarity, self-help, and urban political incorporation but was enabled through white privilege; periods of stable mass production; the New Deal social safety net; generous public expenditures on primary and secondary education; and participation in trade unions, party politics, and democratic social movements.[64] Second, although political incorporation carried a certain symbolic timbre, white ethnic succession was not always universally beneficial in material terms. Although the seizure of city hall by ethnic politicians often delivered some substantive rewards for supporters of the new governing regime, such returns were limited in creating social mobility for the majority of any one ethnic group.[65] Third, this focus on ethnic identity obscures the fundamentally issue-based character of politics and the temporal and porous nature of political constituencies. Cruse's *The Crisis of the Negro Intellectual* and subsequent books and essays built an intellectual justification for postsegregation black ethnic politics on this very shaky foundation.[66]

Although Singh effectively illuminates the conservative implications of Cruse's embrace of ethnic politics, his account might underappreciate the political motives behind this shift and overplay the value of the colonial analogy as a viable political alternative. Perhaps more than the renewed popularity of ethnicity in academic circles, Cruse's conservatism was most likely shaped by the changing political arrangements between black citizens and the state precipitated by civil rights reforms. The historic transition within black public discourse from liberal integration to black autonomy/self-determination should be understood within the context of these political and institutional changes, which were ultimately more consequential in shaping postsegregation black political subjectivity than the activities of anticolonial guerillas thousands of miles away from U.S. shores. The passage of major civil rights reforms reshaped public debate over black political development by removing legal and institutional fetters to formal participation and, thus, created the possibility for greater and more effective involvement of black citizens in the formation of public policy.

I would argue that both the ethnic paradigm and the colonial analogy ultimately legitimated a conservative form of black political subjectivity. Both ethnicity and nationality as conceptual categories and political identities inevitably require the suppression of political differences within the group.[67] Although the colonial analogy offered a more systematic view of racial subordination that accounted for its spatial, economic, and political dimensions and undoubtedly engendered a more international political perspective among some black American adherents, both the colonial analogy and the ethnic paradigm share a common tendency to conflate identity and political constituency. Singh may well overstate the incompatibility of these concepts within Cruse's work for his use of the term "ethnic blocs" in fact predates his elaboration of the colonial analogy in 1962.[68] Likewise, Cruse offered passing endorsement of the colonial analogy in *The Crisis of the Negro Intellectual*.[69] This ostensible semantic shift in Cruse's writings conceals fundamental political consistencies. He appears to use these terms interchangeably when discussing American racial matters. Neither the ethnic paradigm nor the colonial analogy fully accounts for intragroup plurality.

Although the ethnic paradigm was certainly riddled with problems, the colonial analogy was not a viable alternative.[70] The colonial analogy possessed some utility as an assessment of African American life, which accounted for its structural/economic, and social dynamics, but the thesis was hobbled by its faulty political solution—national liberation.[71] The social management function performed by "Negro leaders" during the segregation era bears some resemblance to the patterns of indirect rule practiced by British colonial administrators and West African tribal chieftains.[72] Additionally, spatial segregation under Jim Crow was consistent with the "native zones" that Fanon identified in Algeria and throughout colonial Africa.[73] As well, the conditions of racial slavery and subsequent debt peonage and exploitation in the segregated South were virtually indistinguishable from the processes of value extraction in colonial Africa, Latin America, and Asia at corresponding historical junctures. Nonetheless, beyond the unlikely scenario of racial secession, what would national liberation look like in the American context?

The fact of political enfranchisement, desegregation of public schools and accommodations, and increasing federal investment in participatory antipoverty initiatives served to erode the empirical bases and political utility of the colonial analogy. Even though the rhetoric of domestic colonialism possessed a certain allegorical power during the sixties and seventies, with some important exceptions the operational politics of Black Power came to approximate those of the ethnic paradigm—group solidarity, politico-economic incorporation, and self-help. Self-determination and indigenous control came to mean something characteristically different in the American context. In addition to Cruse's work, Stokely Carmichael and Charles V. Hamilton's ambivalent use of the colonial analogy and equally tortured relationship to mainstream social science further suggests that this construct's primary utility was as a rhetorical device rather than reflexive social theory.[74]

Even at the colonial analogy's apex of popularity among Black Power radicals, the achievement of national liberation in the colonial world was beset with glaring political problems. As various analysts of the neocolonial/postcolonial condition from Ghanaian political founder Kwame Nkrumah to French social theorist Jean-François Bayart have noted, national liberation and the arrival of state sovereignty throughout the Third World delivered a hollow independence where the democratic import of formal procedures such as national elections, courts, and parliamentary deliberation were overshadowed by the increasing power and influence of multinational corporations, neoliberal trade agreements, and transnational financial institutions over the determination of fundamental issues of wages, labor, and life and death, throughout the global South.[75] The popularity of the colonial analogy and Third World national liberation struggles among African Americans during the sixties and early seventies coincided with the increasing decline of state sovereignty on a global scale. It appears that Cruse abandoned the colonial analogy as he came to realize the folly of waging a national liberation struggle on American soil.

Von Eschen characterizes Cruse's embrace of ethnic pluralism in *The Crisis of the Negro Intellectual* as a manifestation of American exceptionalism. She writes: "Cruse echoed dominant assumptions of exceptionalism in *The Crisis* asserting that race in America is a fundamentally domestic issue . . . here, race and racism are not products of global processes at the heart of the shaping of the modern world but exclusively an American dilemma."[76] By equating Cruse's effort to comprehend the unique, historical features of the American social order with exceptionalism, Von Eschen may obscure the thread of materialist critique that runs through Cruse's work and its role in the formation of his politics. American racial politics and racism should certainly be understood within the broader context of modernity and imperialism. Strenuous consideration of the uniqueness of the American social order, however, is not only intellectually imperative but is, as Cruse noted again and again, fundamental to the development of any political project desirous of challenging American inequality.

Cruse was concerned with domestic conditions not simply due to Cold War myopia or a failure to appreciate internationalism but rather because the American domestic context was a primary front where the international left had failed to develop significant inroads. In an especially introspective 1966 essay, "Les Noirs et L'Idée de Révolte," he characterized the civil rights movement as "a movement that forges its ideas in action." In a passage that breaks from uncritical application of the colonial analogy, he noted that while the Cuban example was inspirational, "the Negro movement *must* cast its praxis into a theoretic frame in the final analysis."[77] This is because, unlike revolutionary forces in Cuba or the African colonies, "the American Negro does not exist within an underdeveloped country with a large population of tribes and impoverished peasantry."[78] Hence, the distinctive historical and local circumstances blacks faced in the United States called for equally distinctive political strategies. His turn toward ethnic pluralism—though tragic in its own right—reflected this recognition of the colonial analogy's poverty as a guiding political theory for a subaltern group living under late American capitalism. Cruse's problems here run deeper than a failure to fully appreciate the relationship between modernity and racism. Even more troubling, Cruse's articulation of cultural nationalist politics entailed a departure from consistent, substantive critique of the Cold War American social order and black politics.

In many respects, Cruse was an astute critic of the class dimensions of black political life. His description of the class prerogatives of the Afro-American Realty Company in Harlem's formation was especially perceptive. He was keenly aware of the intermediary role performed by middle-class black leaders in local and national politics during the Jim Crow era.[79] Also, although his specific characterizations of numerous black intellectuals were at times deeply flawed, his efforts to tease out the bourgeois appeal of liberal integration were insightful. On these matters, Cruse wrote:

For the middle classes the civil rights drive is aimed at achieving much more than mere "civil rights" for the masses. The prime motivations of the bourgeois leaders of this movement are selfish class interests, because the main objective of the Negro middle class is a status and social position approximating as closely as possible that pre-eminence enjoyed by the great Anglo-American middle class.[80]

In his attempt to defend the correctness of a black nationalist political line, Cruse minimized the implications of these identifiable bourgeois aspirations among African Americans. In the introductory pages of *The Crisis of the Negro Intellectual,* Cruse elided the saliency of class in an interpretive move that would become a hallmark of postsegregation black nationalist discourse and much nationalist-derived black studies scholarship—the tendency to project an ahistorical, cultural, or political unity onto the black social formation. Cruse wrote that "Negroes are certainly divided into classes—a fact white liberals and radicals often overlook when they speak of 'the Negro.' There is, however, a broad strain of Negro social opinion in America that is strikingly cogent and cuts through class lines."[81] This "rejected strain" in black social opinion is decidedly nationalist according to Cruse. Here, he conflates the diverse, shifting sense of racial alienation experienced by African Americans with a coherent, shared ideology—nationalism.[82] Furthermore, there is little in Cruse's own narrative of twentieth-century black intellectual history to support the notion that the black population constitutes a cohesive political constituency. His view of black ethnic particularity informed this interpretative sleight of hand.

Cruse's focus on black particularity derived from a static, reified notion of culture. His valorization of black folk culture is reminiscent of some early-twentieth-century Irish, Finnish, Polish, and Czech nationalists who viewed peasant culture as the wellspring for a new national identity that might oppose imperial culture.[83] Cruse has a difficult time accounting for patterns of interchange, syncretism, and acculturation that transgress rigidly defined ethnic or racial boundaries. The most famous manifestation of this quality appears in his derogation of the West Indian influence over New Negro art and politics.[84] As well, from his denunciations of white artists such as George Gershwin, Richard Rodgers, and Oscar Hammerstein, one might conclude that all black–white cultural exchanges were characterized by relations of white predation and appropriation—a view that neglects black "appropriations," e.g. Irish folk hymns as a constitutive element in the formation of the Blues and the linguistic, technical, and lyrical cross-fertilizations between Cajun folk music and black Zydeco in segregated southwest Louisiana. As noted above, Cruse was attentive to how the mass culture industry was rapidly transforming "the ordinary" and "the local" in American life, but his view of culture all too often retreated to nostalgic and chauvinistic views of black culture.[85] This tension is reflected in his claim that the "Negro" artist must "fight for the over-all democratization of the American apparatus of cultural communication in order to make a place for the unrestricted expression of his own ethnic personality, his own innate creative originality."[86] Yet despite his democratic intentions, Cruse's notion of a black ethnic personality placed new restrictions on the artistic production of African Americans.

Cruse's personal recollections and the substance of his own artistic work reveal a longing for the temporal cultural forms that accompanied the early-twentieth-century black mass migration. In his scattered autobiographical comments, Cruse celebrated his boyhood exposure to the black vaudeville shows of Harlem during the 1930s. Along with his unique educational experiences in southern segregated schools and northern majority-black and integrated institutions, he attributed the vibrant cultural milieu of Harlem with shaping his aspirations to become a writer. Cruse recalled:

> Little did I realize that I had already received a seminal kind of education and exposure that would prove extremely valuable for the kind of career I would naturally drift towards—that of a cultural and social critic. . . . As a teenager in Harlem my relatives introduced me to the exciting and impressionable black vaudeville world. . . . The great personalities of this world were Duke Ellington, Cab Calloway and his sister Blanche, Earl Hines, Chick Webb, Count Basie, Fletcher Henderson, Jimmie Lunceford, Lucky Millinder, Noble Sissle and Eubie Blake, Ethel Waters, Gladys Bentley, Ivy Anderson, Earl Tucker, the Cotton Club Revue, Bill Robinson, Ella Fitzgerald, and many others, all of whom left me with the indelible impression that black theatrical art was not only unique but inimitable.[87]

These recollections provide some insight into the motives behind Cruse's view of black cultural particularity as well as its limitations. Early jazz and black vaudeville were not merely derivatives of southern black peasant culture, but rather these forms were artifacts of segregation, the developing mass culture industry and Fordist urbanity. As Cruse himself noted, these cultural forms provided newly arriving migrants with refuge and inspiration amidst the disorienting process of urbanization, the shock of metropolitan racism, and deprivations of the Great Depression. Cruse wrote:

> There were many magic worlds in Harlem; the theater was one which was a reflection of many others. These magic worlds helped to shield the minds of youths from many of the grimmer realities of adult segregation. Even the desolation of Harlem's depression years could not blot out the will of most of the black youth to make dreams out of their own spiritual inheritance. This was true despite anger, revolt, crime, poverty and despair.[88]

Once again, on the crest of the second wave of black migration that followed World War II, late-sixties black public discourse was characterized by aesthetic debates that rehearsed the nostalgia and fetishism of southern black peasant culture that accompanied the New Negro era.[89] On one hand, such celebrations of working-class artistic production denoted a radical democratic sensibility that broke from the politics of bourgeois respectability which pervaded the southern civil rights movement. On the other hand, evocations of the "folk" during both the New Negro and Black Power eras sometimes granted a working-class patina to an otherwise elite-driven discourse.

This renewed conversation around blackness and the black aesthetic during the sixties was affirming for many African Americans and served as a powerful antidote to racist caricatures in popular culture. Throughout the Jim Crow era, the notion that blacks were biologically inferior and incapable of self-governance was promoted in every corner of society. From the silver screen to children's books, commercial advertising and home décor, Americans were surrounded by images and words that portrayed blacks as bestial and subservient. Yet despite its restorative properties, the renewed focus on black cultural particularity in the immediate postsegregation context invited canonization, new orthodoxies regarding black artistic production, and waves of purification of those artists who did not meet the repressive criteria of artistic merit and aesthetic judgment established by a handful of vocal artists and activists. As well, some attempts to define the parameters of black culture mirrored and valorized Jim Crow mythologies of black life. Cruse helped to resuscitate this pattern of cultural cleansing with his bitter denunciations of "integrationist" artists such as James Baldwin, Lorraine Hansberry, and Robeson.[90] This interpretative contradiction in *The Crisis of the Negro Intellectual*—acknowledgement of internal class politics and assertion of black cultural particularity—is unfortunately one of its most enduring legacies. The mythic notion that the black population constitutes a corporate political subject continues to inform black political engagement over three decades after the publication of Cruse's masterwork. This idea of a singular black political subject is intimately wedded to the maintenance of black elite privilege in both Cruse's work and postsegregation black politics.

Leading with the State: Cruse's "New Class" Project

In a sense, Cruse's political expectations for African American intellectuals might be read as a rendition of what the nineteenth-century anarcho-socialist Mikhail Bakunin referred to as the "New Class." Although he supported the International, Bakunin was leery of the privileged role assigned to intellectuals in Marx's revolutionary politics. Marx and Engels asserted that the most highly skilled and articulate strata among the working class would serve as the revolutionary core of the proletariat—those who would seize state power and initiate the transition to communism, a stateless and classless society. Bakunin feared that after this group seized power they might betray the struggle for working-class democracy. Within the revolutionary project of building the "People's State," he discerned the reactionary motives of a "new aristocracy." Instead, he pinned his hopes for a radically democratic future on "the great mass, those millions of non-civilized, disinherited, wretched and illiterates" who were "unpolluted by all bourgeois civilization."[91] Although Marx and Engels viewed these masses as the "lumpen proletariat," Bakunin argued that they carried "all germs of the socialism of the future, and which alone is powerful enough today to inaugurate the Social Revolution and bring it to triumph."[92] As Lawrence Peter King and Iván Szelényi note, the quarrel between Bakunin and Marx reverberated throughout the twentieth century and across continents.[93] Echoes of this basic contradiction between the power plays of intellectual elites and the autonomous, democratic aspirations of popular struggles can be heard in the perennial debates over the Vanguard Party, the Johnson–Forest Tendency's critique of state capitalism, the Frankfurt's critiques of both Soviet and American technocracy and the New Left's efforts to outrun the undemocratic tendencies of the Old. In a big way, Cruse advances his own new class project, which minimizes the relevance of popular struggles and the self-activity of workers and carves out a unique historical role for the most articulate, educated sectors of the African American population. Indeed, in *The Crisis of the Negro Intellectual* Cruse expresses disdain for the "black Bakuninism" he senses among sixties radicals.[94]

Cruse was less concerned with the class composition of black politics than the relative effectiveness of black leaders in achieving their prescribed race advancement objectives. He did not develop a sustained critique of the leadership category—although his work illuminates the hidden class prerogatives animating certain historical racial agendas. He argued:

> What is really crucial about Negro leadership is not its class origins, but its program. So far the only programs (good, bad or indifferent) have come from bourgeois Negroes or those with bourgeois aspirations. The real problem, then is that even when more militant and effective leadership does arrive from other than bourgeois class origins, it must have bourgeois support or else it can get nowhere. This is because effective social movements require educated people with knowledge and technical skills which the proletariat or the masses, do not possess. It is only the educated, trained and technically qualified who can lead directly with the state apparatus. In America, when members of the masses acquire education and skills, they cease

forthwith, to be proletarians. Even if the Marxists would rather evade these facts about class differences, they are crucial truths of the Negro Struggle.[95]

This passage devalues the historical significance of black working-class political struggles and proceeds to legitimate a technocratic version of politics premised on expertise and insider negotiation rather than popular participation. The fact of contemporaneous social struggles against Jim Crow segregation and their success in generating landmark reforms during the very years in which this text was penned makes his conservative conclusions especially ironic. Cruse reasserted the centrality of elites within postsegregation black politics at the very moment when their traditional legitimacy under the Jim Crow regime was under siege, and more open, participatory democratic approaches to organization were promoted by militant civil rights activists and the wider New Left.

Cruse trivialized the efficacy of the civil rights movement and disruptive protests asserting that "as long as these uprisings are sporadic, the American capitalistic welfare state will absorb them and more than that, pay for the damage in the same way the government pays for the destruction caused by hurricanes and floods. Uprisings are merely another form of extreme protest action soon to be included under the heading of natural calamities."[96] Cruse correctly identified the social management dynamics of the welfare state, but his categorical dismissal of protest activism signaled his own capitulation to the new institutional arrangements created by civil rights reforms. Like Adam Clayton Powell, Carmichael and Hamilton, Bayard Rustin, and others, Cruse articulated a vision of postsegregation black politics that sought to end racial inequality through conventional political methods.[97] In his two-part essay for *Liberator* magazine "Rebellion or Revolution?," Cruse reveled in Rustin's waning faith in nonviolent civil disobedience and his increasing advocacy of formal politics. Cruse's embrace of Rustin is especially curious given Rustin's staunch commitment to liberal integration and Cruse's well-known animus for such. Still, the two shared a budding appreciation of brokerage politics, and their convergence illustrates how the emerging form of elite-driven, black politics united those in liberal and black nationalist camps.

Rustin's paradigmatic 1965 *Commentary* essay, "From Protest to Politics: The Future of the Civil Rights Movement," signaled his own departure from radical protest toward a more conservative politics of insider negotiation. Rustin's 1965 essay was not a work of "objective" sociological or political analysis. Here, Rustin described his highly partisan view of what precise form postsegregation era black politics should take. Effectively relegating extrainstitutional tactics to a passing stage in the maturation of the civil rights movement, Rustin concluded that "It is institutions—social, political, and economic institutions—which are the ultimate molders of collective sentiments." At the time of the article's publication, Rustin had completed the conservative metamorphosis he was now advocating for the civil rights movement at large. That Rustin would openly advocate insider politics was especially remarkable and frustrating for some of his comrades-in-arms given his long-held role as political gadfly and chief architect of some of the most crucial civil rights protests.

By the time he was summoned to assist in the 1955 Montgomery Bus Boycott, Rustin was a veteran organizer who worked as head of the youth wing of A. Philip Randolph's March on Washington Movement and as field secretary of Congress of Racial Equality's (CORE) forerunner, the Fellowship of Reconciliation (FOR). Rustin was also a conscientious objector during World War II. His gay sexuality and prior affiliation with the Communist Party made him an easy target for anti–civil rights forces and a troublesome presence for conservative clergy and more bourgeois elements among the civil rights establishment. Rustin's historical relegation to a backstage role within movement circles appeared to break down during the late fifties. He finally seemed to achieve some measure of recognition and respect that had been denied so often. Stephen Steinberg argues that the 1963 March on Washington for Jobs and Freedom contained the seeds of Rustin's conversion to the politics of elite entreaty and that of the civil rights movement more generally. He notes that "while the march had all the earmarks of 'protest,' it actually represented the ascendancy of a new brand of 'coalition politics' the antithesis of the politics of confrontation that were at the core of the black protest movement."[98] At the 1963 March on Washington, Rustin and other civil rights leaders urged John Lewis of Student Nonviolent Coordinating Committee (SNCC) to revise his planned speech, which they deemed too radical and potentially damaging to efforts to garner support for President John F. Kennedy's proposed Civil Rights Bill. The following year, at the Democratic National Convention, Rustin once again opposed more militant forces. When the Mississippi Freedom Democratic Party attempted to unseat the all-white state party delegation, Rustin supported the party establishment's compromise which granted the Freedom Democrats non-voting delegate seats.

His shift toward formal insider politics was not without its ambiguities. Rustin continued to criticize brokerage politics, even as he positioned himself as spokesman through the formation of the A. Philip Randolph Institute. He criticized the Community Action Program of the War on Poverty for its mobilization of middle-class leadership. As well, he took issue with the initiative's limited focus on job training and neglect of macrolevel economic issues such as structural unemployment. Unlike Cruse, Rustin was not seduced by ethnic revivalism. He openly criticized the notion that "Black Power" would come through closing ranks and pursuing the formula of group empowerment allegedly used by white ethnics. Rustin asserted that Black Power advocates who accepted the historical myth of ethnic pluralism discouraged honest consideration of the many historical instances of cross-racial solidarity and the prospects for developing such in the present. Against the ethnic paradigm circulating among Black Power advocates and white liberals alike, Rustin concluded "that it was through alliances with other groups (in political machines or as part of trade union movement) that the Irish and the Jews acquired the power to win their rightful place in American society."[99] While he eagerly anticipated the expansion of the black vote, Rustin did not advocate black political independence as an end.[100] Rather, he saw the black vote as one fraction of the Democratic Party electoral equation. Shunning independent leverage politics, Rustin concluded that "the effectiveness of a swing vote depends solely on 'other' votes. It derives its power from them. In that sense, it can never be 'independent,' but must opt for one candidate or the other, even if by default. Thus, coalitions are inescapable, however tentative they may be."[101] Even as he embraced conventional politics, Rustin remained committed to social democracy. Rustin contended that racial inequality could only be ameliorated by "refashioning of our political economy." Challenging the liberal civil rights forces to extend to economic issues, Rustin noted: "I fail to see how the movement can be victorious in the absence of radical programs for full employment, abolition of slums, the reconstruction of our educational system, new definitions of work and leisure."[102]

Although Rustin would be portrayed by more militant Black Power advocates as either a turncoat or Uncle Tom, for his dogged insistence on coalition politics, the basic social democratic reforms he advocated would become the leitmotif of various platforms and agendas crafted by both radical organizers and liberal politicians during the seventies. Although Rustin's ideas were controversial at the time of their publication, his attempts to reconcile radical social reform to institutional politics, his defense of the Democratic party coalition as the only sensible outlet for black political articulation, and his abandonment of popular protest in favor of elite brokerage prefigured the ideological and strategic orientation of the post-segregation era liberal black political regime. His partisan view of pursuing racial justice via institutional politics was recognized and promoted by the state apparatus as an antidote to the mass disruptions of the civil rights movement. On matters of political strategy, Rustin and Cruse represented moderate nodes within the wider constellation of black political thinking during the middle to late sixties.

Enlisting Rustin's public comments to lend authority to his claims, Cruse mocked the viability of protest politics:

> More marches are planned to state capitols and city halls and a proliferation of more "gimmicks." The great sit-in morality crusade will continue in a society predicated on immorality that breeds the pathological martyrdom of the jailhouse. The constant search will go on for new styles of "causes" with new martyrs and other Negro martyred personalities to romanticize in the left-wing press with new "defense" committees.[103]

Cruse's apparent aversion to protest politics was further reflected in the strange conception of creative intellectuals in his work.

Although he is right in pointing out the conservative tendencies of race politicians and civil right leaders, his privileging of creative intellectuals is restrictive. No explicit definition of the term "intellectual" was given in *The Crisis of the Negro Intellectual*.[104] In an analytical style that permeates this work, he imposes a sharp dichotomy between creative artists and political activists. This designation does not capture the zeitgeist of the sixties where the arbitrary boundaries between art and politics collapsed and writers and musicians were swept into the era's social upheavals and, in return, shaped the course of such struggles. As well, Cruse's criticism of civil rights protests neglects the profound creativity that characterized the strategic and tactical aspects of these struggles. This interpretative bias comes into view in the following passage:

> In advanced societies it is not the race politicians or "rights" leaders who create the new ideas and the new images of life and man. That role belongs to the artists and the intellectuals of each generation. Let the race politicians, if they will, create political, economic and organizational forms of leadership; but it is the artist and the creative minds who will and must, furnish the all important content. And in this role, they must not be subordinated to the whims and desires of politicians, race leaders and civil rights entrepreneurs whether they come from the Left, Right or Center, or whether they be peaceful, reform, violent, non-violent or laissez-faire.[105]

Cruse's devaluation of movement activism inevitably supported the processes of institutional incorporation and demobilization that began during the Black Power era.

Conclusion

The expanded role of culture in Cruse's analysis corresponded with the wider cultural turn in left political theory. As some authors have noted, Cruse's work during the sixties was a neglected precursor in the ascendancy of cultural studies during the late seventies and eighties.[106] Although Cruse's conceptualization of culture underwent important revisions between his early political essays and the 1967 publication of *The Crisis of the Negro Intellectual*, his staunch cultural nationalist posture legitimated a politics that contradicted the best of Cruse's critical insights. In fact, Cruse failed to develop a satisfying interpretation of "black culture," which accounted for the historical complexities of acculturation and new social conditions imposed by the culture industry. As well, his major work did not consistently extend his perceptive reading of the internal class dynamics within the black population into his political prescriptions. Cruse's focus on black cultural particularity led away from the kind of home-grown radical social theory he called for and toward a conservative politics. At various moments in *The Crisis of the Negro Intellectual*, his vision of the political is stunted by bourgeois and anticosmopolitan impulses.

At the level of strategy, Cruse opted for elite brokerage over popular mobilization and as such he provides one of the most influential defenses of the new identity politics that congealed during the Black Power era. While Cruse's effort to rethink Marxism was spurred by the bureaucratization of labor and Communist party radicalism at midcentury, his reassertion of elite leadership supported an equally moderate version of black politics. Ironically, this vocal critic of Old Left orthodoxy set in motion a new set of orthodoxies regarding politics, leadership, and identity that would become central to black public discourse during the Black Power movement and beyond. After years of disappointment and marginality, Cruse saw *The Crisis of the Negro Intellectual* as a long-deferred opportunity to influence the direction of black public life in the dawning postsegregation context. Unfortunately, Cruse's notion of politics imposed limitations on the character of black political action. By privileging those "who can lead directly with the state apparatus" in his formulation of black politics, Cruse supported a mode of political organizing that led away from popular mobilization and the kind of public pressure that might have created more substantial democratic changes in American society.

In practice, the calls for black autonomy and indigenous control emanating from *The Crisis of the Negro Intellectual* were compatible with the moderate forms of citizen participation promoted through the War on Poverty initiative. Cruse was well aware of the emerging arrangements of state and corporate investment in black identity politics during the period. He worked momentarily with LeRoi Jones (later Amiri Baraka) at the BARTS. A keystone institution in the Black Arts movement, this cultural nationalist project was funded through Harlem Youth Opportunities Unlimited (HARYOU), a Johnson era antipoverty program led by sociologist Kenneth Clark.[107] Cruse and Amiri Baraka were fellow travelers, but they were never quite comrades. From their 1960 Fair Play for Cuba trip to their membership in On Guard for Freedom, the two men often inhabited the same organizational and intellectual space. In his *Evergreen Review* account of the 1960 trip titled "Cuba Libre," Jones mocked Cruse as being a "1930's type Negro 'essayist' who turned out to be marvelously unlied to."[108] In return, Cruse dug deeper into the generational rift in *The Crisis of the Negro Intellectual* depicting Jones as a young apolitical writer "who was still very impressed with 'name' writers."[109] As well, Cruse added Jones to his long list of American black intellectuals "who did not understand their own social dynamic."[110] Jones succeeded as a playwright and artist in ways that the elder Cruse must have surely envied. In their own ways, both Cruse and Baraka shaped late sixties black cultural nationalism. Moreover, both helped to give form and legitimacy to postsegregation black identity politics. Although Cruse made his mark on sixties black political development at the level of theory, Jones/Baraka would excel in radical practice, creating effective vehicles for popular art and political mobilization.

Return of the Native

Amiri Baraka (LeRoi Jones), the New Nationalism, and Black Power Politics

The Black Artist's role in America is to aid in the destruction
of America as he knows it.
　　—*LeRoi Jones, "State/meant"*

Amiri Baraka (LeRoi Jones) is arguably the most significant
African American intellectual of the late twentieth century. His volu-
minous body of artistic work includes poetry, prose, drama, and visual
arts and spans over four decades—from the heyday of the fifties Beat
generation through the Black Arts movement and into the early
twenty-first century. Even his toughest critics openly acknowledge
Baraka's tremendous influence. Commenting on the younger generation of sixties black radicals, Harold Cruse in *The Crisis of the Negro
Intellectual* concluded, "[o]ne of the most outstanding among them,
Jones, learned in such a personal way to epitomize within himself all
the other things his generation learned either empirically or vicariously."[1] Jerry Watts declares that Baraka's most influential years within
the Black Power movement were characterized by "a quality of political
engagement that has rarely been rivaled in the twentieth century by
traditional American intellectuals."[2] Alongside a panoply of writers,
performance artists and critics including Larry Neal, Addison Gayle,
Don L. Lee (Haki Madhubuti), Gwendolyn Brooks, Sonia Sanchez, Gil
Scott Heron, the Last Poets, Nikki Giovanni, and Jewel C. Lattimore

(Johari Amini), Baraka led an artistic revolution that helped to redefine black aesthetics and popularize Black Power themes.[3]

Baraka and other black cultural workers momentarily forged a
common political language spoken by moderate politicians and
radical activists alike. Equally important, Baraka attempted to operationalize race unity and indigenous control through local and
national political work. He was a chief architect in the creation of
Black Power organizations such as the Committee for a Unified
Newark, the Congress of African Peoples (CAP), and the National
Black Political Assembly. At his most creative moments, Baraka's
charismatic presence, artistry, and organizing skills spurred thousands into meaningful political engagement and transformed African
American politics. The previous chapter examined the evolution of
Cruse's cultural nationalism and the wider social and intellectual
context that shaped its development, whereas this chapter explores
Jones's/Baraka's formidable political achievements and the problems
that emerge from the application of racial authenticity to politics.

The first section of this chapter retraces Baraka's political awakening after his 1960 trip to Cuba. Here I contrast the more open, internationalist racial militancy of the New Afro-American nationalism
during the early sixties with the more strident forms of identity
politics that congealed circa 1965. Between 1965 and 1974, Baraka
increasingly promoted a racialized view of culture that shaped his
political engagement. Although Baraka's artistic work shifted dramatically away from bohemian aesthetic protest toward black cultural
nationalism, the actual contours of his political activism—particularly
at the local level—were complex and contradictory.

Even among the more nationalistic corners of the Black Power
movement, an awareness of class was not altogether absent. Within
sixties black nationalist discourse, class criticism was pitched in racial
or cultural terms, with whiteness and blackness serving as proxies for
bourgeois and proletarian sensibilities. Activists and artists often jux-
taposed the pretentiousness, behaviors, and desires of middle-class
blacks who sought full integration into the white mainstream against
the more authentic lifestyles and manners of the black working class.
Such criticisms, however, did not typically accommodate a more
sophisticated critique of class and capital. By posing class politics in

black-and-white terms, such articulations of black cultural nationalism served to mystify the internal politics of the black population in
ways that undermined the emancipatory aspirations of Black Power.
Although Baraka was critical of the reformist posture of some black
politicians and would eventually abandon identitarian politics, his
advocacy of black vanguardist politics complemented the elite brokerage politics of more moderate black leaders.

The title of this chapter is taken from a poem that first appeared in
Baraka's collection, *Target Study*.[4] The poem "Return of the Native"
recalls the title of an 1878 novel by English writer Thomas Hardy. Just
as Hardy's classic novel emerged from his physical return home to
Dorcester, and his renewed appreciation of its local culture and language, this poem reflects Baraka's awakening to a politicized racial
consciousness and his 1965 move from Greenwich Village to Harlem.
Here Baraka celebrates Harlem as "vicious modernism."[5] Harlem is
"[t]he place, and place meant of black people. Their heavy Egypt."[6] In
this compact, vivacious ode to Harlem, Baraka paints an idyllic place
where "women stare and are in love with themselves. The sky sits
awake over us. Screaming at us. No rain. Sun, hot cleaning sun drives
us under it."[7] For this prodigal son, Harlem is a black space, an
affirming space amidst a majority-white America: "the hearts, the
gentle hum of meaning. Each thing, life we have, or love, is meant for
us in a world like this. Where we may see ourselves all the time. And
suffer in joy, that our lives are so familiar." I evoke this particular
poem here because it is representative of the spirit of much Black
Power artistic production. This poem and much of Baraka's art during the 1960s conveys a sense of alienation and longing for genuine
self-determination that would crystallize in the Black Power movement. Additionally, this poem also captures some of the internal contradictions of black nationalist politics.

This particular native homecoming bore certain antinomies.
Baraka was not an actual native of Harlem. His move to Harlem
and the wider discourses around self-determination concealed complexities of place, class, and politics among African Americans.
Baraka's and his Black Power contemporaries' decision to "go native"
was a progressive turn inasmuch as it signaled their desire to become
more politically relevant. Although Baraka's artistic work announced

a revolutionary rupture from American society, the actual modes of political organizing and assumptions about representation and governance that he promoted during the late sixties and early seventies remained tethered to conventional liberal democratic frames. Indeed, in the spirit of Frantz Fanon, I want to illuminate the "pitfalls of nationalist consciousness" as they were manifested in Black Power politics. Fanon's *The Wretched of the Earth* stands as a classic of sixties radical literature and one of the most influential texts among Black Power radicals.[8] While the first chapter of his book "Concerning Violence" is perhaps the most provocative and often cited one because of his advocacy of emancipatory violence, the most prophetic chapter comes later.

In "The Pitfalls of Nationalist Consciousness," Fanon offers words of caution concerning the aftermath of national independence and, in effect, he foresees the reactionary designs that some native elites pursued throughout the postcolonial world. Independence brought new flags, patriotic anthems, and parliamentary democracy, but genuine progress would only come through sustained revolutionary planning by the new national governments. Fanon concluded, "[i]t so happens that the unpreparedness of the educated classes, the lack of the practical links between them and the mass of the people, their laziness, and let it be said, their cowardice at the decisive moment of struggle will give rise to tragic mishaps."[9] Idealistically, Fanon argued that after attaining national independence "an authentic national middle class ought to consider as its national duty to betray the calling fate has marked out for it, and to put itself to school with the people: in other words to put at the people's disposal the intellectual and technical capital that it has snatched when going through the colonial universities."[10] Fanon lamented that most often the native middle classes construed nationalization of the economy not as a broadly redistributive process that might benefit the greater national public, but rather as "the transfer into native hands of those unfair advantages which are a legacy of the colonial period."[11] As a consequence, the national middle class merely enhances its status and intermediary role between the impoverished populace and the business and political elites of the former mother country. Although the U.S. context, which Baraka and other radicals inhabited during the late sixties, was quite different from that of colonial Algeria, Fanon's brilliant analysis of the limitations of indigenous control is relevant to this discussion of Black Power radicalism. He points out how nationalist consciousness can serve a defensive function during the process of decolonization only to dissolve into an ideological mist the moment that elements of that struggle achieve institutional power. After colonial independence was won, nationalist consciousness often masked parasitic behaviors of some native political elites. Similarly, in the American context, black radicals' promotion of an affirming black consciousness served as a powerful source of mobilization and led to the transformation of public and corporate institutions during the sixties and seventies. Nevertheless, some black radicals advocated a form of identity politics that papered over meaningful ideological differences and material interests among African Americans.

The Cuban Revelation

Baraka's radicalization follows a trajectory similar to other sixties radicals whose political maturation was framed by Cold War domestic conformity, black urbanization, the civil rights movement, and Third World decolonization struggles. He was born Everett LeRoy Jones on 7 October 1934 in Newark, New Jersey. His father Coyette LeRoy Jones was a high-school graduate who worked as postal supervisor while his mother, Anna Lois Russ, a social worker, attended Tuskegee University. The young Jones attended Newark's Central Avenue School and Barringer High School. The grandson of preachers and teachers, early on he expressed an interest in becoming a minister. Jones attended Howard University, an institution that served as an incubator for his growing antibourgeois sentiments. Jones studied under sociologist E. Franklin Frazier and literary scholar Sterling Brown. After leaving Howard in 1954, Jones enlisted in the U.S. Air Force—or as he would later recall, the "Error Farce." While stationed at Ramey Field, Puerto Rico, he served as a weatherman and a gunner on a B-36 intercontinental bomber. There he established the Ramey Air Force Salon, a multiracial collective of photographers, painters, and intellectuals. Jones was undesirably discharged from the military in 1957 under charges of communist sympathy. He recovered from these setbacks and settled into the new bohemian milieu of Green-wich Village.[12] In October 1958, he married Hettie Roberta Cohen at a New York Buddhist temple. Together they created and edited a literary magazine, *Yugen* (a Japanese aesthetic term meaning "elegance, beauty, grace, transcendence of these things and also, nothing at all").[13] Between 1958 and 1962, they published eight issues that showcased a broad swath of literary stars from the local Beat scene including Jack Kerouac, William Burroughs, Diane DiPrima, Allen Ginsberg, Frank O'Hara, among others. The magazine also featured up-and-coming writers, such as Jones's former Howard classmate A.B. Spellman.

By most accounts, a principle catalyst in his politicization was Jones's 1960 sojourn to Cuba sponsored by the Fair Play for Cuba Committee (FPCC) led by former Columbia Broadcasting System (CBS) journalist, Richard Gibson.[14] His trip to Cuba would pro-foundly affect his identity as an artist—transforming his curiosities about the southern civil rights movement and anticolonial struggles into a full-blown commitment to activism and a highly political art. As he recalled much later, "I carried so much back with me that I was never the same again. The dynamic of revolution had touched me . . . Seeing youth not just turning on and dropping out, not just hiply cynical or cynically hip, but using their strength and energy to change the real world—that was too much."[15] A partial impetus for his inclu-sion in the 1960 FPCC delegation was Jones's poetic tribute to the Cuban Revolution "For You" that appeared in a small poetry col-lection *January 1st 1959: Fidel Castro,* which also included contribu-tions by Kerouac, Ron Loewinsohn, Joel Oppenheimer, and Gilbert Sorrentino.[16] His visit to Cuba marked the beginning of Jones's departure from the aesthetic rebellion of the Beats toward more openly political protests and racial militancy.

Originally, invitations were issued to well-known black writers, Langston Hughes, James Baldwin, and John Oliver Killens, but each declined. The delegation included other artists whom Jones had encountered in various New York circles, such as Harold Cruse; the abstract-impressionist painter Ed Clark; the writer and historian John Henrik Clarke; novelist Sarah Wright and her husband; and writer Julian Mayfield and his wife Dr. Ana L. Cordero, a Puerto Rican–born physician. Also accompanying Jones on this trip was

Robert F. Williams, the leader of the Monroe, North Carolina National Association for the Advancement of Colored People (NAACP) and advocate of armed self-defense. During the trip, Jones met other poets such as the Afro-Cuban poet Nicolás Guillén, Pablo Armando Fernández, and Jaime Shelly as well as the French novelist, Françoise Sagan. Although he would briefly exchange words with Castro during the anniversary commemoration of the July 26th movement, his conversations with other young artists from Cuba and throughout Latin America during the journey to the Sierra Maestra seemed to have made the most substantial impact on his conscience.

Jones was deeply impressed by the socialist realist perspectives of young artists who asserted both the political utility of art and the revolutionary obligations of intellectuals. Jones spent much of the 14-hour train ride to Oriente province conversing with Senora Rubi Betancourt, a graduate student in economics and Mexican delegate to the Youth Congress. Betancourt challenged his use of "American" to refer only to U.S. citizens. In response to her implicating him with American imperialism and her incessant criticism of U.S. anti-communism, Jones scrambled to defend himself citing his agreement with her claims, his innocence, and the fact that he was a poet and not a politician. His weak defense only enraged Betancourt who called him a "cowardly bourgeois individualist."[17] With equal passion, Shelly chastised Jones for his political sins of omission: "You want to cultivate your soul? In that ugliness you live in you want to cultivate your soul? Well, we've got millions of starving people to feed, and that moves me enough to make poems out of."[18] Through these exchanges, Jones was forced to reevaluate his own place as an artist and upon returning he sought to make his creative work more relevant to ongoing political struggles. Recalling this confrontation years later, he wrote, "It was the first time I'd been taken on so thoroughly and forcefully and by people my own age, my contemporaries. I was not Eisenhower or Nixon or Faubus, I protested, I was poet . . . For twelve or fourteen hours on the train I was assailed for my bourgeois individualism. And I could see, had seen, people my own age involved in actual *change,* revolution."[19]

Jones's trip to Cuba marked the beginning of the end of his disengaged, bohemian lifestyle and the dawn of his racial militancy.

Increasingly, Jones would integrate more extensive criticism of white racism and Cold War liberalism into his drama and prose. In "Cuba Libre"—Jones's journalistic account of the FPCC trip—he conveys both his frustration with Bohemianism and his longing for more meaningful political opposition.[20] Indicting himself along with his cynically chic peers, Jones wrote: "The rebels among us have become merely people like myself who grow beards and will not participate in politics. Drugs, juvenile delinquency, complete isolation from the vapid mores of the country, a few current ways out. But name an alternative here. Something not inextricably bound up in a lie. Something not part of liberal stupidity or the actual filth of vested interest. . . . Even the vitality of our art is like bright flowers growing up through a rotting carcass."[21] Jones's burgeoning nationalist consciousness and sense of urgency are reflected in a 1962 essay entitled "'Black' Is a Country" where he warns African Americans, "we must act now, in what I see as an extreme 'nationalism,' i.e. in the best interests of our country, the name of which the rest of America has pounded into our heads for four hundred years, *Black*."[22]

Jones's growing racial militancy should be understood within the context of what might be referred to as the New Afro-American Nationalism, a militant political tendency that evolved alongside the southern desegregation campaigns after the 1954 *Brown* decision. The New Afro-American Nationalism was defined by its northern, metropolitan origins, anticolonial politics, critique of the civil rights establishment, and rhetorical posturing toward revolutionary violence. This political tendency emerged from the organizational and intellectual remnants of the New Negro militancy of the interwar period. The novelty of the New Afro-American Nationalism lay in its proponents' intense political affinity with the Third World decolonization movements that gained momentum after the 1955 Bandung Conference.

Harlem-based writer and historian, John Henrik Clarke noted that the organizational cornerstones of this movement were the On Guard for Freedom Committee, the Provisional Committee for Free Africa, and the Liberation Committee for Africa, which published *Liberator* magazine.[23] Other formations such as the Detroit-based Group of Advanced Leadership (GOAL); the Freedom Now Party; the Bay Area's Afro-American Association; and its successor, the

Revolutionary Action Movement (RAM) reflected this tendency as much as the New York–based groups that Clarke mentions. These organizations bore the distinctive imprint of post-Bandung anticolonialism. Cruse asserted that "[t]he rise in the fortunes of colonial self-determination has intensified many an American Negro's sense of alienation and isolation in the West. For those who adopt it, Afro-Americanism serves the purpose of placing them in close rapport with the content and spirit of world revolution."[24] The new nationalists embraced an international pantheon of heroes including Dedan Kimathi, leader of the Kenyan Land and Freedom Army; Congolese premier, Patrice Lumumba; Ghana's first president, Kwame Nkrumah; Guinean anticolonial, Sekou Toure; Cuban revolutionary architect, Fidel Castro; Malcolm X and Williams of the United States; and Chinese Communist Party leader, Mao Tse-tung.[25] Clarke claimed that the new nationalism was essentially proletarian in origin. While it might have been antibourgeois in consciousness and political sentiments, this tendency was populated by middle-class intellectuals, entertainers, writers, and students. More than any other figure, Malcolm X personified the new Afro-American nationalism.

Malcolm's 1963 "Message to the Grassroots" conveys the critical spirit of the New Afro-American nationalism. In late 1963, Reverend Albert Cleage, Milton and Richard Henry of GOAL, Grace and Jimmy Boggs, and other local Detroit activists organized the Grassroots Leadership Conference. This meeting was organized as a more radical alternative to the more mainstream Detroit Council on Human Rights's Northern Negro Leadership Conference. The latter conference organized by Reverend C. L. Franklin excluded black nationalist factions. At the more radical Grassroots Leadership Conference, Malcolm X delivered his influential "Message to the Grassroots" address, which introduced his memorable "house negro/field negro" analogy to map the class and ideological tendencies within black political culture. Moreover, in the address, he offered a scathing critique of mainstream civil rights leadership and attempted to expose the conservative dynamics underlying the 1963 March on Washington.

Malcolm cited a breakdown in the preeminence of Martin Luther King, Jr., and the stewardship of the Southern Christian Leadership Conference (SCLC) over the southern movement following the unsuccessful desegregation campaign in Albany, Georgia. This defeat precipitated a rising tide of militancy among many blacks and violent eruptions in places like Birmingham. Malcolm argued that the Kennedy administration and the "Big Six" civil rights leaders organized the 1963 March on Washington in an effort to subdue the groundswell of dissent while consolidating support for Kennedy's proposed civil rights reforms.[26] While the particulars of Malcolm X's account may be debatable, his claims point to both real ideological cleavages within the black population at that historical juncture and, more importantly, to the genesis of a postsegregation race management regime. Malcolm's staccato reprisals of civil rights leaders, his accessible social theory, and charismatic manner served to popularize a militant politics of black nationalism. Although his early thinking fell within the parameters of the Nation of Islam's (NOI's) doctrines, Malcolm, in his capacity as the NOI's national spokesman, increasingly crafted a popular critique of the limits of liberal integrationism. Unlike the NOI's apolitical mysticism, his public sermons spoke directly to ongoing crises in American race relations. Among others, Jan Carew argues that during his last year Malcolm X was seeking to refine his initial formulations into a more internationalist, revolutionary politics.[27] Only days before Malcolm X's assassination, in an address at Columbia University, he asserted "[i]t is incorrect to classify the revolt of the Negro as simply a racial conflict of black against white . . . Rather we are today seeing a global rebellion of the oppressed against the oppressor, the exploited against the exploiter."[28] After his death in 1965, thousands of African Americans embraced his demands for black self-determination and militant rhetoric although some downplayed his budding affection for left internationalism.[29]

Jones's earliest activism upon returning from Cuba took place within new nationalist mobilizations. He joined the Organization of Young Men (OYM), a small group of downtown black artists including Cruse, Archie Shepp, Spellman, Leroy McLucas, Steve Cannon, Walter Bowie, Bobb Hamilton, and Calvin Hicks. As Jones later recalled, the group's purpose and direction were unclear: "We weren't certain just what we wanted to do. It was more like a confirmation of rising consciousness. We issued at least one statement, but the sense of it was that we knew it was time to go on the offensive in the civil rights movement. We did not feel a part of that movement."[30] Perhaps,

partially due to this lack of clear direction and purpose, the OYM
merged with the On Guard for Freedom committee, an organization
led by Hicks and closely aligned with the FPCC. In February 1961,
Jones was beaten and arrested during a raucous demonstration at the
United Nations following the assassination of Congolese Premier,
Patrice Lumumba.[31] The protesters were drawn from On Guard for
Freedom and the Cultural Association for Women of African Heritage, a group led by singer and actor, Abby Lincoln. As Clarke asserts,
many activists compared Lumumba's death to that of Emmett Till, the
fourteen-year-old Chicago youth who was murdered in Mississippi in
1955 for transgressing Jim Crow social conventions. Lumumba's
death was, according to Clarke, "the international lynching of a black
man on the altar of colonialism and white supremacy."[32] This dramatic response to the Congolese coup d'etat was only one episode in
the development of Cold War anticolonial politics among African
Americans. Following the attempted Bay of Pigs invasion in April
1961, Jones joined the swelling opposition to U.S. intervention in
Cuba. He signed two petitions in response, which mirrored his Beat
roots and developing racial allegiance. One letter published in the
Evergreen Review was undersigned by Jones, DiPrima, Lawrence
Ferlinghetti, Ginsberg, Norman Mailer, and Paul Goodman. A second
letter appeared in the *Afro-American* with signatures from Clarke,
Cruse, Gibson, Mayfield, Robert Williams, Ossie Davis, and the exiled
W.E.B. DuBois. Jones's art surged with this new militancy as well.

Increasingly, Jones's dramatic works appropriated the literal political intentions of anticolonial struggles. Paralleling Fanon, Jones's
plays were imbued with a sense of Manichean racial struggle that
could only be resolved through political apocalypse—the complete
destruction of the old order and the creation of a new one.[33] Jones
achieved his greatest commercial and critical success within New
York theatre circles through plays that interwove absurdist elements,
theatrical violence, and erotic racial imagery. Although his earlier
plays *The Baptism* and *Toilet* found some critical praise, *Dutchman*—
a play that Mailer deemed "the best play in America"—catapulted
Jones into stardom. On the heels of the play's success, he was show-
ered with literary accolades and was invited to teach poetry and
drama at Columbia University, the New School for Social Research,

and the University of Buffalo. His subsequent play *Slave* further
solidified his reputation as the foremost black protest writer of his
generation. His prose reflected his on-going, post-Cuba political
transformation as well. Jones offered a rendition of the black vanguard thesis that was more akin to that of Kerouac and Norman
Mailer's "White Negro" than the claims offered by Cruse or Herbert
Marcuse. In his 1962 essay "City of Harlem," Jones portrays a "community of nonconformists."[34] Harlem was, according to Jones, "a
colony of old-line Americans, who can hold out, even if it is a great
deal of the time in misery ignorance, but still hold out, against the
hypocrisy and sterility of big-time America, and still try to make their
own lives, simply because of their color but by now, not so simply,
because that color now does serve to identify people in America
whose feelings about it are not broadcast every day on television."[35]
Like Cruse, Jones increasingly celebrated the "Negro folk idiom" as an
antidote to the integrationist aspirations and politics of respectability
practiced by the black middle class. Jones valorized streetgeist and
vernacular casting these elements of black working-class culture as an
affirming, normative "blackness." These celebrations of blackness were
accompanied by increasingly venomous rhetorical attacks on whites.

As he would later concede, during this period Jones developed the
reputation of being "a snarling, white-hating madman."[36] One regret-
table instance of his anti-white hostility took place at the Village
Vanguard between a group of white liberals, Jones, and jazz saxo-
phonist Shepp.[37] Jones scorned the contributions of Jewish, CORE
(Congress of Racial Equality) activists Michael Schwerner and Andrew
Goodman who were martyred along with James Chaney in Mississippi in 1964. According to Jones, "[t]hose white boys were only seeking to assuage their own leaking consciences."[38] Jones rejected white
liberals' desire to support antiracist struggles, saying "[y]ou can help
by dying. You are a cancer. You can help the world's people with your
death."[39] Watts contends that Jones's increasing anti-white tirades
were driven by his own sense of racial guilt. He concludes "In denounc-
ing whites, Jones was actually condemning himself for his lack of
involvement in the black movement. The whites he vilified as 'poseur-
liberals who sashayed safely through the streets of Greenwich Village,
the behind-the-scenes bleeding hearts' were essentially transferred

and detested images of himself. Ironically, it was Jones and Shepp, not Goodman and Schwerner, who were trying to assuage leaking consciences."[40]

Watts is right in condemning Jones's hateful dismissal of the sacrifices made by "outside agitators"—as Jones himself would later renounce this misbehavior.[41] His interpretation of these events is enticing because it highlights the peculiar contradictions of the new Afro-American nationalism's emergence among northern black middle-class intellectuals who were both estranged from Jim Crow segregation and very much enmeshed in white artistic circles. Equally significant, Shepp's and Jones's comments took place outside the context of actual, concrete political mobilizations that might have disciplined such irresponsible language. Nonetheless, Watts' retrospective psychoanalysis hinges on an overstatement of Jones's lack of political engagement at mid-decade. He suggests a more insightful line of argument where he notes the budding currency of public white flagellation within mid-sixties liberal discourse. Baraka's success as a playwright increasingly thrust him into the role of a racial spokesman especially in liberal intellectual circles. Other black writers and intellectuals such as Baldwin, Malcolm X, and, later, Stokely Carmichael became routine fixtures on the college lecture circuit, radio, and television as critics of racism, and, for some, exorcists of white guilt. Moreover, this particular episode also reveals an appetite for abusive speech that would typify much of Jones's public rhetoric and ultimately undermine his political influence and personal relationships with blacks as well as whites. This pattern of misdirected ad hominems and invective that often marred Jones's public stature represents the ultimate irony—the influential man of words who has not carefully mastered the power of his own utterances.

Jones's efforts to kill the memory of interracialism during the Village Vanguard fracas signaled a transition from the new nationalist militancy to the more adamant, late sixties arguments for black autonomy. During the immediate years after his Cuban sojourn, Jones's expressions of black identity were less strident than they became after 1965. Although certain writings such as his "Letter to Jules Feiffer" and the aforementioned Village Vanguard episode would express strong anti-white sentiments, these were exceptional and did not completely reflect the character of his actual relationships with whites—his wife,

publishers, actors, theatre patrons, etc. Other works were marked
by an ambivalence toward interracialism. Additionally, many of the
new nationalist activists associated with the OYM and later with On
Guard for Freedom were either married or in sexual relationships
with whites and were embedded in white, liberal social networks. As
Werner Sollors concludes, "Baraka's specific and personal espousal of
'Blackness' and indeed, his very definition of Blackness, however grew
out of literary positions he had adopted in the 1950s. Furthermore, his
ethnocentric tendencies in the first half of the 1960s were neither systematic nor did they exclude other literary, philosophical and political
vantage points in his works."[42] Other reflections on the new nationalism of the early sixties convey a sense of cosmopolitan black militancy.

In a 1963 essay "Negro Nationalism's New Wave" that appeared in
The New Leader, Cruse wrote that while the new nationalists will
"undoubtedly make a lot of noise in militant demonstrations, cultivate beards and sport their Negroid hair in various degrees of la
mode au naturel, and tend to be cultish with African- and Arab-style
dress," these activities would not necessarily give rise to a narrow
racial outlook. The new nationalist intellectuals, according to Cruse,
"will not frown on interracialism, if only to prove that nationalism
must be made acceptable on their own terms . . . Today it is not
uncommon to see Albert Camus' *The Rebel* protruding the hip
pocket of a well-worn pair of jeans among the Afro-American set."
Contrary to his predictions, this fluid alchemy of racial militancy,
internationalism, and coalition politics that characterized early sixties black radicalism was superceded by a more fundamentalist
politics of racial self-assertion in light of the juridical recognition of
civil rights movement demands, the limited reach of state reforms,
and the wave of urban rebellions that followed.

The New Afro-American nationalism arose alongside the early sixties flowering of the southern civil rights struggle. The relationship
between these two movements was more contrapuntal than sheerly
adversarial. The strength of civil rights forces and the disruptive
protests that garnered national attention opened up space for more
radical black voices. In return, the threat of more militant activism
added legitimacy to the political demands of civil rights moderates in
the eyes of state actors and mainstream American public. Jones's successful protest plays of the middle sixties found their most supportive

and adoring audiences among liberal whites. The mid-1960s saw
the calcification of a politicized racial consciousness in Jones's artistic and political work—a rejection of all things white. According
to Sollors, during the latter half of the decade, "His antibourgeois
opposition was now rephrased as a black-white antagonism." Furthermore, his early affection for socialist realism's insistence on a
politically committed art was increasingly recast in terms of racial
authenticity. A writer, according to Jones, "must have a point of view,
or he cannot be a good writer. He must be standing somewhere in
the world, or else he is not one of *us* and his commentary then is of
little value."[43] Ultimately, the tensions between his racially charged
public rhetoric and his interracial personal and professional life
proved to be too much to reconcile. In the wake of Malcolm X's assassination in 1965, Jones severed personal and professional ties with
the village literary circles, left his wife and their two daughters, and
moved uptown to Harlem—"Seeking revolution!"as he recalls.[44]

In a ceremony performed by the same orthodox Muslim who conducted Malcolm X's funeral, Jones adopted the Arabic name Ameer
Barakat or "blessed prince" and later embraced the Kiswahili version
of this name, Amiri Baraka.[45] From 1968 to his renunciation of black
cultural nationalism in 1974, he used the title Imamu, a Kiswahili
variation of the Arabic "Imam" or spiritual leader. In 1966, he created
the influential, though short-lived, Black Arts Repertory Theater/
School (BARTS) in Harlem and helped to christen the Black Arts
movement.[46] Baraka met Sylvia Robinson (later Amina Baraka), a
dancer and actor who was active in the Newark's Black Arts movement.[47] The couple married in August 1967 and began an enduring
personal, artistic, and activist partnership. Baraka recalls being drawn
to Robinson's efforts as a black cultural worker outside the exclusive,
temperamental New York City art circles he frequented. He writes of
Robinson:

> her own cultural work was . . . against much heavier odds . . . in
> those cities like Newark, grim industrial towns in the real world,
> these kinds of projects are necessarily smaller but at the same
> time tougher and blacker because they are rooted in the
> absolute necessities of people's desired sensibility.[48]

He concluded that "[p]eople must fight to bring art to a place like Newark . . . with usually a great deal more of a sense of responsibility than their average New York counterparts."[49] When BARTS collapsed amidst financial turmoil, sectarianism, and the shooting of Larry Neal, Baraka returned home to Newark and began a period of vigorous community activism and institution building that stretched into the next decade. Such local cultural institutions included Spirit House, Jihad Productions, the Afrikan Free School, and a cooperative book and record store.

Baraka met Maulana Karenga (formerly Ron Everett) in 1966 and eventually adopted his Kawaida philosophy.[50] Much of Baraka's political work was built upon the four areas of political power emphasized under Kawaida: (1) elected or appointed public office; (2) community organizing; (3) alliances and coalitions; and (4) the threat or use of disruption. Personal and political ties between Baraka and CFUN (Committee for a Unified Newark) activists and Karenga's Us organization were strained as some New Jersey–based nationalists expressed opposition to Karenga's treatment of women, advocacy of polygamy, and hierarchical leadership. These tensions led to a "near deadly showdown" between armed cadre from CFUN and Us organization at the 1970 CAP meeting in Atlanta.[51] However, Baraka's charismatic oratory, penchant for grassroots mobilization, and Karenga's 1971 conviction of assault charges and subsequent imprisonment served to elevate Baraka as the chief proponent of black cultural nationalism during the late sixties and early seventies. Though his foray into active political work predated the 1967 Newark Black Power Conference, this meeting helped to push Amiri Baraka into the forefront of developing a more radical presence in national black politics.

Between Negro Politics and the "Black Revolution": The Black Power Conferences

Although the introduction of this phrase is most often attributed to SNCC activists Willie Ricks and Stokely Carmichael, Harlem Congressman Adam Clayton Powell's call for an "audacious Black Power" predated their usage. The paper that Powell described as his "life's philosophy" was first delivered in May 1965 and became a routine fixture of his public addresses.[52] In the text, Powell stresses the value of racial pride and the necessity of black self-determination and full racial equality. While he called for "black revolution," Powell's "Black position paper" in fact advocated the pursuit of racial justice ends through peaceful, conventional means. Economic self-help and business development, which might alter what he viewed as blacks' perennial status of consumerism and dependency, were central strategies within Powell's theory of black empowerment. Likewise, he stressed the importance of achieving the full potential of the black vote. Though Powell's adamance and messianic rhetorical delivery lent an air of militancy to his position paper, his conceptualization of Black Power as institutional access was rather conventional. On 3 September 1966, Powell conducted a one-day national Black Power planning conference in the Rayburn House Office Building in Washington, D.C. The principal intent of the meeting was to lay the groundwork for a large-scale Black Power conference to be held the following year.

Powell invited major civil rights leaders Roy Wilkins of the NAACP, Martin Luther King of SCLC, and James Farmer of the CORE but each declined, citing prior commitments. Wilkins went further to demonstrate his suspicion of and disagreement with the Black Power theme as articulated by young militants. In a letter to Powell, Wilkins reasserted the historical position of the NAACP on integration and racial progress: "We of the NAACP do not believe that integration is 'irrelevant,' that white persons should be excluded from participation in the civil rights movement (they created and help maintain the problem and owe it to themselves and to the nation to help rectify racial wrongs), that civil rights legislation is a 'sham,' or that Negroes cannot successfully compete with non-Negroes given an equal opportunity."[53] In spite of Wilkins disapproval of Powell's alignment with young radicals, Powell's efforts to draw diverse leadership elements together around the Black Power theme was met with resistance from radical quarters. SNCC activists declined to participate in the planning conference. Though Carmichael later mobilized support for Powell after his removal from Congress, he offered a critique of Powell's notion of Black Power. Carmichael complained in private that "Powell is talking about stopping the throwing of

Molotov cocktails and not about stopping the causes that bring about the throwing of the cocktails."[54] Additionally, Carmichael lamented that the elder politician's rendition of Black Power was not an advocacy of black independent politics, but rather black Democratic party incorporation. In spite of such dissent, however, Powell's Black Power conference drew significant support and marked the first national-level meeting organized around the Black Power theme.

Over 169 delegates from thirty-seven cities, eighteen states, and sixty-four organizations took part in the proceedings. Powell's biographer Wil Haygood summed up the historic character of the gathering noting that "[n]ever before had so many blacks gathered inside the Capital in such a daring expression of both rage and hope."[55] The conference delegation issued a position paper that called for increased federal aid to urban areas, stronger voting rights enforcement, and greater self-assertion among blacks regarding political involvement. A continuations committee was created to facilitate planning for the 1967 conference. The original committee included well-known Washington, D.C.–based, political activist, Jewel "Mother" Mazique (who later resigned); executive director of the Department of Urban Work for the Episcopal Diocese of Newark Dr. Nathan Wright, Jr.; Omar A. Ahmed of Bronx, New York; cultural nationalist and founder of Us organization, Ron Karenga of Los Angeles; Isaiah Robinson of New York City; and the noted journalist and former aide to Representative Powell, Chuck Stone. Their planning efforts culminated in the 1967 Newark Black Power Conference.

The National Conference on Black Power began on Thursday, 20 July 1967 while much of the host city lay in smoldering ruins. Newark was wracked by a major urban revolt which subsided only a few days before the opening of the conference. When the violence ceased on 17 July, twenty-six people lay dead and over 1,000 were injured. Official reports cited approximately three hundred fires and an estimated $15 million in insured property losses.[56] Baraka was beaten by the police and charged with unlawful possession of firearms. His initial conviction was later overturned. This unfortunate series of events, however, drew national attention and thrust Baraka into the media spotlight. Speaking to reporters on 22 July, he asserted, "Again and again . . . we have sought to plead through the reference to *your opponent / must / have / consciousness...*

progressive humanism . . . again and again our plaints have been denied by an unfeeling, ignorant, graft-ridden, racist government."[57]

The fresh drama of the Newark rebellion helped to contextualize and accelerate leadership certification dynamics between conference participants, mass media outlets, and other mainstream institutions. As sociologist Todd Gitlin argues, the emergence and decline of the New Left and Black Power radicalism must be understood within the context of post–World War II America's increasingly floodlit culture.[58] Mass media provided a platform for the articulation of oppositional programs and, in turn, shaped the self-concept of movement organizations. Major television and news outlets were instrumental in garnering broader support for southern desegregation campaigns as images of police brutalization of peaceful marchers were broadcast into living rooms across the country. There were certain drawbacks to this relationship between mass media and political opposition as sixties popular struggles gained momentum. The desire of radical groups to reach television audiences often led to the retooling of their agendas and the selection of "spokesmen" who complemented the prevailing framing practices of major media outlets and maximized the opposition's public exposure. Consequentially, the most charismatic, telegenic personalities within the New Left were often certified as the voice of the movement writ large. Baraka, H. Rap Brown, Karenga, and other militant activists were thrust into the limelight at the 1967 Newark conference.

The widespread social and physical devastation of the city and the ensuing clashes between black civilians and police as authorities attempted to quell the rebellion added a sense of urgency to the conference proceedings. Despite his formidable role in initiating this national conference and a flurry of rumors that he would address the delegates, Congressman Powell did not attend. Recently deposed on charges of misuse of public funds and facing possible arrest for a criminal contempt citation, Powell remained in exile on the island of Bimini as the conference began.[59] The conference chairman Dr. Nathan Wright, Jr., and the continuations committee voted unanimously against tabling or relocating the meeting in spite of pressure from state and local officials to do so. Against this backdrop of urban rebellion, much of the conference dialogue revolved around the strategic and ideological choice between reform-oriented, black ethnic politics and more radical alternatives.

The conference drew some 1,100 participants representing 26 states, 126 cities, 286 black organizations, and 2 foreign countries.[60] Journalist Chuck Stone asserted that this meeting sharply contrasted "traditional" gatherings by black leaders in that it was more open and democratic—in Stone's words, "[t]he National Conference on Black Power was not a leaders' conference but a peoples' conference."[61] A closer examination of the conference delegation, however, reveals that its participants were drawn from the ranks of middle-class politicos and full-time community organizers. The following partial listing gives a sense of the rich diversity of organizations who supported the 1967 conference: NAACP, CORE, Better Business Investors, Black Liberation Center, RAM, Committee to Seat a Negro Congressman in Brooklyn, A. Philip Randolph Institute, Catholic Interracial Council, the National Association of Black Social Workers, Fisk University Poverty Research Group, Mau Maus, Mississippi Freedom Democratic Party, *Muhammad Speaks,* Zimbabwe African People's Union, Us organization, National Urban League, Socialist Workers Party, Reformed Church of America, New England Grass Roots Organization (NEGRO), SCLC, National Medical Association, Kappa Alpha Psi Fraternity, Inc., Greater Hartford Council of Churches, *Indiana Herald,* New York Police Department, *Liberator* magazine, the City of Rochester, New York's Department of Urban Renewal, National Council of Negro Women, Washington Mobilization to End the War in Vietnam, and the United Auto Workers.[62] Vincent Harding's recollections give some insight into the conference milieu. He notes that "[t]he speeches, clothing and variety of visions and commitments showed that every strain of black radicalism was represented at this meeting . . . The entire scene was filled with a sense of angry, outraged determination, and sometimes one could sense an air of millenarian expectation."[63] Harding's keen observations allude to the Black Power conference's intense psychological value and, yet, deep political impotence.

The Newark Black Power Conference and the string of similar conferences and conventions held in the seventies were critically important for reinforcing the values of activists who often found themselves working in isolated, hostile environments with meager resources. As such, conference participants must have cherished these opportunities to interact with others who expressed comparable commitments to racial advancement. The sense of camaraderie and catharsis that pervaded these conclaves may have also given birth to exaggerated feelings of movement strength and amplitude. Activists who attended the Newark conference were reassured of the validity and ultimate value of their undertakings. Likewise, workshops allowed for practical dissemination of relevant knowledge and tactical skills among participants. Nonetheless, the conference format itself was ill-equipped to facilitate practical political action among participants after adjournment. The Black Power conferences were organized around an inherently ambiguous notion of black unity politics that elided issue-specific organizing. Whereas conference success was determined by the diversity and volume of attendance, few of the organizers possessed the labor power or financial resources to maintain concerted action among the geographically dispersed participants beyond the weekend mobilization. The Black Power conferences and the many other "agenda-setting" conferences that were convened during the seventies and early eighties routinely produced and circulated policy platforms. In retrospect, these documents might be more accurately characterized as surveys of the discordant policy aspirations of African American elites, both radical and moderate, rather than workable agendas, which might guide political action.

The 1967 Newark Conference produced a *Black Power Manifesto*, which included some eighty resolutions.[64] The *Manifesto* featured both gestures toward political revolution and more reformist emphasis on black indigenous control. The *Manifesto*'s predominant, underlying critique of the American order was chiefly directed against white racism and exclusionary practices. As such, indigenous control was offered as the most logical, practical response. On these matters, the *Manifesto* states:

> Black People have consistently expended a large part of our energy and resources reacting to white definition. It is imperative that we begin to develop the organizational and technical competence to initiate and enact our own programs . . . Control

of African communities in America and other black communities and nations throughout the world still remains in the hands of white supremacist oppressors . . .[65]

This emphasis on indigenous control informed much of the substance of the *Manifesto*'s resolutions. Economic resolutions proposed, among other things, the establishment of neighborhood credit unions, a guaranteed annual income, advocacy of "buy black" campaigns, the creation of a Black economic power fund to finance nonprofit and cooperative enterprises and the "upgrading" of black workers. Most of the economic resolutions featured a rhetorical ultimatum—the threat of selective buying campaigns and a potential "move to disrupt the economy" if demands were not forthcoming. Political resolutions emerging from the conference included establishment of a Black Power lobby, advocacy of compulsory black school boards and education administrators in majority-black jurisdictions, election of twelve additional black Congressional representatives, and the mandatory assignment of black police captains to majority-black precincts. The *Manifesto* also contained a resolution proposing a "national black grass roots political convention" to be held during the 1972 presidential election year following those of the major political parties.

The rhetoric of unity permeated the meeting, obscured substantive disagreement and helped to undermine discussion of practical political work. Conference Chair Wright's press statements exemplified this tension between maintaining facile black unity and developing a meaningful political alliance. In his remarks on the conference's objectives, Wright asserted, "We're not interested in consensus. Black people, when they come together, have decided to reject any white definition of what they are doing. Consensus means you gather right down the middle. But our purpose is to reach out to the widest possible embrace. We're interested in inclusiveness, in operational harmony."[66] In an additional effort at clarification, Wright noted that the summit "was not designed to implement programs, but to lay foundations for the development of programs that could later be implemented." Not surprisingly, the unity that was achieved at the Newark Conference was largely cosmetic. Throughout the proceedings, ideological conflicts surfaced. The site of the convention workshops—the

white-owned, Military Park and Robert Treat hotels— and the mandatory registration fee for delegates drew dissent from some delegates
who felt that such choices betrayed the key themes of black autonomy and grassroots, democratic participation.[67] Such protests clearly
illustrated that there was no consensus, before or after the conference, among delegates regarding the precise meaning of the Black
Power slogan. The disjuncture between moderate and radical delegates became more apparent as the conference wore on. During a
press conference, a brief melee erupted when a militant group of delegates asserted their discontent with "white racist press." Tactical differences within the delegation also arose when some radical activists
urged a spontaneous march to confront police patrols and protest the
incarceration of hundreds of black citizens following the recent
riot.[68] Debates over self-defense versus nonviolent resistance, cultural
resistance versus assimilation, the need for building multiracial
alliances versus autonomous black ones, and other ideological fissures, which distinguished black militants from moderate leaders,
were neither consolidated nor resolved under the broad, amorphous
slogans uttered before and after the Newark Conference.

The conference's chief organizer Wright offered a view of Black
Power as a wry blend of ethnic group pluralism and black capitalism
in a book he published shortly before the Newark Conference.[69] In
contrast to the more radical elements within the Black Power movement, Wright was touted in one major news story as representing
"sophistication, scholarship and meditation."[70] For Wright, Black
Power was essentially the fulfillment of the deferred process of black
assimilation into American political, cultural, and economic institutions. "The need now—to close the gap between where we are and
America is as a whole—is for us to have a black purpose, to have
Black Power. It is the most creative social concept in our present century. We will add to American society, not take from it."[71] In contrast
to more radical interpretations of the Black Power slogan, which
placed the source of black subordination in historical-structural
causes—chattel slavery, debt peonage, labor and educational discrimination and apartheid—Wright attributed persistent inequality
to behavioral–cultural deficiencies of the black population. He
argued, "The root of our problem in the United States is not prejudices of the white community against the black community, it is

the faulty power dynamics exercised by black people . . ."[72] In his comments regarding the 1967 Newark rebellion, Wright offers comparable sentiments, "The immediate cause of our so-called riots is white oppression. *The basic cause is pathology in the experience of black people*" [emphasis mine][73] Proceeding from these conservative assumptions regarding black subordination, Wright articulated a vision and strategy of black empowerment consonant with conventional ideas about ethnic politico-economic incorporation. In spite of Wright and other Black Power advocates' public repudiation of white support, the linkages between the Black Power conference and the corporate sector were both ideological and financial with fifty major corporations underwriting the budget for the conclave.

Some delegates dissented against these liberal, pro-corporate views. In numerous workshops, participants debated the relative merits of capitalism, the viability of cooperative economic ventures as alternatives to capitalism, and the merits of black assimilation.[74] One participant, Julius Hobson—a former civil rights activist with the Washington, D.C., CORE chapter—summed up radical discontent with the reformist overtones of the conference and offered a critique of the notion of indigenous control that permeated the 1967 Black Power conference. In reference to the Economics committee workshops, Hobson noted that the "general concensus [*sic*] of this gathering was that we need to transfer the economic power wielded by white men in the Black ghettoes of America to Black men."[75] In light of this generic orientation among the delegates, Hobson lamented in the aftermath of the Newark Conference that many "were completely unaware of the degree to which they have already been 'endarkened' by the status quo," and as a consequence, "had little or no understanding of the nature of their political and economic surroundings."[76] Additionally, Hobson concluded that the conference suffered from the absence of a clear, consistent philosophical base. His remarks on these matters are significant for two reasons.

First, Hobson was alert to the inherent problems of racial unity. He was able to see past the cathartic features of the 1967 conference and examine the extent to which facile commitments to race unity muted open democratic debate. Second, Hobson's comments concerning the Newark Black Power Conference are suggestive of a feature of black radical discourse that would assert itself in an

increasingly destructive fashion during the 1970s. While Hobson
rightfully wished to alert activists to the inherently bourgeois features of reformist Black Power rhetoric, his suggestion to "go left" and
employ a Marxist ideological framework as the principal basis of
political work would become more commonplace and more problematic within black radical circles. Rather than serving as a source of
mobilization, the catechism of ideology, whether Marxist or nationalist, would have the opposite effect during the mid 1970s. Radicals'
injunctions that ideology serve as the centerpiece of organization
would increasingly isolate them from one another, fostering bitter
sectarianism and estranging radical activists from vast sectors of the
African American population for whom doctrinaire ideologies have
little meaning and even less everyday utility. Hobson's comments
reflect fundamental tensions within Black Power radicalism that
would persist well beyond the adjournment of the 1967 Newark
Conference.

At the 1968 Philadelphia Black Power Conference, the efforts of
Baraka and other Newark activists to field local political candidates
were touted as a model to be emulated in other parts of the country.
The third International Black Power Conference was convened at the
Benjamin Franklin High School in Philadelphia from Thursday, 29
August through Sunday, 1 September 1968. Approximately 4,000 per-
sons took part in its proceedings. Baraka appeared on the conference
dais, along with a number of prominent radical activists and political
leaders, including Maulana Karenga, Michigan Congressman John
Conyers, SCLC's Reverend Jesse Jackson, the Urban League's Whitney
Young, longtime Harlem activist Queen Mother Audley Moore, and
Black Studies advocate Nathan Hare. Dr. Wright continued to serve
as the chairman of the continuations committee that was formed two
years earlier at the first conference in Washington, D.C. The deliberations of the conference were organized around a total of ten workshops: Politics, Education, History, Economics, Culture, Community
Organization, Religion and Mythology, Students and Youth, Black
Women, and Communications. Some of the most significant conference resolutions emerged from the section on politics coordinated
by Philadelphia activist Richard Traylor and RAM organizer Max
Stanford. The series of resolutions drafted and read on the final day

of the conference by Traylor centered on the necessity of developing a national black political force. As such the resolutions of the politics workshop capture the militant cries for self-determination and political independence that permeated the 1968 summit.

The workshop participants called for the establishment of a durable, black political party organization since the major political parties and formal system did not meet the needs of black people. This party would be created "in every Black community for the development of radical social change and for the liberation and survival of Black people." It would not be a "crisis organization," but instead the new party would "be capable of having a mass-base of on-going activities which would seek the total empowerment of the Black community."[77] The politics section's resolutions also decreed that successive regional and national conventions be held to build support for the proposed black party. It was suggested that a campaign to recall the "present government system" by referendum and petition be pursued as a means of garnering mass support for the new party. Despite the militant posturing of the Politics workshop reports, much of its substance complemented the pursuit of black indigenous control. The ultimate objective of the proposed party was, in fact, the development of a "national black government."[78]

Tensions between reformist and radical tendencies persisted at the Philadelphia Black Power Conference. Some of the most poignant manifestations of these cleavages involved debates over interracialism and black advancement. At one point in a discussion led by Jim Thomas as part of the Economics section, a debate emerged between participants over union organization and leadership legitimacy. Edward Bragg, a member of District 1199, Hospital Workers Union of New York City, spoke about the majority-black character of the organization and of its Jewish president and founder, Leon Davis. Bragg characterized Davis as being "John Brown–like" because in Bragg's estimation the union leader's commitments to eradicating inequality rivaled those of the martyred abolitionist. Some workshop participants challenged Bragg's acceptance of interracialism with one person asking, "With white leadership at the top, how can a Black organization progress?"[79] After Bragg noted that the organization did include blacks in other leadership positions, another audience member queried "How do you expect to build the power of Black people if the power you use is other than Black?" Others questioned whether there was any real power in Bragg's union given its affiliation with the AFL-CIO (American Federation of Labor-Congress of Industrial Organizations). The contours of this particular exchange reflect concerns about black control central to Black Power discourse. Likewise, the questions raised from the floor spoke to the historical reality of racism within liberal and progressive left organizations. Yet, this particular debate serves as evidence of the double-edged nature of the indigenous control rhetoric. More precisely, it illuminates the fashion in which the rhetoric of black control might obscure the necessarily issue-based nature of political organizing. Serious consideration of the quality of the union's programs, its organizational activities and campaigns, and their implications for the material well-being and social mobility of its black members were overshadowed by concerns over whether blacks controlled the organization's head post. Although these concerns about white leadership and paternalism are justifiable within certain contexts, in other instances the rhetoric of black control becomes unhinged from the struggle against inequality.

Many Black Power advocates were willing to stomach conservative politics, but not color. According to Robert Allen, little effort was made by conference organizers to mask its corporate sponsorship. Conference invitations appeared on Clairol Company stationary and included a copy of a speech given by the company's CEO in which he offered his support of "Black Power" as "ownership of apartments, ownership of homes, ownership of businesses, as well as equitable treatment for all people."[80] The Clairol executive further delineated the role to be played by the corporate sector in this rendition of Black Power, asserting that "[o]nly business can create the economic viability for equity. And only the businessman can make equity an acceptable social pattern in this country."[81]

Like its predecessor, the 1968 Black Power Conference succeeded in drawing together a broad sampling of black leaders and in producing a bold statement of political goals and strategies to redress contemporary problems. The 1968 conference also replicated the celebration of cathartic, symbolic unity at the expense of open, principled debate and initiation of issue-based collaboration. No viable organizational form emerged from the Philadelphia conference nor would any materialize at the 1969 Regional International Black Power Conference in Bermuda. The latter summit was essentially derailed by fearful local government administrators and an equally unfriendly local press core.[82] The Black Power summits were significant as attempts by activists to create space for public dialogue, networking, and exchange. Nonetheless, important conflicts between moderate and radical participants were not adequately addressed. Dissent was often tabled or suppressed for the sake of symbolic unity. Most often, the ritual act of public congregation served as a surrogate for sustained collaboration, planning, and work. While bold proclamations punctuated each of the major Black Power conferences, with each subsequent meeting the capacity of the delegation to advance programmatic actions grew progressively worse. Without an organizational framework to implement its programs, develop real political campaigns, and operationalize its resolutions, the documents emanating from these conferences fell short of being actual political agendas. Temporal collaboration between radical, grassroots activists and moderate, establishment politicians was clearly manifested in numerous local electoral mobilizations. Protracted cooperation between disparate leadership elements, however, proved more troublesome. While radicals and moderates expressed commitment to such broad objectives as indigenous control, various leadership elements pursued such ends with decidedly different sets of expectations. The limited success of the late sixties Black Power conferences in achieving operational unity spurred Baraka and other activists towards the creation of the Congress of African People.

a group of ppl leading the way in new developments or ideas

A Vanguard within a Vanguard

According to Baraka, black nationalists were responsible for acting as a political vanguard capable of radicalizing more moderate sectors of the African American population and advancing the cause of national liberation. Baraka hoped to achieve nationalist hegemony within black political culture through a Trojan horse strategy of direct engagement with nonradical and conservative leadership and organizations. Baraka admonished blacks generally and nationalists in particular, "You must control everything in the community that needs to be controlled. Anything of value: any kind of anti-poverty program, politicians, celebrities, anything that brings money, resources into your community, you should control it."[83] Black nationalists, he argued, "must take what movement actually exists and give it identity, purpose and direction."[84] Furthermore, by participating in conventional organizations such as the NAACP and working toward broad-based operational unity, nationalists would be able to affect concrete, visible change. When defining his view of operational unity, Baraka revealed the crux of the dilemma facing radical intellectuals who wish to be politically relevant and engaged—that is, how does one participate in conventional politics without becoming a part of its machinations or absorbing status quo values. He argued, "We will not be manipulated by anything but the purest Black need. Though the new nationalist must believe and practice, to a sometimes maddening degree of aggravation, operational unity, we cannot lose our values and become negroized [sic]. Our task is to nationalize our brothers and operational unity is one way of getting close enough to them to do it."[85] This passage reflects the generational and ideological tensions within late sixties black political culture and, by extension, reveals the limits of the race unity as political strategy. He deploys "Negroized" and "Black" as shorthand for distinguishing liberal integrationist politics from Black Power militancy. The appearance of such linguistic markers denotes a key contradiction in Baraka's rhetoric—in particular, the tension between black nationalist aspirations for race unity and the fact of political diversity among African Americans.

Like Cruse's arguments regarding the historical responsibility of black intellectuals, Baraka's claims shuttle back and forth between democratic politics and an elite project. At certain moments, Baraka proceeds from more radically democratic impulses noting that the struggle for national liberation "must be a struggle that is organically connected to our lives. No one can pin a revolution button on you, an ideology and say now blood, you know about revolution, here's your copy of the 'Red Book.' It has to come out of the lives of the people themselves."[86] Elsewhere, he expresses an evangelistic faith in nationalist ideology even when such ideas are rejected by blacks themselves:

> Ideas are relevant only in proportion to how much of this material force they can mobilize along a broad but nevertheless, specific path toward national liberation. So that even if the theories of nationalism might say, as theories, alienate negroes, as working stratagems they must have exactly the opposite effect.[87]

This vanguardist posture was valuable as stimulant to local and national activism among many Black Power radicals. The highly skilled and committed cadre of CFUN, CAP, African Liberation Support Committee, the National Black Political Assembly, and many other local Black Power organizations organized successful electoral campaigns; created vibrant public spheres through underground newsletters, pamphleteering, and public forums; and galvanized local communities to confront poverty, inadequate public schools, and other relevant concerns. The efforts of activists to consolidate power in the form of national race institutions, however, would eventually deflate such popular and local social struggles.

Baraka's signal contribution to the development of sixties black cultural nationalism was his effort to operationalize racial unity and indigenous control. In a fashion clearly reminiscent of Malcolm X's Organization of Afro-American Unity, Baraka called for the achievement of "domestic Pan-Africanism" as an indispensable, prerequisite to effective group power. He argued:

> We will not achieve any positive transformation to the world, as Europeans have shaped it unless, we are *unified* and *organized*, personally in our families, our communities, our cities, our nations, and our race. A major part of our work must be institution building, whether we are already evolved to the stage of African unity and have begun to link up, federate, collectivize with other organizations, in expressions of concrete Pan-Africanism, or we still struggling to bring into existence local cadres or organizations around more limited objectives. A nation is simply a large institution.[88]

While the Black Power conferences fell short of creating a durable united front, their failures and limitations stimulated many radical activists to pursue such ends with renewed vigor. Following the fiasco of the 1969 Bermuda Conference, Baraka and other activists began to plan for a similar international meeting in 1970, the Congress of African People that would establish a more permanent organizational base for black radical politics. Baraka called for more progressive engagement with mainstream political forces and institutions. Consequentially, his articulation of Black Power radicalism fused both cultural nationalist politics—with its emphasis on the adoption of alternative lifestyles, black aesthetics, and African value systems—and the goal of black political integration.

Baraka thought that Newark could serve as a model of black control. Newark would be the yardstick of black nationalism's relevancy—"A test of how 'fluidized' [sic] pure nationalism can be and still prove effective at raising the race."[89] Further, he thought the city—with its sizable, spatially concentrated black population—was poised to achieve black indigenous control: "Newark, New Ark, the nationalist sees as the creation of a base, as an example, upon which one aspect of the entire Black nation can be built. We will build schools or transform present curriculum to teach national liberation. We will create agencies to teach community organizing, national, and local politics and send brothers all over the country to re-create the model. We will nationalize the city's institutions as if it were liberated territory in Zimbabwe or Angola."[90] Baraka's ideological commitment to black indigenous control and his penchant for grassroots mobilization were highly instrumental in the historic 1970 election of Newark's first black mayor, Kenneth Gibson.[91]

Gibson was a mild-mannered, Alabama-born engineer who began his political career as vice-president of a local community-action program. Gibson made a strong showing in the 1966 Newark mayoral contest finishing third in the balloting. The successful defeat of incumbent Mayor Hugh Addonizio, however, required some revision of Black Power notions. In 1968, United Brothers organized a black political convention to draft a platform and nominate two black candidates for the city council. The United Brothers was a diverse group of local black male Newark residents organized by Baraka and Spirit

House in the wake of the 1967 Newark rebellion. The convention del-egation crafted resolutions calling for a commuter tax on nonresi-dents, opposition to a proposed interstate highway that would divide standing black neighborhoods, community control of schools, and the development of community-police relations programs.[92] On election day, the United Brothers' candidates were defeated after garnering tepid support from the city's black voters. The ethnic com-position and local political terrain in Newark complicated adherence to a rigid racial identity politics and stimulated the development of more pan-ethnic solidarity between blacks, Puerto Ricans, and other liberal and progressive forces within and beyond Newark.

To win the election, Baraka and CFUN skillfully integrated con-ventional campaign tactics with an assertive grass roots politics.[93] The Newark Black and Puerto Rican Convention held in November 1969 emerged through an alliance between CFUN and the Young Lords. The convention delegation produced a "community choice" slate of candidates for a range of local offices. The New Ark fund was created as a fund-raising apparatus for the 1970 campaigns. During the course of the campaign, public endorsements for the community choice slate were obtained from nationally recognized leaders—both black and white—including Julian Bond, Richard Hatcher, East Orange Mayor William S. Hart, Percy Sutton, George McGovern, John Conyers, Powell, and Shirley Chisholm. Additionally, a host of celebrity personalities such as Stevie Wonder, Ossie Davis, Ruby Dee, Sammy Davis, Jr., Flip Wilson, Dustin Hoffman, and Bill Cosby lent their talent and influence to the campaigns. As a consequence of extensive voter education and mobilization drives, the commu-nity choice supporters achieved a host of watershed electoral victo-ries for Newark's black and Puerto Rican communities. Sharpe James and Dennis Westbrooks won city council seats in the city's South and Central wards. In a run-off election, Kenneth Gibson defeated incumbent Addonizio, 55,097 to 43,086 votes, to become the city's first African American mayor. His success as "king-maker" in Newark served to link Baraka to an emerging network of elected and civic leaders and bestowed him with a level of visibility and notoriety uncommon to radical intellectuals. Additionally, he succeeded in helping to develop a dense regional network of political and cultural organizations and in assembling a cadre of highly disciplined, talented activists from the New York metropolitan area. Such assets proved invaluable as he attempted to forge operational unity among national black elites.

Originally slated to take place in Barbados, the 1970 Congress of African People meeting proposed by Baraka and others was met with resistance by Barbadian government officials—apparently for reasons comparable to those offered by the Bermudian administration during the 1969 Black Power conference. Consequentially, Atlanta was chosen as the site for the inaugural meeting of CAP. In promotional materials distributed before the summer meeting, CAP chairman Hayward Henry, Jr., summed up the intentions of the organizers.[94] Like Baraka, Henry was a staunch black nationalist. At twenty-seven years of age, the precocious CAP chairman was also a Harvard University lecturer, a doctoral candidate in biochemistry at Boston University and chairman of the National Black Caucus in the Unitarian Universalist Church. Setting the tone for the 1970 CAP meeting, Henry noted that "[u]nlike previous Black Power Conferences, the Congress is viewed as a 'working session' rather than a 'rapping session.' We intend to plan and develop specific models for institution-building at the local, national and international levels, and to create the structures of implementation and post conference follow up."[95] Slated for Labor Day weekend, the Atlanta meeting was envisioned by Henry and other organizers as an opportunity for participants to "labor for the nation." As such, the Congress's general direction and underlying purpose represented a significant break from that of the preceding Black Power conferences. Likewise, this meeting reflected the momentary hegemony of nationalist activists within early seventies black political culture.

CAP's inaugural meeting convened from 3–7 September 1970 at the Atlanta University Center. Over 2,700 persons participated. Congress organizers were successful in drawing together a broad cross-section of leaders, including renowned civil rights leaders, such as Reverend Ralph Abernathy, Jackson, and Whitney Young; politicians such as Bond, John Cashin, Gibson, and Hatcher; radical activists such as Howard Fuller of Malcolm X Liberation University and Imari Obadele of the Republic of New Africa; and educators Acklyn Lynch,

Preston Wilcox, and Clarke. The summit also attracted representatives of organizations and countries in Africa and other parts of the Third World, including Roosevelt Douglas of the Organization of Black People's Union (OBPU) and McGill University in Montreal, Canada; Evelyn Kawanza of the Zimbabwe Action Group; Raymond Mbala, representative of the Revolutionary Government of Angola; and Hajj Abdoulaye Touré, Guinean Ambassador to the United States. Also among the international delegation were representatives of Australia's indigenous population including Bob Maza, publicity director for the Aborigines Advancement League in Victoria.

Black nationalist sentiments were articulated by moderate civil rights leaders and politicians. In their respective addresses to the congress, Jackson and Hatcher described African American's social status in colonial terms. Beginning his address with a "Nationtime" call and response intonation taken from Baraka's poetry, Jackson went on to tout the analytic value of the colonial analogy:

See, ghetto is a sociological concept that assumes that we are voluntarily staying somewhere for social reasons. We live in a colony based on economic presupposition. And we ain't judged based on good and evil, intelligent or unintelligent—we've always been judged based on profit and loss, asset and liability.[96]

Hatcher drew direct parallels between the conditions experienced by African Americans and Africans:

You cannot understand what is going on in Mississippi if you do not understand what is going on in the Congo. You cannot be interested in what is going on in Mississippi if you are not also interested in what is going on in the Congo. The're both the same—the same interests are at stake, the same ideas are drawn up, the same schemes are at work. Same stake, no difference whatsoever.[97]

Former SNCC activist and Georgia politician Bond told the delegation: "we reaffirm that we are first and foremost Black nationalists."[98]

Newark Mayor Kenneth Gibson spoke of black nationalism in terms of survival and self-reliance:

> You have to understand that nobody is going to deal with our problems but us. We have to understand that nobody is going to deal with the realities. And the realities and the basis that we are talking about those realities—are the basis of nationalism. And so, nationalism is simply the expression of our recognition of the fact that in the final analysis it is Black people who must solve the problems of Black people.[99]

A number of speakers such as SCLC head Abernathy called for operation unity as well. Perhaps the lone member of the civil rights and political leadership elite to speak critically and openly of certain aspects of the growing nationalist sentiment was Young.

In sharp contrast to anticolonial statements and calls for Pan-Africanist solidarity and revolutionary change, which characterized many of the speeches, Young's address featured advocacy of a practical, incrementalist agenda for black advancement that was tempered by the realities of American society. Rejecting violence as a means of achieving black goals, Young spoke on the virtues of black economic and political power. He encouraged black economic control, support of cooperative economics, credit unions and labor unionization, as well as integration of blacks into management of corporate institutions as sound methods of ameliorating economic inequality. Additionally, Young repudiated the notion that black economic development should occur without formal governmental assistance in the form of subsidies, public capital, and private transfers. Blacks who preached self-help and rejected state support, "reflect[ed] economic naivete" and "invit[ed] economic disaster" according to Young.[100] On political matters, Young expressed support for community control and self-determination as a means of improving local governance and responsiveness to constituencies. Unlike Baraka and most other nationalists, Young, however, did not envision community control in purely racial terms. Rather, he advocated that urban administrators should be elected or hired on the basis of superior qualifications and should, likewise, reflect the diversity of American society. Consequentially, Young argued that there was a need within black public discourse to distinguish between nationalism and chauvinism. Young was, however, in the minority at the meeting as many within the delegation voiced strong support for cultural nationalist ideals and, equally, for the creation of an independent black party.

In an adamant resolution supporting the formation of a black party, the Philadelphia Council claimed that a black party would be a "first step toward building a nation." While the Philadelphia Council's resolution closely mirrored aspects of Baraka's Pan-African party idea, its content was also informed by a recent *Black Scholar* article by Stone.[101] The historical political integration of white ethnics served as the template for Stone's vision of Black Power politics. He argued that "proportionate control of the political process has been manipulated by Irish, the Italians, the Jews and the Polish in virtually every major city in America. Ethnic bloc voting and ethnic political loyalty has been a feverish adjunct to every ethnic group in America except black people."[102] Stone went on to define Black Power primarily in terms of the seizure of public authority. He argued: "we should examine how black people can rise to a position of massive political empowerment that does three things[:] controls the black community, proportionately controls the decision making apparatus of a white racist government and guarantees black survival."[103] Stone's arguments for black political independence echoed elements of the segregation era "balance of power" thesis authored by the NAACP leader Henry Lee Moon.[104] Essentially, Stone argued that the expanding black electorate could act as a "third force" in national elections "which oscillates at will between the candidacies of a Democrat, a Republican or a Third Party black man, depending upon which one the black Third party can more effectively control." Unconditional racial loyalty would not be extended to black politicians under Stone's formula, but, rather, black elected leaders would be equally subject to punishment and reward based on their support of racially germane issues. "Where black politicians elect to work within the system by remaining a Democrat or Republican, black people should only support them if—and this is important—they are responsive first to black people . . ."[105] Following Stone's lead, the Philadelphia Council resolution outlined steps toward party formation.

This proposed black party would be fashioned from the existing CAP structure of councils. Representatives from each council would convene to plan actions for the next election cycle. In localities where a full operative party was not feasible, the council advocated the establishment of a "pseudo-party structure ... through which the Black political agenda can be expressed."[106] Hence, the black party would be generally engaged in "community control of institutions such as health, welfare, housing, land, or any struggle deemed important by Black people."[107] The Council's resolution concluded by charting a political agenda of objectives and aims including full registration of the black voting-age population; black control of ten cities where 39 percent of total black population is located; employment of students and workers in party's work; and the release of all political prisoners. The level and intensity of debate around the black party idea signaled the growing focus of radical activists and intellectuals on the need for national political institutions. The prospects of initiating such a large-scale effort were however tempered by the relative financial troubles encountered by Congress organizers.

Unlike the preceding Black Power conferences, expenses related to the 1970 Atlanta Congress were not underwritten by large corporations. Rather, 90 percent of the $32,200 raised to cover the meeting's cost was drawn from private black donors. CAP activists tried to remain free of white or corporate support and to develop alternative funding bases for their work, but this strategy encountered some difficulty. In a published appeal to Atlanta delegates, CAP finance chairman Traylor spoke of these problems. Unexpected cost incurred during the Congress caused organizers to exceed the initial budget. Due to venue changes for evening entertainment and difficulty in securing low-cost university campus housing for delegates, the Atlanta meeting incurred a $40,000 deficit. Traylor complained of the difficulty in soliciting financial and political support for CAP initiatives from more politically moderate blacks noting, "Since Atlanta our main problem has been getting some of the classical funding sources to relate to the Congress which is the most promising nationalist effort in the history of Blackamerica [sic]. Many of these folks have watched our work in *operationalizing* programs of Black unity; *they know its for real and that's why we can't get funding from classical sources!*"[108] Likewise, he noted the administrative difficulties created in the absence of any paid staff in CAP offices. Traylor concluded by urging all CAP delegates to pay their "self-tax"—1 percent of annual gross income. Perhaps partially due to these financial woes, CAP activists stepped up efforts to build a broad-based alliance with mainstream black elites around the idea of holding a national black political convention, a movement that would culminate in the historic 1972 Gary Convention.

Conclusion

The effective coalition building and political organizing skills of Newark's nationalist forces produced the city's first generation of black elected officials. The 1970 Newark election and subsequent elections in other urban areas ended long histories of political exclusion for African American communities. The ideology of black indigenous control inhibited the development of critical perspectives on power and the public policy-making process. The nationalistic underpinnings of much Black Power organizing confounded racial authenticity with political representation. Too often, Black Power radicals promoted the specious notion that racial loyalty—and not conservative ideology, party discipline, corporate power, or countervailing electoral pressure—would determine the agenda priorities of the new black political elite. Consequentially, many organizers proceeded from the view that the election of black officials would, at minimum, reorient municipal patronage streams in a more racially progressive fashion and, optimally, provide the space for more enduring, substantial redistribution of wealth and power to distressed, black urban citizens. In the absence of a consistent, critical perspective of the American political-economy, activist focus on indigenous control helped to engender consensus among potentially disruptive elements within the black population and consolidate a sizable black political regime.

SNCC activist Phil Hutchings may have summed up the limitations of black control best during his speech at the 1968 Newark Black Political Convention. Hutchings argued that black municipal control would not deliver the kinds of fundamental changes radicals desired because of regional demographic trends and powerful political and economic interests. The movement of more affluent residents to suburbia and the advent of regional planning and metropolitan government schemes undermined the ethnic incorporation model implied in notions of indigenous control. Hutchings concluded that black control would not resolve racial inequalities. In an especially prophetic moment, he foretold the mid-seventies shift toward left politics that would follow as the new black political elite took shape: "It may be that black people will have to have blacks in power over them within the confines of this system before they can truly recognize the necessity to organize against capitalism as well as the racist aspects of America."[109] Indeed, the pitfalls of nationalist consciousness became more apparent as black indigenous control became a reality in many American cities. Following the election of Gibson, many activists complained of enduring problems of police brutality against blacks. By the mid-seventies, latent tensions between radical activists and the Gibson administration grew into open confict over a CAP-sponsored urban development project.

The Kawaida Towers project epitomized the practical, progressive edge of Black Power politics.[110] CAP organizers assembled a talented, multiracial team of architects, attorneys, and contractors to address immediate housing shortages and to carve out more meaningful, livable space in Newark. Baraka and CAP activists secured funding from both the U.S. Department of Housing and Urban Development and New Jersey's Housing Finance Agency to build a sixteen-story, low-to-moderate-income housing complex in Newark's predominantly Italian North Ward. A political crisis quickly unfolded over whether the city should grant tax abatement to the project. As pressure from local reactionary whites mounted, support from local black politicians unraveled. Gibson's initial endorsement wavered while city councilman Earl Harris's opposition to the project was unequivocal. The Newark city council's eventual rejection of CAP's abatement proposal in February 1975 derailed the project and marked the end of black radical influence within Newark's local politics and the stunning realization of the limitations of black indigenous control.

Although his electoral base was derived primarily among black and Puerto Rican residents, in Gibson's day-to-day governance of a city grappling with population loss, industrial decline, and an eroding tax base, racial loyalty was superceded by administrative rationality, *realpolitik,* and pro–growth development schemes. A 1972 essay published by Gibson offers a glimpse of his anxious efforts to pursue certain social democratic policy ideals while balancing the conflict between his electoral constituency and the powerful, vested interests of Newark. Pointing to the mixed economies of Norway, Denmark, and Sweden, Gibson asserted that "competitive, profitable, private enterprise can exist side by side with a socially responsible system. In fact, an elevated social system is private enterprise's best security for the future."[111] Gibson was critical of exclusionary governance and planning schemes designed to "keep the powerless powerless." In a few veiled references, however, he criticized the grassroots, radical forces represented by Baraka, CFUN, and CAP cadre and the exceedingly high expectations of black political leaders engendered by Black Power and the material hardship endured by Newark's black and Latino communities. Gibson asserted, "In times of dire need, people will expect an elected administrator to be a miracle worker. When people need help they will expect department heads of city government to become Houdinis who can unravel the entangled bureaucratic structure."[112]

The disappointments surrounding the Gibson administration and the breakdown of national efforts to develop intraracial political unity would compel Baraka, CAP cadre, and other black radicals to abandon black ethnic politics for "Third World Marxism." By the mid-seventies, Baraka characterized his beloved hometown as a "classic neo-colonial creation."[113] Although he was among the foremost black radical advocates of practical political activity, Baraka became an increasingly vocal critic of black identity politics. Baraka's efforts to move from local organizing toward the creation of a national black political institution achieved marginal success with the 1970 CAP meeting. Largely as a consequence of strong nationalist support, CAP emerged as a potentially more viable formation than the Black Power conferences. Baraka and CAP cadre's dream of creating a national black political institution was deeply challenged by the presence of substantive cleavages within the leadership strata that could not be reconciled within the body of a single bureaucratic organization. The debates and outcomes that characterized the 1972 Gary Convention brought the limits of operational unity into sharper relief.

PART II

RACIAL TECHNOCRATS, DEMOCRATIC STRUGGLES

3

The Convention Strategy and Conventional Politics
The 1972 Gary Convention and the Limits of Racial Unity

The seventies will be the decade of an independent black political thrust. Its destiny will depend on us. How shall we respond? Will we walk in unity or disperse in a thousand different directions? Will we stand for principle or settle for a mess of pottage? Will we maintain our integrity, or succumb to the man's temptations? Will we act like free Black men or timid shivering chattels? Will we do what must be done? These are the questions confronting this convention. And—only we—can answer them. History will be our judge.

> —Richard G. Hatcher, 1972 Gary Convention speech

Before we can have any further movement, we must have unity. Before we can have self-determination, we must have a self, a unified body, which itself demands independence. Splintered, disunified, we are millions of separate, often warring egos, straining to outdo each other, while our actual enemy sits somewhere "above," jiggling the strings. Giving some gold, some "leg," some prestige, some ideology, just scaring some others, and the ugly circus goes on.

> —Amiri Baraka, "Toward the Creation of Political Institutions for All African Peoples"

In his proto-Black Power rhetoric, Malcolm X asserted that the commonality of racial oppression mediated all other social or idiosyncratic differences among African Americans. In his "Message to the Grassroots" speech, he argued:

> What you and I need to do is to learn to forget our differences. When we come together, we don't come together as Baptists or Methodists . . . You don't catch hell because you're a Methodist or a Baptists, you don't catch hell because you're a Democrat or a Republican, you don't catch hell because you're a Mason or an Elk and you sure don't catch hell because you're an American; because if you were an American you wouldn't catch hell. You catch hell because you're a black man. You catch hell, all of us catch hell for the same reason.[1]

Shortly before his death, he attempted to achieve the ideal of intraracial unity through the creation of the Organization of Afro-American Unity (OAAU) modeled after the continental Organization of African Unity (OAU). The OAAU's mission statement asserted that "the future of Afro-Americans is dependent upon our ability to unite our ideas, skills and organizations and institutions . . . We, the Organization of Afro-American Unity pledge to join hands and hearts with all people of African origin in a grand alliance by forgetting all the difference that the power structure has created to keep us divided and enslaved. We further pledge to strengthen our common bond and strive toward one goal: Freedom from oppression."[2] Malcolm X's advocacy of black unity and his short-lived effort to create a black united front organization served as the skeleton for much Black Power rhetoric and practice.

Although some black radical left organizations such as the League of Revolutionary Black Workers and the Black Panther Party acknowledged the importance of building a multiracial, revolutionary popular front, many Black Power advocates viewed race as the paramount basis of political organizing and mobilization. Stokely Carmichael and Charles Hamilton asserted that intraracial unity was the fundamental premise of Black Power: "Before a group can enter the open society, it must first close ranks."[3] Others like Floyd McKissack summed up the growing sentiment that group unity was a precursor to black advancement in the American political system. Echoing elements of Malcolm's rhetoric, McKissack cast the black population in familial terms. He said:

> We must accept it as an on-going problem (white resistance to black unity) one that will not be eliminated unless blacks complete the process now begun of pulling together, of establishing common interests and ideologies based on race. For in the eyes of the surrounding world, we are defined by our race . . . Our infighting will have to be done at home.[4]

Throughout the late sixties and early seventies, calls for black unity were expressed in a variety of popular slogans: "Unity without Uniformity," "Operational Unity," "It's Nationtime,"—and often in Kiswahili phrases—*Pamoja Tutashinda* (Together we will win), *Harambee* (Let's Pull together), *Umoja Mweusi* (black unity), and *Sisi Tuna Watu Wafrika* (We are an African People).

The 1972 Gary Convention was the culmination of tireless efforts of activists to build a black united front. Through various meetings and diplomatic work, Amiri Baraka and CAP cadre pulled together activist intellectuals and black politicos around the idea of holding a national black convention in 1972 as a vehicle for agenda setting, crafting a unified political strategy, and maximizing black influence in the presidential election process. Yet, the convention and its outcomes revealed sharp, substantive cleavages, which posed a serious challenge to the pursuit of operational unity. Debates surrounding the content of the *National Black Political Agenda* and the question of black party formation deeply divided radicals and moderates during the convention. Despite these difficulties, the convention proceeded with the formation of the National Black Political Assembly. Likewise, a few months after the convention, nationalist activists triumphed again through the 1972 African Liberation Day (ALD) mobilization, which drew together thousands of protesters across the western hemisphere in anti-imperialist demonstrations. To a considerable extent, the year was a high watermark in the struggles

of radical activists to muster broad-based support for their programs. The looming 1972 presidential election inspired a greater
sense of urgency among many regarding the need for unity among
black political elites and activists. The debates over presidential strategy that transpired as activists attempted to build support for the
Gary Convention highlighted the distance between the unitarian
ideal and actual politics. As the Convention unfolded, divergent
interests, partisan loyalties, and matters of constituent representation, and leadership preeminence deeply problematized the pursuit
of black united front politics. Such problems would intensify once
nationalist activists attempted to institutionalize this black united
front and solicit more long-term political commitments from established leadership.

In this chapter, I want draw a distinction between *racial solidarity*
as a spontaneous form of consciousness emerging from racial stratification and *racial unitarianism* as a discrete political aspiration of
Black Power politics. As noted in the previous chapter, racial consciousness is often a powerful source of political mobilization whose
collectivist sensibility can serve as a more progressive alternative to
atomistic individualism. Racial affinity does not translate into common political interests. The racial unitarian views articulated by
Black Power radicals and moderates alike embraced the tendency
within segregation era discourse to treat African Americans as a corporate political entity. This recurrent view that black political disagreement should be handled "behind closed doors" or that blacks
should "close ranks" is a repressive tendency derived from nationalist
discourse that hinders the development of open, principled debate.
Under this perspective, ideological or political differences among
blacks were treated like lines in the sand—lacking depth and perma-
nence. Furthermore, many activists held that such ephemeral differences were drawn by outside hands. From this logic, many concluded
that political and ideological lines could be swept away with effective
organization and the development of proper "black consciousness"
to reveal a solid core of racial interests that connected all African
Americans and, for many, all peoples of African descent. The debates
and outcomes that characterized the 1972 Gary Convention brought
the limits of operational unity into plain view.

The Road to Gary

Following the 1970 Congress of African Peoples in Atlanta, black leaders convened a series of regional and national strategy sessions. Increasingly, the content of these meetings centered around the 1972 national elections and the development of effective black political strategies. Many felt the stakes were especially high in the 1972 presidential election given the resurgent conservatism and anti–civil rights fervor of the period. Although the Nixon administration was comprised of a record number of black appointees, its record on social policy was viewed by many as adverse to black interests. Nixon's "Southern Strategy" in the 1968 election, his advocacy of "law and order" approach to policing, and his administration's war against the War on Poverty provided an empirical basis for some liberal black leaders' uneasiness. Rumblings inside the Democratic Party were equally noteworthy. The intraparty split between Dixiecrat conservatives and Northern liberals around looming questions of civil rights enforcement and the pace of desegregation served as a continuing threat to the party's presidential efforts. Alabama governor George Wallace had stirred simmering conservative sentiments among Democrats and demonstrated their electoral utility in his presidential campaigns. Under these conditions, black leadership met to debate which strategies might bolster group influence in the coming election and avert further erosion of social policy gains relevant to black communities.

The series of meetings held during 1971 were divided among those convened by radical activists, which tended to be larger and open to all comers, and those organized by mainstream politicos, which were more exclusive. As a consequence of Baraka's work and that of CAP cadre, these two currents were drawn together around the idea of holding a national black political convention. In late June 1971, CAP hosted the "Strategy for Unity: '72 and Beyond" at Howard University's School of Social Work. Some fifty leaders attended this conference, including Imari Obadele; Hayward Henry; Howard Fuller; Nelson Johnson, Student Organization for Black Unity (SOBU); Reverend Charles Koen, United Front of Cairo, Illinois; Imamu Vernon Sukumu, the CAP West Coast coordinator; Reverend David Eaton of All Souls Church in Washington, D.C.; Les Campbell of the

"East" cultural center in Brooklyn, New York; John Cashin; Carl Holman of National Urban Coalition; Alexander Allen, eastern regional director of National Urban League; former Student Nonviolent Coordinating Committee (SNCC) activist, Cleveland Sellers; Clifford Alexander, former director of Equal Employment Opportunity Commission (EEOC); Mel Turner, National Welfare Rights Organization (NWRO); Dr. Vincent Harding, Institute of the Black World (IBW); Yvonne Price, NAACP; Harold Sims, acting executive director of National Urban League; Richard Traylor and Lou Gothard of Black Affairs Council of Philadelphia; and Balozi Zayd Muhammad, chairman of International Affairs of CAP and its Non-Governmental Organization office at the United Nations. The elected leaders included Kenneth Gibson; Thomas Fortune, an elected official from New York; and Basil Patterson, former New York state senator and candidate for Lieutenant-Governor. Burt Rudasill attended as a representative of Congressman John Conyers. U.N. ambassador S.A. Salim of Tanzania was represented at the June 1971 conference by E.W. Mwasakasfyuka.

In drawing together such a broad swath of leaders, CAP activists hoped that the meeting would develop an institutional means for greater coordination of programs, protection of leadership from external attack, and facilitation of conflict resolution among leaders.[5] In keeping with the spirit of the 1970 Atlanta Congress of African Peoples meeting, a heavy emphasis of the discussion was placed on the development of a national institution to foster operational unity. CAP chairman Henry asserted, "Our movement must create a mechanism to unify all of its diverse elements."[6] In a similar vein, historian Harding argued that "most social change movements have generated some kind of united front capable of unifying divergent groups for the accomplishment of specific objectives."[7] While much of the conversation focused on how unity might be concretized, a number of radical activists pierced the dialogue with cynicism regarding the utility of broad-based unity for progressive action. As Baraka would recall, some activists expressed concern over whether the positions taken to maintain the support of moderate leadership was too great a concession on behalf of radical factions. According to Baraka, "At the D.C. meeting the issue of unity was raised, but also the question of at what point did the attempt at some kind of unity, even an operational unity, become a compromise too heavy for a so-called revolutionary to sustain? Would positions taken for the sake of unity be so weak as to actually hold the race back, or at least render it without a vanguard to take always the correct positions, no matter how 'radical' they might seem, to the mainstream?"[8] Yet while some nationalists questioned the utility of a black united front, the strongest resistance to this idea came from black political elites.

On 24 September 1971, Richard Hatcher called together a meeting of black leaders at Northlake, Illinois, near the O'Hare airport. Willie Brown, Charles Diggs, Coretta Scott King, Jesse Jackson, Julian Bond, and Baraka were co-hosts. Brown did not attend, but the other co-hosts were joined by well-known politicians and civil rights leaders, including Maynard Jackson, Roy Innis, Vernon Jordan, Representative Augustus Hawkins, Barbara Jordan, James Gibson, Antonio Harrison, Percy Sutton, Reverend Channing Phillips, Cashin, Walter Fauntroy, Merv Dymally, George Wiley, and John Conyers, among others. In contrast to the various themes addressed at previous summits, the discussion at Northlake focused on the subject of black presidential strategy in the upcoming 1972 election. During the previous presidential election cycle, many of the same players sought to influence the Democratic Party platform through a variety of tactics. At the 1968 Democratic National Convention (DNC) in Chicago, black partisans had supported the nomination of Channing Phillips for president and Bond for vice president.[9] The three major strategies discussed at the Northlake summit were the "favorite son" strategy, the black presidential campaign, and the black party.

Bond offered the "favorite son" strategy. Under this proposed scheme, popular black candidates would run for the presidency in their respective states and, thus, create black delegate blocs for the DNC.[10] The ideal implementation of this strategy would be the creation of a bloc of 1,200 black delegates to the 1972 DNC in Miami. Bond held that this strategy would be more cost-effective than a singular black presidential campaign. He also argued that the "favorite son" strategy would allow greater local autonomy among black politicos and inhibit egocentric clashes.[11] During his presentation, Bond argued aggressively against the black party idea.

In contrast to Bond's state-by-state strategy, Percy Sutton advocated a single black presidential candidacy. Sutton argued that such a candidacy would serve to nationalize the black vote and, as a consequence, create a more advantageous bargaining situation between that candidate's campaign organization and the Democratic Party. For Sutton and other observers, the 1968 presidential campaign of comedian-activist Dick Gregory was evidence of the potential leverage of a black presidential run. Gregory received over 500,000 votes in the general election with limited financial backing, meager organization, and ballot qualification in only a few states. Consequentially, votes cast for Gregory eclipsed the margin of victory (less than 400,000 popular votes) between Democratic hopeful Hubert Humphrey and Richard Nixon.[12] Before and after Northlake, other politicians such as Conyers and Carl Stokes voiced support for the black presidential strategy.[13]

At Northlake, Baraka was the principal supporter of the black party idea. Since the 1970 Atlanta congress, he had consistently advocated for the formation of such an entity in various position papers.[14] Only a few months earlier, at a political convention held at "The East" organization—a major black cultural center in the Bedford-Stuyvesant neighborhood of Brooklyn, New York—Baraka outlined his party idea in a position paper titled "Strategy and Tactics for a Pan-African Nationalist Party."[15] In contrast to The East organization's political convention where radical activists were dominant, at Northlake, Baraka's audience was more ideologically moderate and politically homogenous. Perhaps anticipating resistance to his black party idea, Baraka presented a more modest proposal—a national black political convention. This convention would be "somewhat like the Atlanta conference, but bigger, and particularly oriented toward Black political development."[16] Baraka envisioned that a national convention of this type "would try to bring all the tribes of Black people together to talk about our political priorities. Certainly about 1972, and what an American Presidential year meant to the national black community; but also what kind of continuing priorities should be sounded for Black people. And as always, we hope that there would be some talk of a continuing mechanism, some structure upon which to build what we still feel absolute *sine qua non* of Black political movement, i.e., a permanent structure, or party."[17] Baraka's advocacy of the black convention idea was met with caution by other attendees. Nevertheless, the Northlake conference concluded not with a call to convention, but rather with the creation of a continuations apparatus that would oversee development of a financial base and convene larger meetings around the issue of black presidential strategy. Of the various strategic planning meetings to occur after Northlake, the first National Conference of Black Elected Officials was a decisive turning point in the initiation of the 1972 National Black Political Convention.

The Congressional Black Caucus (CBC) hosted the inaugural National Conference of Black Elected Officials on 18–20 November 1971 at the Sheraton Park Hotel in Washington, D.C. Over 300 persons attended this meeting. On the first day of the conference, the question of presidential strategy took center stage. During a session chaired by William Clay, "The Development of Black Political Power in the Seventies," Florida state representative Gwendolyn Cherry asked why New York Congresswoman Shirley Chisholm—the only black presidential candidate in the race—was not included on the panel. In response, Chisholm delivered an impromptu speech whereby she confronted members of the CBC for their cool attitude toward her candidacy. She later recounted, in no uncertain terms, what she perceived as a deliberate effort on behalf of most of the Caucus to withhold support for her candidacy in general and to marginalize it within established black leadership circles. Reflecting on the events that transpired during the November 1971 meeting, she lamented, "It seemed to me clear that there had been a subtle but unmistakable attempt to keep me out of the limelight and there was no possibility that I would ever gain the unified backing of the [C]aucus."[18] The debate surrounding Chisholm's candidacy and the turmoil it engendered within the conference forced the issue of black presidential strategy and the idea of the 1972 convention squarely onto the table.

The conference featured a closed session entitled "National Political Strategy Sessions for 1972" chaired by Congressman Diggs. The panelists included Coretta Scott King, Hatcher, Percy Sutton, and Amiri Baraka. Sutton reiterated his position on the utility of a black presidential candidacy. Coretta Scott King presented a paper titled

"The Transformation of the Civil Rights Movement into a Political Movement" coauthored by political strategist Antonio Harrison of the National League of Cities/National Conference of Mayors. Hatcher called for a national fund-raising mechanism to support black candidacies. Baraka reasserted the necessity of a mass political convention in 1972. As chair, Diggs appointed a four-person committee to evaluate the merits of these proposals. The committee included James Gibson of the Potomac Institute in Washington, D.C.; Howard Robinson, executive director of the CBC; Antonio Harrison; and Congressman Clay.

Baraka contends that there was initially "a general air of rejection about the proposal" at the November 1971 meeting. Echoing concerns raised at the "Strategy for Unity" meeting hosted by CAP the previous year, some radical activists criticized the convention idea noting that differences of interests will undermine the productivity of the meeting. Suspicion and concern regarding the convention idea were also voiced by activists of other ideological persuasions as well.

The unease felt by some more moderate activists and politicians regarding the planned convention is evident in a letter that Bond wrote to Baraka in autumn 1971. In his letter, Bond expressed his disagreement regarding the efficacy of the convention idea. At the heart of Bond's complaint were issues of constituency and leadership accountability. Baraka recalls the substance of the letter:

> [Bond] in effect asked why should he be put into a position to be made responsible for some views with which he might not be in total agreement, feeling that, say a brother like Roy Innis, who does not have to answer to any formal constituency might endanger his, Julian Bond's, ability to answer to his constituency. And this answer is always given by Black Elected Officials—that they have constituencies to be responsive and responsible to, whereas nationalists, activists, other radicals, "have no constituencies," therefore, they can feel freer in taking way-out positions.[19]

Essentially, the decision to hold a national black convention emerged as a means of placating conflicting interests both between radicals and moderates and within the ranks of national black politicos. Consequentially, the ad hoc committee assembled by Diggs to evaluate the proposals from the presidential strategy session endorsed the convention idea. Clay recalled the substance of the report, "It approved of the 'black agenda' and rejected the idea of a national black political party, which satisfied the members of the Congress. It also called for a national black political convention, which appeased the militant black elected officials."[20] Thus, the report represented a compromise between the moderate and radical factions.

In his keynote address during the conference dinner, *Ebony* magazine's chief editor and noted historian Lerone Bennett anticipated the 1972 convention, defining its rationale and touching upon a number of familiar Black Power themes. He urged the development and implementation of a black agenda arguing:

> We can no longer avoid the challenge of creating and disseminating a common black agenda . . . It is imperative, it is a matter of life and death, for us to develop a series of comprehensive plans identifying the black interest and the black position in every field. We must plan now not only for the 1972 election but also for the 1976 election and the 1980 election. We must plan now not only for the Nixons [*sic*] and Agnews [*sic*] of today but for the Nixons and Agnews and Rehnquists of tomorrow.[21]

Bennett argued that this agenda be organized around five major themes: survival, empowerment, renewal, mass mobilization, and societal transformation. Throughout the speech, he asserted a view of Black Power where mainstream politics was seen as a means of transforming both entrenched, unresponsive institutions and asymmetrical power relations within American society. Bennett contended that "[p]olitical power is not garbage collection or petty patronage in a rotten political system but the ability to transform political structures so that people will not have to be aliens and adversaries for resources and services that governments should provide routinely."[22] Bennett offered an explanation of racial inequality that sharply contradicted liberal and conservative formulations: "The problem is not the poor; the problem is the powerful. The problem is not the distribution of contraceptives; the problem is the distribution of income.

The problem is not the ghetto; the problem is the white system which created the ghetto and which permeates it."[23]

At the close of the conference, Diggs issued the formal call to convention. He told participants and the press that the planned black convention would take place either in April or May 1972 for the purposes of "developing a national black agenda and the crystallization of a national–black strategy for the 1972 elections and beyond."[24] Diggs added that this convention would produce "strategies for maximum practical unity in the national participation of blacks in the Democratic and Republican conventions and in local, state and national elections." Along with Baraka and Hatcher, Diggs would be a central figure in promoting the convention and soliciting support from various leaders and organizations.

Diggs was in many ways emblematic of the emerging national elected leadership. A native of Detroit, Diggs's personal history bridged the old guard black elite with that of the postsegregation era.[25] He was educated at the University of Michigan and Fisk University. He was trained in mortuary science at Wayne State University and ran his family's successful funeral home business. During a period when there were few black politicians at the state and national level, Diggs was a pioneer. From 1951 to 1954 he served as the first African American member of the Michigan State Senate. In 1954, Diggs became the first black Congressman from his home state. In 1955, he attended the Emmett Till murder trial in the hopes that his presence might leaven the proceedings and increase the likelihood of a fair trial.[26] Diggs was a founding member and first chairman of the CBC. He became the first African American to chair the House Subcommittee on Africa in 1959. Spurred by the growing anticolonial sentiment in African American political culture, Diggs became the foremost advocate of African foreign policy issues in the halls of Congress.[27] Like many other black elected officials, Diggs was attuned to the positions articulated by radical activists, and his legislative work was shaped by the energies of the sixties social struggles. The convention was organized by staff associated with the Joint Center for Political Studies, the National Urban Coalition, the IBW, the CBC, the CAP cadre, and volunteers operating across the country. The date would eventually be moved up to March, giving organizers even less time to pull off an event of this scale. Robert C. Smith contends that the March date was a mistake given that "there were the typical logistical problems of inadequate convention meeting rooms, insufficient and poorly allocated floor space for the state delegations and inadequate hotel accommodations and transportation . . . [and] the principal problems that resulted from the time constraints were in terms of committee work and delegate allocation and selection."[28] Balancing the countervailing forces attending the convention was another key challenge faced by Diggs, Hatcher, and Baraka. Although they were outnumbered with respect to representation in leadership of state delegations, nationalist forces were well organized and poised to make a definitive impact on the convention.

In preparation for the convention, Baraka and Henry organized a meeting of radical cadre. On 9 March, approximately 100 activists met at Gary's Downtown Holiday Inn. Some of the various leaders and organizations represented at the meeting included Sukumu, Zayd Muhammed, Dick Traylor, Cheo Majadi, Johnson, Mark Smith, and Tim Thomas of SOBU; Fuller of Malcolm X Liberation University (MXLU); James Garrett and Courtland Cox of the Center for Black Education; and Reverend Douglas Moore and Absalom Jordan of the Washington, D.C. Black United Front. The centerpiece of discussion was a position paper drafted by Baraka, entitled "The Nationalist Overview," which outlined some core concerns that nationalists might unify around during the convention deliberations.

At the core of the "Nationalist Overview" was a call for the creation of a postconvention national black political structure.[29] Baraka argued that the convention would serve as a "continuing structure" and as the "functioning central structure of a black political party."[30] Although the "Nationalist Overview" spoke in the prevalent language of the popular mobilization and even the threat of disruption, in essence this statement called for an exhumation of historical models of bureaucratic race organizations such as the interwar era Negro Sanhedrin and the National Negro Congress, which sought to consolidate black elite support for a specific race advancement agenda.[31] According to the "Nationalist Overview," the convention would be "a national organ of black will" and perform the "brokerage and bargaining, officially and unofficially between the white structure and the national black community."[32] Everyone in attendance did not look favorably on the paper. Some SOBU and MXLU cadre were opposed to the pro-establishment orientation of the proposal and its failure to explicitly call for the formation of an independent party. Despite tensions around specific aspects, the "Nationalist Overview" was generally supported by the activists who took part in the preconvention meeting. As a consequence of the strong internal organization of nationalist forces, much of the "Nationalist Overview" was adopted at the Gary Convention. In addition to the challenge of obtaining support from moderate leadership elements for their programs, radical black activists faced state surveillance and repression.

State Repression, Leadership Legitimation, and the 1972 Gary Convention

The efforts of American ruling elites to extinguish democratic brushfires that spread during the late fifties and sixties should be understood as part of the Cold War strategy of containment. In the international arena, Cold War foreign policy was guided by the "domino theory"—the view that once socialist revolution triumphs in one country the neighboring states will fall like dominoes toward communism. The Federal Bureau of Investigation's (FBI's) counterintelligence program (COINTELPRO) was intended to monitor and police "hostile foreign governments, foreign organizations and individuals connected with them."[33] When the Bureau was created, its foes were anarchists, communists, socialists, and union leaders. During the sixties, COINTELPRO initiatives targeted the student New Left, the Communist Party USA, the Socialist Workers Party, Martin Luther King, Jr., SCLC, Black Power radicals, and leadership within the civil rights movement. Some of the strategies used to contain and subdue radical forces included eavesdropping, proliferation of bogus mail, fabrication and distribution of propaganda that misrepresented the positions of certain groups to discredit them and foster dissension among radical organizations, harassment arrests, use of agent provocateurs, and the assassination of movement leaders.[34] In their study of state repression, Ward Churchill and Jim Vander Wall contend that black radical organizations bore the brunt of Hoover's COINTELPRO initiatives. In a 1967 memorandum, Hoover announced the initiation of an intensive, national counterintelligence program targeting "black nationalist-hate groups," which was intended to "expose, disrupt, misdirect, discredit or otherwise neutralize the activities of black nationalist, hate-type organizations and groupings, their leadership, spokesman, membership and supporters."[35] Furthermore, according to the memo, a chief goal of the initiative was to "prevent the coalition of militant black nationalist groups" and to "prevent the rise of a 'black messiah.'" A series of developments during the late sixties led to COINTELPRO's official disbandment. However, the post-COINTELPRO period was marked by ideological continuity and modest policy change in the Bureau's relationship to radical organizations.

The successful burglary of an FBI agency office by an antiwar group—the Citizens' Committee—and their subsequent release of confidential files to the media created a firestorm of criticism from Hoover's political rivals and the wider public. As a consequence of such pressures, COINTELPRO was officially suspended in April 1971. Hoover's death less than a month later signaled the end of an era of intense repression of radical dissent. In light of these developments, efforts to challenge the legality of the FBI's covert operations materialized. The CBC held hearings on government lawlessness. Support also grew for Congressional investigation of the Bureau's COINTELPRO campaigns.[36] These developments had a moderating effect over state repression of black radical forces. However, to a considerable extent, ideological and programmatic elements of the COINTELPRO era persisted in subsequent initiatives.

Hoover's immediate successor L. Patrick Gray III vowed to preserve the late director's legacy. In a speech to the fourth annual Crime Control Conference of the governor of Mississippi, Gray promised to continue the FBI's increasingly controversial investigations of those organizations that posed a threat to public safety and security. He defended the legality of the Bureau's activities saying that: "FBI electronic surveillances are instituted and maintained in a manner designed to afford the fullest protection of individual liberties, while at the same time, upholding society's right to protect itself against the ravages of organized crime."[37] Although Gray was replaced by Clarence Kelley shortly afterward, his comments indicate that some agents still saw the tactics of the Hoover era as necessary for the maintenance of national security. The FBI files pertaining to the 1972 National Black Political Convention and subsequent meetings convened by the National Black Political Assembly suggest that intensive intelligence gathering activities targeting "black extremists" continued.

Informants were utilized at a number of the meetings described in this chapter, particularly those nationalist gatherings that were closed to the public. FBI files pertaining to the National Black Political conventions and the Assembly included a variety of data sources such as fact sheets and meeting summaries drafted by informants, newspaper articles on key events, and activists' communiqués—position papers, agendas, official propaganda, organizational correspondences. Given the united front character of these formations, however, investigatory activities were not directed at all participants. Rather, explicit differentiation between "legitimate" and "extremist" activities is made throughout various internal FBI correspondences contained in the files.

In light of mounting criticism, internal FBI memoranda concerning these united front formations reflect some degree of restraint. More important, official memos often justify surveillance with an expressed concern for protecting the normal operation of "legitimate political activities" among blacks. The explicit targets of the Bureau's activities were Black leftists and nationalists. Baraka, Owusu Sadaukai (Fuller), Johnson, and various activists affiliated with the CAP, the MXLU, the SOBU, and other radical organizations were identified by Bureau agents via the use of the black nationalist photo album—a remnant of the late sixties' COINTELPRO initiatives. One pre-Gary convention FBI memo summarized the targets of monitoring activities as follows:

> It is known that black extremists will attend this [c]onvention because we have received information that members of the Cleaver faction of the Black Panther Party (BPP) are sending

a delegation; LeRoi Jones, a black extremist who is affiliated with the Congress of African Peoples (CAP), will attend; and information has been received that the Republic of New Africa (RNA), a black extremist organization, has been requested to supply security guards for the above convention. The CAP is a black separatist group infiltrated at the leadership level by black extremists.[38]

A memorandum from the FBI director to SAC (Special Agent in Charge), dated 16 October 1972, vividly illustrates the distinction between moderate and radical black leadership elements that recurs throughout the Bureau's internal communication concerning the conventions and the Assembly. This memo addressed the first meeting of the National Black Political Assembly convened in Chicago in October 1972. Its instructions to the agents assigned to the meeting were as follows: "Be certain this informant clearly understands that the Bureau is not concerned with legitimate political activities and [e]nsure his reporting is confined to extremist aspects only."[39]

Although the files do not allow one to draw definitive conclusions regarding the execution of specific activities designed to thwart radical activists' initiatives, the text is clearly suggestive of an official posture that served to legitimate and protect the pursuit of black political goals through conventional channels. Generally, the materials contained in the FBI files on the national black conventions and the Assembly reflect this official policy of monitoring radical forces within the Assembly to limit and undermine their influence. The Bureau's policy of selective targeting was allegedly intended to protect "legitimate political activities" among blacks. In promoting moderate forms of black politics, state investigatory activities worked hand in hand with other state maneuvers like the community action programs of the War on Poverty initiative to shaped the black political life in a more conservative direction.

The 1972 Gary Convention

Inasmuch as it embodied the prospects of black political power, the city of Gary, Indiana, was an appropriate site for the 1972 convention.

Hatcher became the first black mayor of Gary in 1967. He was born in Michigan City, Indiana, in 1933 and grew up in a predominantly black working-class community known to locals as "the Patch." Hatcher won an athletic scholarship to Indiana University. As a collegian, he participated in an NAACP-sponsored protest of a local restaurant that refused to service black patrons. He transgressed racial boundaries in private life as well, openly dating a white coed to the vocal disapproval of some and uncomfortable silence of others on Indiana's campus. Upon completing his undergraduate studies, Hatcher attained a jurist doctorate from Valpraiso University Law School, eventually settling in Gary to practice law. Soon after, he became intimately involved in local civil rights struggles and, eventually, formal politics.

Hatcher built up an impressive resume of public service in Gary's local civil rights struggles. He served as counselor for the NAACP young adult branch and as lawyer in the landmark 1962 Gary desegregation case. He participated in the Fair Share movement and led a delegation from Gary to the 1963 March on Washington. Hatcher helped found Muigwithania—a Gikuyu phrase for "Come together and go forward." Named after a newspaper published by Kenyan decolonization leader Jomo Kenyatta, Muigwithania was created to bolster black empowerment and challenge the entrenched, local political machine. In 1962, this organization challenged party regulars and won seats in the Lake County Democratic Party organization's delegation to the Indiana state party convention. Shortly thereafter, Hatcher, with the support of Muigwithania and the Lake County party organization, won an at-large seat on the city council. He served as council president and acquired a reputation for being an outspoken, free-thinking member.[40]

As the city's population approached a black majority, the prospects of electing a black mayor became more plausible. In 1944, Gary's total population was 120,000 with blacks comprising 20 percent (24,000) of the city's residents. Between 1950 and 1960, the city's black population grew five times faster than that of whites. By 1967, black in-migration and white flight from the central city combined to create a black majority (55 percent) in Gary. Within this context,

Hatcher emerged as the prime challenger to incumbent Mayor A. Martin Katz.[41] In the Democratic primary, white voters split between Katz and Bernard Konrady—17,190 to 13,133 votes, respectively. Consequentially, Hatcher garnered 20,272 votes to defeat Katz and advance to the general election. Winning the city's general election proved difficult as many white Democrats voted for Republican candidate Joseph Radigan who mobilized racist, nativist sentiments within the electorate with his campaign slogan "100 percent American." In the face of intense racial polarization, Hatcher won by a slim margin receiving 39,812 votes against Radigan's 37,947. In 1971, Hatcher won a second term despite opposition from a black challenger Dr. Alexander Williams who received the endorsement of the Lake County organization. Hatcher enlisted the support of numerous nationally renowned leaders such as Jesse Jackson and black celebrities such as Bill Cosby, Dick Gregory, Harry Belafonte, and Nancy Wilson to build support for his reelection campaign. He defeated Williams 34,000 to 21,000 votes in the Democratic primary. For many Black Power activists, the city of Gary and Hatcher's mayoral administration symbolized the potential of indigenous control.

From 10 to 12 March 1972, 2776 delegates and 4000 alternates gathered at Gary's Westside High School for the National Black Political Convention. This historic meeting was the product of strenuous organizing on behalf of the various steering committees created in the wake of the the 1971 National Conference of Black Elected Officials. Politicians occupied the leadership of the seven steering committees, but much of the preconvention grunt work and mobilization was conducted by CAP cadre and other grassroots organizations in various states. Although state delegations were composed in an uneven and imperfect manner, the end result was significant. Official delegations from thirty-eight states, the District of Columbia, and the Virgin Islands were represented. In a fashion similar to the convention committees, the delegate selection process was designed to include representation from both elected and non-elected leadership. Each of the fifty states and the District of Columbia was allocated a baseline of five delegates regardless of the size of its black population. Two thousand additional delegate slots were divided among the states and the District according to their respective black population's percentage of the total U.S. black population. Guaranteed delegate slots were extended to both black elected officials and leadership of major black organizations. Elected officials received an automatic berth while some 150 delegate slots were subdivided equally among recognized major organizations. The precise manner in which delegations were formed in each state was not uniform. Some states such as Massachusetts, Maryland, Ohio, and New Jersey held state conventions to select delegates. Other states such as Louisiana solicited delegates on a voluntary basis via radio advertisements.[42] Despite this unevenness, this process of building state delegations yielded one of the most broadly representative summits in twentieth-century African American political history. Nevertheless, the Gary Convention was principally a meeting of black political elites. In fact, some participants expressed discontent that the $25 registration fee deterred the broad participation of "the welfare poor, the union members and the government workers."[43] Equally significant, public officials occupied a disproportionate share of leadership slots within state delegations.

The meeting reflected considerable ideological and political variety despite of its decidedly elite character. The convention program featured a wide range of black political and cultural personalities including Motown recording artist Kim Weston; People United to Serve Humanity (PUSH) director Jackson; Greensboro, North Carolina, activist Sadaukai; Black Panther Party chairman Bobby Seale; Betty Shabazz; Coretta Scott King; and actor Richard Roundtree. The recollections of Reverend Benjamin Chavis—community organizer for the United Church of Christ's Commission on Racial Justice in Wilmington, North Carolina—captures the hopeful tone of many delegates. Chavis recalls:

I had never been to Gary, Indiana, before, although I had heard about Mayor Hatcher being the mayor. And I remember when we first saw the sign saying "Welcome to Gary," and we got to downtown Gary, I mean, we thought we were in a different country. To see a city in the United States, given the backdrop now of all this Nixon repression going on, all this sense of disillusionment in some quarters of the nation, to drive into Gary, Indiana and see streamers, red, black and green and "Welcome National Black Political Convention," it was a fulfillment of what a lot of our dreams were.[44]

Many viewed the meeting as the dawning of a new era in black politics. Diggs compared the convention to the founding of the two major parties and to the NAACP.[45] Colorado state representative Jerome Ross said of the convention, "[T]his is a new advent for blacks. This meeting is the beginning of black unity and we must seek a meaningful platform. Never before have we been able to get black people thinking together."[46] Similarly, Ohio Congressman Louis Stokes noted, "This day is historic for black people in America. Out of this will come a meaningful, constructive program to alleviate some of the black problems of black people. The compilation of a national black agenda is a most important thing." New York state assemblyman Thomas Fortune captured the high optimism of many attendees when he exclaimed to reporters in a hotel lobby that, "We met—therefore, we won!"[47] As was the case with its predecessors—the Black Power conferences and the 1970 Congress of African Peoples—Gary was successful in drawing together a broad sampling of African American political activists. As former director of the Northern Student Movement and cofounder of the Institute of the Black World, William Strickland soberly recalled, however, "Gary has been the victim of a number of interpretations, because different people came to Gary with different motives."[48] Despite the euphoria that characterized many of its organizers' appraisals, the outcomes of the Gary Convention graphically illustrated the limits of racial unity. Debates surrounding the content of the *National Black Political Agenda* and the question of black party formation deeply divided radicals and moderates during the convention.

In an especially perceptive analysis of the Gary Convention and its aftermath that appeared in the October 1975 issue of *Black Scholar*, Strickland recalled the class dimensions of the conclave. Strickland noted, "Bourgeois politics then, whether of the liberal or radical variety, is actually hostile to true mass oriented independent black politics . . . Gary failed to reach and move the masses because it failed to incorporate their needs (or presence) within its structure. Instead it reflected the aspirations of its convenors and participants who were, whether young or old, in office or out, sincere or opportunist, members of the petty bourgeoisie." He added, "The class factor in black politics is not by itself an insuperable obstacle, but it must be admitted if it is to be successfully transcended."[49]

The Making of the 1972 National Black Political Agenda

One of the chief accomplishments of the convention was the drafting of the *National Black Political Agenda*.[50] Historian Manning Marable concludes that the *Black Agenda* was in fact "one of the most visionary and progressive statements ever issued by Afro-Americans about their position in this country."[51] The *Black Agenda* was a wide-ranging set of programmatic resolutions drafted and endorsed by the delegation. To a considerable extent it was comprised of many of the progressive political demands and goals that had been articulated at the various Black Power conferences. The "Gary Declaration" which served as the opening statement of the *Black Agenda* was authored by Vincent Harding and Strickland of IBW and ratified by the convention delegation.

A vital force in black intellectual life during the seventies, IBW was a direct by-product of the civil rights movement. After Martin Luther King, Jr.,'s assassination in 1968, the King family solicited the support of civil rights activist and historian Harding to direct the Martin Luther King, Jr. Memorial Center in Atlanta. One early idea entertained by Harding and Steve Henderson, the chair of Morehouse College's English Department, was the creation of a black research institute in the Atlanta University Center—to be called the Institute for Advanced African American Studies. Around 1969, this idea evolved into IBW first as a project of the King Center and eventually as a free-standing entity.[52]

From its conception, IBW was intended to have an activist focus. As Harding notes, the institute's staff and supporters "made a commitment to the idea that our academic work, our intellectual work, be carried on in the service of the continuing struggle, that there must be an integration of struggle and scholarship."[53] In developing this pioneering independent black think tank, Harding drew a host of social scientists, artists, and activists into IBW's orbit, including Joyce Ladner, Bennett, Robert Hill, Walter Rodney, Margaret Walker, St. Clair Drake, Horace Cayton, C.L.R. James, Grace Lee Boggs, and Jimmy Boggs, among others. The draft preamble for the *Black Agenda* evolved out of IBW's vibrant intellectual milieu.

The "Gary Declaration" was drawn from previous abbreviated agendas Strickland and Harding had outlined in the *IBW Monthly Report*. Of their intentions, Strickland recalled: "we said there wasn't anyone doing an independent black think tank that was trying to think about issues and how the issues nationally and internationally affected black people."[54] In its structural critique of racial oppression, call for systemic transformation, and assertion of a vanguard role for blacks in the struggle for democracy in the United States, the *Agenda*'s preamble clearly bore the imprint of IBW's leftist orientation.

The general tone and ideological hue of the "Gary Declaration" reflect a strong fusion of antiracism and anticapitalism. This preamble declares that "[t]he Crises we face as Black people are the crises of the entire society. They go deep to the very bones and marrow, to the essential nature of America's economic, political and cultural systems. They are the natural end product of a society built on the twin foundations of white racism and white capitalism."[55] In summarizing the state of black life in the early seventies, the preamble paints a bleak, dystopian portrait:

> Our cities are crime haunted dying grounds. Huge sectors of our youth—and countless others—face permanent unemployment. Those of us who work find our paychecks able to purchase less and less. Neither the courts nor the prisons contribute to anything resembling justice or reformation. The schools are unable—or unwilling—to educate our children for the real world of our struggles. Meanwhile, the officially approved epidemic of drugs threatens to wipe out the minds and strength of our best young warriors. Economic, cultural and spiritual depression stalk Black America and the price for survival often appears to be more than we are able to pay.[56]

The preamble goes on to state that "[t]he profound crisis of Black people and the disaster of America are not simply caused by men or will they be solved by men alone. These crises are the crises of basically flawed economics and politics and of cultural degradation." Its elaboration of these stark realities was, however, tempered by considerable optimism. Throughout the preamble and the *Agenda*'s various resolutions, one senses the high feeling of political efficacy that characterized the convention body. The "Gary Declaration" envisioned a vanguard role for African Americans in the movement to transform American democratic institutions. As the preamble states bluntly, "The American system does not work for the masses of our people and it cannot be made to work without radical fundamental change."[57] Finally, the "Gary Declaration" insists on the promotion of new humanistic values to guide American society:

> Here at Gary we are faithful to the best hopes of our fathers and our people if we move for nothing less than a politics which places community before individualism, love before sexual exploitation, a living environment before profits, peace before war, justice before unjust "order" and morality before expediency.

The succeeding portions of the *Black Agenda* outline practical steps for realizing the ideals espoused in the preamble.

The skeletal core of the agenda was drafted on the weekend of 6 March 1972 at a meeting convened by the platform committee chair Fauntroy and hosted by Howard University's Political Science Department. The final agenda was the product of vigorous floor debate, late-night state caucuses, and revision and ratification procedures during and after the convention. The task of presiding over the large delegation and ensuring democratic protocol at times proved extremely difficult. Initially, Congressman Diggs presided over the convention. However, after an apparent misreading of a voice vote, resistance to Diggs's leadership emerged.[58] Consequentially, Baraka took over the role of facilitator. Through charisma and diplomatic skill, he restored a measure of order to the proceedings. In that regard, Baraka was instrumental in facilitating whatever success the convention achieved.

The finished document was subdivided into two major sections—"Action Agenda for Black People" and "Action Agenda for Political Office Holders and Seekers." Both sections contain agenda items organized under the following issue categories: (1) Political Empowerment; (2) Economic Empowerment; (3) Human Development; (4) International Policy and Black People; (5) Communications; (6) Rural Development; (7) Environmental Protection; and (8) Self-Determination for the District of Columbia. The agenda contained both civil society initiatives and policy reforms. With regard to political participation, the agenda contained resolutions calling for a constitutional amendment to provide for compulsory black proportional representation in Congress; enactment of policies that would guarantee black enfranchisement and the right to self-governance under regional and metropolitan governmental arrangements; and a proposal to hold plebiscites in majority black cities whose populations exceed that of the smallest state to determine whether black citizens want to secede and form a new state. In the area of criminal justice, resolutions demanded a new bill of rights to further protect black defendants; the release of all black political prisoners; extension of conditional amnesty to all black draft resistors; support for the abolition of capital punishment; and the elimination of federal, state, and local surveillance campaigns against black leaders and organizations.[59] A relatively detailed package of special resolutions germane to the District of Columbia was handcrafted under Fauntroy's leadership.

The section on self-determination for the District of Columbia began with a resolution supporting a congressional bill that would transform the district's local government in the following ways: (1) creation of an elected mayor–city council government; (2) delegation of broad legislative power to the city government with authority over budgetary matters including power to institute a commuter tax; (3) provision of a compulsory federal payment to the city government each year based on a fixed percentage of locally generated revenues; (4) and delegation of power to the elected mayor to appoint local judges and other local appointive offices and commissions pending the council's confirmation. Additionally, the plan called for allotment of full, equitable congressional representation for the District of Columbia—two senators and as many representatives as it would be entitled if it were a state.[60] The remaining portions of this section of the *Black Agenda* addressed the following policy areas: health; criminal justice; housing and economic development; the environment and transportation; the elderly; jobs and income; education; civil rights; and labor relations.

On economic matters, the *Agenda* included numerous resolutions demanding increased development of black economic infrastructure. One such resolution called for the establishment of a publicly funded national black development bank. This resolution stipulated that the proposed bank would be run by blacks and would operate on an initial budget of $2 billion for each five-year cycle after 1973. Other resolutions called for a Homestead Act to facilitate black land acquisition; the creation of a black-controlled community development bank to assist in the planning and construction of low-to-moderate-income housing; and the enactment of legislation to legally require private foundations to disburse a minimum 8 percent of their assets per annum, with 4 percent directed toward blacks. The Black Agenda endorsed the Community Self-Determination Bill of 1968 (HR 18715) to "provide for the establishment of *community development corporations, community development banks and other supporting programs and provisions* in order to mobilize the talent and resources of the people of this 'nation within a nation' to help them play a more meaningful and rewarding role in building better, stronger and more confident Black communities in America."[61] Hewn from the Congress of Racial Equality's three-part program for black advancement, the proposed legislation would create community corporations— defined as "unit[s] in a community designed to stimulate Black economic development."[62] These community corporations would be piloted by a private corporation, which would provide technical expertise about management, production, and marketing. The bill also called for special tax incentives to encourage industrial development in black communities.

While the aforementioned economic planks were tilted in a decidedly corporate liberal direction, other resolutions were more redistributive in nature. One resolution supported a guaranteed minimum income of $6,500 for a family of four with a built-in cost-of-living adjustment, and a $3.13 per-hour minimum wage with a mandated increase every three years to "provide every American family of four with an income not less than that defined as the lower standard budget".[63] Another resolution spoke to the question of chronic unemployment among the black poor by encouraging manpower legislation that would create African American–designed and controlled national training programs. In a similar vein, one plank supported a renewed national commitment to building and improving efficient, affordable mass transit systems and, where necessary, provide lower transit fares or public subsidies for transportation to ensure black access to employment sites. Additional resolutions sought to improve the overall quality of life for poor, working-class Americans through progressive income tax reforms; an increase in estate and gift taxes to a maximum rate of 90 percent; a 50 percent decrease in defense and space budgets with the transfer of surplus to social, educational, and economic development programs; implementation of national health care insurance for all from birth to death; and free medical care for families whose annual income is less than $10,000. Taking direct aim at big business, other agenda resolutions called for a 50 percent reduction of corporate welfare and for the expansion and more effective enforcement of antitrust laws.[64]

With respect to international affairs, the agenda outlined a slate of antiwar and anticolonial resolutions. Such agenda items called for an end to the Vietnam War and the immediate withdrawal all foreign troops from Asia and Africa; the withdrawal of U.S. military, corporations, and communications facilities from southern Africa and the Third World; support for provisional governments and revolutionary movements in Africa; support for self-determination of Puerto Rico and the Virgin Islands; U.S. compliance with the United Nations sanctions against trade in chrome and other commodities from Rhodesia; an end to U.S. sanctions against Cuba; and the closure of the American military base at Guantánamo Bay.[65] Additional agenda items called for an increase in U.S. financial and technical assistance to developing nations.

While many issues received ecumenical support, two of the *Agenda*'s resolutions drove sharp wedges through the delegation. Some convention participants complained publicly that the disagreement over these resolutions was overstated by the mainstream media. They noted how various newspapers focused disproportionately on these two resolutions while neglecting others that enjoyed widespread support among the delegates.[66] While the media coverage of the conclave did overemphasize these two agenda items their significance should not be downplayed nor should opposition to these items be explained away as being externally driven. Public debate over the anti-busing and pro-Palestine resolutions revealed substantive differences between liberal integrationists and black radicals.

One of the resolutions sponsored by the South Carolina delegation called for an end to court-ordered busing and the implementation of a community-control school plan.[67] Although other resolutions called for community control in other spheres of black public life, this resolution was controversial because it questioned the conventional remedy to inequality in public education which was widely embraced by the civil rights establishment. The idea of community control as an alternative to busing had achieved considerable support among nationalists during the late 1960s.[68] The "Nationalist Overview," prepared by Baraka and circulated among nationalists before the Gary Convention, endorsed community control of schools. The original resolution condemned school busing as "a bankrupt, suicidal method of desegregating schools, based on the false notion that Black children are unable to learn unless they are in the same setting as white children."[69] Instead, the resolution called for "quality education in the Black community through control of our school systems, school districts and a guarantee of an equal share of the money." CORE's executive director Roy Innis defended the resolution in news interviews characterizing busing as "obsolete" and "dangerous."[70] In response negative media and pressure from some moderate leaders, a rider was drafted and incorporated into the final version of this resolution, which softened the original stance. It read:

> Busing is not the real issue in American education today, and we condemn the dishonesty of the Nixon administration and other forces in making busing an issue when in fact, busing had officially been used to maintain segregation for many years in

> many sections of the country . . . we disassociate ourselves from
> the positions put forth by Nixon and Wallace.[71]

This revised language attempted to distance the antibusing resolution from conservatives and segregationists while placating the concerns of liberal integrationists.

Like the busing issue, the resolution concerning the Arab–Israeli conflict was characterized by a position that had become common to black nationalist discourse in the late sixties. The opposition of black radicals to Israel was a product of post–World War II developments. In earlier eras, Zionism was widely supported by black nationalists and African American leaders generally. Throughout the nineteenth century, many black intellectuals and clergy drew parallels between the Old Testament narrative of Hebrew enslavement, persecution, and deliverance and the plight of Africans under modern racial slavery. Edward Wilmot Blyden, the foremost Pan-Africanist of his age, characterized Zionism as "that marvellous movement."[72] In his 1898 pamphlet *The Jewish Question,* Blyden endorsed the politics of Zionism as outlined in Theodor Herzl's 1896 work *The Jewish State.* At one point in the text, Blyden advocates the advantages of creating a Jewish settlement in Africa. On this matter, he wrote: "Africa appeals to the Jew . . . to come with his scientific and other culture, gathered by his exile in many lands, and with his special spiritual endowments."[73] In this way, Blyden imagined Jews and blacks from the western hemisphere acting side-by-side as modernizing forces on the African continent. Though they are typically remembered as bitter arch-nemeses, both W.E.B. DuBois and Marcus Garvey championed pro-Zionist politics at certain junctures. Each drew parallels between their respective formulations of Pan-Africanism and Jewish diasporic politics.[74]

In spite of support by well-known African American public figures, a discernible shift in pro-Zionist attitudes among nationalist and Pan-Africanist members of the black intelligentsia occurred after World War II and the establishment of a sovereign Israel in 1948. Relationships between some black and Jewish intellectuals were showing signs of strain during the mid-sixties. As noted in the previous two chapters, intellectuals such as Cruse and Baraka offered harsh criticism of Jewish participation in the civil rights movement.

Cruse was especially irritated by the contradictory stance of some Jewish leftists who scorned nationalistic sentiments among black Americans while openly supporting Israel.[75]

A critical turning point in the growth of vocal black opposition to Israel was the Six Day War. On 5 June 1967, the Israeli military attacked Iraq, Jordan, Syria, and Egypt. In less than a week, these military campaigns enabled Israel to acquire the entire Sinai Peninsula and the Gaza Strip, Syria's Golan Heights, and the West Bank of the Jordan River. This display of military might helped to transform Israel's global image of vulnerability. Increasingly, black radicals voiced their solidarity with the Palestinian people as an oppressed Third World nation. Furthermore, Israel's economic and military ties with South Africa's racial dictatorship further cemented the view among many radical activists that in the international arena the state of Israel was a partner in Western imperialism. In the wake of the Six Day war, SNCC activists openly condemned the Israeli government in a newsletter that featured anti-Zionist position statements, political cartoons, and graphic photographs depicting the 1956 Gaza Massacres.[76]

In 1967, black delegates to the National Conference for a New Politics (NCNP) in Chicago demanded that white leftists accept a thirteen-point platform that included a statement condemning the "imperialist Zionist war." The NCNP had been organized primarily by white members of the New Left in an attempt to create a national, multiracial radical front. The NCNP had emerged from an ad hoc organization designed to support reform-minded political candidates. Among the black delegates to the 1967 convention were SNCC activists James Forman and H. Rap Brown. The black delegation splintered early on. Some members felt that such a multiracial effort was futile and staged an impromptu black people's convention instead. The small, remaining contingent of black participants at the NCNP drafted a set of militant demands, including equal voting power for the black minority caucus. Although such demands were met with resistance from white participants, the overall platform and the anti-Zionist plank were ratified by the conference barring language, which called for the return of all captured land to Arab control.[77] Despite these revisions, some Jewish participants walked out in protest of the resolution. At the 1968 Black Power Conference in Philadelphia and the 1970 Congress of African Peoples in Atlanta, comparable pro-Palestine resolutions were read and adopted. Thus, by the 1972 Gary Convention, opposition to the state of Israel and support for Palestinian self-determination were widely embraced international policy stances among Black Power radicals.

At the 1972 convention, a proposal sponsored by the District of Columbia delegation called for the "dismantling of Israel." The original text of the resolution was formally read by Reverend Douglas Moore, de facto chair of the D.C. delegation and leader of the D.C. Black United Front. Moore's activist roots ran deep into the postwar civil rights movement. He had been a classmate of Martin Luther King, Jr., during graduate school at Boston University. Moore later served as the North Carolina Representative on SCLC's board. Having led a 1957 sit-in at an ice cream parlor in Durham, Moore was a pioneer in the efforts to desegregate public places in North Carolina.[78] Although he was approached by King with an offer to become more integral to the leadership of SCLC, Moore opted to relocate to Central Africa. During his tenure in the Congo, he gravitated towards a radical anticolonial politics as he witnessed first hand that nation's tumultuous independence struggle and subsequent coup d'etat and assassination of Patrice Lumumba.[79] Moore and other supporters of the pro-Palestine resolution maintained that they were not motivated by anti-Semitism, but rather they wished to demonstrate support for the basic human rights of Palestinians. The proposal cited that the "illegal establishment" of the Israeli government was "a clear violation of the Palestinian traditional right to life in their homeland."[80] Furthermore, the proposal demanded that the U.S. government cease all military and economic support to Israel, that all lands be returned to the Palestinian people, and that "the negotiations be ended with the freedom of the representatives of the Palestinians to establish a second state based on the historic right of the Palestinian people for self-government in their land."[81]

The language of this resolution was toned down in subsequent drafts. Two weeks following the Gary Convention, at a meeting at Howard University's School of Social Work, activists engaged in vigorous debate regarding the language of the Palestinian resolution.

The final version of the *Agenda* was revised in Greensboro, North Carolina, on 6 May 1972. The completed *Black Agenda* was officially released at the Sonesta Hotel in Washington, D.C. on 19 May in commemoration of Malcolm X's birthday. This final version contained a platform plank that endorsed the OAU and the United Nation's Commission on Human Right's official position that Israel should relinquish territory acquired in the Six Day War of 1967 and acknowledge the self-determination of the Palestinian people. Hence, the *Agenda* resolution asserted that the Israeli government be condemned for "her expansionist policy and forceful occupation of sovereign territory of another state."[82] Such concessions did not repair the ideological breach between some moderate leaders and the convention organizers. On the final day of the convention, the majority of the Michigan delegation walked out of the meeting. Led by state legislator Coleman Young, this faction was composed of activists from the NAACP and the United Auto Workers union. Young felt that the nationalist orientation of the *Agenda* would severely jeopardize their relationships with the state and national Democratic Party structure.[83] He later described the convention platform as "completely off-target and unacceptable" and "a blatant separatist document."[84] Young also charged that Baraka and other nationalists sought to muffle deliberation over the draft agenda items pushing instead for a rapid adoption of agenda. After the convention, moderate civil rights leaders and politicos generally distanced themselves from the nationalistic agenda items and the convention apparatus.

One of the most vocal opponents of these two resolutions and the general thrust of the convention effort was the NAACP's executive director Roy Wilkins.[85] Wilkins's disparaging views of Black Power radicalism were no secret. Amidst the initial fervor surrounding Black Power, Wilkins had characterized the politics of racial self-determination in pathological terms. In the elder Wilkins's mind, the racial militancy that permeated black political culture was "a reverse Mississippi, a reverse Hitler, a reverse Ku Klux Klan."[86] Not surprisingly, after reviewing a draft of the "Gary Declaration," Wilkins expressed disagreement with the convention's political direction. In a preconvention memo to John Morsell, Wilkins laid out the basic criterion for the NAACP's support of the conclave, warning that "[i]f the agenda adopted by the convention turns out to be consistent with the draft preamble, the agenda also will be impossible for NAACP to endorse."

Although the NAACP leadership lauded the agenda's progressive social and foreign policy planks, Wilkins strongly denounced its nationalist features and the prominence of black nationalist forces in the convention itself. In a letter to the convention co-chairs, Wilkins stated his opposition to the anti-busing and Israel-related resolutions and to the "separatist and nationalist intent" of the conclave.[87] Wilkins noted that there were points of agreement between the NAACP and the convention's *Agenda*. He commended the *Black Agenda*'s calls for guaranteed annual income, an end to capital punishment, an end to the Vietnam War, the withholding of tax dollars from agencies and institutions that discriminate, strengthening of the EEOC, formation of civilian review boards, increased economic aid to African states, support for the U.N. genocide treaty, and the creation of a national health insurance program. On the matters of Israel and busing, Wilkins argued that the Black Agenda was "repugnant" to the basic principles of the NAACP and that the organization's objection to them "is not reduced by half-hearted and awkward revisions which they have undergone subsequent to the Gary meetings."[88] In the midst of outlining the NAACP's opposition to the convention agenda, Wilkins offered a thoughtful critique of the community-control thesis undergirding both the busing resolution and other aspects of the Agenda. He contended:

At almost no point does the Agenda also demand an equitable black share of control in institutions and agencies now controlled and dominated by whites. Yet these are the real repositories of American wealth and power. In foregoing a share in them, Negro Americans would sell themselves short; in focusing all its concern upon controlling the meager, poverty ridden institutions of the ghetto, the Agenda would fetter black America forever into the poorest and least influential sectors of the national life.[89]

The issues of leadership legitimacy and ideology, that characterized the 1971 exchange between Baraka and Bond resurfaced in public debate over endorsement of the *Black Agenda*. The then director of branches and field administration for the NAACP Gloster Current recalls the organization's official rejection of the convention's over-arching mission and attributes their policy to basic disagreement with nationalist aims but equally to the matter of accountability. He argued:

> Baraka and his group ideologically were not in step with what we considered to be the solution to the problems of blacks in America then and now. If you take a close look at what Mr. Wilkin's statement on the NAACP and the Black Political Convention, you will clearly understand why we can't become a party to these maverick groups who announce and call for a meeting and they don't have to be responsible for what they decide to do because they go out of business. You just can't create an ad hoc group and then tomorrow go in another direction. Otherwise, we [the NAACP] wouldn't have existed since 1909.[90]

In response to the NAACP's official withdrawal from the convention, Baraka publicly decried Wilkins's actions as "irresponsible" and not genuinely reflective of the sentiments of the organization's rank and file membership.[91] Responding to the NAACP leadership's claim that clear differences of interests and ideology precluded their endorsement of the *Agenda,* Baraka reasoned that "Teddy Kennedy doesn't withdraw from the Senate when the Goldwater forces out vote him on an issue . . . He stays in the organization to fight on other issues."[92] Subsequently, Baraka personally appealed to Wilkins by letter asking him to reconsider his disapproval of the *Black Agenda*.

Wilkins's opposition and Baraka's vain attempts to secure support from the elder civil rights leader illustrate the faultiness of the race unity logic that undergirded the convention strategy and nationalist politics more generally. Though differing in partisanship and on some matters of ideology, Kennedy and Goldwater share a basic faith in American liberal democratic institutions. Baraka and Wilkins did not share either ideological unity or the institutional centrifugalism provided by the U.S. Congress. Furthermore, while the U.S. Congress is a form of constituted, sovereign power with long standing rituals, traditions and legitimacy, the fledgling black convention did not possess any real mechanisms for maintaining loyalty or punishing detractors. Baraka's reasoning in his letter to Wilkins exposes a core, flawed assumption of the convention strategy—that ideological and political differences were subordinate to race identity and as such could be disciplined through bureaucratic organization.

These conflicts over leadership legitimacy and ideology between civil rights and nationalist activists also erupted between elected leaders and nationalists. Many nationalists asserted that they should receive proportional representation within the convention body. Generally, elected leaders vigorously challenged this proposal. Sharing the sentiments of the NAACP leadership, Representative John Conyers argued that "[t]here are many nonpolitical people at Gary with little responsibility to a constituency."[93] Likewise, Bond, in a similar fashion, asserted that "[t]here are two types of political activists: those who have a constituency and those who don't."[94] These conversations about "types of political activists" and constituency represent much deeper struggles over leadership preeminence and who should serve as the legitimate brokers of black interests in the wider political system. The assertions of Wilkins, Conyers, and Bond represented an emerging discourse within black public life, which insisted that the only suitable brokers of black political interests were those leaders who derived their legitimacy from the electoral process, the New Deal democratic coalition or formal governing institutions rather than popular struggles.

The Formation of the National Black Assembly

No clear consensus defined the black political elite's strategic outlook regarding the 1972 presidential election. Some supporters of Chisholm felt that the conclave should endorse her candidacy. Despite direct appeals from convention organizers, Chisholm decided to forego the meeting sending representatives instead. She later remarked that her decision was based on the presence of significant opposition to her campaign among the more militant segments of the delegation and the potential problems negative media might create for her campaign.[95] Some black supporters of major party candidates—namely, Democratic hopefuls George McGovern and Hubert Humphrey—attended in hopes of gaining endorsements from the convention participants. Still other more nationalistic participants sought the establishment of a black political party.

In their addresses to the Saturday evening plenary sessions, Hatcher and Jackson threatened to support a third-party effort if the major parties were not more responsive to black demands.[96] Each delivered fiery jeremiads in support of an autonomous, progressive black politics. Both rebuffed the two major parties for their historical neglect of African American constituencies. Of the two speeches, however, Hatcher's was more politically astute and intellectually keen. Although he generally stirred the audience with his calls for racial solidarity and political independence, Hatcher's address—unlike Jackson's—raised key criticisms of the black party idea. While he agreed that the mainstream parties were dreadfully unresponsive to black demands, Hatcher did not defend a race-specific party as a viable remedy.

Hatcher called for an end to "hip-pocket politics" noting that "[w]e are through believing. We are through hoping. We are through trusting in the two major white American political parties. Hereafter, we shall rely on the power of our own Black unity. We shall no longer bargain away our support for petty jobs or symbolic offices."[97] Furthermore, Hatcher sharply criticized the disproportionate influence of private capital over party politics and state policy. On this matter, he concluded that "[n]o political party which represents the interests of America's giant corporations, rather than the urgent needs of the people, may enlist Black political power in its support . . . Hereafter, every political party must make up its mind. It cannot represent both the corporations and the people."[98] He issued an ultimatum: "We say to the two American political parties: this is their last chance. They have had too many already. These are not idle threats. Only servile fools think them so. The choice is theirs. To ignore our demands is to will the consequences."

Hatcher repeatedly asserted the need for a new organizational form to carry out the *Black Agenda*. He warned his listeners, "we must not leave this convention until we have built the mechanism to implement our program . . . For this we must create a living organization and we must deliberate as we plan as we work—the banner waving over our head must proclaim 'unity.' Without that unity all is lost."[99] While he too voiced support for the development of a national black political organization, Hatcher noted the reality of blacks' minority status and the problems this posed for the utility of an all-black party. Likewise, he ruffled the black nationalist sensibilities of the delegation when he suggested that race-first organizing was not enough. Though generally receptive to Hatcher's remarks, loud disapproval erupted from some audience members when the mayor suggested that the convention develop a multiracial, populist movement. To the dismay of some, Hatcher argued, "If they leave us no choice—and we form a third political movement we shall take with us Chicanos, Puerto Ricans, Indians, Orientals, a wonderful kaleidoscope of colors. And that is not all. We shall also take with us the best of white America. We shall take with us the white youth nauseated by the corrupt values rotting the innards of this society; many a white intellectual revolted by the mendacity of the ruling ideology; many of the white poor who have nothing to lose but their poverty which binds them; many a white ex-G.I. who dares say 'Never Again'; yes and many of the white working class, too."[100]

Hatcher's veiled reference to the closing lines of Marx and Engel's *Communist Manifesto*—"They have nothing to lose but their chains"—reflects the wide rhetorical berth and militancy that characterized the more maverick black elected officials of the immediate postsegregation era. Moreover, Hatcher's insistence on more cosmopolitan modes of political organizing was perceptive and ahead of its time. His hecklers registered the anti-coalition sentiments prevalent in the more nationalistic corners of the Black Power movement. While Jackson would eventually embrace the rainbow vision articulated by Hatcher, at Gary he chose to go with the grain of black public discourse at that moment. In contrast, Jackson brought the delegation to its feet in his call for a black party.

Jackson asserted that without "the option of the black political party we are doomed to remain in the hip pocket of the Democratic Party and the rumble seat of the Republican [P]arty."[101] The consummate public speaker, Jackson employed the metaphor of childbirth to describe the inevitability of the black party's creation. Jackson said to the delegation:

> I don't care how much confusion we have here today it is a beautiful occasion . . . when the baby is about to be born everybody gets scared . . . These Black leaders who called us together did not originate the idea, they innovated the idea which has evolved in our growing Black consciousness . . . And so we are pregnant, we are ready for change and whether there is a doctor or not the water has broke![102]

In combination, the speeches of Hatcher and Jackson reflected a vocal bloc within the convention delegation, which sought an independent black politics.

The idea of creating an independent black political party was not new and activists often pointed to some immediate historical examples of black party activity to defend the potential of such an organization. The Freedom Now Party evolved momentarily in New York and Michigan during the early sixties. More successful black party efforts came on the crest of civil rights movement organizing with the Mississippi Freedom Democratic Party (MFDP), the Lowndes County Freedom Organization (LCFO), and the National Democratic Party of Alabama. The aspirations of such party organizations were more modest than that of organizers who hoped to create a national black party organization through the Gary Convention. Each of these early formations was regional or local in scope. The MFDP activists challenged the Democratic Party regulars by staging a protest at the party's 1964 Atlantic City convention. The LCFO was formed in 1966 by SNCC organizers as a vehicle for registering black voters in rural Lowndes County. In a similar vein, activists led by Dr. John L. Cashin created the National Democratic Party of Alabama to contest Dixiecrat rule in that state. These efforts were distinct from the aspirations of convention participants. Each of these black parties was a transitional organization created to address local conditions of political exclusion during the slow death of the Jim Crow system. In each of these historical instances, blacks constituted a numerical plurality and could hope to achieve some electoral success through effective mobilization.

Rising political efficacy among blacks and the popularity and influence of national liberation struggles among Black Power activists engendered even more radical proposals during the early seventies. In addition to Amiri Baraka's consistent advocacy, others such as veteran activist and former member of the Johnson–Forest Tendency James Boggs, IBW founder Strickland, and Revolutionary Action Movement (RAM) founder Max Stanford all penned arguments in favor of the black party idea.[103] Like Baraka's writings, these writers sought a party that would pose an alternative to the two mainstream parties but also an organization that would transcend the narrow parameters of electoral politics. In a 1969 pamphlet "Manifesto for a Black Revolutionary Party," Boggs called for the formation of a party that would "establish and keep before the movement and society as a whole the revolutionary humanist objectives of the Black Revolution."[104] Strickland argued in favor of a black party "that sees its essential historical task as the challenge to govern this society."[105] Such a party for Strickland would draw elements from revolutionary Third World sources such as the Algerian National Liberation Front (FLN), the African Party for the Independence of Guinea-Bissau and Cape Verde (PAIGC) in Guinea Bissau, the Lao Dong Party in Vietnam, and the Chinese Communist Party. Basing his blueprint for a "Pan-African Party" on Lenin's notion of democratic centralism, Stanford argued that only a "centralized leadership is capable of uniting all the forces, directing them toward a single goal . . . strict party discipline means subordination of the minority to the majority."[106]

A large portion of the convention delegation sought the establishment of an independent political party to serve as a vehicle for realizing the tenets outlined in the *Black Agenda*. The Louisiana delegation introduced a resolution calling for the immediate formation of political party. However, despite many delegates' advocacy of third-party formation, the National Black Political Assembly emerged as a compromise between nationalist forces that desired a party and those leaders who sought some form of autonomous black organization but were leery of severing ties with the New Deal Democratic party coalition. While he had articulated the need for a "World African Party" in the years immediately preceding the Gary Convention, Baraka backed down from this idea during the preconvention planning sessions he orchestrated between grassroots activists and mainstream elected leaders during 1971. Sensing resistance from establishment figures around the party idea, Baraka drafted a compromise that was circulated in a pre-Gary position paper titled "The Nationalist Overview." The national black political structure outlined in this text was a blueprint for the organization that was created at Gary.

As the language of the *Black Agenda* clearly states, many delegates sought a divorce from "conventional white politics" and the development of a "permanent political movement that addresses itself to the basic control and reshaping of American institutions that currently exploit Black America and threaten the whole society."[107] The resolution to create the Assembly received the overwhelming endorsement of 2,404 delegates. Under the convention resolution, the Assembly would be a representative body of 427 members drawn from forty-six states and the District of Columbia equal to 10 percent of the total convention delegation. The forty-three-member National Black Political Council (NBPC) was created to serve as the Assembly's administrative arm—10 percent of the Assembly. Baraka, Diggs, and Hatcher assumed co-leadership.[108] This council would be elected by the Assembly. The official formation of the Asembly would take place during an October 1972 follow-up meeting in Chicago. Baraka noted that the Assembly would function ideally as both a racial congress and a party-like structure that would "endorse candidates, support candidates, run national voter education and registration drives, lobby for Black interests, assess Black progress, make recommendations to the national convention and become the focal point of Black politics in the United States, moving to more concrete relationship with our brothers and sisters on the continent. *It should also be a chief brokerage operation for dealing with the white power political institutions.*"[109] Baraka and other nationalist intellectuals hoped that the Gary convention might circumvent the new black political class as the principal arbiter of race advancement. The actions of black political elites in the months following the Gary Convention threatened the brokerage role that Baraka envisioned for the Assembly in black civic life.

In light of the high attendance and media exposure garnered by the Gary Convention, many leaders such as Basil Patterson saw a unique opportunity for black insiders to exercise influence over mainstream processes if they used the strength of these popular mobilizations as leverage. Patterson, in fact, warned of the potential consequences for the basic legitimacy of mainstream black leaders. Speaking specifically of black delegates to the upcoming DNC, he noted that "[i]f they do not (respond to the unity invoked at Gary) I have serious doubts whether they could ever call themselves community leaders."[110] Within months of the Gary Convention, the elite brokerage strategies employed by black politicos during the 1972 DNC clearly illustrated their inability or unwillingness to strictly adhere to the ideals of operational unity and collective bargaining advocated by nationalist forces.

The allegiance of black politicos to the mandates of the Gary Convention were problematized by cross-cutting partisan, ideological, and political obligations. Richard Hatcher summed up these conflicting responsibilities at the close of the convention. He cautioned against the unrealistic expectations many convention delegates attached to black elected leadership. Hatcher warned, "You can be very black and very unified in Gary . . . but when you get back home, your life, your patronage and your political future depend really on how well you fit into the pattern of the very white regional machine."[111] Previously, Hatcher had offered sharp criticism of the Black Power logic of indigenous control, noting the presence of institutional and political constraints that undermined the capacities of black elected leadership to advance either race-based or redistributive policy agendas. Citing his own first-hand experiences as a black municipal leader, Hatcher argued:

> There is much talk about black control of the ghetto. What does that mean? I am a mayor of a city of roughly 90,000 black people, but we do not control the possibilities of jobs for them, of money for their schools or state-funded social services. These things are in the hands of the United States Steel Corporation and the County Department of Welfare of the State of Indiana.[112]

The CBC broke away from the collective leverage strategy articulated at the Gary Convention by crafting its own alternative platform. Less than a month after the *Agenda* was published, the CBC rolled out its "Black Declaration of Independence and Black Bill of Rights,"—a considerably milder, more pragmatic platform in comparison to the *Black Agenda*. As the language of the "Black Declaration" states, its authors sought to establish the CBC as the "legitimate spokesm[a]n on national issues" for the broader black population. In contrast to the nationalist forces assembled at Gary that sought an independent black political structure, the CBC's "Black Declaration of Independence" did not demand black autonomy, but rather black recogition, and influence within the Democratic Party. In fact, the CBC's document appropriates the strength of the black nationalist movement as leverage for its demands. It states: "The new political mood permeating Black America makes it imperative that the Democratic Party address itself to the hopes, aspirations, concerns and rights of Black Americans—if that Party expects to continue to receive the support of black voters. Benevolence and paternalism are unacceptable and will not be tolerated. The torch is being passed to a new generation of blacks who no longer accommodate but confront." This platform was made public at a press conference held by Congressmen William Clay, Diggs, Louis Stokes, and Charles Rangel. The CBC distanced itself from the more volatile policy stances outlined at Gary. In contrast to the *Black Agenda,* the Caucus's "Black Bill of Rights" did not contain a policy plank on Israel. Likewise, in regard to education, the Caucus asserted the need to move beyond "the sterile issue of busing to the basic issue of redistribution of educational wealth and control."[113] Additionally, the Black Bill of Rights called for increased aid to African nations, guaranteed health care delivery systems, black proportional representation in appointed offices and judgeships, and opposition to welfare reform that does not set a one-year guarantee of $6,500 as the annual payment for a family of four.

Although they broke from the Gary Convention and crafted alternative agendas, many black political elites mobilized the event as political capital in the 1972 party conventions. While Baraka attended the DNC in Miami as an official representative of the National Black Convention, numerous other politicos who participated in the Gary

Convention took part in the DNC as voting delegates.[114] As part of its nonpartisan strategy, the leadership of the Gary Convention also sent Baraka as an official representative to the Republican National Convention, which also took place in Miami. Members of the Black Republican Caucus were already firmly committed to Nixon and championed his administration's record.[115] It became quite clear that Baraka's role as the Gary Convention's official observer was largely perfunctory as partisan delegates at both conventions proceeded to broker individually and not in the collective fashion that he and other more radical activists anticipated. Baraka's assessment of what transpired at the major conventions was published in the October 1972 issue of *Black World* magazine. Robert C. Smith characterized Baraka's account of the 1972 DNC as being "some of the most vitriolic language in recent American political discourse."[116] The following passage from Baraka's *Black World* essay is exemplary of its overall tone of outrage and betrayal:

> But in Miami it was ugly to see how the sellout works. Niggers ranted and raved about white folks and Shirley Chisholm . . . Black people in Miami acted about Mrs. Chisholm as if she were actually running for President and not in reality running to line up at the McGovern paywindow!!! But some other niggers were even more reprehensible. The Humphrey niggers led by Arnold Pinckney of Cleveland and Charles Evers of Mississippi were the lowest of all. They s . . . physically! Like old winded rats dizzy from their treadmills they bumped into people trying to form words Black on their s . . . -out mouths . . . Even though they had this ol' p . . . dressed niggle-o preacher from Los Angeles who shouted and wiggled and chanted 'Blackness' (something they would despise and say was a naive concern any other time and place) all for Hump.[117]

To some extent, Baraka gave voice to the frustration and disappointment experienced by many who saw the 1972 elections as an opportunity to compose a progressive political agenda and collectively lobby the major political parties. Baraka's acrid public denunciation of black politicians' actions at the DNC further sealed the possibility of their future cooperation with the fledgling Assembly structure.

In his address at the Assembly's founding meeting in October 1972, Diggs attempted to allay fears and concerns among activists regarding public officials' apparent lack of commitment to the new organization.[118] Diggs told the audience that after the presidential elections were over many of the public officials who had distanced themselves from the Gary Convention would renew their support. Diggs' comments suggest that those black politicos who broke from the convention strategy shared the same goals and agendas as convention organizers but took alternative routes due to partisan and institutional constraints. This view, however, reduces authentic ideological, partisan, personal, and strategic differences, which separated many black politicians and civil rights leaders from the convention idea and radical forces to consequences of external pressure. Despite Diggs's wishful thinking, these political differences among blacks were substantive and consequential. The departure of these forces from the convention strategy signaled the ascendancy of the black political regime as the principal race brokers within national politics and their ecumenical commitment to insider negotiation over movement politics.

Conclusion

In a 1972 *Black World* essay titled "The New Black Political Culture," Howard University political scientist Ronald Walters offered a comparative assessment of the Gary Convention and the ALD mobilizations of May 1972. Walters argued that these two events reflected an emergent duality within postsegregation black civic culture.[119] He contends that both events emphasized mass mobilization and represented a challenge to the more conventional politics of elite brokerage pursued by establishment figures. This chapter's revisiting of the circumstances and outcomes of the 1972 Gary Convention, however, challenges Walters's conclusions. Although these events clearly reflected the popularity of black nationalist and Pan-Africanist ideals, the 1972 Gary Convention and ALD demonstrations represented two distinctive forms of politics and as such yielded equally divergent outcomes.

In contrast to the cumbersome Gary apparatus, the ALD mobilization was an issue-based alliance, which utilized movement-style disruptive tactics. The African Liberation Day Coordinating Committee (ALDCC) was a more fluid organizational form that developed a popular campaign against imperialism. Of the two organizational models, the ALDCC proved to be the most effective means of building broad-based support among disparate sectors of the African American population. The ALDCC format allowed for differences of ideology, tactics, and style to be meaningfully expressed. The ALDCC represented a more efficacious method for pursuing social justice ends than the convention strategy because the ALD's popular mobilizations did not require long-term commitments from participants, allowed for decentralized leadership and grassroots participation, and was focused around a single-issue aim—indigenous rule for Southern and Portuguese Africa. The Gary Convention, on the other hand, was plagued by conflicts throughout. In the months following the convention, the majority of black politicos distanced themselves from the progressive agenda created at the meeting.

The 1972 Gary Convention was a shotgun wedding of the radical aspirations of Black Power and conventional modes of politics. This marriage would not last nor would it produce the kinds of offspring that black radicals desired. Although it possessed the aura and rhetoric of movement politics, in essence the Gary Convention was an attempt to form an elite, race brokerage apparatus. To operate effectively, the convention and its subsequent Assembly structure required the discipline and legitimacy of established parliamentary bodies. Without the effective means to ensure the support of black politicians—particularly mainstream party regulars—the convention's agenda could not be an effective bargaining tool with the major parties as the organizers envisioned. Although the strength of radical forces threatened both the legitimacy and the preeminence of old guard civil rights forces and the emergent black political elite, these same radical forces helped to bolster the position of black political moderates within mainstream institutions. Inasmuch as black politicos were in a more advantageous position to negotiate directly with the Democratic Party and major public institutions, they readily established themselves as the chief race brokers in the post-segregation context.

The dynamics surrounding the 1972 Gary Convention helped to accelerate that process. Black public officials continued to promote many of the domestic and foreign policy issues advocated by radical forces. The agendas produced by the CBC throughout the seventies onward and those crafted by mainstream black leaders at the 1976 Charlotte Black Issues Conference and the 1980 Richmond Conference for a Black Agenda all share a basic commitment to the kind social democratic reforms embodied in New Deal and Great Society legislation. The more moderate policy perspectives of black political mainstream appeared increasingly progressive within the context of a surging New Right and corresponding evaporation of the New Left and Black Power alternatives. The strategic emphasis of black politicos, however, was antithetical to the achievement of their expressed goals. The politics of insider negotiation alone are ill-suited to the realization of the type of left progressive policies voiced during the Black Power conferences, the 1972 National Black Political Convention, and other agenda-setting events. Barring major economic crises or mass pressure, the substantive policy outputs of the modern American state are generally characterized by institutional inertia and the inordinate influence of corporate power. Moreover, the growth and success of right-wing electoral coalitions from the seventies onward; the breakdown of the New Deal Democratic Party coalition; and the corresponding legislative trends of devolution and privatization in education, health, and social welfare policy further problematized the pursuit of social justice ends singularly through conventional channels. The ALD demonstrations represented another path to political power, that of popular struggle.

From Popular Anti-Imperialism to Sectarianism

The African Liberation Day Mobilizations and Radical Intellectuals

Defeated . . . in Southeast Asia, America will develop greater designs for Africa as a source of raw materials, markets and cheap labor . . . Giant corporations, such as General Motors, Polaroid, Gulf . . . are expanding their investments in Southern Africa. Slave jobs that once were available to Blacks in the US will no longer be available now that these corporations can work our people in Southern Africa for less than a $1.00 a day . . . *We must see the connection between oppression here and in Africa. We want African Liberation Day to emphasize that there is a concrete relationship, not just a romantic one.*

> —Owusu Sadaukai, African Liberation Support
> Committee, 1973

Always bear in mind, that the people are not fighting for ideas, for the things in anyone's head. They are fighting to win material benefits, to live better and in peace, to see their lives go forward, to guarantee the future of their children . . .

> —Amilcar Cabral, Revolution in Guinea, 1969

131

Though commonly neglected in discussions of African American influence over U.S. relations with Africa, the African Liberation Support Committee (ALSC) made an indelible impact on American public consciousness of African politics and U.S. state policy toward the continent during the 1970s. Like the National Black Political Assembly (NBPA) and the Congress of African Peoples (CAP), ALSC was an attempt to develop an institutional space for black oppositional politics. At various historical moments, blacks in the western hemisphere have marshaled their resources and political clout to influence the shape of modern Africa. The African Liberation Support Committee efforts were in some ways reminiscent of the international, mass mobilizations to restore Ethiopian sovereignty following the 1935 Italian invasion. Mussolini's imperialist aggression spawned various organizations and campaigns throughout the diaspora, such as the Ethiopian Research Council, the Provisional Committee for the Defense of Ethiopia, the Friends of Ethiopia, the Medical Committee for the Defense of Ethiopia, and United Aid for Ethiopia among others.[1] During the postwar period, African decolonization figured prominently within African American political discourse and organizational activity. Groups such as the Council on African Affairs and the American Negro Leadership Conference on Africa supported the cause of decolonization on the continent.[2] Additionally, transatlantic tours of newly elected African heads of state, the cross-fertilization of ideas and elite personnel between the continent, and the diaspora and advances in mass communication technology helped to cement political ties and patterns of interchange between African and African American leaders and activists during the period.

ALSC emerged within the wake of these developments and was formed against the peculiar historical canvas of postsegregation American society. Its appearance is framed by the rising tide of dissent in American society embodied in popular mobilizations against Jim Crow segregation and the escalation of the Vietnam War and the burgeoning political optimism of black citizens that accompanied the sixties and early seventies. ALSC's ideological and organizational character was in many ways distinct from previous anticolonial movements. Although self-determination and antiracism were salient features of the rhetoric and programs of ALSC activists, they articulated a vision of postcolonial Africa that fused the standard claims of state sovereignty and democratic rights—goals that had become policy norms within most postwar African American elite circles—with a radical critique of the post–Bretton Woods global political economy and the inordinate influence of transnational corporations within this emergent configuration. Furthermore, ALSC activists were able to craft a political campaign that made radical ideals and interpretations relevant to the everyday lived experiences of thousands of blacks throughout North America. ALSC began as a genuinely mass-based organization that drew together radical intellectuals, welfare recipients, homemakers, artists, industrial workers, service workers, politicians, students, professionals, and civil rights activists of various political persuasions. Albeit momentarily, ALSC organizers articulated a popular anti-imperialism that effectively connected American corporate and state practices to the relations of production, conditions of labor exploitation, and political repression on the African continent, and constructed concrete expressions of a trans-Atlantic solidarity.

This chapter rehearses the origins and development of ALSC with particular attention to the African Liberation Day (ALD) mobilizations and their effectiveness in popularizing radical anti-imperialism. The strength of the 1972 ALD mobilization—similar to the 1972 National Black Political Convention at Gary, Indiana—reflected both the momentary hegemony of radical and Pan-Africanist ideals within black political culture during the early seventies and the heightened sense of political efficacy among African Americans from various walks of life. Across the western hemisphere, thousands gathered to protest the injustices of Portuguese colonialism and white-settler regimes in Southern Africa. Unlike the Gary Convention, which was intended to serve as an in-gathering and agenda-setting affair among political leaders and activists, the ALD mobilization was a broad-based frontal assault on U.S. corporate-state complicity in African oppression.

This chapter probes the sources of ALSC's demise as well. I argue that the conversion of many activists to Marxism-Leninism and the subsequent ideological conflicts within the organization stemmed from contradictions within Black Power discourse. The turn to Marxism was partially facilitated by the political limitations of Black Power programmatic emphasis on indigenous control and race unity.

Many activists' faith in identity politics was tested when the ascent of black public officials yielded only marginal substantive returns for some local black constituencies. Increasingly, some former nationalists embraced Marxism and, in many instances, openly admonished their former allies as "bourgeois nationalists." Vigorous ideological warfare ensued as activists debated the relative merits of capitalism, socialism, and racial nationalism on the pages of black intellectual journals such as *Freedomways*, *Black Scholar*, *Black World*, and *Black Books Bulletin*. To the extent that the mid-seventies race-class debate was characterized by doctrinaire ideology and ad hominem attacks versus reflexive political theory and constructive engagement, this development degraded the character of public debate within radical circles and deeply undermined ALSC's viability and the maintenance of radical opposition more generally. Given their overlapping memberships and organizing personnel with ALSC, I also explore developments in the 1974 National Black Political Convention, which paralleled and nourished ALSC's sectarian conflicts. From around summer 1973 through the 1974 Sixth Pan-African Congress in Dar es Salaam, ALSC's programmatic work was increasingly characterized by proselytization rather than the wearisome tasks of organizing actual constituencies around real issues.

The Context of Radical Black Anti-Imperialism

Stimulated by the acceleration of anticolonial activity following the 1945 Manchester Pan African Congress and World War II's politico-economic repercussions throughout the West, a major wave of decolonization movements swept across the African continent during the fifties and sixties.[3] International pressure, diplomatic overtures, parliamentary deliberations, and, in some cases, armed struggle had given birth to political independence throughout many of the former British, French, and Belgian colonies and protectorates. As other regions across the continent experienced transitions to indigenous rule, in the Portuguese colonies of Guinea-Bissau, Cape Verde, Angola, and Mozambique and the white-settler regimes of Rhodesia, Namibia (South-West Africa), and South Africa, the resolve of reactionary forces only deepened. While formal party politics and constitutional reform were effective methods of achieving decolonization elsewhere on the continent, many engaged in more militant, confrontational tactics in the last bastions of colonial rule. Some of the indigenous organizations comprising a second wave of national liberation struggles in the Portuguese colonies included PAIGC (Partido Africano de independência da Guiné e Cabo Verde/African Party for the Independence of Guinea-Bissau and Cape Verde); Frelimo (Frente de Libertação de Moçambique/Mozambique Front of Liberation); MPLA (Movimento Popular de Libertação de Angola/The People's Movement of Angolan Liberation), and UNITA (União Nacional para a Independência Total de Angola/National Union for the Total Independence of Angola). In the white-settler regimes of Southern Africa, other organizations demanded black self-rule, such as ZANU (Zimbabwean African National Union) and ZAPU (the Zimbabwean African Peoples Union) in Southern Rhodesia; SWAPO (the South West Africa People's Organization) in Namibia; and PAC (the Pan African Congress) and ANC (the African National Congress) in South Africa.[4] Foremost in the minds of many American-based Pan-Africanists was the extent of the U.S. state and transnational corporations' involvement and support of Portugal and Southern African settler regimes.

The Nixon administration's reactionary policies toward Africa provided the context and impetus for the 1972 ALD mobilization. The Nixon administration's support of the Rhodesian settler regime was, in many respects, the international elaboration of the "Southern strategy" he employed to mobilize anti–civil rights sentiments, solidify white electoral support, and win the 1968 elections. Profitable returns on U.S investments in Southern Africa and the Cold War strategic objective of inhibiting African communist sympathizers from attaining influence served as the chief justifications for the White House's support of Rhodesia's herrenvolk democracy. Historian Gerald Horne argues that racism lay at the heart of pro-Rhodesia attitudes among many American political elites. Discontent over the implementation and enforcement of liberal integrationist policy throughout the American South compelled many politicians including Congressmen Jesse Helms of North Carolina and Strom Thurmond of South Carolina to doggedly support white minority rule throughout the Southern African region.

Both Helms and Thurmond viewed the United Nations as international carpetbaggers. Commenting on the U.N. Security Council–
imposed sanctions against Rhodesia and South-West Africa, Helms
defended white supremacy in Southern Africa and rejected the ethics
of international intervention. His arguments echoed the disdain for
federal government activism, which always characterized southern
segregationists' cries for "states rights" and the sanctity of local ways.
Helms candidly lamented:

> It's a good thing there was no United Nations at the time when
> Patrick Henry and some other rebellious souls decided to
> declare the independence of a new nation back in 1776 . . .
> African tribes in the back bushes of Rhodesia that have no
> knowledge of or appreciation for civilized society. If that absurd
> position had prevailed in 1776, the American Indians would
> own and be running America today.[5]

Helms's comments represent the most vulgar manifestation of American ruling class support for white supremacy in Southern Africa, but
many others in the White House and Congress shared his sentiments if
not his segregationist manner. By 1969, Nixon broke from UN sanctions on Rhodesia and South-West Africa arguing that the United States
should "normalize our relations with all governments in the area." On the
crest of such sentiments, the Congress legalized the importation of
Rhodesian chrome into the United States with the passage of the Byrd
Amendment.[6] The American-based corporation Union Carbide was
responsible for 20 percent of South African chrome production in addition to owning a large chrome mine in Rhodesia. Therefore, Union
Carbide, Allegheny Ludlum, Foote Mineral Company, the American
Colloid Company, and other major chrome importers were highly
instrumental in the passage of the Byrd Amendment.[7] Given its multi-
tude of industrial usages and its specific relevance to arms production,
such coordinated corporate-state efforts to protect transnational circuits of capital accumulation at the expense of humanitarian interests
and democracy in the region were both predictable and tragic.

The Nixon administration's support of Portugal during the bloody
independence movements of its African colonies was perceived as

being equally inflammatory in the eyes of many Black Power radicals. Nixon had promised Portugal nearly a half billion dollars in financial aid. Vocal opposition to such aid emerged from former ambassadors who charged that such overtures served to delay the emergence of indigenous rule and sovereignty.[8] One dramatic response to these linkages and the relations of domination they sustained was the 1972 ALD mobilization.

1972 African Liberation Day and the Birth of African Liberation Support Committee

The ALD mobilization was the brainchild of activist Owusu Sadaukai. Sadaukai was born Howard Fuller in 1941 in Shreveport, Louisiana. When Fuller was a child, his family moved to Milwaukee like thousands of other Southern blacks in search of economic opportunity in the industrial North. Fuller's earliest political activism was through the civil rights movement. A standout basketball player at Milwaukee's North Division High School, Fuller earned an athletic scholarship to Carroll College. He was among the first class of black students to integrate the college. Fuller graduated from Carroll in 1962 with a BS in sociology. He went on to pursue graduate studies at Western Reserve University in Cleveland. After receiving a master's degree in social administration in 1964, he worked for the Urban League and the Congress of Racial Equality (CORE). His radicalization was facilitated by his immediate experiences as a social worker in the Deep South and the mid-1960s sea change in black public discourse from liberal integration to Black Power militancy.

Sadaukai's experiences as a community organizer were critical to his political maturation. He moved to North Carolina in 1964 and became involved in union activism and other community struggles. Ever since the historic 1960 lunch counter sit-ins, the Greensboro area had been a locus of militant black political activity and was, therefore, home to dense local network of organizations and activists.[9] The region provided a politically rich, supportive environment for the young activist who became head of the Foundation for Community Development, a statewide organization committed to fostering political activism among the poor. The stifling poverty Sadaukai encountered in the region and the challenges to progressive work posed by the local power structure provided him with a second education in political activism:

> It was really in North Carolina that I learned everything that I know today about politics and so forth. And I learned most of it from the people that I was working with . . . I started out doing grass roots organizing at the neighborhood level trying to get streets paved, have houses fixed and get rid of rats. So that really shaped my opinion about the need for power.[10]

During his North Carolina sojourn, Sadaukai became a confidant of Student Nonviolent Coordinating Committee (SNCC) activists Cleveland Sellers and Stokely Carmichael and served as a major player in the development of the Student Organization for Black Unity (SOBU). He later helped to found the Malcolm X Liberation University (MXLU) in Durham, North Carolina (later relocated to Greensboro), which was intended to facilitate social change through the training and development of radical cadre. A skilled orator, resourceful and experienced community organizer, and an erudite intellectual Sadaukai stood poised at the close of the decade to exercise considerable influence within national black politics. In concert with other black nationalist activists such as Newark-based poet, Amiri Baraka, he was instrumental in convening the 1970 CAP meeting in Atlanta. Likewise, Sadaukai, MXLU, and SOBU cadre were central in the series of planning meetings and activities that gave rise to the 1972 National Black Political Convention. Just as Baraka had arisen as the foremost radical figure on domestic matters, Sadaukai quickly established himself as a principle force in the movement to end Portuguese colonialism and white oligarchy in Southern Africa. Like Baraka, Sadaukai also strove to devise a popular language and creative organizing methods that might reconcile radical ideals with pragmatic politics.

Partially due to Carmichael's influence, Sadaukai's ideological direction shifted toward Pan-Africanism by the turn of the decade. In September 1970, Sadaukai embarked on a tour of the African continent as a representative of SOBU and MXLU. SOBU was already engaged in support activities for anticolonial struggles and initiated the Pan-African Medical Program (PAMP) in late 1970.[11] While traveling across the continent, Sadaukai met with leaders of national liberation struggles in Mozambique, Guinea-Bissau, and Angola. Samora Machel and Frelimo rebels urged Sadaukai and other members of the delegation to go back to the United States and build solidarity for anticolonial struggles on the continent. Upon returning, he published a six-part chronicle of his trip in the Greensboro-based movement organ *The African World*.[12] Sadaukai's resolve to assist in indigenous opposition to colonialism and apartheid gave rise to the ALD mobilization.

In a letter dated 17 February 1972, Sadaukai described the motivations and intent of the ALD mobilization and extended a formal invitation to others to become involved. He asserted that this campaign was designed to accomplish the following things:

(1) help make the masses of African (black) people in the United States, the Caribbean, and Canada aware of the political conditions in Southern Africa and the armed struggles being carried out by the brothers and sisters there; (2) to educate African (black) people in these countries about the relationship between what is happening to our people in Africa and what is happening to us in the United States and other places; and (3) to organize a national protest demonstration against the United States foreign policy which supports European colonialist rule in Southern Africa. This planned action is a result of meetings with liberation movement leaders in Mozambique during a prolonged trip to the continent last fall, during which I was able to witness the hard daily struggle our brothers and sisters are waging to regain control of their land. When asked how the masses of our people in the United States could best support them, I was advised that the most useful thing we can do at this stage is to provide them with strong moral support by showing the world our concern through massive Black protest and demonstration against U.S. involvement in Southern Africa.[13]

Upon returning from his trip to the continent, Sadaukai founded the African Liberation Day Coordinating Committee (ALDCC).

The core organizing was carried out by the following ALDCC personnel: Antoine Perot, chairman of supporting council; Florence Tate, Information Director; Mark Smith, director of operations; Mwanafunzi Hekima, logistics coordinator; Juadine Henderson, secretary-treasurer; and Cleveland Sellers, field coordinator. The ALDCC headquarters were established at 2207 14th Street, NW in Washington, D.C. The march was planned to coincide with the annual May 25 observation of the Organization of African Unity's formation in 1963. Organizers ultimately chose Saturday, 27 May 1972 since a weekend date might allow for greater participation. Rapidly, the ALDCC developed a broad, diverse base of support. Sadaukai assembled a national steering committee to pilot the mobilization efforts. This committee contained a broad cast of activists, intellectuals, and politicians. The steering committee included such familiar personalities as Reverend Ralph Abernathy of the Southern Christian Leadership Conference (SCLC); Georgia State representative Julian Bond; H. Rap Brown; Carmichael; Ruwa Chiri of United Africans for One Motherland International (UFOMI); Representative John Conyers; Daniels of the Mid-West Regional Black Coalition of Youngstown, Ohio; Angela Y. Davis; Representative Ron Dellums; Vincent Harding of the Institute of the Black World (IBW); Nathan Hare, editor of *Black Scholar*; Reverend Charles Koen of the United Front of Cairo, Illinois; Don L. Lee, a Chicago-based poet; Reverend Douglas Moore of the Washington, D.C. Black United Front; Huey Newton of the Black Panther Party; Betty Shabazz, activist and widow of Malcolm X; Inez Reid, Washington, D.C. activist; Representative Louis Stokes; and George Wiley, the National Welfare Rights Organization (NWRO), among others. While the ALDCC attained a considerable breadth of support among mainstream black leaders, it did not receive endorsement from the NAACP executive director, Roy Wilkins.

Apparently, Wilkins's opposition to the ALD thrust stemmed from his on-going feuds with black radicals. His disapproval of Black Power sentiments was no secret. Amidst the initial fervor surrounding Black Power, Wilkins characterized the politics of self-determination in pathological terms.[14] Wilkins's differences with Black Power radicals extended to African affairs as well. Reportedly, in March 1972 during a visit to South Africa Wilkins publicly criticized the use of sanctions on the grounds that such actions would adversely affect black South African workers. In an ALD-related press conference, Baraka denounced Wilkins as "criminally irresponsible" and "catatonic" and further as "[a] puppet head of the NAACP."[15] To a considerable degree, Wilkins was a lone dissenting voice even among the mainstream black political elite. As 27 May drew closer, the ALDCC was gaining considerable momentum for its planned anti-imperialist demonstrations.

A measure of the ALDCC's organizing strength was its success in drawing together ideological rivals such as the Black Panther Party and Karenga's US Organization around a common cause. Some of the organizations that formally sponsored the mobilization included SCLC; the National Welfare Rights Organization (NWRO); SOBU; student organizations from various historically black colleges; CORE; CAP; National Council of Negro Women; Delta Sigma Theta Sorority, Inc.; and Alpha Phi Alpha Fraternity, Inc. Additionally, a considerable portion of the mobilization's expenses were underwritten by Inter-religious Foundation for Community Organization (IFCO).

IFCO was established in 1967 in the wake of major urban rioting in Detroit and Newark. In light of white backlash within many church congregations, IFCO's founders sought to develop a mechanism to facilitate positive relations and communication between black and white communities. IFCO Action was formed on 15 March 1972 as a non–tax-exempt offshoot designed to influence public policy and promote social change. Upon its inception, IFCO Action made support of African liberation struggles a top priority and consequentially served as a major funding reservoir for the ALD mobilization.

Additional public endorsements were offered by the National Black Political Convention; Maryland Congressman Parren Mitchell; Socialist Worker's Party (SWP) vice-presidential candidate Andrew Pulley; the National Conference of Black Political Scientists; the New York Black Panther Party; college educator Andrew Billingsley; Concerned African Women; concerned black students of Kent University; and the Black Student and Faculty Coalition of the University of Maryland. Many of these organizations sponsored groups of marchers and assisted in the ALD mobilization by providing transportation to the main march in Washington and other regional demonstrations in New Orleans, San Francisco, and Toronto. The end result of the ALDCC's efforts was the largest, post–World War II demonstration concerning Africa affairs held in the North America.

Although local police and news reports estimated that 10,000 to 15,000 persons attended the ALD demonstration in Washington, D.C., the event's organizers reported over 30,000 participants.[16] Marchers began to assemble at Malcolm X (Meridian Hill) Park during the early morning hours and proceeded on a winding route through embassy-dense northwest Washington. The procession halted briefly at the Portuguese embassy, the Rhodesian Information Center, the South African Embassy, and the U.S. State Department where protestors read aloud statements of indictment, which variably condemned Western imperialist powers and illuminated their direct involvement and support of economic exploitation and political disenfranchisement throughout Africa. These statements were written and delivered in a bold, confrontational language, which vividly described the deplorable living and working conditions of African peoples.

In front of the Portuguese embassy, Ohio activist Ron Daniels and CORE leader Roy Innis read a statement that charged the "murderous state of Portugal" with the "criminal invasion of Mozambique, Angola and Guinea-Bissau," involvement in the modern trans-Atlantic slave trade, cultural imposition throughout the colonies, and "continuing the slave trade in the thinly disguised form of agreements between Portugal and South Africa for the provision of stated numbers of black men from Angola and Mozambique to work in the gold and diamond mines of South Africa in return for cash payments and trade kickbacks to the Portugal [sic] government."[17] Near the South African embassy, Reverend Moore and Lucius Walker indicted South Africa's minority regime with the genocide of aboriginal peoples of the Southern African cape and the imposition of an exploitative, contract labor system on African miners "which forces them away from home without their families, into cattle-like compounds and unsanitary working conditions, for slave wages."[18] Their statement also called attention to the regime's role in the appropriation of mineral wealth from the region, the institution of an unjust system of racial apartheid and the brutal repression of antiapartheid protesters during the 1960 Sharpeville massacre. During the brief rally outside the

U.S. State Department, Jitu Weusi (Les Campbell) of the East cultural center in Bedford-Stuyvesant section of Brooklyn and Dowlu Gene Locke of Houston's Africans in America for Black Liberation outlined the extent of U.S. "collusion with the white minority groups" in the maintenance of inequality and political subordination.[19]

The route of the march ended near the Washington Monument grounds at Lumumba Square (Sylvan Park Theatre) and concluded with a mass rally. The speaker's platform embodied the diverse cross section of African American political and ideological tendencies that the march mobilized. Washington, D.C., Congressman Walter F. Fauntroy served as the master of ceremonies in a closing program interspersed with political sermons and entertainment, including poetry by Don L. Lee, songs by the Harambee Singers, and a performance by the Spirit House Movers. Elaine Brown offered greetings from the Black Panther Party, decried the on-going American war against Vietnam, and called for black domestic unity. Mounting the podium wearing a dashiki atop his shirt and tie, Congressman Diggs visually represented the pervasive influence of radical Pan-Africanism over mainstream black political culture during the early seventies. Diggs had, in fact, arisen as the foremost spokesman among black national politicians on questions of U.S. foreign policy toward Africa. In his address to the marchers, he condemned the Nixon administration's stance on Southern Africa and the role of transnational corporations. He urged white activists from the peace movement to join in the efforts of the ALD organizers and support the cause of African liberation. Likewise, Diggs called on the marchers to initiate a massive letter-writing campaign to pressure Congress and facilitate the passage of more progressive legislation on African affairs. In their speeches, Baraka and Sadaukai insisted on the need for organization and mass mobilization to improve the plight of African peoples domestically and throughout the diaspora. Although the Washington ALD demonstration was the largest event, other concurrent demonstrations were held in New Orleans, San Francisco, Toronto, and the Caribbean. Like the Washington demonstrators, participants in other cities turned out in a mass expression of anticolonial solidarity.

To stimulate support among local citizens for anticolonial struggles, many activists worked strenuously to illuminate tangible linkages between distant political crises on the African continent and familiar local institutions. In New Orleans, the local ALD demonstration was organized by the Black Workers Congress (BWC), an organization that developed out of the Detroit-based League of Revolutionary Black Workers. BWC cadre circulated a promotional flyer in the run-up to the ALD demonstration that drew specific linkages between colonial oppression and local businesses that catered to black New Orleanians. The tract titled "We Got the Same Enemy" appeals to blacks as citizens, workers, and consumers:

> New Orleans Wholesale Jewelry imports diamonds from South Africa at the expense of overworked and underpaid black workers and sells them through Adler's and Hausmann's Jewelry. Polaroid industry—another brutal big boss sells some of its products at Fox and Bennet Photography Stores. Yeah we do have the same enemy which is why a state wide rally is being held. . . . The purpose of ALD is to bring together a national demonstration to show the relationship of oppression in Africa and oppression in America.[20]

Reflecting the desire for territorial sovereignty at the heart of anti-colonial struggles, marchers attempted to "free the land" by renaming demonstration sites after race heroes and heroines. Marchers symbolically claimed public space and linked their contemporary struggles to longer traditions of resistance. In San Francisco, the ALD demonstration convened at Raymond-Kimball Park, which organizers renamed "DuBois Savannah." The San Francisco ALD actions were initiated on 25 May when twelve activists staged a midday demonstration at the Portuguese consulate. The march culminated with a mass rally over which California state assemblyman (and later, San Francisco Mayor) Willie Brown presided. The speaker's platform featured addresses by Black Panther Party leader Bobby Seale; Guyanese Marxist, Pan-Africanist intellectual Walter Rodney; Communist Party, activist Angela Y. Davis; Nelson Johnson of SOBU; Reverend Koen; and Gary Mayor Richard G. Hatcher. The rally also featured performances by the Nairobi Messengers, the Pharaoh Sanders trio, the Umoja Dancers, and the Freddie Hubbard Jazz

Band. Likewise, in Toronto a sizable contingent of West Indian–born émigrés marched past the French, British, Portuguese, U.S., South African, Israeli, and Italian consulates in protest of colonialism and in solidarity with marchers elsewhere. The march culminated at Christie Park, which was rededicated to Marcus Garvey by the demonstrators. Speeches were given by Rosie Douglas, Bond, and Conyers. Additionally, smaller demonstrations were held throughout the Caribbean in Antigua, Dominica, and Grenada. While these demonstrations were the focal point of the ALDCC's activities, they were part of a broader offensive that fused both formal political strategies and movement-style tactics.

Congressman Charles Rangel sponsored an amendment to a $3.43 billion NASA reauthorization bill that forbade any additional spending in South Africa. Such legislation was intended to halt the operation of U.S. satellite tracking stations in South Africa. In April, the Congressional Black Caucus in coordination with private organizations sued the U.S. government in an attempt to stop the importation of Rhodesian chrome ore.[21] Under the leadership of Maxine Maye and Eddie Wilson, employees of the U.S. Department of Health, Education and Welfare (HEW) established a Health and Welfare Committee for African Liberation to distribute funds through the Organization of African Unity (OAU) for public health and education purposes in Southern Africa.[22] Congressman Charles Diggs sponsored a major public policy conference shortly before the ALD mobilization. Some four hundred delegates converged at Howard University for the African American National Conference on Africa. The meeting featured a two-day series of workshops intended to foster discussion and craft practical strategies for hastening the demise of white-settler regimes. In press interviews, Diggs asserted that an immediate purpose of the gathering was to advance legislation that would repeal authorization of Rhodesian chrome imports to the United States.[23]

Other activists displayed their support for national liberation struggles through civil disobedience. Students at Columbia University took over four campus buildings to protest the university's investments in corporations involved in South Africa and the Vietnam War. Likewise, forty members of Government Employees

United Against Racial Discrimination (GUARD) demonstrated at the State Department in protest of the U.S.'s violation of the U.N. Security Council sanctions.[24] At John Hopkins University, an organization of students, faculty, and administrators demanded that the institution investigate its linkages with South Africa. In Philadelphia, members of CAP and the Southern African Committee staged a demonstration outside the Barclay Hotel during the annual meeting of the Foote Mineral Company. Activists sought to dramatically publicize the corporation's on-going importation of Rhodesian chrome. In New Orleans, Southern University students convinced members of the predominantly black Local 1419 of the International Longshoreman's Association to halt the delivery of Rhodesian chrome into Burnside port (Louisiana) in April 1972. Consequentially, Sadaukai, Reverend Walker of IFCO, and members of SCLC joined the students and union members in an unsuccessful effort to stop importation of the commodity.[25]

Given the success of the ALD mobilization, organizers decided to transform the ALDCC into a more permanent organization—the African Liberation Support Committee.[26] Under ALSC's banner, activists embarked on local campaigns to generate funds, medical supplies, clothes, and other essential supplies for donating to liberation movements throughout Western and Southern Africa. In 1973, ALSC organizers staged a second ALD mobilization in honor of Amilcar Cabral, the revolutionary intellectual and PAIGC leader, who was assassinated by Portuguese agents on January 20, 1973. At the time of his death, Cabral's writings on revolution and national culture were part of the general lexicon of American black radicals, and his leadership of the PAIGC afforded him iconic status within the hearts and minds of many activists throughout the diaspora. His murder was a grim reminder of the forces arrayed against revolutionary politics and his death stimulated renewed efforts to organize support for decolonization and the spread of racial democracy throughout the continent. Like the original ALD demonstrations, the goal of the 1973 mobilization was to educate the public, engender greater consciousness of the war in Southern Africa, and raise support funds for dissidents. In contrast to the previous year, the 1973 ALD was designed with a more intense local emphasis. Demonstrations were planned to occur concurrently in twenty cities to encourage greater grassroots participation and to focus attention on the culpability of local governmental and corporate institutions in African oppression.

Nationwide, some 100,000 marchers demonstrated as part of the 1973 ALD observations.[27] The Washington, D.C. demonstration was once again the largest and drew 4,500 participants. Chanting and bearing picket signs with slogans such as "Africa for Africans" and "Down with Imperialism," demonstrators retraced much of the previous march route past the Portuguese, British, and South African embassies. In what was a bold, daring effort to call attention to the inequalities fostered by the global economic order, the 1973 demonstration concluded with a rally at the corporate offices of International Telephone and Telegraph (ITT) at 1707 L Street, NW. In his address to the marchers, activist John McClennon asserted that ITT "symbolizes the multinational corporations that every day plunder and ravage black Africans." He continued, "These corporations are the heart of world capitalism and they make their profits by exploiting other people. If Africa is to be liberated, multinational corporations must be eradicated."[28] Throughout 1973, ALSC local affiliates organized intensely to assist in that eradication and to solicit financial support for African revolutionary organizations. By the end of 1973, ALSC cadre had raised over $40,000, which was evenly distributed to Frelimo, PAIGC, UNITA, and ZANU. Some activists hoped to move ALSC from a diverse, ad hoc alliance to a formal organization with a standard ideological outlook.

The Advent of the "Two-Line" Struggle

For many ALSC activists, the efficacy of race unity politics began to unravel as they came to terms with both the domestic limitations of indigenous control and the nature of Cold War geopolitics on the African continent. During the Nixon years, race remained a powerful axis of inequality in American life, but the strength of the nationalist rhetoric buckled under the new contradictions produced by political integration. As the events of the 1972 Gary Convention illustrated, the race unity ideal often mystified the extent of political differences among blacks. Many activists sought to build alliances that were not predicated on racial affinity but on ideological commitment to revolutionary working-class struggle. Sadaukai, Abdul Alkalimat, Johnson, and other leftward-leaning members of ALSC moved to adapt an official Marxist-Leninist organizational line at a Frogmore (South Carolina) meeting in summer 1973.[29] Although activists based in Greensboro and Nashville tended to form the leading edge of the push for stronger, radical leftist line in ALSC, the Marxist wing of the organization was subdivided into three principal clusters of activity. Johnson and Sadaukai of Greensboro and Alkalimat and Ron Bailey of the Nashville Peoples College formed one node. The Houston chapter led by Dowlu Locke formed a second, while the Atlanta and New Orleans ALSC chapters combined to make up a third group. Although the New Orleans ALSC was organized by members of the Black Worker's Congress and the Atlanta chapter was anchored primarily in the political science department of Atlanta University, both chapters converged in their preference for local organizing and their opposition to participation in the Sixth Pan-African Congress.[30] The actions taken at the 1973 Frogmore meeting provoked heated opposition by the more nationalistic ALSC cadre with some withdrawing their support in the months thereafter. These tensions between nationalists and new advocates of "scientific socialism" permeated ALSC and the wider Black Power movement.

During the late sixties, Black Power radicals routinely offered sharp criticisms of the black establishment but such arguments were usually bridled by a sense of common racial interests. Consequentially, at both the Gary Convention and the inaugural ALD demonstration, organizers actively tried to recruit a broad cross section of African Americans. During planning deliberations for the 1974 Little Rock Black Political Convention, however, this ecumenical view was superceded by a more discerning approach predicated not so much on racial identity but on ideological commitments. Many activists increasingly employed class analysis and cast a more skeptical eye on the political allegiances of newly emerging black political elites in the United States, the Caribbean, and Africa. For some American black radicals, "domestic imperialism" needed to be rooted out and destroyed as much as that in the Third World. These emerging tensions are evident in the organizational life of the NBPA, which was formed out of the 1972 Gary Convention and shared overlapping membership with ALSC. Atlanta Mayor Maynard Jackson was originally invited to address the Assembly's 1974 Little Rock Convention. His invitation, however, was almost annulled at the urging of some organizers who questioned Jackson's and others' commitments to radical ideals.[31] Sadaukai was among those who felt that Maynard Jackson and other prominent political figures such as Jesse Jackson should not be included. Sadaukai charged that "neo-colonialist, petit-bourgeois black elected officials are as much the enemy as their white counterparts."[32] This more selective posture was not reserved solely for African American politicians. Rather, administrators of newly independent African and Caribbean nations were subjected to scrutiny of radical activists within the Assembly.

Before the 1974 Little Rock Convention, Sadaukai, in a letter to Baraka, expressed his reservations regarding a pending invitation to Guyanese Prime Minister Forbes Burnham.[33] During the late sixties, Burnham had emerged as a key proponent of Black Power in Guyana. Like his U.S. counterparts, his appeals to black solidarity and self-determination were central to his electoral campaigns and the official program of the Peoples National Congress (PNC).[34] Increasingly, Burnham was criticized by the Working People's Alliance (WPA), a multiracial, socialist organization.[35] WPA activists accused Burnham of deploying racial rhetoric and gestures as a means of distracting public attention away from the limited import of black indigenous control. They held that while his election offered psychological rewards to black Guyanese, the material conditions of the rank and file had not improved measurably under the Burnham regime. Contrary to the popular slogans of Burnham supporters, WPA organizers charged that black control of the state apparatus had not made the "little man a real man."[36] One staunch critic of the PNC's politics was Walter Rodney.

A Guyanese native, Rodney was a key figure in the Black Power movement in the Caribbean. He was the author of *How Europe Underdeveloped Africa*, a highly influential critique of European imperialism, which was originally published by Bogle L'Ouverture Press in London in 1972 and reissued by Howard University Press in

1974.[37] Rodney joined the WPA upon returning to Guyana in 1974 and remained an important figure in the opposition movement until his assassination by a car bomb in 1980. In a November 1974 *Black Scholar* interview with S. E. Anderson, Rodney criticized Stokely Carmichael's insistence that Africa be the main focus of struggle for blacks throughout the diaspora. Rodney noted: "The impracticalities of [Carmichael's argument] are so huge that they scarcely need emphasizing. Some of us can get to Africa. The vast majority of our people will, in fact, not be able to go there, and struggle takes place where people live and work. That's the locus of struggle."[38] Equally important, Rodney warned against Pan-Africanist politics based on racial sentimentalism. He argued: "we cannot romanticize the situation in Africa. We must draw distinctions. Who is who in Africa? What are the state structures? What are the classes?"[39] He called for a more discerning posture that cut through superficialities and built alliances on the basis of a commonly held vision of society:

> We will have to be more selective in [e]nsuring that our relations are nurtured with particular progressive governments, with particular liberation movements, with particular social organizations—whether they be trade unions, women's movements, student unions—various groups that develop a perspective on African struggle. One must see as the goal of our international activity, itself conditioned by the fact that the struggle is taking place in these various African territories is to develop a perspective that is anticapitalist, anti-imperialist, and that speaks to the exploitation and oppression of all people.[40]

Rodney's perceptive critique of neocolonialism converged with the evolving ideology of many American black radicals.

In addition to their mounting criticism of politicians such as Burnham and Maynard Jackson, some radical activists within the Assembly increasingly challenged the legitimacy of former nationalist allies. Consequentially, some black nationalists were excluded from the 1974 National Black Political Convention program as well. One controversial incident surrounding the composition of the speaker's platform involved Nation of Islam minister Louis Farrakhan. The decision to exclude Farrakhan undoubtedly stemmed from looming questions regarding his influence and role in the assassination of Malcolm X.[41] Some convention participants were dismayed by this decision. "One of the greatest things that brought dissolution to the convention," asserted Reverend Roy Laird, a member of the Arkansas delegation, "was that the heads of the convention were totally disagreeable with the convention in hosting Minister Farrakhan as one of the speakers."[42] Laird estimated that some 80 percent of the convention delegation shared his discontent regarding the convention organizers' practice of what he termed "unity with exclusion."[43] Such internal debates surrounding the 1974 Little Rock Convention stemmed from Baraka's and CAP's official adoption of what they termed "Marxism-Leninism-Mao Tse-Tung thought." Baraka and Sadaukai held that their embrace of Marxism stemmed from their earlier advocacy of cultural nationalism and the revelation of its inadequacies. In his efforts to explain his journey toward Marxism, Baraka revised his stance on black indigenous control noting the limits of this core strand of Black Power discourse:

> those of us who were still determined to serve the people began to understand that merely putting Black faces in high places, without changing the fundamental nature of the system itself, served to make that system more flexible and more dangerous, since for the masses of us . . . the hardship, exploitation and oppression continued.[44]

Eschewing black indigenous control, Baraka now increasingly advocated that black liberation would only come through socialist revolution. In an effort to clarify CAP's position, he argued: "We remain patriots, struggling for the liberation of Black people, but we must understand that liberation will come only with the destruction of the system of capitalism."[45]

Although Cruse and others have criticized Baraka's "ideological vacillation," I would argue that Baraka's embrace of socialism was not as abrupt or as inconsistent as many have claimed.[46] A more attentive reading of Baraka's political development clearly suggests that he had entertained elements of Marxism at previous points in his life. Baraka was "undesirably" discharged from the U.S. Air Force for holding sympathetic views toward communism—charges based on his eclectic diet of reading materials, subscription to the *Partisan Review*, and prior affiliations with civil rights groups.[47] Although the charges were an exaggeration, they indicate that even during his formative adult years Baraka engaged leftist theory and politics to some degree. Likewise, as I discussed in an earlier chapter, a key catalyst in his politicization was his 1960 trip to revolutionary Cuba under the sponsorship of the Fair Play for Cuba Committee. His decision to visit Cuba reflected Baraka's intense curiosity regarding the newly formed revolutionary government. Equally, Baraka noted that his artistic and activist work was deeply influenced by the socialist realism espoused by the Cuban intellectuals he encountered. Once more, Baraka and CAP had incorporated various elements of Marxism into their propaganda before 1975.

CAP's formative engagement with socialism was typically secondary to its promotion of nationalist ideals. Moreover, CAP cadre's flirtation with socialism was always tempered by their view of black cultural particularity. CAP entertained Marxist ideas somewhat indirectly via the political thought of African left intellectuals, namely, Julius Nyerere's Ujamaa/African socialism and Cabral's writings on culture and revolutionary movements. Drawing upon these and other theorists, Baraka outlined the organization's official position on socialism:

> We also believe, as Mwalimu Nyerere, whose progressive government of Tanzania is a living model of positive development that black people all over the world can learn from, that socialism is an "attitude," a way of addressing the world. We believe our address to the world is as African people and so we speak of Ujamaa or cooperative economics, because we understand that at the base of any people's development is their cultural awareness, that is, their understanding of who they are (how they live and what such knowledge means as social definition and responsibility).[48]

Baraka also questioned the universal character of socialism noting that "in any living context ideas take on the qualities of their creators and users. Such ideas in the way they are actually practiced became part of a people's way of life (their culture)."[49] Baraka and CAP cadre held that no ideas or ideologies would be effective unless they were rooted in the Black Value System as outlined under Kawaida's doctrine. Speaking of Kawaida's *Nguzo Saba* or seven values, Baraka wrote, "Their value is that they focus on specific moral qualities black people need to liberate ourselves. But these moral qualities are also political directions and economic attitudes, necessary psychological states and critically important goals for the creation of a revolutionary culture and people."[50] Increasingly, however, Baraka and CAP cadre shed the culturalism of these early positions.[51] More often, the constructs of class, imperialism, surplus value, and alienation were used to refine CAP's analysis of racial oppression.[52] On the revisions of CAP cadre's earlier cultural nationalist positions, Baraka argued:

> We went so far as to try to impose continental Afrikan mores and customs, some out of the precapitalist feudalist Afrika, upon Black people living in North America whose culture actually is that of Afrikans living in America for three centuries, Afro-Americans. We thought of culture in too many ways as a static quality, not in all ways and at the base directly shaped by the economic and political systems in which it developed . . . But from Cabral we also began to understand that even our concern for culture had to be re-examined and that finally our culture here in North America, if it was going to be a national culture had to be a culture of the Black working class, urban and country, as well as the progressive nationalist projections of the urban *petit bourgeoisie*, which did include a determination to identify with Afrika.[53]

On the heels of these growing left sentiments, ALSC organizers expanded their programmatic thrusts for 1974 and declared May as "African Liberation Month." In addition to the annual ALD demonstration, special programs were organized around Malcolm X's birthday (19 May) and the first national ALSC conference was slated to take place before the 25 May ALD demonstration. Throughout May, local ALSC affiliates planned to host programs on the energy crisis, police repression, and the Nixon impeachment. Likewise, ALSC activists hoped to raise $75,000 in support funds during 1974.

Organized under the theme "Which Road Against Racism and Imperialism for the Black Liberation Movement?," ALSC's first national
conference proved to be a critical turning point in the development of
the organization and seventies black radicalism generally. The meeting took place during 23–24 May 1974 at Howard University and drew
approximately 800 participants. In addition to Sadaukai and other
ALSC organizers, the delegates included Baraka, Carmichael, and
scores of activists affiliated with CAP, the Youth Organization of
Black Unity (YOBU), the NBPA, and the Socialist Worker's Party. In
his published report on the conference, the former SNCC national
chair Phil Hutchings noted that while the meeting reflected a strong
student base, the delegation was characterized by a decidedly leftist
orientation with the majority of the participants converging around
the slogan "black workers take the lead." This desire to make ALSC
more relevant to working-class people was, however, undermined by
the growing emphasis on ideological clarification within movement
circles.

Hutchings' report on the conference is significant because his take
on its rationale, objectives, and outcomes reflects the shifting political sands that defined the meeting. His comments convey a keen sensitivity to class contradictions that were rendered more visible by
black political integration. According to Hutchings, the conference
was held "in recognition of the fact that black people are at a stage in
the struggle which required regroupment and the development of a
new approach." Hence, ALSC national conference was "a new kind of
conference, specifically designed to place before black activists alternative theoretical positions and to combat ideological deficiencies or
in some cases a total lack of ideology." Unlike the previous Black
Power conferences and the 1972 Gary Convention, which emphasized unity between radical forces and the black establishment and
the need to impact the two-party system, this conference, according
to Hutchings, "dealt with problems of a theoretical nature as a pre-
condition for base-building and renewed emphasis on organizing
new strata within black communities, particularly, black workers."[54]
However, contrary to Hutchings' claims that ideological clarity was
necessary for the development of a viable opposition, the increasing
preoccupation of many radical activists with developing the "correct

line" had the opposite effect. Instead of popularizing radical ideals, the "two-line struggle" between black nationalists and Marxists descended into parochialism and marginality. The advent of virulent ideological debate among American black radicals capsized ALSC and bore significant ramifications for Black Power radicalism, generally.

After the 1974 ALSC national conference, the remaining leftist ALSC cadre fractured into even sharper ideological camps. The level of sectarian splintering was most dramatically manifested during the 1975 ALD observations. Once a broad-based, diverse demonstration of anticolonial solidarity, the ALD mobilization fractured sharply along ideological lines. The same year, three rival ALD demonstrations were held in Washington. One march was held by the All African Peoples Revolutionary Party (AAPRP) led by Carmichael (Kwame Ture), while the other two demonstrations were sponsored by the Socialist Worker's Party and by Baraka and CAP cadre. Perhaps more than any other event that year, the multiple ALD demonstrations illustrated the devastating effects of sectarianism on the Black Power movement. Clearly these marches reflected Black Power radicals' retreat from a politics that sought to impose mass public pressure on governmental and corporate institutions and advance relevant issues toward a politics that was centered on ideological education. Coming to terms with the origins, content, and limitations of the Marxist–nationalist debate within the postsegregation black public sphere is critically important for understanding the factors responsible for Black Power radicalism's demise and for strengthening future efforts to forge a viable, popular movement for social justice in the United States. It is to these internal debates and contradictions that I now turn.

The Race-Class Debate and the Retreat from Politics

Tensions between Marxists and black nationalists had surfaced at earlier moments during the Black Power era. SNCC activist James Forman had emphasized class analysis in his speeches, writings, and political work and was often met with angry resistance from staunch nationalists who resented any reliance on the ideas of white theorists.[55] In a similar fashion, Julius Hobson, CORE activist and participant in the early Black Power conferences, had openly criticized the bourgeois tendencies within Black Power discourse and advocated that black radicals adopt sharper leftist positions.[56] Struggles for ideological and leadership preeminence contributed to legendary, fatal clashes between Karenga's cultural nationalist US Organization and the revolutionary nationalist BPP on the West Coast.[57] Among the black intelligentsia, vigorous debate over the relative merits of cultural nationalism and Marxism were stimulated by the publication of Harold Cruse's *The Crisis of the Negro Intellectual* in 1967. Cruse's heavy-handed criticism of black participation in prewar Communist Party politics garnered stern rebuttals from many black leftists such as Robert Chrisman and Ernest Kaiser, among others.[58] While such ideological schisms were ever present in Black Power discourse and, for that matter, in much of twentieth-century black political thought, changing political and social conditions during the early seventies served to throw these existing ideological differences into sharper relief. The emergence of a sizable, self-conscious tier of mainstream black political elites and the eroding prospects of operational unity between them and radical activists helped to facilitate a leftward shift of many former nationalists.

Although other intellectuals had offered Marxist critiques of nationalist politics, the mid-seventies' adoption of Marxist-Leninist-Maoist ideology by Baraka and others sent shock waves through movement circles since many radical activists and intellectuals viewed such ideological converts as traitors.[59] Contending positions in the Marxist–nationalist debate were published in response to a series of particularly strident articles penned by Chicago-based, cultural nationalist and poet Haki Madhubuti (formerly Don L. Lee).[60] Madhubuti served as publisher and chief editor of Third World Press, director of the Institute for Positive Education, and editor of the quarterly journal *Black Books Bulletin*. He had been at the heart of the evolving Pan-Africanist and Black Power artistic movements since the late sixties and, therefore, was a close ally of both Baraka and Sadaukai. Madhubuti's vitriolic denunciation of their turn toward Marxism reflected the sentiments of many other devout black nationalists.

In developing his criticism of the newly converted black Marxists, Madhubuti essentially restated the anti-interracialist themes and credos that had been common to much of Black Power discourse since the mid-sixties. More precisely, Madhubuti reasserted the durability of white supremacy and, by extension, the futility of multiracial coalition politics. Likewise, he adamantly defended the need for black autonomy in thought and practice. Madhubuti argued that race was more fundamental than class as both a cause of black oppression and basis for political work. He spurned Marxists' arguments concerning the structural causes of black oppression. Baraka, for instance, summarized the view held by many black leftists at the time that capitalism gave rise to modern forms of racism. He argued:

> It was capitalism that caused our national oppression in the first place. It was capitalism that created the slave trade . . . It was capitalism expanding to imperialism that caused colonialism. It is a continuing capitalism that has reaped super profits by super exploiting its colonies and oppressed nationalities wherever they are and in the United States very clearly.[61]

For Madhubuti, such arguments removed the onus of racial oppression from whites. He argued:

> We now talk about the "system" as if the "system" is void of people or better yet a specific people. This "system" for the "masses" has become defined by the intellectuals as monopoly capitalism or world imperialism . . . Our speech is sprinkled with terms like global influence, international fraternity, multinational corporate structures, spheres of influence, internationalist, world revolution, petty bourgeoisie, black lackeys, lumpen proletariat and the ever present *comrade*. The important fact to remember here is that people develop "systems" not vice versa.[62]

Accordingly, Madhubuti rejected the argument posed by some black Marxists that racism is an outgrowth of capitalist society. He contended:

> The Marxist position is that white racism—which to us is the only functional racism in the world—is result of the profit motive brought on by the European slave trade and that white racism or anti-Black feeling didn't exist before such a time . . . It is

important to understand that the ideology of white supremacy precedes the economic structure of capitalism and imperialism the latter of which are falsely stated as the cause of racism. To believe that the white boy mis-used [*sic*] and manipulated us for centuries up until today for purely economic reasons is racist and void of any historical reality.[63]

To further rebut those who held that racist thought and behavior were superstructural elements of capitalist socioeconomic organization, Madhubuti evoked Carlos Moore's writings. Moore was Afro-Cuban and vehemently anti-Castro. His advocacy of race-first politics and direct experiences in revolutionary Cuba gave him considerable authority as a critic of socialism especially among American black nationalists. For Madhubuti, Moore's arguments concerning the persistence of antiblack racism in postrevolutionary Cuba were evidence enough that the Marxist turn among American black radicals was misguided and could not serve as a means toward black liberation.[64]

Other intellectuals defended Madhubuti's arguments concerning the primacy of race. Echoing Madhubuti's claims, Howard University political scientist Ronald Walters argued that "[r]ace has been, is now and will continue to be dominant over class for the foreseeable future as the key determination of oppressive behavior exercised by Whites, especially in places like the United States, where Blacks are an identifiable, powerless, minority of the entire population."[65] Walters reiterated Madhubuti's contention that black oppression was the result of "peoples of a different civilization than ours" and not structural-economic forces. Additionally, he shared Madhubuti's skepticism regarding the prospects of socialist revolution and its potential to improve the position of blacks given the unique character of American race relations. Kalamu Ya Salaam (Val Ferdinand), a poet and founding member of the New Orleans-based cultural nationalist organization Ahidiana asserted that Madhubuti's statements were "fundamentally correct." Although he conceded that "race alone is an insufficient criterion for determining friends and foes" Salaam argued that "race is one of the determinants that defines the focus, goals and conditions of our relationships with other peoples, ourselves and the world."[66]

Like Madhubuti, Salaam viewed the spread of Marxist ideology within the black radical circles as being driven by external agents. He asserted:

> What we are seeing/hearing from many of our would be leaders is a white backlash led by black faces! . . . The assumption is that some *white boy* or *group of white boys*, have, did or will provide the ultimate solution to our problems . . . always there are *white boys* at the center/core pulling the strings, pushing the buttons, providing the money and thoughts and ultimately the identity purpose and direction.[67]

Salaam's rehearsal of this common nationalist critique of black leftism did not go unanswered.

A handful of critical responses to Madhubuti's "Latest Purge" article were featured in the *Black Scholar*.[68] Perhaps the most thoughtful, meticulous rebuttal to Madhubuti was issued by Mark Smith, director of operations for the 1972 ALD mobilization and past vice-chairman of YOBU. Smith sought to dispel distortions in Madhubuti's presentation of Marxism. As Smith noted, there is little direct reference or critique of actual Marxist texts and arguments in Madhubuti's essay. Instead, Smith accused Madhubuti of utilizing a straw man–debating style built on fallacious representations of the subject of criticism.[69] Others pointed out glaring contradictions and weaknesses in Madhubuti's dismissals of black Marxists. As Alonzo 4X (Cannady) argued, Madhubuti's arguments utilized "ad hominem arguments as refutation."[70] Baraka also noted that while Madhubuti ridiculed black leftists for engaging political writings by nonblack authors, much of the dietary and lifestyle regimen he advocated was predicated on white hippie counter culture.[71]

For Smith, Madhubuti's view of black people was not affirming or liberating but rather contemptuous. Smith noted that in spite of Madhubuti's claims that racism was the consequence of people and not structural forces, much of his discussion rests on a thesis of black subordination wherein blacks receive everything "life-sustaining" from the majority white culture. For Madhubuti, all areas of black people's lives "except love of ourselves and recreation of ourselves,"

exist in a web of dependency. Stemming from this view of racial relations, Madhubuti offered an interpretation that, though stated in
clearly racial terms, ironically mirrors the Marxist notion of false
consciousness. He asserted: "Our thought patterns, our frames of references are not black but white, and we can't back off of this fact . . .
We never redefine from a black perspective not because we don't have
one, but only because we are not aware of one."[72] To a considerable
extent, Madhubuti's characterization of the black people is indicative
of what Daryl Michael Scott has termed "damage imagery." Scott
holds that historically black and white, liberal and conservative social
scientists, and politicians have emphasized the view of blacks as being
psychologically scarred as a consequence of slavery and racial segregation. In turn, this image has been deployed by liberal and conservative black leaders at various junctures as a means of eliciting support
for various race advancement schemes.[73] The following passage by
Madhubuti is illustrative of this tendency: "We have, whether we
admit it or not, been molded into beings that are mentally—in terms
of our existence—just above animals, and just as we are ruled by
instincts which govern us from day to day."[74]

Madhubuti's characterization of the black masses echoed the worst
of early-twentieth-century racial uplift ideology. In addition, this tendency within nationalist rhetoric to emphasize the putative low self-
esteem and self-worth of the black working class and poor anticipates
neoconservative explanations of poverty that would underpin the dissolution of Great Society reforms during the eighties and the nineties.
Like Madhubuti, right wing and liberal intellectuals alike would argue
that durable inequality was not the product of systemic factors such as
discrimination and industrial flight, but rather the result of a weak
work ethic or other dysfunctional behaviors and antisocial values,
which are assumed to circulate among the urban poor.[75] Madhubuti's
arguments were a desperate reassertion of black nationalist themes at
a moment when black ethnic politics was revealing itself to be an
inadequate means for addressing the vital needs of many black working class and poor citizens. Also implicit in this portrait of black people as being "just above animals" is an implicit claim to the role of
either shepherd or ringmaster. Madhubuti was not alone in his reassertion of a privileged place for black elites in race politics. Although the

race-class debate represented a major fissure in seventies' black activist culture, the generic embrace of more sectarian outlooks carried with it a muted form of elitism. Despite their rhetorical attention to capital–labor conflicts and perceptive critiques of bourgeois black politicians, some black left activists also retreated to political tactics and methods, which served to buttress their privileged status. This muted elitism within black radical discourse is evident in leftists' and cultural nationalists' increasing advocacy of ideological education rather than populist political strategies.

Both Marxists and nationalists emphasized the need for ideological education and the formation of localized study circles. For instance, Madhubuti asserted that a "black national ideology is desperately needed" and called for the formation of study groups focusing on key nationalist thinkers. The following materials made up his suggested reading list: *The Destruction of Black Civilization* by Chancellor Williams; *Garvey, Lumumba, Malcolm* by Shawna Maglanbyan; *The African Origins of Civilization: Myth or Reality?* by Cheikh Anta Diop; *Lumumba Speaks* by Patrice Lumumba; *The Crises of the Negro Intellectual* by Cruse; *Introduction to African Civilization* by John H. Jackson; *The Philosophy and Opinions of Marcus Garvey* edited by Amy Jacques-Garvey; *The Appeal* by David Walker; the speeches of Malcolm X; and *The Autobiography of Malcolm X*.

On the left, the Nashville, Tennessee-based Peoples College under the direction of Abdul Alkalimat (Gerald McWhorter) proposed a reading program as a means of developing black popular resistance to imperialism. The proposed course/study group on "Imperialism and Black Liberation" suggested the following "basic texts": *Imperialism* by V. I. Lenin; *Monopoly Capitalism* by Paul Baran and Paul Sweezy; *Capitalism and Slavery* by Eric Williams; *How Europe Underdeveloped Africa* by Walter Rodney; *Black Reconstruction* by W. E. B. DuBois; *Class Struggle in Africa* by Kwame Nkrumah; *The Demand for Black Labor* by Harold M. Baron; *Black Bourgeoisie* by E. Franklin Frazier; *Negro Liberation* by Harry Haywood; *Selections from V. I. Lenin and J. V. Stalin on National Colonial Question*; *The Age of Imperialism* by Harry Magdoff; *Neo-Colonialism* by Nkrumah; *Imperialism in the 1970s* by Pierre Jalee; and *On the Transition to Socialism* by Paul Sweezy and Charles Bettleheim.

Other Marxists such as S. E. Anderson and Mark Smith also stressed the need for regimented study among black activists. Anderson responded to Madhubuti with his own required readings:

In the same manner we *should* study the basic writings of Marx, Engels, and Lenin in order to study and practice the evolving more advanced Marxist-Leninist theories . . . Folks like Guyanese Walter Rodney (see his *How Europe Underdeveloped Africa*: Bogle-L'ouverture or Howard University Press), Egyptian Samir Amin (see his *Accumulation on a World Scale*: Monthly Review Press) and Mexican Rodolfo Stavenhagen (see *Les Classes Sociales Dans les Sociétés Africaines*: Paris, France 1969) for example have advanced Marxist analysis . . . [76]

Smith also encouraged the need for serious study, but cautioned that black radicals must develop theory and strategy tailored to the unique conditions of their own times. His comments echoed the sentiments offered by Cruse, James, and Grace Lee Boggs, among others, regarding the need to develop a revolutionary politics that was unique to American soil.[77] Smith noted:

We, also, think that black activists should study, especially the works of Marx, Engels, Lenin, Stalin, Mao, and Enver Hoxha. In addition, though, we need to study the history of the labor movement and of black people in *this* country. A knowledge of 1900 Russia or 1940 China *alone* (much less ancient Egypt) cannot guide our struggle here. Our task is to learn the *general* laws of revolution and the past and present of our *specific* circumstances; the combination is revolutionary strategy.[78]

Smith's wisdom was eclipsed by more conservative approaches to organizing and popular education.

The common emphasis of these programs on grassroots education stemmed from a faith in mass mobilization that defined sixties radicalism. As the postwar civil rights movement and subsequent political demonstrations by antiwar, student, and Black Power activists had dramatically illustrated, popular pressure could compel languid public institutions into action and foster progressive reforms. The emphasis on "the masses," "the people," and "the grass roots" in these proposals reflects a desire to build broad support for their respective agendas. Additionally, these study programs convey radicals' desire to popularize critical orientations toward the American social order. Likewise, such curricula were attempts to combat the anti-intellectualism inherent in late-twentieth-century American mass culture.[79] Nonetheless, despite their progressive veneer, these varying approaches to popular education were equally grounded in undemocratic pedagogy that maintained status hierarchy. Each is driven by an antidemocratic orientation that is perhaps best summarized in the Maoist aphorism commonly uttered during the era—"No investigation, no right to speak."[80] Essentially, the mid-seventies turn to ideological education favored a mode of politics that inhibited principled political debate and issue-driven, temporal collaboration. Instead of galvanizing public sentiment around discrete policy matters or programmatic efforts capable of generating identifiable gains, Marxist and cultural nationalist activist intellectuals became mired in esoteric debates that rarely had anything to do with issues of immediate concern to the broader black citizenry.

Consequentially, the manner in which such educational programs are proposed and designed tends to privilege intellectuals in relation to nonelite participants. Both Madhubuti's and the Peoples College's proposed study programs emphasized the mastery of radical canons. Neither of the programs proceeds from a more democratic view of education that encourages genuine grassroots participation where traditional teacher–student dynamics are reorganized in a more egalitarian fashion and participants develop curricula and determine what is important and relevant. Instead, each proceeds from the assumption that full-time employees, parents or homemakers possess the leisure, energy and the desire to consume lengthy or esoteric texts. Both programs rest on the detrimental assumption that ideological clarity must precede political work and that familiarity with the radical canon—either nationalist or Marxist—is a prerequisite to meaningful participation in public life. To a considerable extent this pedagogical approach was an unfortunate departure from the more genuinely democratic initiatives of only a decade earlier during the Southern civil rights movement. The Highlander Folk School, the Citizenship Schools, and the participatory democratic impulse that guided SNCC and the Students for a Democratic Society (SDS) through their early years all reflected an approach to popular education and organizing that was not informed primarily by idiosyncratic intellectual tastes but by local needs and the lived political struggles of ordinary people.[81] The democratic models of organizing championed by Ella Baker, Myles Horton, and others sought to subvert the leadership category by nurturing the knowledge, skills, and confidence of ordinary people. The muted elitism inherent in the strategy of ideological education and its implications for black radical politics during the seventies and beyond was not completely unacknowledged within movement circles.

Gwendolyn Patton offered a brilliant critique of the fetishization of ideology within movement circles. She was a veteran SNCC activist and founder of the Student Mobilization Committee Against the War in Vietnam (SMC) and the Third World Women's Alliance, a path-breaking black radical feminist organization that evolved from SNCC's Women's Caucus. In a brief but searing piece that appeared in the April 1975 *Black Scholar* titled "An Open Letter to Marxists," Patton rebuffed the notion that ideological clarity was a prerequisite to effective political work. She asserted that such a view was grounded rather uncritically in notions of expertise and management derived from technocratic capitalism. This problem was not merely one of bourgeois nationalists as some Marxists claimed. Rather, Patton held that this form of elitism permeated the ranks of black radical activists. She argued, "This need for subjective identity, to belong to a 'fan club' as opposed to a political, honest form has its root in the capitalist version of leadership, management and administration of work."[82] As a consequence of these vanguardist tendencies, Patton saw the major obstacles to the development of viable oppositional movements as "the inability to deal with honest, political criticism of racism, the inability to join and to practically work in a struggle on a sustained basis and the inability to shed the elitist role."[83] For Patton, the advent of the Marxist–nationalist debate to a considerable extent facilitated the breakdown of critical, principled debate and interchange among radical forces.

Other ALSC activists such as Florence Tate, who had served as information director for the original ALD mobilization, was troubled by the turn to doctrinaire ideology as well. Although Tate wrote dismissively of the white left, she reiterated the need for movement politics: "The 'masses' are very intelligent. If you're going where they want to go, they'll follow you. They don't follow you because you're going somewhere you want to go."[84] She noted that the 1972 ALD mobilizations did not evolve because of the charisma or talent of a few activists, but rather "consciousness-raising had taken place and taken root and been nourished by many, many organizations and individuals long before ALSC and the current 'movement' organizations came along."[85] Like Tate, Salaam also sought to reassert the need for popular mobilization and a more ecumenical posture. Although Salaam would side with the ultranationalist arguments offered by Madhubuti, in his 1974 *Black World* essay "Tell No Lies, Claim No Easy Victories," he advocated a return to "kazi" or practical work as a way for radicals to mend the ideological divide. Salaam called for ALSC to create a program "that would allow for unprincipled participation in a demonstration and fund-raising effort. Unprincipled in the sense that a participant would not be asked to believe in anything in particular but rather simply to show up and give support."[86] Stressing the importance of movement building, Salaam argued that "[o]ur efforts as organizers must be to find ways to include more and more people into the arena of struggle rather than simply to develop strategies and tactics that exclude more and more people from meaningful participation because of what they do or do not believe/espouse."[87] Against such warnings, both sides of the race-class debate drifted farther away from meaningful politics.

Race operated as a conceit in mid-seventies nationalist discourse as did class among some black Marxists of the period. Both concepts were often treated as unfractured political categories. The mid-seventies' nationalist arguments were largely a reiteration of pre–World War II interpretations of *race as culture*.[88] Equally detrimental, the Marxism articulated by some black activists within ALSC and related organizations—though by no means all—sagged under the conceptual language and arguments inherited from earlier historical moments and national contexts. With few exceptions, both sides of this debate offered little room for the resolution of historical conflicts and the formation of new forms of political community among former adversaries. Mark Smith was one such exception. In his critique of Madhubuti's discussion of people versus systems, Smith offered a more dialectical alternative noting that "[p]eople make systems and systems in turn make people." Likewise, he argued that while many Marxists within ALSC acknowledged that white racism was ubiquitous, it was surmountable. Smith's views on these matters left the door open to both personal and social transformation. Inter-racial coalitions, alliances, and community were attainable through social struggle. Unfortunately, Madhubuti's unequivocal restatement of anti-interracial and anti-left politics may have left a deeper imprint on postsegregation black political culture.

Madhubuti and his supporters posed the argument that white racism is a fundamental, unchanging feature of world history. To develop this claim, he employed Howard University professor Chancellor Williams' magnum opus *The Destruction of Black Civilization*. Yet, the meta-narrative of white supremacy presented in this work tends to read the complexity out of history and to project modern ideas, biases, and political concerns onto premodern times. For Madhubuti, white racism is "natural" and, therefore, immutable. Madhubuti's "Latest Purge" essay signaled a departure from the kind of politically engaged black nationalism that had characterized much of the Black Power movement. Even more than Cruse's earlier insistence on black cultural particularity, Madhubuti's arguments and those of his allies foreclosed the possibility of social transformation. His fatal-istic reading of American political landscape encouraged racial self-help and unity politics as the only viable antidote to racial inequality.

The dogmatic racialism offered in his essay would be superceded in the eighties and nineties by a subgenre within Africana/black studies rooted in reified notions of race and culture. One argument that achieved cultish notoriety on college campuses and activist circles was psychiatrist Frances Cress Welsing's "Cress Theory of Color Confrontation." She workshopped these ideas amidst the Marxist–nationalist debate in a series of articles in *Black Books Bulletin* and the most sustained expression of her claims came in her 1991 book *The Isis Papers*, which was also published by Madhubuti's Third World Press.[89] She attempted to explain white supremacy through pseudoscientific notions of "melanin deficiency" and a "neu-rochemical basis for evil." Other more respectable, but no less problematic, works such as Temple University professor Molefi Asante's string of writings on Afrocentricity and former SNCC activist Marimba Ani's (Dona Richards) 1994 tome *Yurugu* updated elements of sixties black nationalism, in particular its overly racialized view of culture.[90] Whether posed in the language of genetics/biology or culture, these reassertions of black particularity carried a certain emotive power for some black audiences. Like the Nation of Islam's Yacub myth that inverted the Jim Crow racist culture to assert the "true" superiority and divinity of blacks, these more recent expressions of black nationalism possessed a special allure amidst the deteriorating social conditions that accompanied deindustrialization and the Reagan–Bush era assaults on Great Society liberal reforms. Although these and other neo-black nationalist arguments may provide temporary succor to some, such attempts to define race in terms of either genetics or ahistorical cultural traits are not only impoverished as social theory but these views are politically fatalistic and lead away from public engagement.

Those activists working within ALSC, CAP, and the Assembly who embraced "scientific socialism" were liberated from the mystifications of racial identity politics. Nonetheless, they faced other challenges. The bitter irony of the Marxist turn taken by ALSC radicals was their corresponding loss of popular resonance. The more loudly activists voiced commitments to working-class struggle, the more often they found themselves speaking in amen corners or, worse, in monologues. In retrospect, part of these problems stemmed from the failure to develop reflexive social theory that might comprehend the unique social conditions of the historical moment. Although ALSC activists were prescient in grasping the dynamics of neoliberal restructuring and global mobility of capital, they encountered more difficulty in devising language that could illuminate domestic-class inequalities and forms of organization that might popularize alternative visions of society and oppose the emerging New Right bloc.

Whereas nationalists asserted that white racism was like a disease, some Marxists clung to sluggish formulas that absolved white workers of responsibility. At various junctures in the Marxist–nationalist debate, black leftists cited the ruling class as the principal instigators of racism in U.S. society. Earl Ofari, activist and author of *The Myth of Black Capitalism*, argued that "The biggest single roadblock to worker's unity still remains racism . . . Racism is pushed openly through every social and cultural medium by the ruling class. The material base of racism lies in the estimated $22 billion in super profits taken in off of black labor. Racism is sustained because it means both profit and control."[91] In a similar vein, Baraka offered a split-labor market account of racism, "By exploiting oppressed nationalities even more than white workers and using that double oppression as the basis for calling us inferior, the capitalists re-enforced the gap created between white workers and oppressed nationalities creating and exploiting a chauvinism in them and a narrow nationalism in us."[92] Likewise, Smith argued: "Racism is a tool used by the capitalist class to divide the people who have a common interest in overthrowing them, and to attack the wages and organization of the working class through the super-exploitation of blacks and other minority workers."[93] Such interpretations failed to adequately address the problematic of American racism in critical terms and to acknowledge the agency of white workers in the maintenance of racist ideology and practices.

The Marxism articulated by some ALSC activists tended toward economic determinism and a rather uncritical wedding to the conceptual language, and organizational forms of pre–Cold War Marxism. The following passage concerning the "undermining logic" by Baraka is reflective of this tendency:

As the economic crises in the U.S. and throughout the capitalist world intensifies (for instance, over 100,000 were laid off one recent week in the auto industry alone) layoffs, speedups, inflation, the growing depression will worsen, especially in big cities which is where most Black people in the U.S. live. As the economic crises worsens, repression will increase. People will not merely lay down when they are told that they must stay jobless or routinely unemployed. They will strike back and with that 'strike back' which the State glibly calls crime, police brutality and repression will rise and the entire political fabric of the U.S. will move openly to the Right. As capitalism goes deeper into crises, one depression after another, until it stretches into one vicious economic earthquake that creates the undermining dynamic that will enable the enraged masses to toss the entire capitalist system into the garbage can of history.[94]

Although Baraka's claims and other such arguments are powerful as an ethical condemnation of capital's pernicious effects, such claims veer toward millennialism and founder as viable social theory that might inspire and guide political struggles. The economic pressures he cites did not lead to the kind of working-class anger and action he anticipated. In lieu of a viable alternative left politics, certain strata of the American working class moved to the Right during the seventies. The Marxist turn within Black Power radical circles helped to reorient black political debate around the critique of capital in valuable ways, but the new historical conditions unfolding during the seventies required fresh thinking and creative forms of organization.

In a sense, the turn to Marxism within ALSC, CAP, and the Assembly coincided with the increasingly visible effects of deindustrialization in American cities. During the early seventies, existing patterns of inequality and racial discrimination were compounded by the oil crisis, the exodus of capital investment and jobs from former manufacturing centers, the erosion of municipal tax bases in many central cities, and the proliferation of low-wage service-sector jobs.[95] This shift from centralized, Fordist production toward flexible accumulation was a counterrevolutionary move by the Western ruling classes in response to pressures from democratic popular struggles, rising real wages throughout the industrialized world, and falling rates of profit.[96] As ALSC cadre noted, the new accessibility of cheap labor pools throughout the Third World provided a golden opportunity for many transnational corporations. The hollowing out of the manufacturing base bore disastrous consequences for many black neighborhoods and communities across the United States. The living and working conditions of many Americans were reshaped by the increased use of computerized and automated systems; lean production schemes; and the heightened use of overtime, part-time, and temporary contracting by employers to avoid additional hiring.[97]

The tectonic shifts taking place in the American economy during the seventies not only decimated factory work, but such forces also rendered obsolete notions of revolutionary subjectivity and organization that activists borrowed uncritically from either the bygone Fordist era or the Third World liberation struggles. The seventies saw the parallel developments of intensified labor exploitation in the Third World by Northern-based firms and the U.S. domestic proliferation of retail strip malls, discount outlets, and national department store chains catering to lower-middle and modest-income clientele. This period was also characterized by the intensification of corporate marketing campaigns tailored to all black consumers and not just the "comprador class" whom radicals despised. The Marxist–nationalist debate in many ways derailed the development of popular social theory tailored to the conditions of late-twentieth-century African American life, which might have advanced social justice.

Conclusion

In their intellectual work and programmatic efforts, radical intellectuals maintained an unwavering commitment to race advancement and to the necessity of leadership responsiveness to the most dispossessed citizens within the African American populace. Common to radical parlance during the period, Fanon's theory of the native intellectual and Cabral's notion of "class suicide" served as guiding axioms underlying radical intellectuals' self-conception and social theories.[98] Although there are important exceptions, the intellectual practice of activists operating within the orbit of ALSC and the Assembly increasingly mirrored technocratic notions of expertise and leadership. The turn to Marxism among many black activists was progressive to the extent that it encouraged the development of critical perspectives regarding the limits of black indigenous control and, more generally, racial identity politics. Nonetheless, Sadaukai's, Baraka's, and other radicals' fundamental premise that doctrinaire ideology—and not historically specific, temporal political issues—should serve as the principal basis of political work was essentially flawed. The advent of the Marxist–nationalist debate marked the end of anti-imperialism as an umbrella theory uniting black leftist and cultural nationalist tendencies. The sectarian struggles among radical forces fragmented organizations, and potential allies in many instances, sealing off the possibility of cooperation around discrete issues. Much of the crucially important media infrastructure that had sustained black public debate during the late sixties and early seventies imploded under the weight of these developments.

A monthly showcase of political commentary, international news, art, and cultural criticism, *Black World* magazine was discontinued by publisher John Johnson. To the dismay of many readers, editor Hoyt Fuller was fired. When confronted with a boycott of his company organized by John Henrik Clarke and Madhubuti, Johnson explained that his decision was due to pressures from white financial backers who disapproved of the journal's radical content, especially editorials in support of the Palestinian and African liberation struggles.[99] The protest was aborted and some demonstrators supported Fuller in the creation of the short-lived journal *First World*. The Oakland-based *Black Scholar* saw the resignation of Nathan Hare who expressed discontent over what he viewed as the increasingly Marxist orientation of the magazine. With the passage of publications such as *Black World* and weakening of other movement organizations, many artists, intellectuals, and activists lost a valuable platform for the articulation of alternative political programs and social visions. Sectarian politics isolated radical activists from each other, and perhaps, more critically, the retreat toward doctrinaire ideology alienated radicals from vast sectors of the African American population.

ALSC expressed a prototypical antiglobalization politics decades before the construct of "globalization" attained popular currency in the West. During the ALD mobilizations of 1972 and 1973, ALSC cadre were able to compel thousands of people into action, to raise public awareness of U.S. corporate-state practices and their adverse effects on African peoples, and to advance a radical democratic vision for postcolonial Africa embodied in the various guerrilla organizations fighting colonialism and white oligarchy. Although ALSC fractured along sectarian lines by 1975, many of the ideals it promoted came to fruition. By mid-decade, Angola, Cape Verde, Guinea-Bissau, and Mozambique would gain national sovereignty. Likewise, Southern Rhodesia underwent racial democratic reforms and, in 1980, was officially renamed Zimbabwe after the medieval Southern African society. To a considerable extent, ALSC prefigured the rise of more formalistic pro-African lobbies such as TransAfrica and Constituency for Africa. Likewise, ALSC activists' efforts to publicize the horrors of racial apartheid in South Africa through their educational work, community seminars, mass demonstrations, and civil disobedience anticipated the antiapartheid activism of the eighties and the achievement of democratic reform. The formative success of the ALD mobilizations rested in their fluid, ad hoc structure, which allowed for participation of people from all walks of life. Such participation was not predicated on the religious adoption of any political faith, but rather on principled opposition to colonialism. Differences of opinion or motivation did not preclude those of diverse educational, political, and ideological backgrounds from working in solidarity. The success and strength of the early ALD mobilizations was rooted in the capacity of organizers to develop propaganda hewn from black vernacular culture and commonsensical notions of justice, fairness, and equality; to convey the complexities of the emergent transnational politico-economic system through references to those institutions that organize black life in the United States; and to construct tangible, ways for black citizens to act in solidarity with democratic social struggles on the African continent. The Marxist–nationalist debate represented the negation of this political methodology and, thereby, signaled the abandonment of populist anti-imperialism by many black activists.

In many respects, the NBPA was the domestic twin of ALSC's international activism. Coming out of the Gary Convention, Assembly activists hoped to establish a broad-based, progressive presence in American political life. The Marxist–nationalist debate swept through the Assembly, eventually leading to the expulsion of Baraka from the leadership. Unlike ALSC, however, the Assembly weathered this ideological storm. After the most heated debates of 1974 cooled, a loose network of activists stretching across the country continued to push for the development of an autonomous black politics. Their efforts led to important local campaigns, the formation of the National Black Independent Political Party in 1980, and eventually to the Jesse Jackson Presidential candidacies during the Reagan years. Assembly activists attempted to realize the most progressive, democratic ideals espoused at the Gary Convention. Like ALSC, however, the Assembly project could not transcend technocratic style of politics and build a popular democratic movement to achieve social justice ends.

Radical Departures

The National Black Political Assembly, the National Black Independent Political Party, and the Struggle for Alternatives

To those who say that such an Agenda is "visionary", "utopian" and "impossible", we say that the keepers of conventional white politics have always viewed our situation and our real needs as beyond the realm of their wildest imaginations. At every critical moment in our struggle in American [*sic*] we have had to press relentlessly against the limits of the "realistic" to create new realities for the life of our people. This is our challenge at Gary and beyond, for a new Black politics demands new vision, new hope and new definitions of the possible. Our time has come. These things are necessary. All things are possible.

    —*The National Black Political Agenda (1972)*

[handwritten: —same year as Miami rebellion]

The year 1980 *[handwritten circle around 1980]* marked a critical turning point in the history of the National Black Assembly, an organization established at the 1972 *[handwritten: (est. 1972)]* Gary Convention as a continuations apparatus and, some hoped, the beginnings of an independent political party. In the eight years after Gary, activists habitually tabled party formation. In 1976, the organization attempted to draft a prominent black politician to run for president, but was unsuccessful. Calls for a black political party gained momentum in 1979 within the context of high inflation, Ronald Reagan's neoconservative presidential campaign, and the embattled Democratic presidency of James "Jimmy" Carter. The 1980 election presented a "lesser of two evils" dilemma for many black political activists, who saw both candidates as variations on the prevailing neoconservative mood.

Both Carter and Reagan shared similar anti-New Left origins. Carter ran for governor of Georgia on a pro–George Wallace ticket. Once elected, he adopted a more conciliatory posture on racial matters, but his core politics still remained right of center. Carter organized part of the anti-McGovern campaign during the 1972 election. In retrospect, he was a clear forerunner of the New Democrats, who found institutional expression in the mid-1980s with the formation of the Democratic Leadership Council. Carter began the rightward drift of Democratic leadership and helped to nudge portions of the party's traditional base away from commitment to the liberal social policy legacies of Franklin Roosevelt and Lyndon Johnson. Although Reagan was a New Deal democrat as a young adult, he switched parties because he thought the Republican Party was tougher on communism. During his acting career, he collaborated with the FBI to identify "disloyal" Hollywood actors. He also testified before the House Committee on Un-American Activities. Like Carter, Reagan was an antagonist of sixties' social struggles. In his run for Governor, he pledged to "put the welfare bums back to work."[1] In June 1969, he dismissed activist professor Angela Y. Davis from her post in the philosophy department at the University of California, Los Angeles, under the pretext of a 1949 California state law that prohibited Communist Party members from holding public jobs.[2] After he took office, he fulfilled his campaign promise of cleaning up the University of California, Berkeley, by taking a hard line on student protest activities. His historic clashes with the Black Panther party, fiscal conservatism, and anti–Great Society posture gave many black activists reason to worry that a crisis was at hand. Reagan's avuncular style and rhetorical gifts helped him to make the conservative rage of Barry Goldwater and George Wallace both respectable and electorally viable.[3] As National Black Independent Political Party (NBIPP)

activist Kathryn Flewellen aptly concluded, the vision of America
that Reagan promised was "anti-black, anti-worker, anti-woman."[4]

This backdrop of rising neoconservatism, industrial decline, and
grinding economic hardship in many black communities rekindled
debate among Assembly activists about the need for an independent
black political alternative. In a 1980 memo to her fellow National
Black Political Assembly Co-chair Ron Daniels, Mashariki Kurudisha
(formerly Bernadette Ross) called for the development of new organizational forms commensurate with changing historical conditions:

> the nature of the struggle in which we are engaged like the
> nature of the world is changing. Therefore the tools of struggle
> which we use must be adopted to the task at hand. We cannot
> expect a strategy used in the 60s or early 70s to produce the
> same results or in some case to even serve a useful purpose
> because the System has had time to adjust. The beast has again
> changed its spots. The struggle as we approach the 80s must
> move to define a new set of tools which will assist us in reaching
> our ultimate goal—the total liberation of our people. However,
> we cannot achieve the broad objectives of this goal without call-
> ing forth our greatest genius in our efforts to create and modify
> the instruments of struggle.[5]

Building her argument for new organizational forms, Kurudisha spoke
critically of the botched efforts of radical activists to fill this void noting
that: "there is within our community a failure by progressive forces to
provide concrete models of institutions, issue development and/or
strategy implementation. This void forces our community to turn less
productive and less useful models in developing organizations and
institutions to serve the community's needs."[6] Kurudisha's memo
revived enduring questions regarding new historical conditions and
the necessity of revising radical political practice. This chapter
rehearses the historical development of the National Black Political
Assembly and the NBIPP and explores the tension within these
formations between effective political mobilization and a form of
vanguardism that approximated the technocratic approaches of the
American political mainstream.

Assembly activists sought to promote operational unity among disparate leadership elements and to refashion state policies and civic culture in accordance with radical ideals. During its creation at the 1972 Gary Convention, activists envisioned that the Assembly and its administrative arm—the National Black Political Council (NBPC)—would serve as a routinized, national consensus–building apparatus that would facilitate open dialogue among diverse leaders and aggregate the various policy initiatives and programs of locally based constituencies and organizations into a coherent racial agenda.[7] As stated in the *National Black Political Agenda*—a document constructed and ratified during the Gary Convention—organizers desired a "permanent political movement that addresses itself to the basic control and reshaping of American institutions that currently exploit Black America and threaten the whole society."[8] To a considerable extent, the Assembly and NBIPP bridged the Black Power period and Jesse Jackson's 1984 campaign for the Democratic presidential nomination.

Sociologist Paulette Pierce characterizes the Assembly and NBIPP as "social movement abeyance organizations" drawing on the work of Verta Taylor.[9] These organizations preserve movement values during downward cycles of political retrenchment. Such organizations sustain social networks that allow activists to maintain solidarity, socialize newcomers into movement subculture, and devise new strategies. While acknowledging the preservative function that Pierce identifies, I wish to go beyond a focus on abeyance because the temptation to find a silver lining amidst periods of demobilization might discourage critical attention to the sources of movement failure. Although Assembly activists across the United States labored diligently to foster cooperation among diverse leadership elements and to build an institutional space for Black Power radicalism, their efforts yielded only marginal successes. Subsequent national conventions were held under the auspices of the Assembly at Little Rock, Arkansas, in 1974, at Cincinnati in 1976, and at New Orleans in 1980. Although Assembly leadership attempted to reach out to mainstream politicos, with each of these subsequent meetings support from politicians and civil rights leadership waned steadily. Consequentially, moderate leadership elements developed their own parochial rendition of operational unity by convening more exclusive agenda-setting meetings. By the early 1980s, the Assembly's influence at the national level was negligible. The Assembly and its offspring, NBIPP, proved ineffective in either influencing or challenging the stature of the emergent black political regime as the legitimate arbiters of black interests.

Like the African Liberation Support Committee (ALSC), the Assembly and NBIPP were wracked by sectarianism at various turns, but a more vexing problem within these formations was the failure to break free of what amounted to a more radical version of elite brokerage politics. The strategic choices and organizational priorities that characterized the Assembly during the late 1970s suggest that many radical cadres accepted the strategic shift from "protest to politics" as an irreversible trend in black public life and, by extension, abandoned the propensity to utilize disruptive methods to pursue social justice ends. The Assembly and NBIPP maintained outspoken commitments to progressive political vision but were equally tied up in a bureaucratic politics predicated more on meetings, conferences, and conventions than in the mobilization of real constituencies outside the ranks of radical activist intellectuals.

Organizing for Political Power: The National Black Political Assembly

The first National Black Assembly was elected and seated at an inaugural meeting in Chicago held during October 21–22, 1972.[10] The expressed purpose of the meeting was to establish an organizational framework and procedures for leadership selection. With some four hundred persons in attendance, the meeting reflected much of the optimism and solidarity of the Gary Convention and African Liberation Day (ALD) mobilizations that had taken place the previous spring. The delegates began the meeting with a ritual Black Power salute. In his keynote address, Congressman Charles Diggs vowed to fight what he termed the "new conservative coalition"—that embryonic array of right-wing leadership, organizations, and think tanks aligning against the liberal social policies created by movement pressures and Great Society initiatives. This mounting backlash to social liberalism added a sense of urgency to the proceedings and the desire of many participants to build a strong, progressive political force.

The participants endorsed the tripartite leadership structure outlined in the *Black Agenda* and remained committed to the Gary
Convention's original leadership troika. Charles Diggs was elected
president of the 427-member Assembly, while Richard Hatcher was
chosen chairman of the fifty-four-member NBPC. Amiri Baraka was
tapped for the secretary-general's post, which was charged with coordinating the two bodies.[11] At the state and local levels, Assembly affiliates were formed through state conventions. The constitution of
state organizations and local chapters was not uniform across states.
Rather, these state-level processes reflected the kind of decentralized
and ad hoc processes used to compose state delegations for the Gary
Convention. Hence, state leaders determined how their Assembly
organizations would be configured. For instance, in Ohio, Assembly
chapters were created to coincide with cities and towns, yielding
eleven local Black Assemblies in Columbus, Cleveland, Cincinnati,
Dayton, Springfield, Youngstown, Akron, Canton, Toledo, Lima,
and Bellefontaine. The North Carolina Black Assembly, on the other
hand, was subdivided along Congressional district lines creating
eleven regional Assembly affiliates in that state.[12]

The first major national convention of the Assembly was held
in May 1974 in Little Rock. Some 1,700 registered delegates and
observers gathered at Arkansas' historic Central High School, Little
Rock, for the second National Black Convention.[13] The actual convention turnout fell well below the four thousand participants expected
by organizers. With a much lower turnout than its predecessor, the
Little Rock meeting took on a more intimate feel than the Gary
Convention. Likewise, the scaled-down attendance was more con-
ducive to networking and productive workshop sessions. Despite
these advantages, the declining convention numbers signaled the loss
of support from some more mainstream political forces.

Conspicuously absent from the parley were well-known politicians including Assembly president Charles Diggs, who officially
resigned shortly after the meeting. In a news interview, Charles Diggs
said that he intended to phase out his involvement with the Assembly
in order "to devote more time to Congressional matters."[14] The
politicos who took part included California Congressman Ronald V.
Dellums; Prichard, Alabama, Mayor Algernon J. Cooper; Michigan

Congressman John Conyers; Oklahoma State Representative Hannah Diggs Atkins, and various locally elected officials. The apparent slippage in support from public officials was not ignored by media nor was this development taken lightly by Assembly activists. In his remarks to the convention delegates, Mayor Hatcher offered sharp criticism of absent elected leadership. Although he noted that his continued commitment to the newly formed Assembly was dependent upon whether the group returned to its original emphasis on operational unity, Hatcher openly questioned the legitimacy of those leaders who did not attend the convention. In his keynote address, he lamented that "obviously some so-called leaders, some so-called Black statesmen who have climbed to limited power on the backs of poor Black people would prefer to forget the debt they incurred . . . Where are they now that their people need them here in Little Rock?"[15] Hatcher proceeded to call out the names of prominent, yet absent politicians and organization leaders including Charles Diggs, Floyd McKissack, Coleman Young, Roy Wilkins, Tom Bradley, and Vernon Jordan.

The 1974 convention produced a brief political agenda that essentially reiterated some of the positions articulated at Gary and previous Black Power conferences. The agenda included resolutions in support of African revolutionary movements, the creation of a Court of Appeals to aid black political prisoners, the formation of a Black United Fund to finance political activism, the enactment of an Urban Homestead Act that would support black home ownership, and self-determination for the District of Columbia. Additional resolutions opposed psychological testing in schools, the new delegate selection rules of the Democratic National Convention, and American financial aid to Israel. As it had in Gary two years earlier, the issue of black party formation surfaced at the Little Rock Convention. Yet, in spite of vocal support among some delegates, a party did not materialize. Although numerous delegations including those from New Jersey, Colorado, Pennsylvania, and Maryland drafted resolutions calling for the immediate formation of a black third party, the resolution proposed by the Georgia delegates is perhaps the most noteworthy. Similar to early propositions by Baraka, the Philadelphia Congress of African Peoples (CAP) council, William Strickland, and others, the

Georgia resolution called for a party that would embrace both electoral politics and popular struggles. The resolution proclaimed:

A Black party should build struggles against racist education
and for community control of schools. It should support the
strikes and struggles of Black workers. It should champion the
demands and struggles of Black women. It should lead the fight
against Watergate-style victimization and harassment of the
Black Liberation Movement. It should fight police repression
and fight for a police force drawn from the Black community.[16]

Additionally, the resolution called for total independence from the
two major parties. While numerous state delegations voiced support
for creation of an autonomous black political vehicle, some moderate
leadership elements opposed the idea. In fact, Atlanta mayor Maynard
Jackson pressured members of the Georgia delegation to withdraw
the resolution. Consequentially, the language of total independence
was pared from the resolution. In spite of this and other efforts to
build support, the Georgia resolution was halted by a motion to
table. Although Ohio Black Assembly Chair Daniels was generally
supportive of the party idea, he argued that the immediate creation
of a party was premature and that the development of a grassroots
base was a necessary prerequisite to party formation. Much of the
Little Rock Convention's substantive workshops were geared toward
this task of building local organizations and campaigns.

The convention's training-oriented workshops were designed to
enhance political-organizing skills among Assembly activists. Baraka
noted at a pre-convention news conference that while the first convention emphasized an ingathering of blacks of various backgrounds
and political tendencies, the Little Rock Convention would address
more practical political issues and strategies such as electoral campaign organizing, coalition building, and grassroots mobilization.[17]
In a similar fashion, Hatcher asserted that the convention would be a
"working convention" centered on transmission of "how to" kinds of
information.[18] The convention workshop sessions were organized
into three tracts—"Electoral Politics," coordinated by Hannah Atkins;
"Community Struggles" headed by Owusu Sadaukai, the Assembly's

Southern Regional Coordinator; and "Building Black Assemblies," coordinated by Daniels, president of the Ohio Black Assembly.[19]

After the Little Rock Convention, Assembly activists returned home and attempted to develop local organizations that were responsive to the needs of residents in their towns and cities. Assembly activists fashioned a number of strategies for influencing local electoral politics. Many activists engaged vigorously in voter registration drives. Activists rarely used the Assembly structure to run candidates for public office, because some activists worried that full-blown independent campaigns would have jeopardized the relationship of some black elected officials to the Democratic Party and, by extension, discouraged their cooperation with the Assembly. Therefore, some local Assembly activists opted to pursue other methods of influencing electoral and policy outcomes that might avoid direct conflict with black public officials and civil rights leadership whom activists hoped to maintain as allies. One such alternative strategy was the use of candidate-screening forums. Typically, candidates were invited to a public forum in a local African American neighborhood. Assembly activists then facilitated an open discussion between the candidates and the general public.[20] The Louisiana Black Assembly offers an example of this tactic.

In a state whose political history is riddled with incidences of bribery, impeachment, embezzlement, and robust abuse of public authority, Louisiana Assembly activists employed the candidate-screening method during the 1979 gubernatorial campaign as a means of educating the public and influencing candidate stances on relevant political issues.[21] A statewide committee was created to draft a position paper on issues of concern to black Louisianans. A public forum was held on June 21, 1979, with five of the six candidates—including incumbent Republican governor David Treen—appearing for an hour-long question-and-answer period. In addition to these screenings, some state Assembly organizations reviewed state legislative agendas and rated each legislator's performance on policy areas deemed germane to African American constituencies. The Louisiana Assembly developed one such rating system and published the results. Candidates were rated according to their responses during the forum. Likewise, an additional scale was constructed on the basis of the following five criteria: (1) candidate's voting record; (2) black status and participation in campaign organization; (3) past relations with black constituents; (4) institutional ties, and (5) overall impression. Such efforts served to open up local public spheres and create more vibrant, democratic debate among candidates and voters. In addition to more conventional electoral and public policy work, Assembly cadre also moved to organize around pertinent local and regional concerns. The Columbus, Ohio, Assembly chapter's antipolice brutality campaign offers a vivid example of the type of grassroots activism conducted by many local Assembly activists.

A series of disturbing incidents spurred Columbus Assembly activists to address the issue of police brutality.[22] A black couple and their young child were dining at the Kahiki, a Polynesian-themed restaurant on Columbus's east side. When an argument arose over a discrepancy in their bill, police were called and the couple was forcibly removed from the establishment. Photographs taken of the father after his release from police custody suggested excessive use of force according to some Assembly activists. In another incident, a young black man was shot to death by police officers while fleeing in a stolen cab. The Assembly responded with a community forum on police brutality, which featured Louis Taylor, Director of the Civil Rights division of the U.S. Department of Justice and representatives of the National Organization of Black Law Enforcement Executives. Spearheaded by Dr. William E. Nelson and Yolanda Robinson, the forum was designed to "bring together a cross-section of the Columbus community to discuss issues such as police brutality, the legal rights of citizens victimized by police action, and the development of effective mechanisms for establishing community input into and control over the police system."[23] Subsequently, the Assembly formed a coalition, The Citizen Committee on Justice, and attempted to foster support for Ohio State Senate Bill 61 designed to address police brutality. Nelson, in his capacity as president of the Columbus Assembly chapter, testified before the Ohio Senate Judiciary committee in support of the bill. In his testimony, he argued:

> The Columbus Chapter of the Ohio Black Political Assembly takes the position that the actions of all persons in possession of deadly weapons—including policemen—must be tightly

controlled through legal regulations. We are supportive of Senate bill 61 because it spells out in clear language the conditions under which an officer may be justified in using deadly force.[24]

Nelson recalled that the local mayoral administration responded to the Assembly pressures with symbolic gestures. Columbus Mayor Tom Moody initiated a policy stipulating that no officer below the rank of sergeant could carry shotguns, only to promote a number of lower-ranking officers to sergeant shortly thereafter.[25] Despite such dissemblance by local officials, the efforts of Columbus Assembly activists and others across the country increased the level of public dialogue in many local communities around the problem of over-policing of African Americans. Assembly activists worked tirelessly to address other issues such as plant closures, public education, and local corporate divestment in the South African apartheid regime.

Perhaps the chief accomplishment of the Assembly was its truly democratic culture that attempted to operationalize the Black Power ideal of self-determination and develop a politics driven by grassroots concerns. New Jersey Assembly chairperson and veteran of Committee for a Unified Newark (CFUN) and CAP Talaamu Holiday recalled the Assembly's democratic character:

> We attempted to bring together a structure that brought grass roots people in and afforded them an opportunity to present their opinion and raise issues that they thought were important. And to bring forth a discussion on the agenda of how you are going to address it and a plan on how to do it . . . We were effective at doing that.[26]

Louisiana Black Political Assembly Chair Reverend Albert McKnight also credited the Assembly with facilitating greater grassroots involvement in the political arena as well as with altering long-standing patron–client relations between local black functionaries and the Democratic Party in some parts of the state. He argued that before the Assembly "candidates would go to the black person who would deliver the black vote. And I think we changed that. We had an effect on that. I don't think we destroyed it, but we certainly weakened it. I think that's the biggest effect that we weakened that they could go

can't expect Black vote easily / just pander

to one place and have the vote delivered."[27] The activism of local Assemblies during the seventies is testament to their commitment and resourcefulness. Campaigns were often waged on meager budgets. State and local Assembly chapters maintained their work financially through the local dues structure and fund-raising activities, which included raffles, Saturday night discos, guest lecture series, and other public events. In some cases, activists utilized their own personal incomes and resources to assist the creation of viable political alternatives, influence public policy, and confront local problems. These and other small acts characterized the mundane, though crucially important, work of Assembly activists between national and regional conventions. Such local successes were eclipsed by national developments in the Assembly's leadership and within wider movement circles.

The capacity of the Assembly to become a viable political organization was severely challenged by the development of sectarian infighting among radical activists. Much of this trouble stemmed from the prevalence of vanguardist posturing within movement circles. More importantly, the ideological debates that festered within the Assembly, ALSC, and other organizations were inevitably rooted in the denial of ideological differences that had governed much of Black Power discourse during the late sixties and early seventies. The calls for unity without uniformity, operational unity, and the like elided open and honest discussion of political differences of African Americans in favor of black identity politics. Having been bridled for a time beneath the banner of black unity, the political differences among black activists burst out into the open. The Assembly's Economic Conference in August 1975 was the scene of an intense ideological skirmish between CAP cadre and black nationalists.

how damaging ability to act

The conference was held at Ralph Abernathy's West Hunter Street Baptist Church in Atlanta under the theme "The Current Depression and the Survival of Black People: What is to Be Done?" Initially, the conference had been organized to provide a forum for national and local leaders, economists, businesspersons, and activists to discuss strategies and programs for addressing poverty and inequality. In his conference address, Daniels—Charles Diggs's successor as Assembly president—attempted to convey the Assembly's purpose of holding the conference, "The National Black Assembly stands for a new economic order . . . the masses of people are struggling for a change in their material condition . . . Economic Democracy, people participation and control is a must . . . in 1976 we must pose an alternative."[29] Hence the Atlanta summit was intended to facilitate the exchange of alternative economic development schemes and policy solutions. According to news reports, Julian Bond, trade union activist Bill Lucy, and Georgia State Representative and veteran civil rights organizer Hosea Williams were verbally assaulted by CAP cadre.[30] However, the most bitter clashes occurred during a workshop conducted by Dr. Naim Akbar, coordinator of the Nation of Islam's (NOI's) Office of Human development and Attorney Saad El'Amin, NOI business manager.

Akbar and El'Amin outlined an economic development plan that was rooted in NOI's philosophy of self-help and entrepreneurship. Their arguments for small business development and economic self-determination were met with a volley of questions and denunciations from CAP cadre and other Marxists. To a considerable degree, the critical response to Akbar and El'Amin's presentation and their defense of the NOI's economic development strategies rehearsed much of the Marxist–nationalist debate. CAP cadre held that the NOI's programs amounted to "bourgeois capitalism." Baraka characterized the NOI and the black business strata generally as the "new oppressors" because of their adoption of capitalist economic development programs.[31] In their defense, El'Amin and Akbar argued that the NOI combined conventional free enterprise schema with shared ownership and collectivism compatible with theories of socialism. As El'Amin noted, "The difference between the Nation and capitalism is that we are not in business to make profits for self—we are in it to grow and serve." Likewise, Akbar offered a utilitarian defense of capitalism comparing it to a garden tool, which could be used for good or ill intentions. In a stern rebuttal of his Marxist critics, El'Amin asserted that their arguments were essentially academic and bore no immediate benefit to the poor communities, unlike the practical efforts of the NOI. Equally, El'Amin dismissed many activists' embrace of Marxism as tangential and inauthentic. He said, "Marxism is a fad . . . It has supplanted cultural nationalism of the past. It is a new rap, a new terminology and young people have mimicked it." For many Assembly activists, the events that transpired at the Atlanta Economic Conference were the final straw in a series of questionable actions undertaken by CAP cadre. Even before the Atlanta conference, some Assembly activists had voiced concern about Baraka's leadership.

Opposition to Baraka developed in Assembly ranks following his public embrace of communism and charges that CAP cadre was attempting to impose its newfound ideological line on the Assembly's direction. Oklahoma State Representative and Assembly treasurer Hannah Atkins resigned from her position in February 1975 at an Assembly meeting in New York City.[32] Her decision was prompted by the "brutish tactics" employed by Baraka and CAP cadre "to domi-nate the NBPA."[33] Atkins asserted that "[o]pen measures were taken to push out of the organization persons who happened not to express the views acceptable to certain 'Nationalists.'" In its report on the February 1975 meeting, a *Pittsburgh Courier* article cited an anony-mous source who foresaw Hatcher's resignation as being imminent.[34] In fact, Hatcher relinquished his formal leadership role with the Assembly shortly afterward. During the New York meeting, there was an effort to establish a vote of no confidence regarding Baraka's lead-ership. Assembly President Daniels recalls that the motion did not succeed, "not for lack of majority sentiment, but due to anxieties over lack of a well-defined, principled basis for the action."[35] Daniels was growing increasingly leery of Baraka's politics as well. Regarding Baraka's leadership, Daniels said:

> Though I respect Amiri Baraka's right to express his opinion and advocate his ideology, I must express my grave misgivings about the repercussions at this point in time of having an avowed com-munist in the leadership of the NBPA. I have serious concerns about our capacity to grow if, in addition to all of the other problems we confront, we must also be constantly reacting to the fear which communism engenders in the masses of our people.[36]

Although Baraka's misbehavior was well known, Daniels's com-ments reveal a neglected dynamic. On the surface, he professed a certain ecumenical posture, but ultimately his tolerance had limits.

Daniels's interview comments regarding the "fear which communism engenders" confirms CAP's and Baraka's claims of late–Cold War anti-communism within the Assembly ranks.

In his typical style, Baraka chastised his critics noting that while Atkins and other politicians could not stomach his radicalism, they were willing to work alongside conservatives in the Democratic Party.[37] CAP activists rallied behind Baraka and held that efforts to remove him from the Assembly betrayed the foundational tenet of broad-based unity. They argued that "the NBA is a black united front, i.e. an organization of all tendencies and ideologies that can cohere around certain given objectives or goals. It is necessary to stress both the union of all parties and the relative independence of each . . . And no organization can be asked to give up its independent political program, even though that might be at variance with the NBA united front position!"[38] Equally, CAP and Baraka attributed the growing support for his removal as being driven by anti-communist sentiment among more moderate Assembly leadership. Yet, while he may have indeed fallen prey to red-baiting by liberal black political elites, Baraka did not articulate an adequate defense against the looming charges of strong-arm politics on his part and other CAP cadre. At the 1974 Little Rock Convention, members of the black press core complained of intimidation and bullying at the hands of CAP cadre assigned to secure the proceedings.[39] Testimonies in media coverage as well as in articles authored by Assembly activists suggested that CAP's politics had veered away from respect for parliamentary debate and consensus building toward more confrontational tactics. As opposition to Baraka's leadership mounted, a formal initiative materialized to reform the Assembly's organizational structure and, by extension, to neutralize Baraka's and CAP's influence.

These ideological conflicts within the Assembly served as a catalyst for reforming the organization's cumbersome leadership structure and democratizing gender relations as well. The Assembly moved toward greater gender equality due to two principle factors—the abandonment of cultural nationalist ideology by CAP cadre and the development of a women's caucus. Before the 1966 Meredith March, black social life was constituted by gender norms and patriarchy, which were largely indistinguishable from that of mainstream America.

Malcolm X's proto–Black Power sensibility integrated the autodidactic rhetorical style of Harlem radicalism with notions of republican manhood.[40] His rhetoric most often recalled notions of citizenship, which predated the passage of the Nineteenth amendment and equated civic agency and right with economic autonomy and the capacity for masculine self-defense. From its inception, Black Power bore a distinctively patriarchal character. Not surprisingly, some popular Black Power radicals espoused playful sexism and open misogyny ranging from Stokely Carmichael's infamous statement regarding the necessity of women's sexual service within movement circles or Eldridge Cleaver's notorious endorsement of rape as "an act of insurrection."[41] Other manifestations of sexism within Black Power radicalism were less sensational but equally troubling. The 1965 Moynihan report gave a gloss of respectability to black patriarchal assertions.

At the time of his controversial report's publication, Daniel Patrick Moynihan was an Assistant Secretary of Labor for Policy Planning and Research in the Johnson Administration. In Moynihan's 1965 report *The Negro Family: A Case for National Action*, he asserted that "the Negro family in the urban ghetto is crumbling."[42] Drawing on mainstream social science literature and a battery of government statistics, the report located the source of various social problems in the prevalence of the matriarchal family structure among the urban black poor. Although Moynihan wrote as a Great Society liberal who was clearly sympathetic to the plight of the poor, his 1965 report's devaluation of female-headed households and assertions regarding the "tangle of pathology" that ensnared the black urban poor became linchpins in the New Right's assault on the Welfare State. The report garnered a small library of well-deserved criticism from social scientists, feminists, and historians who challenged its ideological agenda and historical credibility.[43] Nonetheless, the report's implicit antifeminism, presentation of patriarchal households as normative, and assertions regarding the degradation of black men helped to shape scholarly and public discourses on sexuality and gender among African Americans from the Black Power era through the 1995 Million Man March.

Some black nationalists attempted to legitimize "traditional" gender roles and patriarchal authority through the re-invention of _but often not accurate_

pre-colonial African cultural practices. One such example was the Kawaida nationalism authored by West Coast activist Maulana Karenga (Ron Everett) and later adopted by Baraka.[44] Instructional materials circulated by Karenga and the US organization, carefully delineated the "proper" organization of the household and women's domestic and marital responsibilities. On the matter of familial decision making, the tract instructs readers as follows: "Discussion and agreements should be considered by both on matters concerning or affecting the family. Due to tradition, reason and acceptance, the man is the ultimate authority. The wife should share in decision making but refrain from making strong statements."[45] This cultural nationalist prescription for correct gender relations also went on to list chief factors contributing to divorce, some of which included, an "unresponding wife," a "selfish wife," an "impatient wife," and a "condemning wife"—described as one who is "always pointing out failures concerning matters outside and in the home including in the bed."[46] As Komozi Woodard points out, promotion of such gender norms faced some opposition within nationalist circles. Activists within the CFUN successfully barred efforts by some members to adopt polygamous practices.[47] Likewise, CAP activists moved toward a more progressive position on gender issues largely at the urging of the Black Women's United Front, which evolved from the activism of Amina Baraka and CAP's Social Organization Council.

The adage often evoked to describe the gendered division of labor within the civil rights movement, "men led, women organized" holds true for much Black Power activism.[48] With some exceptions, Black Power organizations were most often characterized by the same two-tiered leadership structure occupied by an upper stratum of visible male spokespersons and lower stratum of indispensable female organizers who bore the brunt of daily organizational maintenance. Women activists were central to the most successful mobilizations and highly publicized achievements of early seventies black radicalism—the 1970 Congress of African Peoples meeting in Atlanta, the 1972 National Black Political Convention at Gary, and the 1972 African Liberation Day demonstrations. Whereas each of these events is commemorated by footage of stirring speeches of male leaders such as Baraka, Sadaukai, Jackson, and others, the enormous logistical work and technical expertise required to make these conventions and popular mobilizations materialize remains largely invisible. Such unsung women activists included Amina Baraka and Muminina Salimu (Netty Rodgers) of CAP; Joan Thornell of the National Black Political Convention; Mwanfunzi Hekima and Florence Tate of the African Liberation Day Coordinating Committee, among countless others. Not surprisingly, soon after the establishment of the National Black Assembly at the 1972 Gary Convention, many women activists called for reform.

As CAP formally adopted "scientific socialism," activists also endorsed a more progressive analysis of sexual politics. In a 1975 statement published in the Assembly's Newsletter, Baraka wrote of the "triple oppression of black women." In reference to the omission of gender/sexual subordination from the founding documents of the Assembly, he asserted, "It is this kind of blatant male chauvinism that has dominated the Assembly, that has crippled the productivity of its female members. Issues from air pollution to cable television were explored and resolved—but no mention of sex discrimination in hiring practices, equal pay for equal work, ERA, free and voluntary abortions, safe and free birth control or any of the concerns of the millions of working Black women."[49] Baraka's statements reflected the core concerns being raised by the Assembly's Women's Caucus at the time. The Caucus called for 50 percent women's representation on all committees. The issues raised by the Women's Caucus, however, were eclipsed by an intensifying political and ideological struggle between CAP cadre and other Assembly activists. This fray was an outgrowth of the Marxist–nationalist debate that then threatened to destroy the Assembly. Mashariki Kurudisha, then a member of the Assembly's Executive Council, openly questioned the sincerity of Baraka's endorsement of the Women's Caucus. In a letter addressed to "All Interested Black Women," Kurudisha accused CAP cadre of exclusionary and manipulative tactics regarding promotion of the "woman question."[50] She argued that "[i]n light of the behavior of the members of this organization it seems clear to me that their desire is not to build the NBA in the best interest of all Black people but to control it in their interest. At this time CAP is clearly attempting to use the 'women's question' in their best interest."[51]

In September 1975, an open letter proposing sweeping structural reforms was issued by a collective of "Concerned NBA members."[52] The letter expressed the need to redress "structural and organizational defects," which had circumscribed the Assembly's ability to enact meaningful programs. Such problems included the cumbersome tripartite leadership structure or Executive Council (EXCO), which had recently been expanded to nine persons. The letter's authors noted that such reform was significant in that it allowed for more effective decision making and helped to initiate some of the Assembly's more meaningful projects, such as the Atlanta Economic Conference and the organizational newsletter. Yet, the newly expanded EXCO functionally replaced the NBPC, the Assembly's original administrative arm, thus rendering the latter body pointless and creating an unnecessary bureaucratic layer. Underlying the letter's concerns regarding the Assembly's overgrown bureaucratic structure, however, was discontent surrounding CAP's and Baraka's presence within the organization. The letter indicts CAP for "the continual disruption of NBA meetings, harassment of members of the NBA who do not wish to vote as CAP felt they should"; the letter then turns to direct accusations against Baraka citing "the Secretary General's attacks upon everyone and anyone" and "a pattern of behavior which has no place in the leadership of any organization which hopes to move forward and grow." The undersigned concluded sternly, "We will not be an unorganized majority which is used, manipulated and controlled by an organized minority." The letter outlined seven corrective measures that would revise the organization's structure and, in effect, neutralize the influence of Baraka and CAP.

Some of the more substantive, proposed reforms to the Assembly's organizational structure included: (1) the abolition of the existing tripartite leadership structure and its replacement with four more conventional administrative offices (Chairperson, Vice-Chairperson, Secretary and Treasurer); (2) The dissolution of the NBPC and the creation of an expanded EXCO of nineteen persons (four officers, eight regional representatives, five chairpersons of standing committees, and two at-large members); (3) abolition of the Assembly's multiple ministries and their replacement with five standing committees around specific areas of work to be accountable to the EXCO; (4) Reduction of

Assembly meeting schedule from four to three annual meetings to facilitate greater participation and curb financial costs; and the (5) creation of informal state caucuses during national conventions and meetings to ensure that issues are clearly understood. In a clear effort to mediate CAP's influence in subsequent Assembly activities, the letter called for the transformation of the role of national organizations such that their participation may be exercised via state delegations. Likewise, it suggested that meeting protocols be re-crafted to limit "the ability of observers to disrupt NBA meetings."

Tensions over the Women's Caucus and wider conflicts over CAP's influence within the Assembly came to a head at an explosive meeting in Dayton, Ohio, in November 1975. Several constitutional reforms were enacted, which effectively led to Baraka's removal from the leadership and the subsequent withdrawal of CAP support.[53] Assembly President Daniels anticipated the Dayton meeting as "the most important meeting ever to be held by the National Black Political Assembly."[54] Indeed the outcomes of this meeting constituted a decisive moment in the development of the Assembly. In addition to the proposed changes to the charter and organizational structure, consideration of the 1976 presidential election strategy and issues regarding the Women's Caucus were slated on the meeting agenda. These issues took a backseat to the looming confrontation between CAP cadre and reformists within the Assembly. Amidst emotionally charged debate, the terms outlined in the "open letter" were adopted. In the aftermath of Baraka's ouster, a new slate of leaders was chosen. The following individuals assumed leadership of the Assembly under the new structure: Daniels, chairperson; Kurudisha, co-chairperson; John Warfield, secretary; and State Representative Lois Deberry, treasurer.

Both Daniels and Kurudisha brought valuable skills and experience to the national leadership of the organization. A native of Youngstown, Ohio, Daniels was the founder of Freedom, Inc., a community organization dedicated to black self-reliance through creation of independent economic, cultural, and political institutions. He was also a college professor and moderator of "Perspectives in Black," a weekly TV talk show broadcast by Youngstown's WYTV-ABC. Daniels had attended the Gary Convention as a member of the Ohio delegation and, therefore, was involved in the Assembly from its inception. Daniels was sympathetic to both black nationalism and social democratic left politics. Kurudisha was the first woman to ascend to the apex of the Assembly's leadership structure. She hailed from Turner Station, a black enclave in the working-class Baltimore suburb of Dundalk. Her grandfather and other male relatives were active members of the steelworkers local. As a consequence of their union activism, Kurudisha attended the 1963 March on Washington at thirteen years of age. She was also among the first group of black students to integrate Dundalk High School. Later, as a student at the University of Maryland, Baltimore County, she became involved in electoral politics staffing Parren Mitchell's successful campaign for the House of Representatives. Subsequently, she participated in the 1972 Gary Convention as a member of the Maryland delegation. Kurudisha recalls her ability to work within mainstream and radical black tendencies: "I crossed into both camps unlike a lot of other people and was viewed by many people as being nationalist because I came out of the student movement. Locally, I was involved in some of the collective living experiments and in helping to start Kwanzaa celebrations. So I was considered by a lot of people to be a progressive nationalist."[55] Kurudisha, Daniels, and other remaining Assembly cadre such as Kurudisha's husband Mtangulizi Sanyika (formerly Heyward Henry) brought a range of diverse, practical skills and leadership abilities and provided a degree of continuity to the organization during a time of substantial transition.

In the months that followed, CAP denounced Daniels, Kurudisha, and the remaining Assembly leadership.[56] CAP's organ *Unity and Struggle* featured a wave of articles that characterized the Assembly leadership as the "new comprador class," "the petit bourgeois aspirant elite," "democrat lackeys," "social democratic swine," and "the gun-bearers of the front end of that elite who are the elected officials and top bureaucrats." One particularly venomous passage derided Assembly president Daniels as the "black Mussolini." Generally these retorts sought to portray CAP as the victim of anti-communist forces within the Assembly. In Baraka's defense, one of the organization's statements held:

> The Congress of Afrikan People's Chairman is resigning because we do not want to continue to be part of this leadership clique which now sees the National Black Assembly as its own pocket

bauble and instrument to broker money and position from the bourgeoisie and we do not want to allow them to hang their pointed hats upon the lie that the Congress of Afrikan People through the Secretary General is 'trying to impose' our ideology on the National Black Assembly.[57]

Although CAP called for "intensification of the struggle" within the Assembly, the Dayton meeting effectively marked the end of CAP's presence in Assembly politics. The once-prominent efforts of Baraka and CAP cadre to create a progressive, autonomous black politics effectively ended.

Ronald Walters concluded after witnessing Baraka's leadership at Gary that he was not merely a man, but "a movement."[58] Indeed, to a considerable extent, Baraka's personal and political development embodied the possibilities and limitations of the Black Power radicalism. The years spanning 1969 to 1974 marked the most fruitful period of Amiri Baraka's efforts as a political activist. During this brief tenure, he combined progressive stances on domestic and international politics with practical, effective organizing strategies. Equally significant, as a cultural worker, Baraka was central in the development of affirming ideas about black identity, new modes of artistic expression, and creative interpretations of social reality. The period of Baraka's preeminence and his descent in national black politics roughly corresponds with that of Black Power radicalism within black public life generally. Following his departure from the Assembly, Baraka would remain politically active.

He maintained his intellectual restlessness by revising some of his earlier positions. Some Black Power radicals such as Cleaver and Sadaukai abandoned radical ideals for neoconservative politics, while others retreated to the anonymity of private life.[59] Baraka remained a steadfast voice in the New Communist Movement and actively promoted his politics on the lecture circuit and through his creative work. Although Baraka maintained celebrity status in radical circles, he would not wield the same level of influence he had during his leadership of the Assembly and CAP. As a conciliator between diverse leadership elements, Baraka was crucial in the birth of the Assembly. Unfortunately, his leadership became more divisive and detrimental to the maintenance of a viable, autonomous black politics during the mid-seventies.

The Cincinnati Black Political Convention and the "'76 Strategy"

[handwritten: election of '76?]

During the February 1975 meeting where Oklahoma State Representative Hannah Atkins announced her resignation, the Assembly leadership also unveiled its "'76 strategy." This strategy was viewed by some within the leadership as an opportunity to regain lost momentum, build popular support for progressive politics, and to begin the arduous task of challenging the mainstream parties. Assembly organizers viewed the 1976 presidential campaign "as a unique opportunity to raise the question of the need for a new social system based on human needs (not profit), economic and political democracy and self determination." In a move that broke from the anti-interracialism of earlier moments during the Black Power movement, Assembly activists pledged to build a progressive united front that would "involve a broad cross-section of the National Black Community, the Puerto Rican community, the Chicano community, the Native American community, the Asian community and the white community in this effort."[60] While the emphasis of previous work had largely centered on achieving intraracial solidarity and black self-determination, the '76 strategy was characterized by a slightly more cosmopolitan outlook. *[handwritten: — broad coalition botwn racial groups]*

Equally, Assembly activists envisioned that the '76 strategy might serve primarily as a means for popularizing progressive political ideals in a fashion typical of third-party campaigns. Assembly president Daniels argued:

> It is important that we use the 1976 elections as a vehicle to educate the masses of our people to the contradictions and the vicious nature of monopoly capitalism as it relates to our people, and that beyond the election itself, there be an instrument as a repository of that sentiment which can agitate for both reform and reconstruction . . . Now, its obvious that the election will be an important instrument to popularize what we consider to be a new politics.[61]

In spite of the turbulence generated by Baraka's deposition, Assembly leaders forged ahead with planning for the 1976 convention. Sanyika chaired the '76 Strategy committee, which was comprised of twenty-two members (eleven men and eleven women). With the withdrawal of CAP support and the rich human resources it lent to the Assembly's organizational life, the task of mounting a national presidential campaign must have seemed especially daunting. Equally troublesome was the cool attitude toward the Assembly that had developed among many elected leaders.

Despite attempts by Daniels and others to minimize the importance of public officials' support of the Assembly, the selection of a well-known black political leader to serve as the organization's presidential candidate was the linchpin of the '76 strategy. During deliberations over who would serve as the best possible candidate, Assembly activists considered numerous progressive politicians—many who had initially supported the Assembly idea. Early on, Georgia politician Julian Bond appeared to be the front-runner in terms of potential candidates. In 1975, Bond gave some indication that he intended to run as an independent candidate. Bond, however, rejected the Assembly's offer during an interview on a national radio show the day before the Cincinnati convention began. He concluded that the third-party idea was premature because "Black voters are unprepared to support an independent candidacy."[62] Bond opted to pursue a delegate slot to the Democratic National Convention on a slate pledged to Arizona Congressman and presidential hopeful Morris Udall. Also, Congressmen John Conyers and Ron Dellums were considered as potential "first choice" nominees. Others suggested Dick Gregory as a possible choice apparently because of his previous experience as an independent presidential candidate. Nevertheless, as the convention drew closer, Dellums emerged as the clear choice of Assembly leaders. Dellums had distinguished himself through both his antiwar activism and legislative record to be among the more progressive-minded black politicians.[63] Although these potential candidates remained noncommittal in the months preceding the 1976 convention, Assembly organizers continued preparations for the meeting.

Cincinnati was in some sense an appropriate and predictable choice for the 1976 convention. The Ohio Black Assembly had grown steadily into one of the largest, most active, and well-organized forces within the Assembly. The departure of CAP forces solidified the Ohio Black Assembly's centrality in the life of the national organization. Veteran organizer Bailey Turner provided leadership for the convention-organizing committee. A Cincinnati resident Turner was an elder mentor to many younger activists in the state of Ohio. In conjunction with Antioch College, he founded the Institute for Practical Politics. Initially, Turner hoped that the Institute's curricular offerings in political organizing might be expanded into an undergraduate and graduate degree-granting department at Antioch. Turner's wealth of organizing experience and the overall strength of the Ohio Black Assembly helped to partially fill the void created by CAP's exit and he was a key figure in the planning of the convention.

The short-lived effort to develop a multiracial campaign vehicle was one of the most significant developments in the run-up to the 1976 Cincinnati Convention. This attempt reflected both Assembly activists' realization of the limits of black political independence and the persistence of Black Power anxieties around interracial politics. The planning committee of the '76 strategy moved to create the National Committee for a People's Politics (NCPP) as the formal campaign organization for the 1976 presidential campaign. After the Assembly had drafted its presidential candidate, the NCPP would nominate a vice presidential running mate and exercise decision-making power over the campaign. The NCPP was conceived as a multiracial progressive alliance but 51 percent black control would be reserved at the leadership level. Although this measure was taken to safeguard black control, its essentially undemocratic logic surely deterred substantive, lasting cooperation and support from nonblack progressives. Before the convention, some fifty representatives from the following organizations met with Assembly leadership in Cincinnati: the Mass Party Organizing Committee, the Puerto Rican Socialist Party, the American Indian Movement, the Union of Electrical Workers, Fight Back, and the New American Movement. Assembly leaders hoped that this multiracial, progressive alliance could secure ballot status for an independent presidential candidate in thirty states. In an historically significant step, Assembly leaders also agreed to allow nonblack progressive activists to attend the 1976 Cincinnati

part of reason why

part of failure too

Convention as observers.[64] Although many of the activists involved would become more vocal proponents of rainbow politics in the coming years, this formative multiracial united front did not come to fruition. Stipulations that excluded nonblacks from choosing a presidential candidate and ensured majority black control effectively confined nonblack progressives to the role of junior partners in this multiracial coalition. The NCPP signified a timid, incomplete departure from the anti-interracialism that defined much of Black Power discourse.

The third National Black Political Convention was held at the Cincinnati Convention Center during March 17–21, 1976. Representing thirty-two states, some 2,200 formal delegates and 2,500 observers took part in the convention proceedings. Among the nationally known leaders in attendance were Representative Charles Diggs, Jr., C. Delores Tucker, Gregory, and Bond. One newspaper report described the meeting as being distinct in both demographics and overall tone from its two predecessors: "The attitude is calmer and more business like this year. And while youthful intellectuals predominate, there appears to be a significant proportion of middle-aged, working-class blacks, people more likely to be found in a Baptist church or a community organization."[65] The article also noted the low attendance of black elected leaders and cultural nationalist organizations. Indeed, with its more radical and conservative wings pared away, the convention represented the core of dedicated state and local Assembly activists who remained committed to the ideals espoused in the *Black Agenda*. In effect, the convention reflected a more cohesive group than its predecessors.

Still smarting from the effects of ideological struggles, Assembly activists attempted to forge an agenda that might generate more effective, coordinated action. Daniels concluded that owing to the events that transpired before the 1976 convention "the NBPA learned the value of shaping and projecting a popular progressive nonsectarian program which is not congested with academic and ideological jargon or over-burdened with the familiar phraseology of the isms."[66] Consequentially, the 1976 convention adopted a set of practical, progressive goals. The Priority Platform featured a tier of social democratic policy reforms, which would ensure the "Right to a Decent Life"—full employment, national health care, and a National Housing Bill of Rights that guarantees that all people have adequate living facilities. Equally, NBPA's Priority Platform called for Defense spending reductions, public ownership of utilities, and progressive tax reform measures.[67] These items formed the core platform that would undergird the '76 strategy. After Bond declined to run as the Assembly's presidential candidate, convention strategists intensified efforts to draft Dellums as their candidate for what organizers were beginning to call the Independent Freedom Party. He was slated to address the conclave on Saturday, the last day of open proceedings. Many organizers hoped that Dellums' acceptance speech would serve as the convention's climax.

In anticipation of his acceptance, that Friday, hundreds of students and other volunteers fanned out across the majority-black suburb of Lincoln Heights to procure five thousand signatures to place the convention's presidential candidate on the ballot.[68] As Dellums took the podium, he was greeted by over two thousand enthusiastic delegates with many touting placards with campaign slogans "Dellums for President" and "Posing the Vital Alternative, Ronald V. Dellums." During his address, Dellums criticized the absence of his fellow black public officials and endorsed the basic legitimacy of the Assembly's efforts to build an independent black politics: "It is legitimate for a group, based upon its perception of its oppression to pose the alternative. There is nothing controversial about black people coming together as black people to pose the alternative."[69] Dellums also supported the idea of a black presidential candidacy. However, to the shock and disbelief of convention strategists and onlookers, Dellums declined the Assembly's invitation to serve as the Independent Freedom Party's presidential candidate. In an emotional address, he told the delegates, "I'd like to do it but the reality side of me says I have things to do . . . It's not my role, not my moment." Delegates reacted to his decision with anger, betrayal, and despair.

Although Dellums expressed support for the kind of independent progressive politics embodied in the Cincinnati Convention, his decision was essentially a tactical one. Clearly, for Dellums the tangible political influence guaranteed via his continued service in Congress outweighed the symbolic benefits that might be wrought from the Independent Freedom Party campaign. Based on interviews with

Dellums' staff, one news report linked his decision to legal and political considerations. Dellums' staffers wondered whether California law would allow the Congressman to run for two offices simultaneously under two different party banners. More importantly, Dellums did not want to abandon his House seat.[70] There also seems to have been some concern regarding his level of maneuverability after the campaign was initiated. If the presidential contest between the major party candidates was close, would it be possible for him to step aside and encourage supporters to vote for the more liberal candidate? These issues were a major determining factor in the Congressman's decision. In the aftermath of the convention's dramatic conclusion, Daniels attempted to downplay the significance of Bond's and Dellums' rejections. He told reporters that fielding a presidential candidate was not crucial to the Assembly's future.[71] Instead, he argued that the development of strong local and state organizations was the most important task ahead for the Assembly. Contrary to Daniels's media spin, the buildup and decline that characterized the development of the '76 strategy was incredibly consequential. The pre-campaign effort expended a considerable amount of the organizers' intellectual and emotional energies, physical labor, time, and resources.

In light of Dellums' decline, Assembly activists, in an apparent act of desperation, nominated a little-known, New York City activist, lecturer, and folk musician Frederick Douglass Kirkpatrick to serve as their presidential candidate.[72] Kirkpatrick was one of the central organizers of the proto–Black Power organization, the Deacons for Defense and Justice that engaged in armed self-defense in Louisiana and Mississippi during the mid-1960s. He also led a contingent of demonstrators at the 1968 Poor People's Campaign in Washington.[73] Assembly activists originally planned to secure his name on the ballot in the District of Columbia and in six states—New York, South Carolina, Mississippi, Louisiana, Kentucky, and Indiana. There were also plans to initiate write-in campaigns in selected Congressional districts in Pennsylvania, Michigan, and Ohio. Given the organizational strength of the Assembly in these locales, this plan held out the potential to register new voters and elevate key issues within public debate. Despite Kirkpatrick's activist credentials and the faith of some Assembly leaders in the campaign, sentiments among Assembly

activists for his candidacy were typically lukewarm. Indeed, following
the rejections by both Bond and Dellums, many looked upon the
nomination as somewhat of an embarrassment. Consequentially,
some Assembly cadre ceased active participation in the organization
following the 1976 convention. The outcomes of the 1976 convention
depleted the morale of many dedicated activists. To a considerable
extent, the "Frederick Douglass Kirkpatrick for President" impasse
reflected not so much the candidate's lack of viability but that of the
organization.

In its effort to pursue the '76 strategy, the Assembly showed some
signs of moving toward a more cosmopolitan, progressive politics.
Early on, strategists pursued the idea of a multiracial united front and
adoption of nonsectarian platform based on practical, social democratic reforms. Assembly activists' overtures to other radical and marginalized groups who shared their commitments to social justice may
have enabled the organization to build an electoral campaign that
might popularize the ideals contained in the 1972 *Black Agenda*. Likewise, the efforts of Assembly leaders to refocus the organization's
platform around discrete, relevant political issues and to draft its
programmatic statements in an accessible language represented a
genuine effort to move beyond the destructive sectarian squabbles of
only a year earlier. Nonetheless, in practice, the organization remained
dependent on black political elites for support and legitimacy. The
Assembly's strategy for influencing the process rested on a level of
elite entreaty that the Assembly cadre did not possess. Likewise, the
Assembly's continued emphasis on the convention strategy represented a departure from movement-style politics toward conventional
political processes.

The fracas surrounding the '76 strategy raised a number of questions regarding the viability of an independent black party. Both the
idea of fielding a black presidential candidate and forming an all-black
political party were peculiar manifestations of Black Power thinking.
Both ideas endured within radical circles due to their emotive or
symbolic power rather than their demonstrated strategic value. The
rightward drift of the mainstream parties and increasingly precarious
state of social liberalism in American public life helped to give cre-
dence to the view that blacks could not rely solely on the Democratic

Party to advance their interests. The idea of creating a national black
political party was, however, fraught with a number of built-in contradictions and unique challenges. The most obvious problem facing
the black party idea with respect to electoral viability is the minority (1)
status of blacks within the U.S. electorate. This basic numerical fact
greatly diminished the prospects of any party organization that would
only mobilize support among African Americans. Even in states or
cities where African Americans formed the majority of registered
voters, the development of a black party would have to surmount the
entrenched power of local Democratic machinery and the divergent
ideological tendencies and political commitments within African
American communities. As the dynamics and outcomes of the Gary
Convention demonstrated, the black united front idea was powerful
but quixotic. Despite its cathartic power, racial identity alone could
not serve as the adequate basis for sustained political activity. Despite
these and other structural deterrents to the development of viable
third-party organizations, such as the nature of campaign financing (2)
(2) and majoritarian/"winner take all" electoral schema throughout the
United States, some Assembly activists huddled around the idea of
creating a black party and kept this aspiration aflame.

"Revolution by Resolution": The Birth of the National Black Independent Political Party

Perhaps as a consequence of the '76 strategy debacle, the National
Black Political Assembly did not hold a biennial convention in 1978.
Nonetheless, as Daniels hoped, activists continued to work at the
local and state levels to build viable Assembly affiliates. Momentum
began to build during 1978 around the idea of holding a convention
during the 1980 presidential election cycle. Equally, support for the
creation of an independent political party mushroomed both among
Assembly cadre and within the wider black population. In various
position papers and articles, Howard University political scientist
Ronald Walters and Daniels encouraged the formation of an independent party.[74] From the wreckage of the '76 strategy, Assembly
activists regrouped and began to plan for a 1980 convention. During
March 2–4, 1979, one hundred activists converged for a meeting of

the Assembly's EXCO and state chairpersons in Detroit, Michigan. A major outcome of this meeting was the finalization of the 1980 strategy and the development of an organizational timetable. New Orleans was chosen as the national convention site. Kurudisha assumed leadership of the convention organizing apparatus along with King Wells, chair of the Louisiana state planning committee and Reverend Albert J. McKnight, chair of the Louisiana Black Political Assembly.[75] In response to the heightening intellectual dialogue concerning party formation and plans for a 1980 convention, Harold Cruse in his legendary candid style offered a blistering critique of Assembly leadership.

Essentially, Cruse contended that nothing would come out of the 1980 convention. Cruse held that despite Daniels and Assembly cadre's continual advocacy of independent black politics, they were in practice committed to the Democratic Party. He based this claim on a range of personality, leadership, and organizational problems within the Assembly—characterizing the organization itself as "a domestic Black political problem."[76] Regarding the Assembly's programmatic efforts, he wrote: "Here is reflected a rehash of the eclectic platformism [sic] of the Black Sixties, the cacophonic orchestration of clashing agendas, the confused medley of discordant themes about 'blackness' and 'goals of Black militancy.'" Given his own experiences with the short-lived Freedom Now Party in the early 1960s, Cruse's commentary reflected his impatience with the deferred creation of an independent black party. In a two-part article published in the *Black World*, Cruse reprimanded Assembly leadership for not creating a black party at the 1974 Little Rock Convention. Notwithstanding his ad hominem assaults, Cruse's comments point to the lack of originality, bad faith, and bureaucratic entrenchment that characterized the Assembly's national organization and the extent to which such dynamics discouraged progressive action. In retrospect, Cruse was both right and wrong in his predictions concerning the 1980 convention. Contrary to his forecast, a party did emerge. Nonetheless, the historical, political impact of the newly formed party would be modest at best. In fact, the fatal flaw of NBIPP was the inability of activists to transcend their own radical version of elite brokerage politics and develop a more viable left populism, which has historically been the strong suit of progressive and radical forces. Mtangulizi Sanyika, a veteran organizer of CAP and the Assembly, accurately summed up these shortcomings when he later lamented that NBIPP "tried to make revolution by resolution."[77]

The fourth National Black Political Convention took place during August 21–24, 1980, at the Hyatt Regency Hotel in downtown New Orleans. The convention attracted some eight hundred delegates under the theme "Developing a Progressive Black Agenda from the Grass-Roots for the 1980s." With the presidential election less than one month away, the convention organizers made no pretense of influencing its outcomes. Unlike previous election year conventions, which focused on strategies for influencing the major parties, the New Orleans Convention was focused on revitalizing African American politics and ensuring an organizational space for black progressive politics during the next decade. Some argued that the ascendant conservatism of the era and the capitulation of mainstream black leaders demanded more effective efforts on behalf of black radicals. For many Assembly activists, the 1980 convention was an opportunity to create the type of concrete political formation that had been deferred throughout the seventies' black political conventions. The first day of the convention featured workshops organized around the following subjects: Jobs and Employment; Housing; Health Care; Criminal Justice/Police Brutality; Black Women; Black Liberation and the Church; and Black Labor. During the convention's second day, participants took part in more workshops designed to impart relevant organizational and leadership skills. The honored plenary speakers were Ernest "Dutch" Morial, first black mayor of New Orleans, Minister Louis Farrakhan, national spokesman for NOI, and Reverend McKnight. As in Cincinnati four years earlier, the New Orleans Convention participants represented die-hard cadre who, in spite of the various difficulties and failures of the 1970s, remained committed to the progressive vision elaborated at the 1972 Gary Convention. This fact was critical to the outcomes of the 1980 convention. Although pro-party forces faced some opposition, their strength ultimately prevailed.

Farrakhan set the tone of the convention in his opening remarks where he expressed adamant support for the creation of a black party.

Farrakhan asserted that "[w]henever you have an idea that is on time it will find its way into the hearts of many and the idea of a black political party is an idea whose time has come. We blacks have had our marriage to integration and now it's time for a divorce."[78] Nonetheless, during debates over party formation, members of the Louisiana and Texas delegations took issue with the idea. While expressing their support for a black party in theory, some argued, as others had before, that any step toward party formation was premature. One of the more vocal opponents was Louisiana Black Assembly Chair Albert McKnight. He was a key player in southwest Louisiana desegregation struggles who founded the Southern Development Foundation, a producer cooperative among black farmers in the region. McKnight argued that there was too much infighting within Assembly circles and given the strength of Reagan's neoconservative campaign, blacks stood more to gain by supporting Carter in the 1980 presidential race.[79]

The Pennsylvania, New York, Ohio, and Washington, D.C., delegations strongly advocated the creation of a party. Many within those delegations had been present through much of the Assembly's history, had witnessed the various aborted attempts at party formation, and, therefore, viewed the present moment as long overdue. Nonetheless, a compromise resolution was offered that would delay any decision on party formation until after the November elections. In a passionate address to the delegates, Barbara Sizemore denounced the compromise asserting that "the revolution is now *and not in ninety days*."[80] During an EXCO meeting that Friday night, members voted 12 to 3 with 3 abstaining to present a compromise motion to the convention floor. However, by the following morning some among the opposed and undecided voters shifted their support in favor of the resolution calling for party formation.[81] Despite language preserving the Assembly and its autonomy, for all intents and purposes, the state and local network of Assembly chapters was largely absorbed into the emergent party. The resolution also called for a founding or charter conference to be held within a hundred days following the adjournment of the New Orleans Convention. The delegation also passed a resolution that discouraged support of any mainstream presidential candidate in the 1980 election.[82] Instead, the resolution encouraged blacks to support either third-party campaigns or to abstain altogether.

The party's founding convention was held in Philadelphia during November 21–23, 1980. While mainstream news reports estimated one thousand participants, organizers contended that the founding convention drew close to two thousand activists from twenty-five states.[83] The delegation was very young, highly educated, and politically radical, based on the results of a survey of 184 registered delegates conducted by convention organizers.[84] With some difficulty, the delegates succeeded in drafting a party charter that set up a temporary organizational framework. Various names were proposed for the new organization, including the National Independent Black Freedom Party and the African Freedom Party. The new formation was named in accordance with an amendment offered by the Pennsylvania delegates.[85] The conference produced both the National Party Organizing Committee (NPOC) and the Charter Review Commission (CRC). The NPOC was intended to serve as the interim body between the founding convention and the first Party Congress scheduled for August 1981 in Chicago. Therefore, the NPOC was to assist the formation of state and local branch organizations. In turn, the CRC would exist to discuss, review, and revise the charter in response to input from local chapters. The NPOC was comprised of two co-conveners elected at large, two regional co-conveners elected within each of the four regions of the country (Northeast, Midwest, West, and South) and two state co-conveners elected within each state. Two representatives from each national caucus would also sit on the NPOC. In addition to those formed in states and municipalities, local organizing committees were also established in prisons, including the District of Columbia's Lorton Correctional Complex in Northern Virginia; the Maryland House of Correction in Jessup; and the Alderson Federal Prison for Women in West Virginia.[86] The activists took immediate steps to make the newly formed party relevant beyond the ranks of movement elites.

To coordinate the NPOC's organizing efforts among targeted, underrepresented populations, activists created the following four caucuses: Women, Youth/Students, Workers/Labor, and the Elderly. Organizers attempted to democratize the new party along gender lines by requiring co-leadership in all party offices.[87] Elsa Barkely-Brown and Daniels served as national co-chairs, while Barbara Arnwine and Ben Chavis served as NBIPP's national representatives. In addition, each regional and state party affiliate was guided by this male–female co-chair recipe.[88] These efforts to develop institutional means of incorporating gender, class, and age diversity represented important—albeit imperfect—steps and was clearly the end-product of struggles waged during the sixties and seventies within organizations that were traditionally elite and male dominated. However, these changes in organizational design did not transform the wider set of social arrangements and cultural norms in which gender operates. In fact, Paulette Pierce argues that these efforts to bureaucratize gender equality amounted to structural deflection—"an adroit substitution of a formal equality for a true equality that would require fundamentally changing the way things are done, or even changing the goals of the organization or both."[89] Ultimately, Pierce contends, these institutional reforms served to entrench male power by failing to challenge the implicitly masculine norms of leadership and public activism, which inform black nationalism and wider new left ideological currents, and by erecting a sex-paired leadership structure, which deterred any potential direct female challenge to male leadership.[90]

Some activists within NBIPP were well aware of the limitations of bureaucratic reform at the time, but they continued to assert their will and desire for a better, more egalitarian public life nonetheless. One such activist was Kathyrn Flewellen. She came to NBIPP with over a decade of political work ranging from student activism at Macalester College and the African Liberation Support Committee. Additionally, Flewellen worked with Cortland Cox to organize the American delegation to the Sixth Pan African Congress and served as a news reporter for Howard University's WHUR radio station.[91] With respect to her participation in struggles for gender equality within NBIPP, Flewellen recalls her experiences with radical honesty and hope:

I saw it as trying to get the concerns of women on the agenda of the organization. And that it was not okay to have a schizophrenic life. That one could be a leader in NBIPP and beat your

wife or have five different women was not accepted . . . that kind
of behavior was not okay and we needed to set an example of
what it meant to be a transformed human being in the process
of transforming society. That was our challenge.[92]

At the 1981 Chicago Congress, participants ratified NBIPP's
charter and drafted a national platform that was characterized by a
strong radical democratic orientation descendant from the 1972
Black Agenda and subsequent Assembly platforms. The document
employed language almost verbatim from the "Gary Declaration"
issuing a challenge to the "twin evils of racism and capitalism." In certain respects, NBIPP's Platform and Program was more coherent and
focused than earlier Black Power era agendas. The document began
with a defiantly antiracist and anticapitalist statement:

the present socio-economic system in the U.S. severely and
adversely affects the lives of Black and poor people. The disproportionate and unequal distribution of wealth and income in
this society puts unreasonable and excessive amounts of power
in the hands of an elite few, who through giant multinational
corporations, dominate the economic and political life of the
United States.[93]

To redress the problems associated with the current social order,
NBIPP activists called for establishment of a new economic order
characterized by public ownership of land, natural resources, industry, and technology. They also demanded a guaranteed, adequate
standard of living—including right to food, clothing, housing, and
medical care. NBIPP activists argued that such basic needs should be
recognized as human rights in accordance with the U.N. covenant on
human rights. NBIPP Platform/Program also laid out strategies for
abolishing racism in American society. In a fashion similar to earlier
Black Power platforms, NBIPP sought to address racism through a
dual approach, which incorporated governmental action and civil
society initiatives in black communities. NBIPP Platform/Program
supported use of judicial and legislative means to ensure that "racism
and racist practices in all forms should be outlawed and eliminated."

Likewise, it called for a full share of political representation of black communities and protection of social and economic rights. To some extent, the platform planks on racism and economic rights combined elements of community control with redistributive policy. On economic matters, NBIPP's Platform/Program calls for a strategy:

> designed to increase the volume of capital that flows into our community nationwide—and also to increase the amount that is retained in the community, and not allowed to flow out. Tax monies and corporate profits are part of the national income, just as our wages and salaries. Therefore, we believe they must be continuously redirected into programs and services to better the lives of our people in our communities.[94]

(redistribution)

The methods outlined to obtain NBIPP's stated goals heavily emphasized mass mobilization. The party's platform advocated three sets of mass-based strategies: (1) issue-based community organization and mobilization, which utilizes direct action, advocacy, popular education, and research among other activities; (2) institutional and community development, which entails both the design and implementation of alternative forms of social provision (food cooperatives, housing cooperatives, and credit unions) and the creation of cultural institutions that reflect and preserve black culture and identity; and (3) public policy and electoral politics through lobbying, preparation of public policy statements, and running and supporting candidates for elected and appointed public offices.

NBIPP cadre undertook important, progressive political work. They established relationships with socialist governments in Cuba and Grenada and sponsored delegations to these countries. NBIPP cadre also created a task force to conduct research and support action regarding the Atlanta child murders. Likewise, NBIPP activists formally supported and participated in the 1981 Solidarity March sponsored by the AFL-CIO (American Federation of Labor-Congress of Industrial Organizations) to protest Reagan's proposed budget cuts. Like its organizational forerunner, NBIPP served as a mechanism of political socialization into movement subculture and provided a framework for the transmission of organizing techniques from movement veterans to newcomers. Although NBIPP's founding convention pulled together a new generation of radical activists, to a considerable degree the fledgling organization fell prey to the same difficulties that beset the Assembly and ALSC. Essentially, NBIPP's growth was arrested by vanguardist sensibilities that inhibited its capacity to develop broad, issue-based alliances that stretched beyond radical circles and mobilized constituencies among the broader populace.

Writing on the eve of the Chicago Congress, Flewellen offered a perceptive analysis of NBIPP's formative period. Given the depth of her involvement in seventies' radicalism, she hoped that NBIPP would not repeat the mistakes of its predecessors. Having experienced the early growing pains of NBIPP firsthand through her participation in the Philadelphia founding convention, Flewellen surmised that the major problem facing the organization centered on the presence of ideological ambiguity.[95] She argued that in the effort to develop autonomous black organizations ideological debate was most often suppressed to maintain unity. Instead, Flewellen asserted that ideological struggle was necessary and healthy for organizational development. She conceded that during the process of ideological struggle, fissures are inevitable but are most often the result of individual personalities vying for authority rather than a result of principled, open debates on the issues. While warning against the creation of a "bureaucratic monster," she contends that NBIPP must develop an organizational structure capable of facilitating open, democratic debate. Most importantly, Flewellen asserted that ideological clarity "should come from the practical work of the organization." Flewellen's critical intervention and advice regarding the direction that NBIPP should take were insightful and, in some respects, prophetic. To a considerable extent, Flewellen's analysis both embodies and anticipates factors responsible for NBIPP's decline. While Flewellen encouraged the need for open, democratic debate and grassroots participation, to a considerable degree her insistence that "ideological clarity" and "ideological struggle" serve as the motive of organizational development reiterated the vanguardist logic of the mid-seventies' two-line struggles. Flewellen was not doctrinaire in her articulation of radical democratic ideals. Nonetheless, this premise that ideological unity was a prerequisite for effective organizational development entailed a logic prone to breed dissension and to distract organizers from crucially important development of practical political campaigns that might widen overall support for their efforts. Despite Flewellen's injunction that NBIPP cadre learn the political lessons of the previous decade, old problems haunted the organization's efforts to achieve social justice.

During NBIPP's administrative and organizational work, rhetorical conflicts increasingly arose between nationalist activists and members of the Socialist Workers Party (SWP). In contrast to other predominantly white leftist organizations, SWP had stressed the vitality of the black movement in its internal debates and position statements for decades. Although SWP cadre's position was shot through with irony and, at times, sad opportunism, they were staunch advocates of black party formation. As early as 1969, SWP adopted an official policy, which held that: "The indispensable instrument for organizing and carrying on effective struggle for such demands, achieving complete control over the black community and moving forward to black liberation is an independent black political party."[96] At the 1974 ALSC national conference, SWP activists sought to compel the delegation to form a black party to contest the electoral predominance of the two major parties—a proposal that was rebuffed by Stokely Carmichael and Owusu Sadaukai and eventually defeated by the majority of delegates.[97] During the Assembly's deliberations over the '76 strategy, some SWP cadre opposed the multiracial, united front character of the NCPP, demanding a black party instead. SWP's historic support for independent black political action was rooted in the organization's lackluster efforts to reconcile world revolution and American racial politics. The result was an awkward formulation that merely grafted elements of black nationalism onto Troskyist socialism. In other words, SWP cadre did not develop an interpretation of American domestic politics, which approached class composition and social dynamics in an organic, reflexive fashion. SWP cadre adhered to a deferential ideological position that accommodated race-specific politics as an adjunct or transitional dimension in the grander struggle for socialism.[98] Many NBIPP activists shared SWP's anticapitalist orientation. Nonetheless, some black nationalists within NBIPP perceived these efforts to steer the organization as a colonial maneuver, which entailed the same kind of white paternalism that had spurred the cries for Black Power over a decade earlier.

During an April 1981 NPOC meeting in Memphis, conflicts erupted over SWP's role in NBIPP.[99] Pittsburgh-based activist Sala Udin took issue with what he viewed as SWP's attempts to control the direction of the party. He introduced a motion that demanded that SWP discontinue publishing and distributing literature bearing NBIPP's name. It also stipulated that if SWP did not comply, its members would be barred from NBIPP. Supporters of the motion argued that SWP was attempting to mislead the public regarding NBIPP's mission and program. SWP supporters retorted that they were genuinely supportive of NBIPP and were merely utilizing their resources to promote the party. The conflict was resolved through subsequent revision of Udin's initial motion, which deleted language threatening SWP's removal. Ideological conflicts of this sort, however, continued to plague the organization at both the state and national levels and often paralyzed effective organizing efforts. As a consequence of such internecine battles, many NBIPP activists lost faith in the organization and withdrew their support.

The struggles of the Assembly and NBIPP cadre to build an independent black political party helped to lay the organizational foundation for the Jesse Jackson campaigns for the Democratic presidential nomination in 1984 and 1988.[100] An understudy to Martin Luther King Jr., Jackson rose to prominence in the aftermath of King's assassination in 1968 and took on a key role in the Resurrection City movement along with Ralph Abernathy, which attempted to force issues of poverty onto the national agenda. During the late sixties and early seventies, Jackson moved easily among the ranks of Black Power radicals. A gifted preacher, Jackson was a sought-after speaker at some of the Black Power era's major events, including the 1972 Gary Convention and the massive Wattstax concert in Los Angeles organized by Stax Records that same year. Not surprisingly, when building his Rainbow Coalition, Jackson drew upon the residual network of Black Power and New Left activists. Howard University political science professor and veteran of the Assembly, ALSC, and NBIPP, Ronald Walters served as deputy campaign manager for issues and political strategy for the Jackson campaign while former Assembly president Daniels assumed the post of executive director of Jackson's Rainbow Coalition. NBIPP veteran, Hulbert James served as New York State campaign manager for Jackson. Gary, Indiana, mayor Richard Hatcher headed Jackson's presidential advisory board. Bernard Parker and Riley Smith, past chairmen of the Detroit Assembly, served as co-chairs for the Jackson campaign in the 13th Congressional district of Detroit. As well, Ohio Black Assembly activists Esie Hughes, Dean Lovelace, and Richard Gilbert assumed leadership roles in the Jackson campaign in that state. Baraka also used his access to the lecture circuit to promote the Jackson candidacy.[101]

interesting! not advocating abstaining

The Jackson campaigns represented an important political watershed with respect to postsegregation African American politics. Although Jackson was not the first African American to enter the presidential race, his candidacy garnered more support than any of his predecessors. For Assembly activists who had suffered through the 1976 strategy debacle, the Jackson campaign was long overdue. Many activists hoped that the 1984 and 1988 campaigns would revitalize progressive politics and counter the prevailing neoconservatism in American society and the Democratic Party in particular. The extensive presence of civil rights and Black Power veterans within Jackson's campaign organization engendered a sense of political movement, but in many respects the campaigns signaled a radical departure from movement building. Not only did the campaigns reflect an overinvestment in messianic politics, they also revealed a renewed faith in systemic politics among many radical intellectuals and activists.[102] In the 1988 election cycle, Amiri Baraka called for popular mobilization, but he was very much a lone wolf. Baraka's call to arms was undoubtedly triggered by flashbacks of the 1972 Democratic National Convention in Miami, where he had witnessed black party regulars leverage the momentum of the Gary Convention for modest concessions and individual mobility within the party establishment. In addition to electoral mobilization during the primaries, Baraka threatened to stage a mass demonstration at the 1988 Democratic National Convention as a way to ensure a progressive party platform. Baraka argued: "*We've got to hit Atlanta with more impact than General Sherman!* We've got to organize a Political, Cultural/ Artistic and Economic 'pyramid' of activity and presence. We must create an alternative presence to that brought by the Democratic party."[103] Unfortunately, Baraka's proposed "March on Atlanta for Democracy and Peace" never happened. Baraka did not command the resources and influence of his Black Power years and many other activists thought that the strength of the electoral mobilization would be sufficient to influence the direction of the Democratic Party.

In both campaigns, Jackson ran on a progressive left platform that promised to reduce military spending; protect affirmative action; increase domestic spending on job training, health care, and public housing; and take steps toward nuclear disarmament with the Soviet Union. Although Jackson's bid for the presidency succeeded in energizing the black electorate, it could not halt the retreat of the Democratic Party from the policy legacies of Great Society liberalism. Jackson garnered 3.5 million popular votes in 1984 and more than seven million in 1988. In the 1988 campaign, he achieved electoral victories in one hundred congressional districts. Despite these significant inroads, Jackson's campaigns had little progressive impact on the policy platforms of the Democratic Party. The Democratic Party responded to the electoral pressures generated by Jackson with symbolic patronage to black and left-leaning constituencies, namely, the appointment of Ron Brown, Jackson's campaign manager to lead the Democratic National Committee (DNC). This gesture allowed Democratic Party officials to deflect charges of racism and create the illusion of progress while continuing its efforts to appeal to more moderate and conservative constituencies. This style of progressive gesture and conservative politics within the Democratic Party reached its apex under the administration of Bill Clinton. He was a key figure in the formation of the Democratic Leadership Council, which developed amidst the Jackson campaigns and vowed to steer the party rightward. Clinton's single-parent upbringing, folksy charisma, virtuosity on tenor saxophone, appetite for fast food, rainbow cabinet appointments, and mastery of a performative liberalism would lead author Toni Morrison to deem him "our first black President."[104]

Conclusion

The Assembly and NBIPP activists attempted to carve out a space for progressive black politics during an era of ascendant conservatism. The convention strategy and black party ideal led away from the kinds of popular democratic politics their architects advocated. As the brief case histories of this chapter illustrate, the declining influence of radical activists was attributable to both their continued commitment to both the black united front strategy and a muted form of elite politics. Despite many black politicians' departure from the organization, Assembly leaders continued to craft strategies that were dependent upon the support and legitimization of mainstream leadership. While the Assembly activists took a bold step in creating the NCPP and moving toward a broad-based, multiracial coalition, such efforts appeared halfhearted and were eclipsed by attempts to draft a mainstream black political leader for the organization's presidential campaign. Moreover, some Assembly leadership remained mired in the anticoalition premise of Black Power radicalism. The unreasonable stipulations regarding black control in a multiracial alliance, in all likelihood, doomed the project from its inception. Although the Assembly and its successor NBIPP maintained a progressive veneer, the actual political strategies employed by these organizations increasingly resembled that of black politicos. Hence, the Assembly and NBIPP's programmatic efforts were increasingly characterized by conventions and meetings more often than actual popular mobilization.

Conclusion
The Ends of Black Politics

The demand for Black Power arose as a challenge to liberal democracy. The landmark civil rights reforms enacted under the Johnson administration helped to close a long chapter of legal segregation in American life, but the problems facing African Americans could not be resolved solely through the assurance of formal constitutional protections. Black Power radicals demanded meaningful self-determination—the power to decide one's political and economic destiny. For some, this meant controlling local government, anti-poverty programs, public schools, businesses, and other institutions that organized black life. Taking aim at Western historiography and deep-seat racist assumptions in American culture, many black nationalists called for a radical redefinition of black history, aesthetics, and culture in ways that elevated black, African, and Third World dress, language, customs, spirituality, knowledge, and ways of being as new paradigms. Some radical left activists saw the inequality and hardship endured by blacks and other American working people and the poor in places like Vietnam, Guinea-Bissau, and Mozambique as being fundamentally rooted in capitalist productive relations. Therefore, they demanded revolutionary change that would abolish capitalism and usher in a new socialist political order. Such idealism stimulated waves of political and cultural work within and beyond African American communities during the sixties and seventies. The most radical promise implied in the Black Power demand, however, was gradually eclipsed by more moderate forms of black political aspiration.

This book offers a critique of the *means* of postsegregation black politics—the strategies and modes of action that have come to define African American political culture over the past four decades. In retracing important intellectual and political currents from the Black Power era onward, I have described how black political life gradually conformed to liberal democratic capitalism in political style and ideological commitments. Whereas most of this book focuses on the means of black politics, in conclusion, I want to turn to the *ends* of contemporary black politics. My argument here is twofold. First, I contend that black ethnic politics has reached its ends or limits as an effective set of political practices. Second, I think that the ends or aims of contemporary African American politics must be radically democratic in form and aspirations. In other words, such politics should not merely seek recognition or influence within the parameters of the current social order, but rather it should pursue the democratic transformation of those politico-economic structures that reproduce inequality in the contemporary world. Although the goals of indigenous control and black unity were powerful modes of politics during the immediate postsegregation context, their utility has faded and, in some instances, these practices serve as barriers to the effective pursuit of social justice.

The Black Power demand for indigenous control created a sizable black political leadership class during the seventies and eighties. In terms of liberal democratic rights, black political integration during the seventies was certainly an advance over the Jim Crow era terms of black political life. The initiation of democratic reforms ameliorated long-standing racial barriers to citizen participation and governance through the extension of direct access to institutions of public authority. In this regard, political incorporation was universally meaningful for African Americans, but its material rewards were uneven. Political integration was not beneficial to the advancement of the interests and agendas of certain sectors of the black population. Rather, the transformation of black politics from radical protests and systemic change toward a politics of insider negotiation and incremental payoffs within the established political order was a recessive development for those who sought to abolish inequality and to reorganize the U.S. political economy along radically egalitarian lines. This historical reality remains partially buried beneath intellectual and popular understandings of postsegregation black life, which were grafted from ethnic pluralism.

Formative expressions of Black Power developed in an antagonistic relationship with liberal integration, but such expressions were shaped by prevailing myths about ethnic political incorporation. Under this formulation, the ethnic group was presented as the primary form of political affiliation, and by extension, group mobility was to be achieved through the seizure of formal political power. During the Black Power era, many activists and ordinary citizens pinned exceedingly high expectations on the achievement of indigenous control. As this study's discussion of the Kenneth Gibson and Richard Hatcher mayoral elections illustrates, the emergence of a sizable, self-conscious coterie of black public officials was electorally and ideologically supported by a wide, diverse network of Black Power movement organizations. As Gibson lamented, many expected new black politicians to be "miracle workers." As activists and politicians quickly came to realize, African American's pursuit of the ethnic paradigm was deeply undermined by the economic and social decline of cities during the seventies.

The first generation of national and local black public officials continued to promote many of the domestic and foreign policy issues articulated by radical forces, but given the mounting assault on the planner state, they found themselves increasingly fighting a rearguard action. The agendas produced by the Congressional Black Caucus throughout the period and those crafted by mainstream black leaders at the 1976 Charlotte Black Issues Conference and 1980 Richmond Conference for a Black Agenda contained many of the social democratic elements articulated at the historic 1972 Gary Convention. Although they were not monolithic in outlook, generally black public officials desired the maintenance of the liberal social policies engendered by the New Deal and Great Society reforms. The moderate strategic orientation of black politicos was in many ways antithetical to the realization of substantial reforms. The kind of popular pressures that might have supported more extensive political change dissolved during the seventies. The strategy of insider negotiation and parliamentary politics undertaken by liberal-minded black and white public officials could not stem the rising neoconservative movement, which sought the total abatement of state interventions to achieve social justice ends.

Both indigenous control and the related pursuit of racial unity were moored in a corrupted notion of politics, which equated ethnic/racial identity with political constituency. As this book's examination of the Gary Convention and other united front efforts has illustrated, the strategy of achieving black unity was predicated on the flawed logic that the different political loyalties, ideologies and material interests animating black activists, politicians, and citizens could be disciplined through bureaucratic race organizations. From the colonial analogy to the more moderate arguments rooted in the ethnic paradigm, late sixties' black nationalist discourses assumed the fact of common interest among African Americans by virtue of a shared experience of marginality. Within any social formation, however, a sense of shared interest is historically contingent and achieved through the course of public debate and political struggle. Like other forms of identity politics, the politics of black unity retains some affirming, emotive power for many African Americans. The idea that race unity is a prerequisite to black political engagement, however, is a political fiction that often distracted organizers from the core basis of political life—the historical tasks of addressing specific social issues and attempting to amass public support for desired solutions through persuasion and organizing. As this book has illustrated, the race unity rhetoric most often masked elite prerogatives and forestalled honest public debate among African Americans. Despite these limitations, the peculiar form of race unity politics that congealed during the Black Power movement continues to shape African American political life.

Like other conclaves held in recent years such as the State of Race Conferences organized by National Black Assembly veteran Ron Daniels during the 1990s and the State of Black Union events convened by talk-show personality Tavis Smiley, the 2006 National Black Peoples Unity convention was rooted in an unfortunate nostalgia for the Gary Convention.[1] Although this latest black agenda-setting convention carried the style and rhetoric of mass politics drawn from sixties black radicalism, this event did not have the same popular resonance or political impact. In his call to convention delivered a year earlier at the national meeting of the Coalition of Black Trade Unionists, Founder and President William Lucy told delegates that "it is time to go back to Gary . . . to talk among ourselves as trade unionists, as social activists, as political leaders, as academics about what it will take to move our communities forward."[2] The convention's organizers hoped to build a movement around "black economic empowerment" that would "build partnerships among the religious community, the trade union movement and the investment community." Do these groups share the same interests? Do they even share the same appreciation of black economic empowerment? Are the political concerns of Republican-friendly, mega-church televangelists such as T. D. Jakes and Eddie Long the same as smaller, more activist-oriented congregations located in economically depressed rural areas or urban neighborhoods? Are the interests of black union members who desire living wages, health insurance, pensions, more leisure, a safe work environment, and opportunities for more education and training reconcilable to the profit motive that animates black corporate executives, middle management, and investors? Diverse constituencies and antagonistic social groups can find common ground, but the black unity rhetoric cannot reconcile such differences because it minimizes their presence. By taking black unity as its starting point rather than the mobilization of real constituencies around some clearly delineated goal, the 2006 National Black Peoples Unity Convention is destined to repeat the same problems as its predecessors.

While autonomous black organization is necessary in specific social and historical contexts, many of the progressive policy goals espoused by black activists from the sixties onward had resonance beyond the immediate circumstances and varied interests of African Americans and demanded more cosmopolitan forms of social action. With some notable exceptions, Black Power radicals' contention that race was the principal basis of politics inhibited the development of effective coalitions and alliances that might have garnered broader public support. From the Black Power movement to the 2006 National Black Peoples Unity Convention, activists have often pointed to the presence of racial stratification and white backlash to rationalize their defense of race-first politics. Racial animus, spatial/residential segregation, and reactionary attitudes remain formidable challenges to interracial organizing. However, these facts of American social life are not immutable.

Some Black Power radicals' diatribes against interracialism often depended on the suppression of an imperfect, but rich history of multiracial social struggles, which expanded the meaning of democracy and achieved concrete forms of social justice. The abolition of slavery, universal suffrage, the eight-hour work day, child labor laws, antitrust legislation, the minimum wage, the right to organize in the workplace, occupational safety laws, consumer protection standards, and the expansion of a social safety net under the New Deal and Great Society legislation all evolved because of public pressures from below. The various local mobilizations against Jim Crow segregation during the fifties and sixties were led by blacks, but such forces were supported by a diverse array of social actors beyond Birmingham, Selma, and Greenwood. The achievement of major civil rights reforms was made possible by popular social struggles that awakened the conscience of many Americans who had never traveled through the Jim Crow South and even those citizens who were previously supportive of racial apartheid.

The deepening of class inequality within the African American population over the past few decades and the conjoining of black and white ruling elites around self-help and carceral solutions to persistent inequality further erodes the utility of the black unity strategy. The Marxist revival among black radicals during the mid-seventies coincided with the expansion of the black middle classes and worsening social conditions of the black poor. Many activists turned to class analysis as the limited import of black political integration exposed the pitfalls of black nationalist thinking. The "race-class" debate spread to academe as well. Largely touched off by William Julius Wilson's 1978 book *The Declining Significance of Race*, mainstream scholars weighed the relative importance of racial discrimination and structural factors such as deindustrialization and urban decline in determining the fate of the black poor. In more recent years, social liberal approaches to racial inequality have been overrun by neoconservative explanations of inequality, which focus on "underclass" behavior. Within everyday parlance, "ghetto," "hood rat," "thug," and, at certain moments, "nigga" are more frequently deployed to distinguish the undesirable behaviors associated with the black poor from that of the black professional–managerial stratum. The popularity of this new class language among blacks and its implicit behavioral explanation of poverty have been aided by insipid debates over the influence of "gangsta rap" on adolescents that are most often animated by middle-class anxieties about how the race is represented rather than sound research. Black nationalists and liberals have converged around advocacy of personal responsibility and behavioral modification as curatives to racial inequality. These political tendencies have departed from their more progressive roots in the fifties and sixties that demanded systemic change over individualistic or market-based remedies. The controversy surrounding actor Bill Cosby's highly publicized denunciations of the urban black poor throughout the summer of 2004 is perhaps the most disturbing instance of black liberal implosion.

In a mix of stand-up comedy and self-righteous indignation, Cosby rehearsed neoconservative platitudes about the behaviors, language, and apathy of the urban "underclass." Ironically, Cosby launched his tirade amidst an NAACP event commemorating the 1954 *Brown v. Board of Education* Supreme Court decision that struck down the "separate but equal doctrine" established in the 1897 *Plessy v. Ferguson* case and stimulated local struggles against Jim Crow segregation. Reflecting on the legacy of the *Brown* decision and the civil rights movement, Cosby charged that "the lower economic people are not holding up their part in this deal."[3]

Those familiar with his wildly popular 1980s sitcom *The Cosby Show*, his best-selling books *Fatherhood* and *Love and Marriage* and his well-publicized charitable contributions to historically black colleges and universities were not surprised by the content of his remarks. His speech included the same rhetoric of patriarchal family values and bootstrap self-help that had endeared him to much of the American public since the dawning of the Reagan era.[4] What distinguished these latest comments was his open class contempt for the black urban poor.

Cosby's polemics help to legitimate the workfare regime and punitive solutions to contemporary inequality. His speech included puzzling apologetics for police brutality and misconduct: "These are people going around stealing Coca-Cola. People getting shot in the back of the head over a piece of pound cake and then we run out and we are outraged, (saying) 'The cops shouldn't have shot him.' What the hell was he doing with the pound cake in his hand?" Cosby also ridiculed other blacks' fashion sense and positive identification with Africa:

> People putting their clothes on backwards: Isn't that a sign of something gone wrong? . . . People with their hats on back-wards, pants down around the crack, isn't that a sign of something, or are you waiting for Jesus to pull his pants up? Isn't it a sign of something when she has her dress all the way up to the crack and got all type of needles [piercing] going through her body? What part of Africa did this come from? Those people are not Africans; they don't know a damn thing about Africa.

He drew absurd linkages between the naming practices of some black parents and criminality: "With names like Shaniqua, Taliqua and Mohammed and all of that crap, and all of them are in jail." Most disturbing was Cosby's willingness to breath new credibility into the long-standing sentiment that black people's behaviors are to blame for persistent inequality—and not documented racial discrimination in hiring and lending practices, poorly funded public schools, declining real minimum wage in many urban areas, exorbitant housing costs, and the negative repercussions of corporate globalization on the character, availability, and wages of American jobs.[5]

Such sentiments were a far cry from the beatnik narrator of the *Fat Albert* cartoon series who wove together the junkyard gang's youthful exploits into life lessons tinged with countercultural values like self-sacrifice, racial and gender equality, fairness, inclusion, and the moral imperative to stand up against big and small bullies. Sidestepping any talk of economic-structural factors or public policy, Cosby preached a gospel of mobility through education, parental responsibility, and philanthropical work as curatives to contemporary inequalities.

After the NAACP address, Cosby carried his soapbox to meetings sponsored by other organizational cornerstones of the postsegregation black political elite—the National Urban League, Rainbow/PUSH coalition, and the Congressional Black Caucus. While some voiced concerns that Cosby's choice of words was inappropriate, with the rare exceptions like Village Voice writer Ta-Nehisi Coates and University of Pennsylvania professor Michael Eric Dyson, few stepped forward to openly contest the truth or validity of his claims.[6] Other high-profile black political figures such as Detroit mayor Kwame Kilpatrick and former Spelman College president Johnetta Cole openly embraced Cosby's neoconservative politics.[7] Despite his appeal among some desperate corners of the left, then Illinois State Senator Barack Obama's celebrated address to the 2004 Democratic National Convention was merely a more tolerable iteration of the conservative themes in Cosby's remarks.[8] In many respects, Cosby's neoconservative speaking tour and its reception within these specific contexts might be read as a eulogy for black politics—an indication of its historical and substantive rupture from the progressive, democratic struggles that gave birth to it.

Ringing endorsements and silent agreement with Cosby's crusade within mainstream leadership circles are evidence of the hegemony of neo-uplift ideology—the prevailing view that black elites are the principal arbiters of race advancement by virtue of their education and institutional access and that self-help and incremental technocratic reforms are more plausible solutions to racial inequality than democratic popular struggles and generous, redistributive social policy. Cosby's narrative recreates a world of the urban poor that more closely resembles stock Hollywood imagery than reality. The most damaging caricatures are exaggerated—drugs, violence, criminality, and sexual licentiousness—while the more complicated, textured rhythms of everyday life in many of America's urban areas are neglected. Voter registration drives; tenants' organizations; local mobilizations against police brutality and predatory lending; union drives initiated by organizations like SEIU (Service Employees International Union) and UNITE HERE! (Union of Needletrades, Industrial and Textile Employees/Hotel Employees and Restaurant Employees International Union); informal networks of mutual aid; neighborhood associations; church-sponsored social activities and community ministries; support networks for families living with HIV/AIDS; Take Back the Streets marches; youth sports leagues; and banal acts of good will in America's poorest, most marginalized urban settings evaporate under Cosby's gaze. In effect, Cosby projects political apathy onto the

urban black poor and, thereby, reproduces the commonsensical notion
that the black urban poor are the objects of elite overtures and benevolence rather than independent subjects possessing agency and political will. His comments, like much of contemporary American public
discourse on inequality, portray the poor as an aberration within
liberal democratic society, rather than a constituent element of capitalist social organization. The ghetto is never represented as a community that can be rebuilt, revitalized, or renewed, but as a zone that
must be escaped, avoided, and policed.

The neoconservative ideas expressed in Cosby's crusade flourish
in an historical context where left social struggles among African
Americans and the wider population are molecular and sporadic.
The circulation and expansion of such struggles could contest hegemonic ideas about mobility, poverty, and public responsibility,
but developing a meaningful progressive left politics that resonates
beyond academic or activist conferences remains a formidable challenge. During the Black Power era, vanguardist approaches helped to
create disciplined, highly committed cadres who built impressive
community development programs and mobilized thousands around
electoral and public policy campaigns. By the mid-seventies, many
Black Power organizations such as ALSC and the Assembly fell prey
to internecine struggles over ideology. Radical activists who once
rooted their work in the quotidian concerns of local communities
and neighborhoods increasingly embraced the politically moribund
strategy of ideological education. This strategy decimated the vibrant,
diverse political culture of the Black Power years and led away from
the kind of movement-styled politics that might have engaged ordinary citizens and built support for political alternatives to the New
Right. The problems that beset the ALSC, the Assembly, and NBIPP
continue to haunt efforts to revitalize black opposition such as the
Black Radical Congress (BRC).

In June 1998, some two thousand activists, students, and scholars
converged in Chicago to form the BRC. Many in attendance were
veterans of the ALSC, the Assembly, NBIPP, and the National Black
United Front. The organization was founded by some 150 activists
from around the country who wanted to build a left political presence

in black public life. Their efforts began in the wake of the 1995 Million Man March orchestrated by Louis Farrakhan and the Nation of Islam and supported by a slew of Black Power veterans and notable public figures. The Million Man March drew together record numbers of black men to the National Mall in Washington, D.C., but carried with it no specific policy demands. The chief impetus of the march—the need for black men to atone for past transgressions and confront antisocial behaviors in their ranks—meshed nicely with the ascendant conservative narratives which locate the roots of urban poverty and crime in the proliferation of female headed households and the loss of patriarchal authority.[9] The organizers of the BRC hoped to develop an alternative to these neoconservative sentiments. The Congress's *Freedom Agenda* echoed the content and spirit of the 1972 *Black Agenda* and founding statements of NBIPP in its calls for radical democratic change.[10] Moreover, the Congress's politics were colored by deeper hues of feminist and gay and lesbian politics than any of the statements produced during the late sixties and seventies.[11] While the BRC served as an important network for activists across the country, it never fulfilled its potential. One of the most insightful assessments of the BRC's limitations was penned by the BRC's national organizer Bill Fletcher.

Fletcher came to the BRC as a veteran union organizer who worked for District 65United Auto Workers in Boston and the national office of SEIU before serving as education director for the AFL-CIO. After attending the founding conference of the BRC, Fletcher sensed some confusion among delegates about what it meant to pose a black radical political alternative. He recalls overhearing one group of organizers discuss support for black business development as an area of local work they hoped to initiate under the BRC umbrella. Fletcher writes, "They saw no inconsistency between the platform of the BRC (which is anticapitalist and pro-worker) and the notion of building, as a first major campaign of the BRC in that particular locale, an initiative around supporting black business."

In a 1999 essay "Can Black Radicalism Speak the Voice of Black Workers?" that appeared in the British journal *Race & Class*, Fletcher called for black radicalism, which put the material interests and desires of black working people at the core of its project. Although the title of his essay draws on a language of race leadership common to the black political mainstream, Fletcher's arguments served as a compelling antidote to the abandonment of popular struggles that had overtaken African American public life. In fact, Fletcher called for the widening of public debate and opportunities for black working people to articulate their political demands. The BRC could help to foster such self-activity but this would not be achieved through bold pronouncements or head counting. Rather, for the BRC, he argued, "it is not enough for economic justice to be an add-on to its programmatic thrust. Economic justice (nationally and internationally) has to be at the core of its work."[12]

He warned that the organization would become obsolete if it did not operationalize its ideological commitment to the black poor and working class through practical work. The BRC according to Fletcher "has to interpret black freedom via the demands of the Black working class and it has to have the Black working class as central to its construction." He suggested that activists develop issue-based campaigns in three core areas—(1) the transition from welfare to workfare; (2) living wage campaigns; and (3) the spread of unionization.[13] Rather than devising viable political alternatives capable of mobilizing support for tangible policy remedies to the problems many blacks face daily, the BRC and other contemporary efforts such as the reparations campaign advanced a mimetic politics that drew on the radical posturing and rhetoric of sixties opposition minus its popular resonance and political efficacy. Fletcher's comments, like the struggles of the Assembly and NBIPP, illuminates an important truth regarding the necessity of anchoring progressive political vision in practical work. Without such work that would make radical pronouncements relevant to the everyday lives of most African Americans, the BRC and comparable efforts will remain echo chambers for academics and Black Power veterans.

A more promising path to a viable left populism can be found in the struggle between mostly poor, black residents of Convent, Louisiana, and the giant multinational firm Shintech during the 1990s. In the democratic spirit of the civil rights and Black Power movements, this struggle began with the most basic desires and needs of local people and sought to create a concrete vision of social justice. In June 1998,

Emelda West, a seventy-two-year-old, retired schoolteacher from Convent, Louisiana, made an uninvited visit to the corporate headquarters of Shin-Etsu Chemical Company in Tokyo. Accompanied by Damu Smith, an NBIPP veteran and then Greenpeace activist, West met with Shin-Etsu CEO Chihiro Kanagawa in an effort to discourage one of the firm's U.S. subsidiaries Shintech from building the world's largest polyvinyl chloride plant in West's hometown in the Mississippi River parish of St. James.[14] Despite support for the $700 million development by Governor Mike Foster and other area politicians, St. James Citizens for Jobs and the Environment was successful in its efforts to halt what many residents considered a serious threat to the health of their community and its natural resources.

This conflict broached a number of related public issues—poverty, environmental quality, public health, and sustainable economic development. The St. James citizen's organization worked in solidarity with Greenpeace; the Oil, Chemical and Atomic Workers union; the Tulane University Environmental Law Clinic; and the Louisiana Environmental Action Network. As the battle with Shintech waged on, many participants' sense of community was enlarged. Old barriers and wounds between local residents that had festered since the desegregation struggles of the sixties were mended as they came to realize their common interests. In addition, the struggle of local citizens against a multinational corporation gave rise to a more global political outlook. The St. James citizen's organization ventured beyond the NIMBY (not in my back yard) impulse that often informs contemporary community organizing in the United States. Instead, local activists embraced the slogan "Not in anybody's back yard" as a core message of their campaign and crafted a cosmopolitan political project that bridged racial, ethnic, and national divides to oppose the most pernicious effects of corporate globalization. As West concluded after traveling through the Japanese countryside with local environmental activists, "When I look around here, I don't see Japan, I just see poor little Convent."[15]

The Shintech battle and many other local campaigns around poverty, affordable housing, police brutality, unionization, living wage ordinances, neighborhood revitalization, public transit, lead paint abatement, and public education, among other issues, constitute the fragments of new popular democratic movement, which might transform citizens and powerful institutions alike. Embedded in such social struggles is an alternative set of values regarding community, altruism, ecology, and work that might form the basis for freer, more democratic society. Future, more democratic forms of society cannot be determined in advance, but are contingent on the aspirations and power amassed by popular struggles. Effective struggles for social justice inevitably require countercultural work that might open up new public spheres and encourage people to connect their own ostensibly personal issues with those of broader publics. By reversing the commonplace tendency to caste public issues in terms of individual self-interest, such activist work might break the hold of conservative notions of self-governance. The history of late-twentieth-century American social movements bears witness that popular social struggles can transform participants and create a new sense of historical possibility. To confront contemporary inequalities within the United States and beyond, activists, workers, and citizens must build a counterpower that challenges state policies and productive relations which reproduce inequality and seeks to remake our world in a more humanistic, democratic image.

Notes

Introduction: All Power to the People?

1. Clayborne Carson, *In Struggle: SNCC and the Black Awakening of the 1960s* (Cambridge, MA: Harvard University Press, 1995), 209; Charles M. Payne, *I've Got the Light of Freedom: The Organizing Tradition and the Mississippi Freedom Struggle* (Berkeley: University of California Press, 1995), 376; Stokely Carmichael with Ekwueme Michael Thelwell, *Ready for Revolution: The Life and Struggles of Stokely Carmichael (Kwame Ture)* (New York: Scribner, 2003), 501–8; John Lewis with Michael D'Orso, *Walking with the Wind: A Memoir of the Movement* (New York: Simon & Schuster, 1998), 370–72.

2. Richard Wright was perhaps the first African American public figure to use the phrase "Black Power" during the civil rights period. In 1954, Wright published *Black Power*, a chronicle of his travels through the Gold Coast during its transition from colonial administration to indigenous rule and sovereignty. Wright did not focus on American domestic race relations in this nonfiction work. Nonetheless, *Black Power* anticipates mid-sixties' black public discourse through its emphasis on the possibilities stemming from black governance. Congressman Adam Clayton Powell used the term in a series of political sermons beginning in May 1965. Also, *The Liberator* articles penned by William Epton in 1963 and by C. E. Wilson in 1964 expressed very clear, proto–Black Power sensibility. Richard Wright, *Black Power* (New York: Harper Perennial, 1995 [orig. pub. 1954]); see also Kevin Gaines, "Revisiting Richard Wright in Ghana: Black Radicalism and the Dialectics of Diaspora," *Social Text* 19, no. 2 (2001): 75–101; Adam Clayton Powell, "My Black Position Paper," in *The Black Power Revolt*, ed. Floyd Barbour (Boston: Extending Horizon Books, 1968), 257–60; Art Pollack, " 'My Life's Philosophy': Adam Clayton Powell's 'Black Position Paper,' " *Journal of Black Studies* 4, no. 4 (1974): 457–62; William Epton, "An Alternative Policy: Political Power," *The Liberator*, September 1963, 15–16; C. E. Wilson, "Towards Black Community Power," *The Liberator*, March 1964, 9–11.

3. Carson, *In Struggle*, 209.

4. Payne, *I've Got the Light of Freedom*, 376.

5. Carson, *In Struggle*, 236–41. The more militant nationalist factions led by Bill Ware and the Atlanta Project staff pushed openly for the expulsion of all whites from the ranks of SNCC. The official purging of white members was achieved by a slim 19-to-18 vote, with twenty-four abstentions, at a December 1966 meeting at black tap dancing legend Clayton "Peg Leg" Bates' resort in the Catskills region of New York state.

6. Roy Wilkins, "Whither 'Black Power'?" *Crisis*, August–September 1966, 354.

7. Peniel Joseph, "Waiting Till the Midnight Hour: Reconceptualizing the Heroic Period of the Civil Rights Movement, 1954–1965," *Souls* 2, (2000): 6–17; Peniel Joseph, *Waiting 'Til the Midnight Hour: A Narrative History of Black Power in America* (New York: Henry Holt, 2006); Rod Bush, *We Are Not What We Seem: Black Nationalism and Class Struggle in the American Century* (New York: New York University Press, 1999); Komozi Woodard, *A Nation within a Nation: Amiri Baraka (LeRoi Jones) and Black Power Politics* (Chapel Hill, NC: University of North Carolina Press, 1999); Jeffrey O. G. Ogbar, *Black Power: Radical Politics and African American Identity* (Baltimore: Johns Hopkins University Press, 2004); Nikhil Pal Singh, *Black Is a Country: Race and the Unfinished Struggle for Democracy* (Cambridge, MA: Harvard University Press, 2004); Scot Brown, *Fighting for Us: Maulana Karenga, the Us Organization, and Black Cultural Nationalism* (New York: New York University Press, 2003); Jerry G. Watts, *Amiri Baraka: The Politics and Art of a Black Intellectual* (New York: New York University Press, 2001); James Smethurst, *The Black Arts Movement: Literary Nationalism in the 1960s and 1970s* (Chapel Hill: University of North Carolina Press, 2005); James Edward Smethurst, "'Pat Your Foot and Turn the Corner': Amiri Baraka, the Black Arts Movement, and the Poetics of a Popular Avant-Garde," *African American Review* 37 (2003): 261–70; James Smethurst, "Poetry and Sympathy: New York, the Left and the Rise of the Black Arts," in *Left of the Color Line: Race, Radicalism, and Twentieth-Century Literature of the United States,* ed. Bill V. Mullen and James Smethurst (Chapel Hill, NC: University of North Carolina Press, 2003); Monique Guillory and Richard C. Green, eds., *Soul: Black Power, Politics, and Pleasure* (New York: New York University Press, 1997); Mike Marqusee, *Redemption Song: Muhammad Ali and the Spirit of the Sixties* (London: Verso, 1999); James C. Hall, *Mercy, Mercy Me: African-American Culture and the American Sixties* (Oxford, UK: Oxford University Press, 2001); Fanon Ché Wilkins, "'In the Belly of the Beast': Black Power, Anti-Imperialism, and the African Liberation Solidarity Movement, 1968–1975" (PhD diss., New York University, 2001); Stephen Ward, "'Ours Too Was a Struggle for a Better World': Activists Intellectuals and the Radical Promise of the Black Power Movement, 1962–1972" (PhD diss., University of Texas, 2002); Stephen Ward, "'Scholarship in the Context of Struggle': Activist Intellectuals, the Institute of the Black World (IBW), and the Contours of Black Power Radicalism," *Black Scholar* 31 (2001): 42–53; Robin D. G. Kelley and Betsy Esch, "Black Like Mao: Red China and Black Revolution," *Souls* 1, no. 4 (1999): 6–41; Kimberly Springer, *Living for the Revolution: Black Feminist Organizations, 1968–1980* (Durham, NC: Duke University Press, 2005); Benita Roth, *Separate Roads to Feminism: Black, Chicana, and White Feminist Movements in America's Second Wave* (Cambridge, UK and New York: Cambridge University Press, 2004); Farah Jasmine Griffin, "'Ironies of the Saint': Malcolm X, Black Women and the Price of Protection," in *Sisters in the Struggle: African-American Women in the Civil Rights—Black Power Movement,* ed. Bettye Collier-Thomas and V. P. Franklin (New York: New York University Press, 2001), 214–29; Duchess Harris, "From the Kennedy Commission to the Combahee Collective: Black Feminist Organizing, 1960–1980," in *Sisters in the Struggle: African-American Women in the Civil Rights–Black Power Movement,* ed. Bettye Collier-Thomas and V. P. Franklin (New York: New York University Press, 2001), 280–305; Cynthia Griggs-Fleming, "Black Women and Black Power: The Case of Ruby Doris Smith

Robinson and the Student Non-Violent Coordinating Committee," in *Sisters in the Struggle: African-American Women in the Civil Rights–Black Power Movement,* ed. Bettye Collier-Thomas and V. P. Franklin (New York: New York University Press, 2001), 197–213; Tracye Matthews, "No One Ever Asks 'What A Man's Place in the Revolution Is': Gender and Sexual Politics in the Black Panther Party, 1966–1971" (PhD diss., University of Michigan, 1998); Joy James, ed., *The Angela Y. Davis Reader* (London: Blackwell, 1998).

8. Giorgio Agamben, *Means Without End: Notes on Politics* (Minneapolis: University of Minnesota Press, 2000), 29. Recalling the French Revolution, Hannah Arendt notes the place of political inequality in the origins of the "people" as well. Arendt writes: "The very definition of the word was born out of compassion, and the term became the equivalent for misfortune and unhappiness—*le peuple, les malheureux m'applaudissent* [the people, the unfortunate ones applaud me], as Robespierre was wont to say; *le peuple toujours malheureux* [the always, unfortunate people], as even Sieyès, one of the least sentimental and most sober figures of the Revolution would put it." See Hannah Arendt, *On Revolution* (New York: Viking Press, 1963), 70.

9. Barbara Cruikshank, *The Will to Empower: Democratic Citizens and Other Subjects* (Ithaca, NY: Cornell University Press, 1999), 2.

10. Ibid., 2.

11. Adolph Reed Jr., "Sources of Demobilization in the New Black Regime: Incorporation, Ideological Capitulation and Radical Failure in the Post Segregation Era," in *Stirrings in the Jug: Black Politics in the Post-Segregation Era* (Minneapolis: University of Minnesota Press, 1999), 131; Robert J. Kernstein and Dennis R. Judd, "Achieving Less Influence with More Democracy: The Permanent Legacy of the War on Poverty," *Social Science Quarterly* 61, no. 2 (1980): 208–20.

12. Senate Committee on Labor and Public Welfare, Subcommittee on Employment, Manpower and Poverty, *Economic Opportunity Amendments of 1967,* 90th Congress, 1st Session, 1967, Report 563, 20.

13. Daniel Patrick Moynihan, *Maximum Feasible Misunderstanding: Community Action in the War on Poverty* (New York: Free Press, 1970).

14. Peter K. Eisinger, "The Community Action Program and the Development of Black Political Leadership," in *Urban Policy Making,* ed. Dale Rogers Marshall (Beverly Hills, CA: Sage, 1979), 129; Peter Marris and Martin Rein, *Dilemmas of Social Reform: Poverty and Community Action in the United States* (Chicago: Aldine, 1967).

15. Michel Crozier, Samuel Huntington, and Joji Watanuki, *The Crisis of Democracy: Report on the Governability of Democracies to the Trilateral Commission* (New York: New York University Press, 1975).

16. In 1968, Harold Cruse claimed that "Black Power is nothing but the economic and political philosophy of Booker T. Washington given a 1960s militant shot in the arm and brought up to date." A year later, Robert Allen described Black Power as "militant reformism." Cruse's and Allen's respective characterizations of Black Power reflect the slogan's declining militancy following its appropriation by moderate political elements. Around the time of these authors' comments, the notion of Black Power as black capitalism was publicly embraced by Republican President Richard Nixon. Harold Cruse, "Behind the Black Power Slogan," in *Rebellion or*

Revolution? (New York: William Morrow, 1968), 201; Robert L. Allen, *Black Awakening in Capitalist America: An Analytic History* (Trenton, NJ: Africa World Press, 1990 [orig. pub. 1969]), 49.

17. Stokely Carmichael and Charles V. Hamilton, *Black Power: The Politics of Liberation in America* (New York: Vintage, 1967); Stokely Carmichael and Charles Hamilton attempted to define Black Power in their 1967 book. The text draws on mainstream American social science, the colonial analogy, and elements of left critique of capitalism to explain the dynamics of racial inequality and to outline a provisional framework for Black Power. Carmichael and Hamilton anchor this analysis in an understanding of racism that is radical by today's neoconservative standards. Rather than focus on emotional injury or errant behaviors of individuals, the authors define racism in institutional terms as "the predication of decisions and policies on considerations of race for the purpose of subordinating a racial group and maintaining control over that group."

18. Carmichael and Hamilton, *Black Power*, 44–45.

19. In one of the book's more remarkable chapters, "Dynamite in the Ghetto," Carmichael and Hamilton explored the interstices of institutional racism and urban industrial decline. They concluded:

Herein lies the match that will continue to ignite the dynamite in the ghettos: the ineptness of decision-makers, the anachronistic institutions, the inability to think boldly, and above all the unwillingness to innovate. The makeshift plans put together every summer by city administrations to avoid rebellions in the ghettos are merely buying time. White America can continue to appropriate millions of dollars to take ghetto teenagers off the streets and onto nice, green farms during the hot summer months. They can continue to provide mobile swimming pools and hastily built play areas, but there is a point beyond which the steaming ghettos will not be cooled off. It is ludicrous for the society to believe that these temporary measures can long contain the tempers of oppressed people. And when the dynamite does go off, pious pronouncements of patience should not go forth. Blame should not be placed on 'outside agitators' or on 'Communist influence' or on advocates of Black Power. That dynamite was place there by white racism and it was ignited by white racist indifference to act justly. (Carmichael and Hamilton, *Black Power*, 161–62.)

20. Robert C. Smith calls attention to this matter in his peerless overview of the literature on African American leadership. See Ronald W. Walters and Robert C. Smith, *African American Leadership* (Albany, NY: State University of New York Press, 1999), 35–58; Robert C. Smith, "Leadership in Negro and Black: Retrospect and Prospect," *The Urban League Review* 9 (1985): 8–19.

21. Mathew Holden, "Black Politicians in the Time of the 'New' Urban Politics," *Review of Black Political Economy* 2 (1971): 56–71; Michael B. Preston, "Limitations of Black Urban Power: The Case of Black Mayors," in *The New Urban Politics*, ed. Louis H. Masotti and Robert L. Lineberr (Boston: Ballinger, 1976); Leonard A. Cole, *Blacks in Power: A Comparative Study of Black and White Elected Officials* (Princeton, NJ: Princeton University Press, 1976); Robert C. Smith, "The Changing Shape of Urban Black Politics: 1960–1970," *Annals of the American Academy of Political and Social Science* 439 (1978): 16–28; Michael B. Preston, Lenneal J. Henderson Jr., and Paul Puryear, eds., *The New Black Politics: The Search for Political Power* (New York: Longman, 1982); Roger Biles, "Black Mayors: A Historical Assessment," *Journal of*

Negro History 77, no. 3 (1992): 109–25; Rod Bush, *The New Black Vote: Politics and Power in Four American Cities* (San Francisco: Synthesis, 1984); T. Cavanaugh and D. Stockton, *Characteristics of Black Elected Officials* (Washington, D.C.: Joint Center of Political Studies, 1982); Georgia Persons, ed., *Dilemmas of Black Politics: Issues of Leadership and Strategy* (New York: HarperCollins, 1993); William E. Nelson Jr., "Black Mayors as Urban Managers," *Annals of the American Academy of Political and Social Science* 439 (1978): 53–67; William E. Nelson, "Black Mayoral Leadership: A Twenty Year Perspective," *National Political Science Review* 2 (1990): 188–95; William E. Nelson Jr. and Philip J. Meranto, *Electing Black Mayors: Political Action in the Black Community* (Columbus, OH: Ohio State University Press, 1977); Martin Kilson, "From Civil Rights to Party Politics: The Black Political Transition," *Current History* 67 (1974): 193–99; Martin Kilson, "Political Change in the Negro Ghetto, 1900–1940s," in *Key Issues in the Afro-American Experience*, vol. 2, ed. Nathan Huggins, Martin L. Kilson, and Daniel Fox (New York: Harcourt Brace, 1971); Bette Woody, *Managing Crisis Cities: The New Black Leadership and the Politics of Resource Allocation* (Westport, CT: Greenwood, 1982); Albert Karnig and Susan Welch, *Black Representation and Urban Policy* (Chicago: University of Chicago Press, 1980); Susan Welch and Albert Karnig, "The Impact of Black Elected Officials on Urban Social Expenditures," *Policy Studies Journal* 7 (1979): 707–14; Lenneal J. Henderson, *Administrative Advocacy: Black Administrators in Urban Bureaucracy* (Palo Alto, CA: R & E Pub, 1979).

22. Ronald Walters, "The Black Politician," *Current History* 67, no. 399 November (1974): 201.

23. Martin Kilson, "Black Politics: A New Power," in *The Seventies: Problems and Proposals,* ed. Irving Howe and Michael Harrington (New York: Harper & Row, 1974), 307. By politicization of ethnicity, Martin Kilson means "to use ethnic patterns and prejudices as the primary basis for interest group and political formations, and to build upon these to integrate a given ethnic community into the wider politics of the city and the nation."

24. Tommie Shelby, *We Who Are Dark: The Philosophical Foundations of Black Solidarity* (Cambridge, MA: Belknap Harvard, 2005), 20.

25. Adolph Reed Jr., *Stirrings in the Jug: Black Politics in the Post-Segregation Era* (Minneapolis, MN: University of Minnesota Press, 1999).

26. Robert C. Smith, *We Have No Leaders: African Americans in the Post-Civil Rights Era* (Albany, NY: State University of New York Press, 1996), 278–79. Robert Smith's title was taken from a lecture Cruse delivered at Prairie View A&M University in 1989. During the question-and-answer period, an unfortunate student asked the curmudgeonly guest speaker to appraise black leaders. Cruse quipped, "What leaders? We have no leaders?"

27. Ironically, the view that more responsive leadership is required is most often and vocally espoused by right-of-center commentators. Far-right commentators routinely criticize black liberal politicians and the institutionalization of the civil rights movement. Neoconservative Dinesh D'Souza refers to professional civil rights activists as "race merchants." Stanford linguistics professor John McWhorter, Christian minister and talk-show personality Jesse Lee Peterson, and welfare-mother-turned-workfare-poster-child Star Parker, among others, criticize black political elites for defending such policies as affirmative action, Aid to Families

with Dependent Children, and other liberal social policies, more generally. With some variation among them, each of these authors wishes to expunge race-based public policy and redistributive measures altogether from the contemporary public agenda. As well, each is guided by the assumption that markets, not government, can assure equality of opportunity to all Americans. The curious thing about the conspicuous appearance of minority neoconservatives who denounce identity politics and redistributive social policy is that each is in fact the beneficiary of racial representational practices and de facto affirmative action. What distinguishes the color-blind conservatism of Ward Connerly, D'Souza, and the like from their white counterparts is the social weight afforded to their claims because of their racial identity. Their criticisms are deemed more genuine because of their first-person racial perspective and avoid the stigma of racism that might accompany an attack on redistributive public policy by white pundits. Recalling Nixon strategist Kevin Phillips' landmark 1969 work, *The Emerging Republican Majority,* McWhorter even engages directly in a form of racial brokerage by claiming to speak on behalf of "the silent black majority" who he contends is not adequately represented by liberal black political leaders. In February 2005, Peterson's Brotherhood Organization of a New Destiny (BOND), the Heritage Foundation, and Roy Innis of the Congress of Racial Equality hosted a conference for black conservatives under the banner "The New Black Vanguard." Black neoconservatives' denunciation of the civil rights establishment stems from their battle for leadership preeminence and desire to maintain their brokerage status within the Republican party circles and neoconservative media networks rather than some principled opposition to elite power. Dinesh D'Souza, *The End of Racism* (New York: Free Press, 1996); John McWhorter, *Authentically Black: Essays for the Black Silent Majority* (New York: Gotham Books, 2004); John McWhorter, *Losing the Race: Self-Sabotage in Black America* (New York: Perennial, 2001); Jesse Lee Peterson, *Scam: How the Black Leadership Exploits Black America* (Nashville, TN: Nelson Current, 2003); Star Parker, *Uncle Sam's Plantation: How Big Government Enslaves America's Poor and What We Can Do About It* (Nashville, TN: Nelson Current, 2003); Kenneth R. Timmerman, *Shakedown: Exposing the Real Jesse Jackson* (Washington, D.C.: Regnery, 2002); Juan Williams, *Enough: The Phony Leaders, Dead-End Movements and Culture of Failure That Are Undermining Black America—And What We Can Do About It* (New York: Crown Publishing/Random House, 2006).

28. Cedric J. Robinson, "Blaxploitation and the Misrepresentation of Liberation," *Race & Class* 40, no. 1 (1998), 1. Cedric Robinson's critique of the culture industry is perceptive, but he may well overstate how these representations were received by black audiences. Were black theatergoers necessarily "degraded" by such silver screen representations? Did they partake of such caricature and satire in discerning fashion? Certainly these representations probably did offend the sensibility of many activists seeking to popularize unconventional political ideals, but less-politicized consumers undoubtedly perceived this cinema's endless string of larger-than-life heroes, villains, pimps, cops, and comedic sidekicks as entertaining fiction rather than a mirror of seventies American society.

29. Jennifer Hyland Wang, "'A Struggle of Contending Stories': Race, Gender and Political Memory in Forrest Gump," *Cinema Journal* 39, no. 3 (2000): 92–115; Thomas B. Byers, "History Re-Membered: Forrest Gump, Postfeminist Masculinity and the Burial of the Counterculture," *Modern Fiction Studies* 42, no. 2 (1996):

419–44; Peter Chumo, " 'You've Got to Put the Past Behind You Before You Can Move On': Forrest Gump and National Reconciliation," *Journal of Popular Film and Television* 5, no. 1 (1995): 2; Judith P. Zinsser, "Real History, Real Education, Real Merit— Or Why Is 'Forrest Gump' So Popular?" *Journal of Social History* 29, no. 1 (1995): 91.

30. Quoted in Byers, "History Re-Membered," 420.

31. Ibid., 431.

32. Gerald Horne, " 'Myth' and the Making of 'Malcolm X,' " *American Historical Review* 98, no. 2 (1993): 440–50.

33. Allan Bloom, *The Closing of the American Mind* (New York: Simon & Schuster, 1987); Robert H. Bork, *Slouching Towards Gomorrah: Modern Liberalism and American Decline* (New York: HarperCollins, 1996); Peggy Noonan, "You'd Cry Too If It Happened to You," in *Backward and Upward: The New Conservative Writing*, ed. David Brooks (New York: Vintage, 1996); Allen J. Matusow, *The Unraveling of America: A History of Liberalism in the 1960s* (New York: Harper & Row, 1984); Myron Magnet, *The Dream and the Nightmare: The Sixties' Legacy to the Underclass* (New York: Morrow, 1993).

34. For a perceptive critique of the neoconservative uses of the fifties and the family values trope, see Stephanie Coontz, *The Way We Never Were: American Families and the Nostalgia Trap* (New York: Basic Books, 1992); Elaine Tyler May, *Homeward Bound: American Families in the Cold War* (New York: Basic Books, 1988); Peter J. Kuznick and James Gilbert, eds., *Rethinking Cold War Culture* (Washington, D.C.: Smithsonian Institution, 2001).

35. Francis Fukuyama, *The End of History and the Last Man* (New York: Free Press, 1992); Daniel Bell, *The End of Ideology: On the Exhaustion of Political Ideas in the Fifties* (Glencoe, IL: Free Press, 1960); Ellen Schrecker, *Cold War Triumphalism: The Misuse of History After the Fall of Communism* (New York: New Press, 2004).

36. Nikhil Singh, "The Black Panthers and the Underdeveloped Country of the Left," in *The Black Panther Party [Reconsidered]*, ed. Charles E. Jones (Baltimore, MD: Black Classics, 1998), 58–59; Elizabeth Martínez, "That Old White (Male) Magic," in *De Colores Means All of Us: Latina Views for a Multi-Colored Century*, ed. Elizabeth Sutherland Martínez (Cambridge, MA: South End, 1998); Paul Buhle, "Madison Revisited," *Radical History Review* no. 57 (1993), 248; Rod Bush, "When the Revolution Came," *Radical History Review* no. 90 (2004): 102–11; Alice Echols, "We Gotta Get Out of this Place: Notes Toward Remapping the Sixties," *Socialist Review* 92, no. 2 (1992): 15.

37. Todd Gitlin, *The Sixties: Years of Hope, Days of Rage* (New York: Bantam, 1987); Todd Gitlin, *The Twilight of Common Dreams: Why America is Wracked by Culture Wars* (New York: Henry Holt, 1995); Todd Gitlin, "From Universality to Difference: Notes on the Fragmentation of the Idea of the Left," *Contention* 2, no. 2 (1993): 31; Tom Hayden, *Reunion: A Memoir* (New York: Random House, 1988); Matusow, *The Unraveling of America*, 345; Elisabeth Lasch-Quinn, *Race Experts: How Racial Etiquette, Sensitivity Training, and New Age Therapy Hijacked the Civil Rights Revolution* (New York: W.W. Norton, 2001).

38. Peniel Joseph, "Black Liberation Without Apology: Reconceptualizing the Black Power Movement," *Black Scholar* 31 (2001): 2; Van Gosse, *Where the Boys Are: Cuba, Cold War America and the Making of a New Left* (London and New York: Verso, 1993).

39. Ibid., 9.

40. Nikhil Pal Singh, "The Black Panther Party and the 'Undeveloped Country' of the Left," in *The Black Panther Party [Reconsidered]*, ed. Charles E. Jones (Baltimore, MD: Black Classics, 1998), 59.

41. Robin D. G. Kelley, *Freedom Dreams: The Black Radical Imagination* (Boston: Beacon, 2002), ix; Cedric Johnson, "Dream On," *In These Times,* March 31, 2003, 24–26.

42. Referring to the work of Adolph Reed, Jerry G. Watts, Dean Robinson, and this author, Peniel Joseph contends that although "all these works offer insightful analysis of the era, they are hampered by their quest to find out why the movement failed, rather than search for the way in which Black Power unfolded historically." See Peniel Joseph, ed., *The Black Power Movement: Rethinking the Civil Rights— Black Power Era* (London: Routledge, 2006), 288–89; Joseph, *Waiting 'Til the Midnight Hour.*

43. W. E. B. Du Bois, *Black Reconstruction in America, 1860–1880* (New York: Atheneum, 1962 [orig. pub. 1935]).

1. The "Negro Revolution" and Cold War America: Revolutionary Politics and Racial Conservatism in the Work of Harold Cruse

1. Christopher Lasch, "The Trouble with Black Power," *New York Review of Books* 10, no. 4 (1968): 4–14.

2. Harold Cruse, *Rebellion or Revolution?* (New York: William Morrow, 1968), 13; Jerry Watts, ed., *Harold Cruse's* The Crisis of the Negro Intellectual *Reconsidered* (New York: Routledge, 2004), 6. Watts describes Cruse in a similar vein: "He aspires to be a Promethean figure who is willing to disturb the mediocre quietude of the black intelligentsia and accept the personal costs of doing so."

3. Harold Cruse, "Black and White: Outlines of the Next Stage, Part I," *Black World* 20, no. 3 (1971): 19–41, 66–71.

4. Jerry Watts, "Escaping the Ghost of Harold Cruse," in *Heroism and the Black Intellectual: Ralph Ellison, Politics and Afro-American Intellectual Life* (Chapel Hill, NC: University of North Carolina Press, 1994); Harold Cruse, *The Essential Harold Cruse: A Reader,* ed. William Jelani Cobb (New York: Palgrave, 2002); Watts, ed., *Harold Cruse's;* Hortense Spillers, "The Crisis of the Negro Intellectual: A Post-Date," *Boundary 2* 21, no. 3 (1994): 65–116; Beverly Guy-Sheftall, "Reconstructing a Black Female Intellectual Tradition: Commentary on Harold Cruse's *The Crisis of the Negro Intellectual,*" in *Voices of the African Diaspora,* vol. IX, no. 1 (1994); Winston James, "Postscript—Harold Cruse and the West Indians: Critical Remarks on *The Crisis of the Negro Intellectual,*" in *Holding Aloft the Banner of Ethiopia: Caribbean Radicalism in Early Twentieth Century America* (London: Verso, 1998), 262–91; Harold Cruse, *The Crisis of the Negro Intellectual* (New York: New York Review Books Classics, 2005 [orig. pub. 1967]).

5. Karl Marx, "For a Ruthless Criticism of Everything Existing" (Letter from Marx to Arnold Ruge) in *The Marx-Engels Reader,* ed. Robert C. Tucker (New York: W.W. Norton Company, 1978), 13. The following passage from volume 3 of *Capital* reflects Marx's contention that materialism serves as a powerful antidote to ideological mystification: "It is always the direct relationship of the owners of the conditions

of production to the direct producers—a relation always naturally corresponding to a definite state in the development of methods of labour and thereby its social productivity—which reveals the innermost secret, the hidden basis of the entire social structure, and with it the political form of the relation of sovereignty and dependence, in short, the corresponding specific form of the state. This does not prevent the same economic basis—the same from the standpoint of its main conditions—due to innumerable different empirical circumstances, natural environment, racial relations, external historical influences, etc., from showing infinite variations and gradations in appearance, which can be ascertained only by analysis of the empirically given circumstances." Karl Marx, *Capital* (Oxford, UK: Oxford University Press, 1999), 459–60.

6. Kevin Mattson, *Intellectuals in Action: The Origins of the New Left and Radical Liberalism, 1945–1970* (University Park, PA: Pennsylvania State University Press, 2002); Daniel Horowitz, "Rethinking Betty Freidan and The Feminine Mystique: Labor Union Radicalism and Feminism in Cold War America," *American Quarterly* 48, no. 1 (1996): 1–42; C. Wright Mills, "The New Left," in *Power, Politics and People,* ed. Irving Louis Horowitz (New York: Oxford University Press, 1963).

7. Nelson Lichtenstein, *State of the Union: A Century of American Labor* (Princeton: Princeton University Press, 2003), 25; Meg Jacobs, "'Democracy's Third Estate': New Deal Politics and the Construction of a 'Consuming Public,'" *International Labor and Working-Class History* 55 (1999): 27–51.

8. See Antonio Negri, "Keynes and the Capitalist Theory of the State," in *Labor of Dionysus: A Critique of the State-Form,* ed. Michael Hardt and Antonio Negri (Minneapolis, MN: University of Minnesota Press 1994), 23–51; Mario Tronti, "Social Capital," *Telos* 17 (1973): 98–121; Timothy W. Luke, "The Modern Service State: Public Power in America from the New Deal to the New Beginning," in *Race, Politics and Culture,* ed. Adolph Reed Jr. (Westport, CT: Greenwood Press, 1986), 184–205; Ruth O'Brien, *Worker's Paradox: The Republican Origins of New Deal Labor Policy, 1886–1935* (Chapel Hill, NC: University of North Carolina Press, 1998).

9. Lichtenstein, *State of the Union,* 35.

10. Harry Braverman, *Labor and Monopoly Capital: The Degradation of Work in the Twentieth Century* (New York: Monthly Review Press, 1974); David Montgomery, *Worker's Control in America: Studies in the History of Work, Technology and Labor Struggles* (Cambridge, UK: Cambridge University Press, 1979); Rosalyn Baxandall et al., eds., *Technology, the Labor Process and the Working Class* (New York: Monthly Review Press, 1976); Mark Wardell, Thomas Steiger, and Peter Meiksins, eds., *Rethinking the Labor Process* (Albany, NY: State University of New York Press, 1999).

11. David Caute, *The Great Fear: The Anti-Communist Purge under Truman and Eisenhower* (London: Secker and Warburg, 1978); Ellen Schrecker, *Many Are the Crimes: McCarthyism in America* (Boston, MA: Little Brown and Company, 1998); Ellen Schrecker, *Age of McCarthyism: A Brief History with Documents* (Boston, MA: Bedford Books, 1994); Victor S. Navasky, *Naming Names* (New York: Viking Press, 1980); George Lipsitz, *Class and Culture in Cold War America: "A Rainbow at Midnight"* (New York: Praeger Publishers, 1981).

12. Cruse, *Rebellion or Revolution?,* 4.

13. Van Gosse, "Locating the Black Intellectual: An Interview with Harold Cruse," *Radical History Review* 71 (1998): 106.

14. Cruse, *Rebellion or Revolution?*, 15.

15. Ibid., 8.

16. Ibid., 13.

17. Ibid., 8.

18. Van Gosse, "More than just a Politician: Notes on the Life and Times of Harold Cruse," in *Harold Cruse's* The Crisis of the Negro Intellectual *Reconsidered*, ed. Jerry G. Watts (New York: Routledge, 2004), 20–21.

19. For varying accounts of this trip, see LeRoi Jones, "Cuba Libre," in *Home: Social Essays* (New York: William Morrow, 1966 [orig. pub. 1960]); Amiri Baraka, *The Autobiography of LeRoi Jones* (New York: Freundlich Books, 1984), 163–67; Harold Cruse, "A Negro Looks at Cuba," in *The Essential Harold Cruse: A Reader*, ed. Harold Cruse (New York: Palgrave, 2002), 7–20; Harold Cruse, *The Crisis of the Negro Intellectual* (New York: William Morrow, 1967), 356–57; John Henrik Clarke, "Journey to the Sierra Maestra," *Freedomways* 1, no. 2 (1961): 32–35; Komozi Woodard, *Nation within a Nation: Amiri Baraka (LeRoi Jones) and Black Power Politics* (Chapel Hill, NC: University of North Carolina Press, 1999), 52–54; Van Gosse, *Where the Boys Are: Cuba, Cold War America and the Making of a New Left* (London and New York: Verso, 1993), 184–88; Cynthia Young, "Havana Up in Harlem: LeRoi Jones, Harold Cruse and the Making of a Cultural Revolution," *Science & Society* 65, no. 1 (2001): 12–38.

20. Cruse, *The Essential Harold Cruse*, xviii.

21. Gosse, "More than just a Politician," 35.

22. Ibid., 360.

23. Cruse, *Crisis of the Negro Intellectual*, 373.

24. Dean E. Robinson, *Black Nationalism in American Politics and Thought* (Cambridge, UK: Cambridge University Press, 2001); Nikol Alexander, "From Endangerment to Atonement: Reading Gender, Race and Nationalism in the Million Man March" (PhD diss., Rutgers University, 1999); Kevin Gaines, "Black Americans' Racial Uplift Ideology as 'Civilizing Mission': Pauline E. Hopkins on Race and Imperialism," in *Cultures of United States Imperialism*, ed. Amy Kaplan and Donald E. Pease (Durham, NC: Duke University Press, 1993); Kevin Gaines, *Uplifting the Race: Black Leadership, Politics, and Culture in the Twentieth Century* (Chapel Hill, NC: University of North Carolina Press, 1996); Judith Stein, *The World of Marcus Garvey: Race and Class in Modern Society* (Baton Rouge: Louisiana State University Press, 1986).

25. Wilson J. Moses, *The Golden Age of Black Nationalism: 1850–1925* (New York: Oxford University Press, 1978), 7. Writing at the height of the Black Power era and in a more sympathetic vein than Moses, James Turner also characterized black political thought as being inherently constitutive of discursive features of American society due to processes of acculturation. In the language of the age, he argued: "The Black man lives in a symbiotic relationship with the white man, held in a subordinate position by the caste system. Furthermore, the black man is governed by the white dominant group, especially in the areas of religion and social morality . . . Thus, an ironic aspect of Black popular movements is the way in which white ideas act as a catalysts [*sic*] of nationalist feelings." See James Turner, "Black Nationalism: The Inevitable Response," *Black World* January (1971): 13.

26. See Mark Naison, "Marxism and Black Radicalism in America: Notes on a Long (and Continuing) Journey," *Radical America* 5, no. 3 (1971): 3–25; Mark

Naison, "Historical Notes on Blacks and American Communism: The Harlem Experience," *Science and Society* 42 (1978): 324–43; Mark Naison, *Communists in Harlem During the Depression* (New York: Grove Press, 1984); Robin D.G. Kelley, *Hammer and Hoe: Alabama Communists During the Great Depression* (Chapel Hill: University of North Carolina Press, 1990); Gerald Horne, "The Red and the Black: The Communist Party and African Americans in Historical Perspective," in *New Studies in the Politics and Culture of U.S. Communism*, ed. Michael E. Brown et al. (New York: Monthly Review Press, 1993); William J. Maxwell, *New Negro, Old Left: African-American Writing and Communism Between the Wars* (New York: Columbia University Press, 1999); Bill V. Mullen, *Popular Fronts: Chicago and African-American Cultural Politics, 1935–1946* (Urbana: University of Illinois Press, 1999); Brent Hayes Edwards, "The 'Autonomy' of Black Radicalism," *Social Text* 67, no. 2 (2001): 1–13; Nikhil Pal Singh, "Retracing the Black-Red Thread," *American Literary History* 15, no. 4 (2003): 830–40.

27. Naison, *Communists in Harlem*, xv.

28. Cruse, *Crisis of the Negro Intellectual*, 347.

29. Despite their later efforts to discourage rigid adherence to any specific formula or program, the ten-point program in Marx and Engels's *Communist Manifesto* has eclipsed other, more radical democratic routes to socialism offered in later writings such as Marx's report on the Paris commune. See Karl Marx, *The Civil War in France* (New York: International Publishers, 1940); Robert J. Antonio, *Marx and Modernity* (London: Blackwell Publishers, 2002), 40–47.

30. Cruse, *Rebellion or Revolution?*, 142–43.

31. Ibid., 140.

32. Harold Cruse, "Revolutionary Nationalism and the Afro-American," in *Rebellion or Revolution?* (New York: William Morrow, 1968), 75.

33. Jonathan Neale, *A People's History of the Vietnam War* (New York: New Press, 2003); Marilyn Young, *The Vietnam Wars, 1945–1990* (New York: Harper Perennial, 1991); James Gibson, *The Perfect War: Technowar in Vietnam* (Boston, MA: Atlantic Monthly Press, 1986); Christian Appy, *The Working-Class War: American Combat Soldiers and Vietnam* (Chapel Hill, NC: University of North Carolina Press, 1993); Jules Roy, *The Battle of Dienbienphu* (New York: Carroll and Graf, 1984).

34. Caroline Elkins, *Imperial Reckoning: The Untold Story of Britain's Gulag in Kenya* (New York: Henry Holt, 2005); David Anderson, *Histories of the Hanged: The Dirty War in Kenya and the End of Empire* (New York: W. W. Norton and Company, 2005); Wunyabari O. Maloba, *Mau Mau and Kenya: An Analysis of a Peasant Revolt* (Bloomington, IN: Indiana University Press, 1998); Roxanne Lynn Doty, *Imperial Encounters: The Politics of Representation in North–South Relations* (Minneapolis, MN: University of Minnesota Press, 1996); Maina wa Kinyatti, ed., *Kenya's Freedom Struggle: The Dedan Kimathi Papers* (London: Zed Books, 1987); Frank Furedi, *The Mau Mau War in Perspective* (Athens, OH: Ohio University Press, 1989).

35. Richard Wright, *The Color Curtain: A Report on the Bandung Conference* (Jackson, Miss.: University Press of Mississippi, 1956).

36. C. L. R. James, "The Revolutionary Answer to the Negro Problem in the USA," in *The C.L.R. James Reader*, ed. Anna Grimshaw (Oxford, UK, and Cambridge, US: Blackwell Publishers, 1992), 188–89; for precursors of the black vanguard thesis within James's earlier writings and that of others within the Trotskyite left, see

C. L. R. James, *C.L.R. James on the "Negro Question,"* ed. Scott McLemee (Jackson, MS: University Press of Mississippi, 1996); Max Shachtman, *Race and Revolution* (London and New York: Verso, 2003).

37. For discussion of the Johnson–Forest Tendency's origins, history, and internal debates, see Grace Lee Boggs, *Living for Change: An Autobiography* (Minneapolis, MN: University of Minnesota Press, 1998); Grace Lee Boggs, "C.L.R. James: Organizing in the U.S.A., 1938–1953," in *C.L.R. James: His Intellectual Legacies,* ed. Selwyn R. Cudjoe and William E. Cain (Amherst, MA: University of Massachusetts Press, 1995), 163–72; Raya Dunayevskaya, *For the Record: The Johnson–Forest Tendency or the Theory of State Capitalism, 1941–1951: Its Vicissitudes and Ramifications* (Detroit: News and Letters Committee, 1972); Paul Buhle, *C.L.R. James: The Artist as Revolutionary* (London: Verso, 1988); Kent Worcester, *C.L.R. James: A Political Biography* (Albany, NY: State University of New York Press, 1996); Bill V. Mullen, *Afro-Orientalism* (Minneapolis, MN: University of Minnesota Press, 2004) 113–62.

38. According to Cruse, Boggs criticized his draft program for the Freedom Now Party, which appeared in the February 1964 issue of *Liberator* magazine. However, the circumstances surrounding this development and Cruse's curious published response cast doubts on the plausibility of his charges. In his characteristic form, Cruse, in *The Crisis of the Negro Intellectual,* dismissed Boggs's alleged criticism: "James Boggs' letter showed the limiting effect Marxist training has on the Negro's social imagination, within the context of American conditions. Marxist conceptions become mechanically rooted in the thinking patterns much as do religious dogmas—so much so that if the Negro Marxist does not free his mind from these dogmatic categories he remains forever unable to deal with new American realities." Cruse does not mention this letter's substantive content nor does he cite specific passages to support his claims. Instead, he reiterates his stock criticism of black Marxists, which hardly applied to Boggs at the time given the convergence of his and Cruse's evolving positions on black autonomy and left political organizing. See Cruse, *The Crisis of the Negro Intellectual,* 418–419; "Freedom Now Party: Draft National Platform," *Liberator* February (1964): 4–5.

39. James Boggs, *The American Revolution: Pages from a Negro Worker's Notebook* (New York: Monthly Review Press, 1963), 33.

40. Boggs, *American Revolution,* 43.

41. Boggs, *American Revolution,* 84–85.

42. Herbert Marcuse, *One Dimensional Man: Studies in the Ideology of Advanced Industrial Society* (Boston, MA: Beacon Press, 1964), 256–57; Norman Mailer's 1957 essay "The White Negro" is also representative of the black vanguard thesis. In an essay that reflected rebel Beat sensibilities and playfully embraced Jim Crow caricatures of black life, Mailer saw "the Negro" as a primal, rebellious force cutting a path out of fifties banality Mailer wrote: "What a man feels is the impulse for his creative effort, and if an alien but nonetheless passionate instinct about the meaning of life has come so unexpectedly from a virtually illiterate people, come out of the most intense conditions of exploitation, cruelty, violence, frustration and lust and yet has succeeded as an instinct in keeping this tortured people alive, then it is perhaps possible that the Negro holds more of the tail of the expanding elephant of truth than the radical, and if this is so, the radical humanist could do worse than to brood upon the phenomenon." Norman Mailer, "The White Negro: Superficial Reflections

on the Hipster," in *Advertisements for Myself* (New York: G.P. Putnam's Sons, 1959), 357.

43. Jean-Paul Sartre's appreciation of anticolonial struggles was not without its limitations. As David Macey and others have noted, Sartre's celebration of Fanon's emancipatory violence sharply contrasted his pro-Zionist politics. Sartre defended Israeli aggression in the Six Day War of June 1967. Because of such stances, Fanon's wife, Josie, insisted that Sartre's preface be removed from a 1968 reprint of *Les Damnés de la terre*. In a telegram to François Maspero, Josie Fanon requested: "Please immediately omit from all future editions Jean-Paul Sartre's preface to Franz Fanon's book *Les Damnés de la terre* because of the pro-Zionist and pro-imperialist position taken by its author with respect to Zionist aggression against Arab peoples." See David Macey, *Frantz Fanon: A Biography* (New York: Picador, 2001), 467.

44. In a subsequent essay, Marcuse alluded to the limitations of the black vanguard thesis while inevitably reasserting its salience: "The long range power of the black rebellion is further threatened by deep division within this class (the rise of a Negro bourgeoisie), and by its marginal (in terms of the capitalist system) social function. The majority of the black population does not occupy a decisive position in the process of production and the white organizations of labor have not exactly gone out of their way to change this situation. In the cynical terms of the system, a large part of this population is 'expendable,' that is to say it makes no essential contribution to the productivity of the system. Consequentially, the powers that be may not hesitate to apply extreme measures of suppression if the movement becomes dangerous. The fact is that, at present in the United States, the black population appears as the 'most natural' force of rebellion." Herbert Marcuse, *An Essay on Liberation* (Boston, MA: Beacon Press, 1969), 58.

45. Enrique Larana, Hank Johnston and Joseph R. Gusfield, eds. *New Social Movements: From Ideology to Identity* (Philadelphia: Temple University Press, 1994). For alternative views of "new social movements," see Antonio Negri and Nick Dyer-Witheford's respective discussions of the socialized worker and Stanley Aronowitz's characterization of these new agents as "modalities of class." Antonio Negri, *The Politics of Subversion: A Manifesto for the Twenty-First Century* (Cambridge, UK: Polity Press, 1989); Nick Dyer-Witheford, *CyberMarx: Cycles and Circuits of Struggle in High-Technology Capitalism* (Urbana, IL and Chicago: University of Illinois Press, 1999), 82–90; Stanley Aronowitz, *How Class Works: Power and Social Movements* (New Haven, CT: Yale University Press, 2002).

46. Harold Cruse, "A Reply to Richard Greenleaf," in *For A New America: Essays in History and Politics from Studies on the Left, 1959–1967*, ed. James Weinstein and David W. Eakins (New York: Random House, 1970), 379.

47. Cruse, *Rebellion or Revolution?*, 147–48.

48. Ibid., 148.

49. Cruse, *Crisis of the Negro Intellectual*, 158.

50. Cruse, *Crisis of the Negro Intellectual*, 357. In his account of the 1960 Fair Play for Cuba Committee (FPCC) trip to Cuba, Cruse wrote: "I was admittedly pro-Castro, but there were too many communists around acting imperious and important. Moreover, there was the obvious and unclarified position of the Cuban Negro to consider ... For [LeRoi] Jones's impressionable generation this revolutionary indoctrination, this ideological enchantment, was almost irresistible. And here,

vicariously, a crucial question was engendered: *What did it all mean and how did it relate to the Negro in America?"*

51. Cruse, *Crisis of the Negro Intellectual,* 371.

52. Ibid., 64.

53. Ernest Kaiser, "The Crisis of the Negro Intellectual," *Freedomways* 9, no. 1 (1969); Marshall McLuhan, *Understanding Media: The Extensions of Man* (Corte Madera, CA: Gingko Press, 2003).

54. Theodor Adorno and Max Horkheimer, *The Dialectic of Enlightenment* (New York: Continuum International Publishing Group, 1976); David Noble, *Digital Diploma Mills* (New York: Monthly Review Press, 2003); Jodi Dean, *Publicity's Secret: How Technoculture Capitalizes on Democracy* (Ithaca, NY: Cornell University Press, 2002); Christine Rosen, "The Age of Egocasting," *The New Atlantis: Journal of Technology and Society,* no. 7 (2004/2005).

55. Cruse, *Crisis of the Negro Intellectual,* 64.

56. Here Cruse's views regarding the emancipatory possibilities of technology and the contingent nature of capitalist development anticipate more recent arguments of "autonomist" Marxism. From the autonomist perspective, new communicative technologies often serve emancipatory ends and even facilitate the expansion and coalescence of social struggles. For example, the New Left made skillful use of televised news coverage, the mimeograph machine, and the Watts telephone line as organizing tools. In turn, civil rights and antiwar activists were able to widen support for localized struggles and coordinate activity across wide geographic regions in ways that were not possible at earlier historical moments. For an engaging overview of the autonomist tradition, see Dyer-Witheford, *CyberMarx,* 63–90; See also, Harry Cleaver, *Reading Capital Politically* (Leeds, UK: Anti/Theses, 2000); Maurizio Lazzarato, "Immaterial Labour," in *Radical Thought in Italy,* ed. Paolo Virno and Michael Hardt (Minneapolis, MN: University of Minnesota Press, 1996); Katie Vann, "On the Valorization of Informatic Labour," Ephemera 4 (3): 246–66; Paolo Virno, "Notes on the General Intellect," in Marxism Beyond Marxism, ed. Saree Makdisi, Cesare Casarino and Rebecca E. Karl (London and New York: Routledge 1996), 265–272.

57. Harold Cruse, "Rebellion or Revolution? Part I," in *Rebellion or Revolution?* (New York: William Morrow, 1968), 114.

58. See James S. Allen, *Negro Liberation* (New York: International Pamphlets, 1932); Harry Haywood, *Negro Liberation* (New York: International Publishers, 1948); Oscar Berland, "The Communist Perspective on the 'Negro Question' in America, 1919–1931," *Science & Society* 63, no. 4 (1999–2000), 411–32, and 64, no. 3 (2000), 194–217; Harvey Klehr and William Thompson, "Self-Determination in the Black Belt: Origins of a Communist Policy," *Labor History* 30, no. 3 (1989), 354–66.

59. Don Freeman, "Nationalist Student Conference," *Liberator* 5, no. 7 (1964), 18; James Boggs, *Racism and the Class Struggle* (New York: Monthly Review Press, 1970); James Boggs and Grace Lee Boggs, "The City is the Black Man's Land," in James Boggs, *Racism and the Class Struggle: Further Pages from a Black Worker's Notebook* (New York: Monthly Review Press, 1970); Stokely Carmichael and Charles V. Hamilton, *Black Power: The Politics of Liberation in America* (New York: Random House, 1967); Eldridge Cleaver, "Revolution in the White Mother Country and National Liberation in the Black Colony," *North American Review,* 26 October 1968 and 30 November 1968; Robert Blauner *Racial Oppression in America* (New York: Harper & Row, 1972);

Robert Allen, *Black Awakening in Capitalist America: An Analytical History* (New York: Doubleday, 1969); Joseph Hannibal Howard III, "How to End Colonial Domination of Black America," *Black World* 19, no. 3 (1970): 9–10. In addition to its currency in African American radical discourse, the colonial analogy was employed by radical Chicano activists and academics during the period. See Rudolfo Acuña, *Occupied America: The Chicano's Struggle Toward Liberation* (San Francisco: Canfield Press, 1972); Tomas Almaguer, "Class, Race and Chicano Oppression," *Socialist Revolution* 25 (1975); Mario Barrera, *Race and Class in the Southwest: A Theory of Racial Inequality* (Notre Dame, IN: University of Notre Dame Press, 1979).

60. Quoted in Harold Cruse, "Revolutionary Nationalism and the Afro-American," in *Rebellion or Revolution?* (New York: Random House, 1968), 76 (originally appeared in *Studies on the Left* 2, no. 3 (1962): 12–26). In his introduction to the reissue of Cedric Robinson's *Black Marxism,* Robin Kelley discusses the influence of Cruse's 1962 essay within the Afro-American Association, an organization of radical nationalist students in California's East Bay. In addition, Van Gosse reports that Donald Freeman encouraged the cadre of the Afro-American Association's successor, the Revolutionary Action Movement to "seriously study" Cruse's article. See Cedric J. Robinson, *Black Marxism: The Making of the Black Radical Tradition* (Chapel Hill, NC: University of North Carolina Press, 2000), xv–xvi; Gosse, "More Than Just a Politician," 26.

61. Milton Gordon, *Assimilation in American Life: The Role of Race, Religion, and National Origins* (New York: Oxford University Press, 1964).

62. Nikhil Pal Singh, "Negro Exceptionalism: The Antinomies of Harold Cruse," in *Harold Cruse's* The Crisis of the Negro Intellectual *Reconsidered* (New York: Routledge, 2004), 88.

63. Cruse, *Crisis of the Negro Intellectual,* 7–8.

64. See Stephen Steinberg, *The Ethnic Myth: Race, Ethnicity and Class in America* (Boston, MA: Beacon Press, 2001); Micaela di Leonardo, " 'Why Can't They Be More Like Our Grandparents?' and Other Racial Fairytales," in Adolph Reed, Jr., ed. *Without Justice for All: The New Liberalism and Our Retreat from Racial Equality* (Boulder, CO: Westview Press, 1999).

65. Stephen Erie, *Rainbow's End: Irish-Americans and the Dilemmas of Urban Machine Politics, 1840–1985* (Berkeley, CA: University of California Press, 1988); Peter Eisinger, "Black Mayors and the Politics of Racial Economic Advancement," in *Readings in Urban Politics: Past, Present and Future,* ed. Harlan Hahn and Charles Levine (New York: Longman, 1984).

66. For his subsequent elaborations of black ethnic pluralism, see Harold Cruse, *Plural But Equal: A Critical Study of Blacks and Minorities and America's Plural Society* (New York: William Morrow, 1987); Harold Cruse, "A New Black Leadership Required," *New Politics* 2 (1999): 39–49.

67. Benedict Anderson, *Imagined Communities: Reflections on the Origin and Spread of Nationalism* (London and New York: Verso, 1991), 7.

68. See Harold Cruse, "An Afro-American's Cultural Views," in *Rebellion or Revolution?* (New York: William Morrow, 1968), 49. In this 1957 essay that originally appeared in the Parisian journal, *Présence Africaine,* Cruse wrote, "An American Negro cannot be understood culturally unless he is seen as a member of a detached ethnic bloc of people of African descent reared for three hundred years in the unmotherly bosom of Western Civilization."

69. Cruse, *Crisis of the Negro Intellectual,* 433. Cruse wrote: "But the fact that the American Negro was also a subject of a special kind of North American domestic colonialism was never fully accepted either by the Negro himself or by Africans or West Indians."

70. For a more recent defense of the relevancy of the colonial analogy, see Robert L. Allen, "Reassessing the Internal (Neo) Colonialism Theory," *Black Scholar* 35 (2005): 2–10.

71. Some more critical assessments of the internal colony thesis include Ronald Bailey, "Economic Aspects of the Black Internal Colony," *Review of Black Political Economy* 3, no. 4 (1973): 43–72; Donald Harris, "Black Ghetto as Internal Colony: A Theoretical Critique and Alternative Formulation," *Review of Black Political Economy* 2, no. 4 (1972): 3–3; Dean Robinson, *Black Nationalism in American Politics and Thought* (Cambridge, UK: Cambridge University Press, 2001), 81–84.

72. Ira Katznelson, *Black Men, White Cities: Race, Politics and Migration in the United States, 1900–1930 and Britain, 1948–1968* (New York: Oxford University Press, 1973); William Grimshaw, *Bitter Fruit: Black Politics and the Chicago Machine, 1931–1991* (Chicago: University of Chicago Press, 1992); Adolph Reed, Jr., "The 'Black Revolution' and the Reconstitution of Domination," in *Stirrings in the Jug: Black Politics in the Post-Segregation Era* (Minneapolis, MN: University of Minnesota Press, 1999); Kevin Gaines, *Uplifting the Race: Black Leadership, Politics, and Culture in the Twentieth Century* (Chapel Hill, NC: University of North Carolina Press, 1996).

73. On the spatial aspect of the colonial condition, Fanon wrote: "The zone where the natives live is not complimentary to the zone inhabited by the settlers. The two zones are opposed, but not in the service of a higher unity. Obedient to the rules of pure Aristotelian logic, they both follow the principle of reciprocal exclusivity. No conciliation is possible, for the two terms, one is superfluous." Fanon goes on to describe the native town as "a crouching village, a town on its knees, a town wallowing in the mire. It is the town of niggers and dirty Arabs." See Frantz Fanon, *The Wretched of the Earth* (New York: Grove Press, 1963), 38–39.

74. Stokely Carmichael and Charles V. Hamilton, *Black Power: The Politics of Liberation in America* (New York: Vintage, 1967).

75. Jean-François Bayart, *The State in Africa: The Politics of the Belly* (London and New York: Longman, 1993).

76. Penny Von Eschen, "The Cold War Seduction of Harold Cruse," in *Harold Cruse's* The Crisis of the Negro Intellectual *Reconsidered* (New York: Routledge, 2004), 170. Von Eschen describes the "Cold War seduction" of Cruse: "[Paul] Robeson and his allies were uncompromising in their insistence on making explicit and visible the lineaments of wealth and power that have shaped the modern world. Cruse, on the other hand, took the Cold War path of concentrating on racism at home while maintaining silence on the United States abroad. Cruse adopted the very assumptions of liberal hegemony that undergirded the deteriorating conditions of urban black Americans and the economic devastation against which he fought and which indeed he was prescient in grasping" (174–75).

77. Cruse, *Rebellion or Revolution?,* 186.

78. Ibid.

79. Cruse wrote: "The middle classes of Harlem that furnish community leadership are neither sovereign nor solvent; neither independent nor autonomous. They

thrive on the crumbs granted them by the power structure for keeping the unruly masses mollified. They are the recipients of those few well-paying jobs from white businesses—both inside Harlem and beyond. Others have gained possession of a few parcels of real estate property, or have opened up a successful business. They are the lawyers, doctors, accountants, public relations experts, etc. who are of the same stamp as others who have made their mark in Democratic or Republican politics. Here is this class-stratum of ghetto aristocrats, the ministers of churches vie with professional social workers and police chiefs over which brand of community uplift is best for soothing the tortured ghetto soul 'twixt Hell on earth and Heavenly hereafter." Cruse, *Crisis of the Negro Intellectual*, 90.

80. Cruse, "An Afro American's Cultural Views," 63.

81. Cruse, *Crisis of the Negro Intellectual*, 4.

82. Although generally critical of the disciplinary and patriarchial dimensions of nineties neo-black nationalism, Wahneema Lubiano's reading of nationalist sensibilities as "black common sense" echoes Cruse's argument and its limitations. She too mischaracterizes the historically contingent expressions of alienation and desires for autonomy circulating among many (but not all) blacks during the Reagan–Bush era and its Clintonian aftermath as transhistorical, essential traits of black political culture. Without fully acknowledging the consonance of these sensibilities within an historically particular neoconservative milieu, Lubiano concludes that black nationalism is "the cultural logic of black peoples' historical self-consciousness." Lubiano's treatment of black nationalism as the "everyday ideology" of African Americans may partially stem from the wide interpretative license afforded by textual analyses of popular culture, e.g. Hip Hop lyrics, Hollywood movies, etc. My point here is not to assert that Lubiano's or Cruse's claims might be better substantiated through other interpretative means, but rather to locate their desire to gauge the "Negro mood" within a longer-standing history of representational practices in black elite political discourse. As Kenneth Warren notes, "discussion and analyzing of literature and culture has been central to ventriloquizing a black collective state of mind . . . what has remained true of much African-Americanist inquiry has been the claim that expressive forms remain more crucial to a consideration of the conditions of black peoples than they do to considerations of other social groups." See Wahneema Lubiano, "Black Nationalism and Black Common Sense: Policing Ourselves and Others," in *The House that Race Built: Black Americans, U.S. Terrain*, ed. Wahneema Lubiano (New York: Pantheon Books, 1997), 232–52; Kenneth Warren, "The End(s) of African American Studies," *American Literary History* 12, no. 3 (2003): 637–55.

83. James Edward Smethurst, " 'Pat Your Foot and Turn the Corner': Amiri Baraka, the Black Arts movement and the Poetics of a Popular Avant-Garde," *African American Review* 37 (2003): 261–70.

84. See Cruse, *Crisis of the Negro Intellectual*, 420–48; James, "Harold Cruse and the West Indians," 262–91.

85. Singh argues that culture carries "different burdens" in *The Crisis of the Negro Intellectual*. The term operates as "the site for (1) articulating cohesive ideologies of group belonging ('cultural identity'); (2) intervening in the discriminatory organization and administration of the U.S. economy ('cultural apparatus'); and (3) rethinking leftist theories of social transformation ('cultural revolution')." Singh, "Negro Exceptionalism," 78.

86. Cruse, *Rebellion or Revolution?*, 124.

87. Ibid., 11.

88. Ibid., 12.

89. Adolph Reed offers a compelling critique of black cultural particularity during the Black Power era and its roots in nostalgia for southern folk culture. He notes: "This yearning was hypostatized to the level of a vague 'black culture'—a romantic retrieval of a vanishing black particularity. This vision of black culture, of course, was grounded in residual features of black rural life prior to migrations to the North. They were primarily cultural patterns that had once been enmeshed in a life-world knitted together by kinship, voluntary association, and production within a historical context of rural racial domination." See Adolph Reed, Jr., "The 'Black Revolution' and the Reconstitution of Domination," in *Stirrings in the Jug: Black Politics in the Post-Segregation Era* (Minneapolis, MN: University of Minnesota Press, 1999), 66–67; A formative version of this essay appeared in the neo-Marxist journal *Telos*. See Adolph Reed, Jr., "Black Particularity Reconsidered," *Telos* 39 (1979): 71–93; J. Martin Favor, *Authentic Blackness: The Folk in the New Negro Renaissance* (Durham, NC: Duke University Press, 1999); Langston Hughes, "The Negro Artist and the Racial Mountain," *The Nation*, 23 June 1926; George Schuyler, "The Negro Art Hokum," *The Nation*, 16 June 1926; W. E. B. DuBois, "The Criteria of Negro Art," *Crisis* 32 (1926) [all reprinted in David Levering Lewis, ed. *The Portable Harlem Renaissance Reader* (New York: Viking Press, 1994)].

90. Harold Cruse, "James Baldwin, the Theater and His Critics," in *The Essential Harold Cruse: A Reader*, ed. William Jelani Cobb (New York: Palgrave, 2002), 27–35; Addison Gayle, ed. *The Black Aesthetic* (Garden City, NY: Doubleday Publishers, 1971); Larry Neal, "New Space/The Growth of Black Consciousness in the Sixties," in *The Black Seventies*, ed. Floyd Barbour (Boston, MA: Porter Sargent Press, 1970); LeRoi Jones and Larry Neal, eds., *Black Fire: An Anthology of Afro-American Writing* (New York: William Morrow, 1968); Amiri Baraka, "The Black Aesthetic: We Are Our Feelings," *Black World* 18, no. 11 (1969): 5–6; Jennifer Jordan, "Cultural Nationalism in the 1960s: Politics and Poetry," in *Race, Politics and Culture*, ed. Adolph Reed (New York: Greenwood Press, 1986), 29–60; Jerry Watts, *Amiri Baraka: Politics and Art of a Black Intellectual* (New York: New York University Press, 2001), 141–258; Smethurst, " 'Pat Your Foot and Turn the Corner,' " 261–70.

91. Mikhail Bakunin, "Marx, the Bismarck of Socialism," in *Patterns of Anarchy*, ed. Leonard Krimerman and Lewis Perry (New York: Anchor Books, 1966), 89–90.

92. Ibid. Bakunin wrote: "There is in this programme another expression which is profoundly antipathetic to us revolutionary Anarchists who frankly want the complete emancipation of the peole; the expression to which I refer is the presentation of the proletariat, the whole society of toilers, as a "class" and not as a "mass." Do you know what that means? Neither more nor less than a new aristocracy, that of the workers of the factories and towns, to the exclusion of the millions who constitute the proletariat of the countryside and who in the anticipation of the Social Democrats of Germany will, in effect, become subjects of their great so-called People's State."

93. Lawrence Peter King and Iván Szelényi, *Theories of the New Class: Intellectuals and Power* (Minneapolis, MN: University of Minnesota Press, 2004).

94. Cruse, *Crisis of the Negro Intellectual*, 365.

95. Cruse, *Crisis of the Negro Intellectual,* 378–79.

96. Ibid., 370.

97. Adam Clayton Powell, "My Black Position Paper," in *Black Power Revolt,* ed. Floyd Barbour (Boston, MA: Extending Horizon Books, 1968), 257–60; Art Pollock, "'My Life's Philosophy': Adam Clayton Powell's 'Black Position Paper,'" *Journal of Black Studies* 4, no. 4 (1974): 457–62; Bayard Rustin, "From Protest to Politics: The Future of the Civil Rights Movement," *Commentary* 39 (1965): 25–31; Bayard Rustin, "'Black Power' and Coalition Politics," *Commentary* 42 (1966): 35–36; Bayard Rustin, "Coming of Age Politically," *Crisis* 79, no. 9 (November 1972): 296–98; Stephen Steinberg, "Bayard Rustin and the Rise and Decline of the Black Protest Movement," *New Politics* 6, no. 3 (1997); See also John D'Emilio, *Lost Prophet: The Life and Times of Bayard Rustin* (New York: Free Press, 2003); Jervis Anderson, *Bayard Rustin: Troubles I've Seen* (New York: HarperCollins Publishers, 1997); Daniel Levine, *Bayard Rustin and the Civil Rights Movement* (New Brunswick, NJ: Rutgers University Press, 2000).

98. Stephen Steinberg, "Bayard Rustin and the Rise and Decline of Protest Politics," *New Politics* 6, no. 3 (1997); See also John D'Emilio, *Lost Prophet: The Life and Times of Bayard Rustin* (New York: Free Press, 2003); Anderson, *Bayard Rustin*; Levine, *Bayard Rustin and the Civil Rights Movement.*

99. Rustin, "'Black Power' and Coalition Politics," 35–36.

100. Ibid., 29. On the value of the black vote, Rustin writes: "the urban negro vote will grow in importance in the coming years. If there is anything positive in the spread of the ghetto, it is the potential political power base thus created and to realize this potential is one of the most challenging and urgent tasks before the civil rights movement."

101. Ibid., 29.

102. Rustin, "Protest to Politics," 65.

103. Cruse, *Rebellion or Revolution?,* 129.

104. Other writers such as Jerry Watts, Beverly Guy-Sheftall, and James Hall note the limited definition of "intellectuals" operative in Cruse's work. Cruse focused on a narrow segment of male literati (with the exception of Lorraine Hansberry) rather than those who work in the visual arts, dance, or music in his critique of intellectuals. See Jerry Watts, "Thirteen Theses Nailed to the Door of Harold Cruse," in *Harold Cruse's* The Crisis of the Negro Intellectual *Reconsidered,* 307–8; Guy-Sheftall, "Reconstructing a Black Female Intellectual Tradition" and James C. Hall, "The African American Musician as Intellectual," in *Harold Cruse's* The Crisis of the Negro Intellectual *Reconsidered,* 109–19.

105. Cruse, *Crisis of the Negro Intellectual,* 96.

106. See Van Gosse, "An Interview with Harold Cruse," 113; Singh, "Negro Exceptionalism," 74.

107. Gosse, "More than just a Politician," 17–41.

108. Jones, "Cuba Libre," 13.

109. Cruse, Crisis of the Negro Intellectual, 356.

110. Ibid., 362. Cruse wrote: "They were interested, after a fashion, in politics, economics and culture, but not at all interested in political, economic, and cultural organization *per se*. The Jones who could set up the Black Arts Theater and School in 1965 was not the Jones of 1961. Although Jones and his trend considered themselves the new wave, once they had set up their organizations they proceeded to do the

exact same thing every other civil rights trend was doing—they went out on protest demonstrations."

2. Return of the Native: Amiri Baraka (LeRoi Jones), the New Nationalism, and Black Power Politics

1. Harold Cruse, *The Crisis of the Negro Intellectual* (New York: William Morrow, 1967), 355.

2. Jerry G. Watts, Amiri Baraka: *The Politics and Art of a Black Intellectual* (New York: New York University Press, 2001), 349.

3. Some of the many literary appraisals of Baraka include the following: Harry Elam, *Taking It to the Streets: The Social Protest Theater of Luis Valdez and Amiri Baraka* (Ann Arbor: University of Michigan Press, 2001); Kimberly W. Benston, Baraka: The Renegade and the Mask (New Haven: Yale University Press, 1976); Kimberly W. Benston, *Imamu Amiri Baraka: A Collection of Critical Essays* (Englewood Cliffs, NJ: Prentice-Hall, 1978); Sandra Garrett Shannon, "Baraka, Black Ethos and the Black Arts movement: A Study of Amiri Baraka's Drama during the Black Arts movement from 1964 to 1969," (PhD diss., University of Maryland, 1986); Werner Sollors, *Amiri Baraka/LeRoi Jones: The Quest for "Populist Modernism."* (New York: Columbia University Press, 1978).

4. See LeRoi Jones, *Black Magic Poetry: Collected Poetry, 1961–1967* (Indianapolis and New York: Bobbs-Merrill, 1969). This volume includes *Target Study* (1963–1965) as well as *Sabotage* (1961–1963) and *Black Art* (1965–1966). The poems in *Target Study* reflect Jones's increasingly strident racial politics and its title conjures the imagery of a looming race war. Jones explains, "Target Study is trying to really study, like bomber crews do the soon to be destroyed cities. Less passive now less uselessly 'literary.' Trying to see, trying to understand . . . 'Will the machinegunners please step forward . . .' trying as Margaret Walker says, 'to fashion a way,' to clean up and move."

5. LeRoi Jones, "Return of the Native," in *Black Magic Poetry,* 108.

6. Ibid.

7. Ibid.

8. The full translation of Frantz Fanon's masterwork was published by Grove Press in 1965 and widely reviewed in the American press. See Donald Mintz, "Find Something Different," Washington Evening Star, 23 April 1965; Perry London, "Multi-faceted Treatise on Colonial Revolution," Los Angeles Times, 23 May 1965; "Speaking for the African Masses," Houston Chronicle, 2 May 1965; Alfred L. Malabre Jr., "A Disturbing Diatribe from the Third World," Wall Street Journal, 23 July 1965; Nat Hentoff, "Bursting into History," The New Yorker, 15 January 1966; William V. Shannon, "Negro Violence vs. the American Dream," New York Times, 27 July 1967. Fanon was born in the French Caribbean colony of Martinique and educated in psychiatry and medicine in Lyon, France. His most fertile intellectual period came after he moved to Algeria to work at that colony's largest psychiatric hospital, Blida-Joinville. Through his experiences as a clinician and his political work with the anticolonial Front de Libération Nationale, Fanon developed a keen analysis of the dynamics of racial alienation under colonialism. His masterwork *The Wretched of the Earth* rapidly became required reading among American black

radicals and the wider New Left. The text is written with an incredible sense of personal and revolutionary urgency—Fanon dictated much of the manuscript to his wife, Josie, as his health deteriorated and literally edited the galley proofs from his deathbed. Surely, American radicals struggling to find alternatives to Cold War liberalism found his brilliant diagnosis of colonial alienation and his prescription of revolutionary violence especially seductive. For Fanon, colonialism was achieved and maintained through violence, and only the comparable violent counteraction by the oppressed could create a new, authentically democratic political community. See David Macey, *Frantz Fanon: A Biography* (New York: Picador, 2000).

9. Frantz Fanon, *The Wretched of the Earth* (New York: Grove Press, 1963), 148. Fanon "slightly stretched" Marxist categories to capture the unique class dynamics of the colonial milieu. Unlike the nineteenth-century industrial European societies with large proletarian populations that inspired and informed Marx's writings, in French Algeria, Fanon encountered a society with a smattering of white settlers, an only slightly larger native middle class, and an expansive peasantry. For Fanon, the native bourgeoisie were pivotal to the process of national liberation. Under colonialism, the native bourgeoisie served a conciliatory function between colonizers and the native peasantry. Fanon heralded the moment when the native intellectuals shattered the myths of their colonial education and placed their expertise in service of national liberation, acting in solidarity with the impoverished masses.

10. Ibid., 150.

11. Ibid.

12. Amiri Baraka, *The Autobiography of LeRoi Jones* (New York: Freundlich Books, 1984); Cruse, *The Crisis of the Negro Intellectual*, 274–75; Fred W. McDarrah and Gloria S. McDarrah, *Beat Generation: Glory Days in Greenwich Village* (New York: Schirmer Books, 1996); A. Robert Lee, *The Beat Generation Writers* (London: Pluto, 1996); Paulette Pennington-Jones, "From Brother LeRoi Jones Through the System of Dante's Hell to Imamu Ameer Baraka," *Journal of Black Studies* 4, no. 2 (1973): 195–214.

13. Hettie Jones, How I Became *Hettie Jones* (New York: E.P. Dutton, 1990); Barrett Watten, "What I See in How I Became *Hettie Jones*," in *Girls Who Wore Black: Women Writing the Beat Generation*, ed. Ronna C. Johnson and Nancy M. Grace (New Brunswick, NJ: Rutgers University Press, 2002), 96–118; Deborah Thompson, "Keeping Up with the Joneses: The Naming of Racial Identities in the Autobiographical Writings of LeRoi Jones/Amiri Baraka, Hettie Jones and Lisa Jones," *College Literature* 29.1 (2002): 83–101.

14. Amiri Baraka, interview with the author, tape recording, by telephone, 13 March 2000. For varying accounts of this trip, its background, and impact on Baraka and African American radicalism, see LeRoi Jones, "Cuba Libre," [orig. pub. 1960], reprinted in *Home: Social Essays* (New York: William Morrow, 1966); Amiri Baraka, *The Autobiography of LeRoi Jones*, 163–67; Cruse, *The Crisis of the Negro Intellectual*, 356–57; Harold Cruse, "A Negro Looks at Cuba," in *The Essential Harold Cruse* (New York: Palgrave, 2002), 7–20; Harold Cruse, "Les Noirs et l'idée de révolte (The Blacks and the Idea of Revolt)," in *Rebellion or Revolution?* (New York: William Morrow, 1968), 168–92; John Henrik Clarke, "Journey to the Sierra Maestra," *Freedomways* (1961): 32–35; Cynthia Young, "Havana Up in Harlem: LeRoi Jones, Harold Cruse and the Making of a Cultural Revolution," *Science & Society* 65, no. 1 (2001): 12–38;

Komozi Woodard, *Nation Within a Nation: Amiri Baraka (LeRoi Jones) and Black Power Politics* (Chapel Hill, NC: University of North Carolina Press, 1999), 52–54; Van Gosse, *Where the Boys Are: Cuba, Cold War America and the Making of a New Left* (London: Verso, 1993), 184–88; Timothy B. Tyson, *Radio Free Dixie: Robert F. Williams and the Roots of Black Power* (Chapel Hill, NC: University of North Carolina Press, 1999), 220–43.

15. Baraka, *The Autobiography of LeRoi Jones,* 165–66.

16. Sollors, *Amiri Baraka,* 4; Watts, *Amiri Baraka,* 52.

17. Jones, "Cuba Libre," 42.

18. Ibid., 42–43.

19. Baraka, *The Autobiography of LeRoi Jones,* 164.

20. Jones's 1960 essay "Cuba Libre" was well received and widely read at least within the budding New Left circles in and beyond New York City. The essay was reprinted numerous times after its initial publication in *Evergreen Review.* "Cuba Libre" appeared in the Winter 1960 issue of *Kulchur.* In January 1961, the essay was published as an FPCC pamphlet. "Cuba Libre" was also included as the lead essay in Jones's 1966 collection, *Home.* In his autobiography, Baraka recalls the spirit of the revolutionary Cuba that he was trying to convey and his awe following this first journalistic success: "When I returned I was shaken more deeply than even I realized. The arguments I'd had with my old poet comrades increased and intensified. It was not enough just to write, to feel, to think, one must act! One could act . . . I remembered that the Cubans had changed the name of the Hilton Hotel in Havana to Havana Libre, and a US telephone operator, in making the hookup of a call there, insisted the hotel was still the Havana Hilton. But the Cuban operator would have none of it. "Havana Libre!" she shouted. "Get used to it!" that was the spirit I wanted to invest in the essay. It won an award after being published in the *Evergreen Review.* The award was $300 and was the most money I'd ever gotten for something I'd written." Baraka, *The Autobiography of LeRoi Jones,* 166.

21. Jones, "Cuba Libre," 62.

22. Quoted in David Llorens, "Ameer (LeRoi Jones) Baraka," in *The Black Revolution: an Ebony Special Issue* (Chicago: Johnson Pub. Co., 1970), 67–68.

23. John Henrik Clarke, "The New Afro-American Nationalism," *Freedomways* (1961): 285–95; Cruse, *The Crisis of the Negro Intellectual,* 355.

24. Harold Cruse, "Negro Nationalism's New Wave," in *Rebellion or Revolution?* (New York: William Morrow, 1968), 68.

25. Cruse, "Negro Nationalism's New Wave," 73.

26. Malcolm X, "A Declaration of Independence," in *Malcolm X Speaks,* ed. George Breitman (New York: Pathfinder Press, 1965), 13–17.

27. Jan Carew, *Ghosts in Our Blood* (Chicago: Lawrence Hill Books, 1994); George Breitman, *The Last Year of Malcolm X: The Evolution of a Revolutionary* (New York: Pathfinder Press, 1970); Albert Cleage and George Breitman, "Myths About Malcolm X," *International Socialist Review* (1967).

28. *Columbia Daily Spectator,* 19 February 1965, quoted in Wilson Jeremiah Moses, *The Wings of Ethiopia: Studies in African American Life and Letters* (Ames, Iowa: Iowa State University Press, 1990).

29. Gerald Horne, "'Myth' and the Making of 'Malcolm X'" *The American Historical Review* 98 (1993): 440–50; Frederick D. Harper, "The Influence of Malcolm X on Black Militancy," *Journal of Black Studies* 1 (1971): 387–402; Adolph Reed Jr., ed.,

"The Allure of Malcolm X and the Changing Character of Black Politics," in *Stirrings in the Jug: Black Politics in the Post-Segregation Era* (Minneapolis, MN: University of Minnesota Press), 197.

30. Baraka, *The Autobiography of LeRoi Jones,* 168.

31. Woodard, *Nation within A Nation,* 54–59.

32. Clarke, "The New Afro-American Nationalism," 1.

33. Lewis R. Gordon, "Fanon's Tragic Revolutionary Violence," in *Fanon: A Critical Reader,* ed. Lewis Gordon, T. Denean Sharpley-Whiting, and Renee T. White (Oxford, UK and Cambridge, MA: Blackwell, 1996).

34. Jones, *Home,* 93.

35. Ibid.

36. Baraka, *The Autobiography of LeRoi Jones,* 194.

37. Ibid., 135–40. Watts reconstructs this exchange from Baraka's *The Autobiography of LeRoi Jones,* and accounts by Cruse and Larry Rivers. See Cruse, *The Crisis of the Negro Intellectual,* 486; Larry Rivers and Arnold Weinstein, *What Did I Do? The Unauthorized Autobiography* (New York: HarperCollins, 1992), 432.

38. Baraka, *The Autobiography of LeRoi Jones,* 194.

39. Ibid., 193.

40. Watts, *Amiri Baraka,* 137.

41. Baraka, *The Autobiography of LeRoi Jones,* 194.

42. Sollors, *Amiri Baraka,* 74; Baraka, *The Autobiography of LeRoi Jones,* 184. Baraka's autobiographical reflections on this period recall a sense of intellectual open-endedness, internationalism, and political optimism amidst the motion of world historical events. He wrote:

It was a bizarre time, in so many ways. Attempts at new ways of life were clashing with the old. India and China had gotten their formal independence before the coming of the 50s, and by the time the 50s had ended, there were many independent African nations (though with varying degrees of neocolonialism). Ghana's Kwame Nkrumah had hoisted the black star over the statehouse in Accra, and Nkrumah's pronouncements and word of his deeds were glowing encouragement to colored people all over the world. When the Chinese exploded their first A-bomb I wrote a poem saying, in effect, that *time* for the colored peoples had rebegun. [sic.] Frantz Fanon's books were popular, Grove Press had brought out *The Wretched of the Earth.* My own reading was broad and wilder than I knew. I was reading people like the right-wing Sorel's Reflections on Violence as well as the Italian Marxist Gramsci. But it was all mixed up and unsorted out. However, I was plodding "forward" at the quickstep.

43. Jones, *Home,* 118.

44. Baraka, *The Autobiography of LeRoi Jones,* 202.

45. Woodard, *Nation within a Nation,* 59.

46. Woodard, *Nation within a Nation,* 63–68; Watts, *Amiri Baraka,* 156–209; Lorenzo Thomas, "The Shadow World: New York's Umbra Workshop and Origins of the Black Arts movement," *Callaloo* 4 (1978): 53–72; James Smethurst, " 'Pat Your Foot and Turn the Corner': Amiri Baraka, the Black Arts movement and the Poetics of a Popular Avant-Garde," *African American Review* 37 (2003): 261–70; James Smethurst, "Poetry and Sympathy: New York, the Left and the Rise of the Black Arts," in *Left of the Color Line: Race, Radicalism and Twentieth Century Literature of the United States,* ed.

Bill V. Mullen and James Smethurst (Chapel Hill, NC: University of North Carolina Press, 2003), 259–78.

47. Baraka, *The Autobiography of LeRoi Jones*, 238–40.

48. Baraka, *The Autobiography of LeRoi Jones*, 239.

49. Ibid.

50. Scott Brown, *Fighting for Us: Maulana Karenga, the Us Organization, and Black Cultural Nationalism* (New York: New York University Press, 2003), 99–106; Woodard, *Nation within a Nation*, 70.

51. Brown, *Fighting for Us*, 125–26.

52. Adam Clayton Powell, "My Black Position Paper," in *The Black Power Revolt*, ed. Floyd Barbour (Boston: Porter Sargent Publisher, 1968), 257–60; Art Pollock, "'My Life's Philosophy': Adam Clayton Powell's 'Black Position Paper,'" *Journal of Black Studies* 4 (1974): 457–62; Lee A. Daniels, "The Political Career of Adam Clayton Powell," *Journal of Black Studies* 4, no. 2 (1973): 115–38.

53. Quoted in Charles V. Hamilton, *Adam Clayton Powell, Jr.: The Political Biography of an American Dilemma* (New York: Atheneum, 1991), 28–29.

54. Carson, *In Struggle*, 224.

55. Wil Haygood, *King of the Cats: The Life and Times of Adam Clayton Powell, Jr.* (Boston: Houghton Mifflin, 1993), 325–27.

56. Richard Reeves, "Hatred and Pity Mix in Views of Whites on Newark Negroes," *New York Times*, 22 July 1967, 1; "Newark Property Loss Is Put at $15 Million," *New York Times*, 22 July 1967, 10; Ron Porambo, *No Cause for Indictment: An Autopsy of Newark* (New York: Holt, Rinehart and Winston, 1971); Tom Hayden, *Rebellion in Newark: Official Violence and Ghetto Response* (New York: Vintage Books, 1967); Woodard, *Nation within a Nation*, 78–84; Robert L. Allen, *Black Awakening in Capitalist America: An Analytic History* (Trenton, NJ: Africa World Press, 1990 [orig. pub. 1969]), 128–40.

57. Allen, *Black Awakening in Capitalist America*, 135.

58. Todd Gitlin, *The Whole World is Watching: Mass Media in the Making and the Unmaking of the New Left* (Berkeley: University of California Press, 1980).

59. Homer Bigart, "Powell Remains in Exile," *New York Times*, 22 July 1967, 10.

60. Earl Caldwell, "Two Police Inspectors from Here Among the Newark Delegates," *New York Times*, 22 July 1967, 26; Thomas Johnson, "McKissack Holds End of Violence Is Up to Whites: CORE Leader at Meeting on Black Power Warns of Further Rioting," *New York Times*, 22 July 1967, 1.

61. Chuck Stone, "The National Conference on Black Power" in *The Black Power Revolt*, ed. Floyd Barbour (Boston: Porter Sargent Publisher, 1968), 189–98.

62. Stone, "The National Conference on Black Power," 191–92.

63. Vincent Harding, "Black Radicalism: The Road from Montgomery," in *Dissent: Explorations in the History of American Radicalism*, ed. Alfred Young (DeKalb: Northern Illinois University Press, 1968), 191–92.

64. The actual workshop topics and their respective coordinators were as follows: (1) The City and Black People—Lee Montgomery and Oswald Sykes; (2) Black Power Through Black Politics—Chuck Stone and Dan Watts; (3) Black Power in World Perspective: Nationalism and Internationalism—Ron Karenga; (4) Black Power Through Economic Development—Robert Browne; (5) The Black Home—Nathan Hare; (6) Black Power and American Religion—Reverend C. Lincoln

McGhee; (7) New Roles for Black Youth—Cleveland Sellers; (8) Black Artists, Crafts and Communication—Ossie Davis and Carol Green; (9) Black Professionals and Black Power—Hoyt Fuller and Gerald McWorter; (10) Developmental Implications of Black Power—Dr. James Comer; (11) Black Power and Social Change—John Davis and Lou Gothard; (12) Fraternal, Civic and Social Groups—Fay Bellamy; (13) Co-operation and Alliances—James Farmer and Vivian Braxton; and (14) New Trends for Youth—William Strickland.

65. Quoted in Stone, "The National Conference on Black Power," 195.

66. Nathan Wright, "Why Black Power? An Interview with Dr. Nathan Wright," interviewed by David Holstrom, *Christian Science Monitor,* 18 September 1967.

67. Allen, *Black Awakening in Capitalist America* (1969), 157.

68. Harding, "Black Radicalism," 345.

69. Nathan Wright, *Black Power and Urban Unrest* (New York: Hawthorn Books, 1967), 62, 92; Wright, "Why Black Power?"; See also Allen, *Black Awakening in Capitalist America,* 161.

70. "Negro Spokesman: Nathan Wright, Jr." *New York Times,* 22 July 1967, 11.

71. Wright, "Why Black Power?"

72. Ibid.

73. Ibid.

74. Allen, *Black Awakening in Capitalist America,* 161.

75. Julius Hobson, "Black Power: Right or Left?" in *The Black Power Revolt,* ed. Floyd Barbour (Boston: Porter Sargent Publisher, 1968), 199.

76. Ibid., 200.

77. *Black Power Conference Reports: Philadelphia, PA, August 30–September 1, 1968; Bermuda, July 13, 1969* (Harlem, NY: AFRAM News Services, 1970), 5.

78. In addition to the black party proposal, the Politics section reports of the 1968 Philadelphia Black Power Conference also included statements on specific policy areas including a pledge of support for the Organization of African Unity, an anti-Vietnam war declaration, a brief proposal for the formation of an organization for black self-defense against white violence, and a statement against Zionism.

79. *Black Power Conference Reports,* 27.

80. Quoted in Allen, *Black Awakening in Capitalist America,* 163–64.

81. Ibid., 164.

82. *Black Power Conference Reports,* 57–58. A number of black radicals from the United States were barred from entering the country to participate in the proceedings. Additionally, those delegates who did obtain entrance into Bermuda complained of discrimination and of subjection to unreasonable scrutiny at the hands of government officials. Conference participants also charged the Bermudian *Royal Gazette* with erroneous reporting and mediocre publicity of the proceedings. The transgressions in news coverage noted by conference participants included inaccurate headcounts of conference attendees, numerous misquotes, and the exclusion of the meeting's most serious, pertinent content in published reports. In fact, in light of such problems the Communications section of the conference recommended the immediate enactment of a black boycott against the *Gazette.* The Bermuda conference followed a comparable, though slightly abbreviated, workshop configuration of previous Black Power summits. The decreased participation of African American radicals due to government-imposed entry restrictions is clearly reflected in the

character of resolutions produced at the 1969 conference. Most of the resolutions submitted by the workshop on politics dealt with local Bermudian issues. Pan-Africanist and socialist theoretician C.L.R. James presided over the Workshop on Politics, which convened at the Pembroke-Hamilton Club Stadium in Warwick Parish, Bermuda. The workshop drafted and submitted six resolutions for adoption at the closing plenary session. The first four resolutions made no mention of U.S. domestic politics, but spoke to relevant Bermudian concerns—job discrimination and negative ramifications of Portuguese contract farm labor; land distribution; dissension and alienation among the black Bermudian population; and government repression of free press. The fifth resolution addressed the arrest and detainment of forty-two black and fifty-five white student activists in Montreal, Canada, and the consequent barring of their legal defense committee chairman Norman Cooke from entering Bermuda to attend the conference. The sixth resolution expressed solidarity with liberation struggles worldwide. This last statement made specific mention of blacks in the United States and invoked the need for greater operational unity. This resolution called for an "open forum" as a means of resolving dissension. The Bermuda conference, therefore, unfortunately offered little—ideologically, strategically, or organizationally—that was novel to the Black Power movement in the United States.

83. Imamu Amiri Baraka, ed. *African Congress: A Documentary of the First Modern Pan-African Congress* (New York: William Morrow, 1972), 96.

84. Baraka, *Kawaida Studies: The New Nationalism* (Chicago: Third World Press, 1972), 36.

85. Ibid., 34.

86. Baraka, *African Congress*, 99.

87. Baraka, *Kawaida Studies*, 35.

88. Amiri Baraka, "Black Nationalism: 1972," *Black Scholar* (1972): 25.

89. Baraka, *Kawaida Studies*, 33.

90. Ibid., 37.

91. For a more extensive discussion of the 1970 Newark elections, see Woodard, *Nation within a Nation*, 138–55; Watts, *Amiri Baraka*, 348–73.

92. Allen, *Black Awakening in Capitalist America*, 141.

93. Ibid., 144.

94. See Alex Poinsett, "It's Nation Time! Congress of African Peoples Proposes Models for Worldwide Black Institutions," *Ebony* 26, no. 2 (1970): 98–106; Carl J. Hayden, "The Congress of African Peoples (Atlanta, Georgia, September 3–7, 1970)," *Black Academy Review* 1 (1970): 61.

95. Hayward Henry Jr. Promotional Brochure for 1970 Congress of African Peoples, c. 1970, Amiri Baraka Collection, Moorland-Spingarn Research Center, Howard University, Washington, D.C.

96. Baraka, *African Congress*, 32.

97. Ibid., 64.

98. Ibid., 88.

99. Ibid., 19.

100. Ibid., 38.

101. Chuck Stone, "Black Politics: Third Force, Third Party or Third Class Influence?" *Black Scholar* 1, no. 2 (1969): 12.

102. Ibid., 8.

103. Ibid.

104. Henry Lee Moon, *Balance of Power: The Negro Vote* (New York: Kraus Reprint Co., 1969 [orig. pub. 1949]).

105. Stone, "Black Politics," 12.

106. Baraka, *African Congress,* 139.

107. Ibid., 140.

108. Dick Traylor, "To the Atlanta Delegates," *Nationtime News,* 1971, 1, 2.

109. Quoted in Allen, *Black Awakening in Capitalist America,* 142.

110. Woodard, *Nation within a Nation,* 219–54; Tex Novellino and Stanley Terrell, "Baraka and Six Are Arrested at Council Meeting," *Newark Star Ledger,* 6 February 1975: 6.

111. Kenneth A. Gibson, "Newark and We," in . *What Black Politicians Are Saying,* ed. Nathan Wright, Jr. (New York: Hawthorn Books, 1972), 114.

112. Ibid., 121.

113. Amiri Baraka, "Newark Seven Years Later: Unidad y Lucha!" *Monthly Review* 26, no. 8 1975, 16–24.

3. The Convention Strategy and Conventional Politics: The 1972 Gary Convention and the Limits of Racial Unity

1. Malcolm X, *Malcolm X Speaks,* ed. George Breitman (New York: Pathfinder Press, 1965), 4.

2. Malcolm X, "Basic Unity Program: Organization of Afro-American Unity," in *Modern Black Nationalism: From Marcus Garvey to Louis Farrakhan,* ed. William Van Deburg (New York: New York University Press, 1997), 108–15; William W. Sales, Jr., *From Civil Rights to Black Liberation: Malcolm X and the Organization of Afro-American Unity* (Boston: South End Press, 1994), 99–132.

3. Stokely Carmichael and Charles V. Hamilton, *Black Power: The Politics of Liberation in America* (New York: Vintage Books, 1967), vii.

4. Floyd McKissack, "The Way to a Black Ideology," *Black Scholar* 1, no. 2(1969).

5. "Black Leaders Hold Unity Conference," *Nation Time News,* July 1971, vol. 1, no. 1, 1.

6. Quoted in "Black Leaders," *Nation Time News,* 1.

7. Ibid.

8. Amiri Baraka, "Toward the Creation of Political Institutions for All African Peoples," *Black World* 21, no. 12 (1972): 54–78.

9. Manning Marable, *Race, Reform and Rebellion* (Jackson, MS: University Press of Mississippi, 1991), 108.

10. Julian Bond, "A Black Southern Strategy" in *What Black Politicians Are Saying,* ed. Nathan Wright, Jr. (New York: Hawthorn Books, 1972), 137–43.

11. Alex Poinsett, "Black Political Strategies for '72," *Ebony* 72 (1972): 66–74.

12. Ibid., 72, 74.

13. Baraka, "Toward the Creation," 57–59; John Conyers, Jr., "A Black Political Strategy for 1972," in *What Black Politicians Are Saying,* ed. Nathan Wright (New York: Hawthorn Books, 1972).

14. Amiri Baraka, "The Pan-African Party and the Black Nation," *Black Scholar* 2, no. 7 (1971): 24–32.

15. Kwasi Konadu, *Truth Crushed to the Earth Will Rise Again: The East Organization and the Principles and Practice of Black Nationalist Development* (Trenton, NJ: Africa World Press, 2005).

16. Baraka, "Toward the Creation," 59.

17. Baraka, "Toward the Creation," 59–60.

18. Shirley Chisholm, *The Good Fight* (New York: Bantam, 1973), 46; Eddie Bernice Johnson, interview with Norma Leonard, 17 July 1972, Ralph Bunche Oral History Project, Moorland-Spingarn Research Center, Howard University, Washington, D.C.; Shirley Chisholm, interview with Edward Thompson III, 2 May 1973, Ralph Bunche Oral History Project, Moorland-Spingarn Research Center, Howard University, Washington, D.C.

19. Baraka, "Toward the Creation," 62–63.

20. William Clay, *Just Permanent Interests* (New York: Amistad, 1992), 197.

21. Lerone Bennett, "A Black Agenda for the Seventies," *Race Relations Reporter* (1972), 13.

22. Bennett, "Black Agenda," 13.

23. Ibid.

24. Thomas A. Johnson, "Black Caucus Calls National Political Convention," *New York Times,* 21 November 1971, 68.

25. Carolyn P. Dubose, *The Untold Story of Charles Diggs: The Public Figure, The Private Man* (Arlington, VA: Barton Publishing House, 1998).

26. Stephen J. Whitfield, *A Death in the Delta: The Story of Emmett Till* (New York: Free Press, 1988), 37–38.

27. Charles C. Diggs, Jr., "The Role of the American Negro in American-African Relations," in *Apropos of Africa: Afro-American Leaders and the Romance of Africa,* ed. Martin Kilson and Adelaide Cromwell Hill (Garden City, NY: Anchor Books, 1971); Charles Diggs, Jr., "The Afro-American Stake in Africa," *Black World* 25, no. 3 (1976).

28. Robert C. Smith, *We Have No Leaders: African Americans in the Post Civil Rights Era* (Albany, NY: State University of New York Press, 1996), 44.

29. Amiri Baraka, "Nationalist Overview," unpublished document, 1972, author's possession.

30. Ibid.

31. Jonathon Scott Holloway, *Confronting the Veil: Abram Harris, Jr., E. Franklin Frazier and Ralph Bunche, 1919–1940* (Chapel Hill, NC: University of North Carolina Press, 2002); Alvin C. Hughes, "The National Negro Congress Movement" (PhD diss., Ohio State University Press, 1982); Lawrence Wittner, "The National Negro Congress: A Reassessment," *American Quarterly* 22 (1968): 883–901.

32. Baraka, "Nationalist Overview," 3.

33. Quoted in Ward Churchill and Jim Vander Wall, *Agents of Repression: The FBI's Secret Wars Agaainst the Black Panther Party and the American Indian Movement* (Boston: South End Press, 1990), 37.

34. See William Pepper, *An Act of State: The Execution of Martin Luther King, Jr.* (London and New York: Verso, 2003); Churchill and Vander Wall, Chapter 2, 37–62.

35. Ibid., 58.

36. O'Reilly, "Racial Matters," 345–47.

37. Sanford J. Ungar, "New FBI Chief Vows to Stress Hoover's Goals," *Washington Post,* 26 May 1972, A2.

38. Memorandum from G.C. Moore to E.S. Miller, captioned National Black Political Convention, 3/72, West Side High School, Gary Indiana, 8 March 1972.

39. Memorandum from FBI Acting Director to SAC, no caption, dated 16 October 1972.

40. Jon Teaford, "'King Richard' Hatcher: Mayor of Gary," *Journal of Negro History* 77 (1992): 126–40; Alex Poinsett, *Black Power Gary Style: The Making of Mayor Richard Gordon Hatcher* (Chicago: Johnson Publishing, 1970).

41. Teaford, "King Richard," 127–30; William E. Nelson, Jr. and Philip Meranto, *Electing Black Mayors: Political Action in the Black Community* (Columbus, OH: Ohio State University, 1977) 166–87.

42. Smith, *We Have No Leaders,* 45; James Stephens, "The State Delegations," *Jet,* 30 March 1972.

43. Gerald West and Jeannye Thornton, "Young Blacks Upset at 3d Party Shunning," *Chicago Tribune,* 13 March 1972, 2.

44. Henry Hampton and Steven Fayer, eds., *Voices of Freedom: An Oral History of the Civil Rights Movement from the 1950s through the 1980s* (New York: Bantam, 1990), 72–73.

45. Thomas A. Johnson, "Blacks Convene National Session," *New York Times,* 11 March 1972, 12; Bryant Rollins, "The Importance of Gary," *Amsterdam News,* 3–11 March 1972; Simeon Booker, "Black Political Convention is Successful Despite Splits and Tactical Differences," *Jet,* 30 March 1972; Edwin Jaffe, "Coming Together at Gary," *Nation,* 3 April 1972; "The Experiment at Gary," *Amsterdam News,* 18 March 1972; Carlos Russell, "A Journey We Must Make," *Amsterdam News,* 18 March 1972; "If We Failed," *Michigan Chronicle,* 25 March 1972; Austin Scott, "Impact of Black Parley Assessed by A.P. Newsman," *Gary Post Tribune,* 14 March 1972.

46. *Chicago Tribune,* 13 March 1972, 2.

47. Thomas Johnson, "'We Met Therefore We Won,'" *New York Times,* 13 March 1972, 3.

48. William Strickland, "The Gary Convention and the Crisis of American Politics," *Black World* 21, no. 12 (1972): 18–26.

49. William Strickland, "What Ever Happened to the Politics of Black Liberation?," *Black Scholar* 7, no. 2 (1975): 25.

50. *National Black Political Agenda* (Washington, D.C.: The National Black Political Convention, 1972); Gerald C. Fraser, "Black Document Sets Downs Goals," *New York Times,* 21 May 1972, 29; Gary Slaughter, "Blacks Ask Radical Changes in System," *Gary Post Tribune,* 13 March 1972.

51. Manning Marable, "Black Nationalism in the 1970s: Through the Prism of Race and Class," *Socialist Review* 50/51 (1980): 57–108.

52. See Stephen Ward, "'Scholarship in the Context of Struggle': Activist Intellectuals, the Institute of the Black World (IBW), and the Contours of Black Power Radicalism," *Black Scholar* 31 (2001): 42–53; Stephen Ward, "'Ours Too Was a Struggle for a Better World': Activists Intellectuals and the Radical Promise of the Black Power Movement, 1962–1972" (PhD diss., University of Texas, 2002); "Institute of the Black World ... Statement of Purpose and Program Fall 1969," *Massachusetts Review* 10 (1969): 713–17; Alex Poinsett, "Think Tank for Black Scholars," *Ebony* 25

(1970): 46–48, 50, 52, 54; "Institute of the Black World," *Negro Digest* 19 (1970): 19–23; Lerone Bennett *IBW and Education for Liberation* (Chicago: Third World Press, 1973); *Education and Black Struggle: Notes from the Colonized World,* Institute of the Black World (Cambridge, MA: Harvard Education Review, 1974).

53. "Biography, Democracy and Spirit: An Interview with Vincent Harding," *Callaloo* 20 (1998): 682–98; MARHO: the Radical Historians Organization, "Interview with Vincent Harding," *Visions of History,* ed. Henry Abelove, Betsy Blackmar, Peter Dimock, and Jonathon Schneer (New York: Pantheon Books, 1983), 231–32.

54. William Strickland, interview with the author, tape recording, by telephone, 14 October 1999.

55. *National Black Political Agenda,* 2.

56. Ibid., 1.

57. Ibid., 2.

58. Paul Delaney, "Conciliator at Black Parley," *New York Times,* 13 March 1972, 30; Virginia Thrower, "Observers Criticize Planning," *Gary Post Tribune,* 3 March 1972; Tom Knightly, "Confusion Normal, Diggs," *Gary Post Tribune,* 12 March 1972; "Emergence of a New Leader," *Newsweek,* 27 March 1972; Ronald W. Walters, "The New Black Political Culture," *Black World* 21, no. 12 (1972): 4–17; Komozi Woodard, *Nation within a Nation: Amiri Baraka (LeRoi Jones) and Black Power Politics* (Chapel Hill, NC: University of North Carolina Press, 1999), 210–11.

59. *National Black Political Agenda,* 25–26.

60. Ibid., 40–47.

61. Ibid., 53; an abstract of the 180-page bill is appended to the agenda.

62. Ibid., 53.

63. Ibid., 28.

64. Ibid., 27–30.

65. Ibid., 34–35.

66. Walters, "New Black Political Culture," 7; "Hatcher Reviews Parley of Blacks," *New York Times,* 16 March 1972, 34.

67. Angela Parker, "Black Parley Comes Out Against Busing," *Chicago Tribune,* 13 March 1972, 1–2; Lu Palmer and Betty Washington, "Blacks Sound Call for Militant Politics," *Chicago Daily News,* 13 March 1972, 1; "Anti-Busing Resolution OK'd," *Gary Post Tribune,* 13 March 1972; Thomas A. Johnson, "Blacks at Parley Divide Over Basic Role in Politics," *New York Times,* 12 March 1972, 1, 38; "Hatcher Reviews Parley of Blacks," 34; "Gary Convention Failed to Live Up to Its Roseate Promise," *Chicago Defender,* 18–24 March 1972; "Moment of Truth at Gary and Beyond," *Chicago Defender,* 18–24 March 1972.

68. Roy Innis and Victor Solomon, "Harlem Must Control Its Schools," *New Generation* 49 (1967): 4; "New Findings–Negro Attitudes on Racial Issues," *U.S. News and World Report,* 5 August 1968, 10; Preston R. Wilcox, "The Community Centered School," in *The Schoolhouse in the City,* ed. Alvin Tiffler (New York: Praeger, 1968); Whitney Young, "Minorities and Community Control," *Journal of Negro Education* 38 (1969): 285–90; Douglas Glasgow, "Black Power Through Community Control," *Social Work* 17 (1972): 62.

69. *National Black Political Agenda,* 11–12.

70. Thomas A. Johnson, "Black Assembly Voted at Parley," *New York Times,* 13 March 1972, 1, 30.

71. *National Black Political Agenda,* 12.

72. Robert Weisbord and Richard Kazarian, Jr., *Israel in the Black American Perspective* (Westport, CT: Greenwood Press, 1985), 8–10; Hollis R. Lynch, *Edward Wilmot Blyden: Pan-Negro Patriot, 1832–1912* (London: Oxford University Press, 1967), 64–65.

73. Weisbord and Kazarian, *Israel in the Black American Perspective,* 10.

74. Ibid., 13–20.

75. See especially Cruse's "Jews and Negroes in the Communist Party," and "Negroes and Jews—The Two Nationalisms and the Bloc(ked) Plurality," in Harold Cruse, *The Crisis of the Negro Intellectual* (New York: William Morrow, 1967) 147–170, 476–497; Alan Wald, "Narrating Nationalisms: Black Marxism and Jewish Communists Through the Eyes of Harold Cruse," *Science & Society* 64 (2000/2001): 400–23; Sid Resnick, "Harold Cruse's Attack on Jewish Communists: Comment," *Science & Society* 66 (2002): 393–400.

76. *SNCC Newsletter,* September–October 1967; Cleveland Sellers with Robert Terrell, *The River of No Return—The Autobiography of a Black Militant and the Life and Death of SNCC* (New York: William Morrow, 1973), 201–3; Clayborne Carson, *In Struggle: SNCC and the Black Awakening of the 1960s* (Cambridge, MA: Harvard University Press, 1981), 267–8; James Forman, *The Making of Black Revolutionaries* (Washington, D.C.: Open Hand Publishing, 1985), 497–503.

77. Weisbord and Kazarian, *Israel in the Black American Perspective,* 37–38; James Ridgeway, "Freak-Out in Chicago," *New Republic* 16 (1967): 9–12; Sid Lens, "The New Politics Convention: Confusion and Promise," *New Politics* 6, no. 1 (1967): 9; Walter Goodman, "When Black Power Runs the New Left," *New York Times Magazine* 24 (1967): 124; Irwin Unger, *The Movement: A History of the American New Left* (New York: Dodd, Mead and Company, 1974); James Miller, *Democracy is in the Streets: From Port Huron to the Siege of Chicago* (Cambridge, MA: Harvard University Press, 1994).

78. See Aldon Morris, *The Origins of the Civil Rights Movement: Black Communities Organizing for Change* (New York: Free Press, 1984) 197–203.

79. Douglas Moore, interview with the author, Washington, D.C., 6 August 1999; Douglas Moore, interview with Robert Wright, 12 December 1968, Ralph Bunche Oral History Project, Moorland-Spingarn Research Center, Howard University, Washington, D.C.; Taylor Branch, *Parting the Waters: America During the King Years 1954–1963* (New York: Simon & Schuster, 1988).

80. National Black Political Convention, National Black Political Agenda Draft Document, 1972, Ronald W. Walters Papers, Moorland-Spingarn Research Center, Howard University, Washington, D.C., 13B.

81. National Black Political Convention, Black Agenda Draft Document, 13B.

82. *National Black Political Agenda,* 15–16.

83. Nadine Brown, "Diggs Peacemaker in Gary Walkout Hassle," *Michigan Chronicle,* 25 March 1972.

84. Recalling the Gary Convention in his memoir, Coleman Young denounced the *Black Agenda* again as the "obvious work of Baraka, the misguided ramblings of a so-called artist who would be dictator. It consisted of bullshit like taking over five states for black people." See Coleman Young and Lonnie Wheeler, *Hard Stuff: The Autobiography of Coleman Young* (New York: Viking Press, 1993), 189.

85. Tony Thomas, "The Meaning of the Black Agenda," in *Independent Black Political Action, 1954–1978,* ed. Mac Warren (New York: Pathfinder Press, 1982) 61;

Nadine Brown, "Diggs Peacemaker in Gary Walkout Hassle," *Michigan Chronicle*, 25 March 1972.

86. Roy Wilkins, "Whither 'Black Power'?," *Crisis* 73 (1966): 354; Roy Wilkins, "Integration," *Ebony* 25 (1970): 58; Roy Wilkins, "Black Nonsense," *Crisis* 78 (1971): 78; Roy Wilkins, "Black Neo Segregationists," *Crisis* 74 (1967): 439–40.

87. Roy Wilkins "Minorities Are the Losers When They Play Ethnic Politics," *Sacramento Bee*, 12 February 1972; Thomas A. Johnson, "NAACP Aide Opposes Draft of Black Preamble," *New York Times*, 10 March 1972, 20; Gary Slaughter, "NAACP Blasts Preamble," *Gary Post-Tribune*, 11 March 1972; Gary Slaughter, "The NAACP and the Black Political Convention," *Crisis* (1972): 229–30.

88. Slaughter, "The NAACP and the Black Political Convention," 229–30.

89. Slaughter, "The NAACP and the Black Political Convention," 229.

90. Hampton and Fayer, *Voices of Freedom*, 571.

91. Les Ledbetter, "NAACP Leaves New Black Group," *New York Times*, 17 May 1972, 9.

92. Ibid.

93. Quoted in Dom Bonafede, "Black Vote Loses Cohesion but Gains Sophistication, Clout in Key Areas," *National Journal*, 24 June 1972, 1060–68. Elsewhere, Conyers is quoted saying "the truth of the matter is that this is an unrepresentative group. The average black is a nice quiet, church-going person who would be scared out of his wits to hear this rhetoric. But this is the vanguard. These are the young leaders who don't have vested interests. It's easier for them to take this position. But this is going to have an electrifying effect." Quoted in William Greider, "Gary Manifesto: Black Politics," *Washington Post*, 19 March 1972, B3.

94. Quoted in Bonafede, "Black Vote Loses Cohesion," 1064.

95. Chisholm, *The Good Fight*, 44–47; Mickey Thrower, "Rep. Chisholm, Busing Hot Issues at Convention," *Gary Post Tribune*, 10 March 1972; Geraldine Fields and Virginia Thrower, "Women Agree: No Endorsements," *Gary Post Tribune*, 13 March 1972; Mickey Thrower, "60 to Continue Parley's Work, *Gary Post Tribune*, 13 March 1972.

96. William Greider, "Hatcher Calls for Blacks to Unite Politically," *Washington Post*, 12 March 1972, A2; Robert P. Mooney, "Hatcher Warns of Third Party," *Indianapolis Star*, 12 March 1972, 1; Richard G. Hatcher, "History Will Be Our Judge," *Freedomways* 12, no. 2 (1972): 134–142; Grayson Mitchell and David Robinson, "Blacks Give Ultimatum and Edge to New Party," *Chicago Sun-Times*, 12 March 1972; Gary Slaughter, "Black 3d Party—Now? Wait?" *Gary Post Tribune*, 12 March 1972.

97. Hatcher, "History Will Be Our Judge," 136.

98. Hatcher, "History Will Be Our Judge," 138.

99. Ibid., 134.

100. Ibid., 141–42.

101. William Greaves, "Nationtime: Gary" 60-minute William Greaves Productions, 1972, videocassette.

102. Quoted in Walters, "The New Black Political Culture," 7.

103. Amiri Baraka, "Pan-African Party and the Black Nation," 24–32.

104. James Boggs, *Manifesto for a Black Revolutionary Party* (Philadelphia: Pacesetters Publishing House, 1969), 2.

105. Strickland, "The Gary Convention," 25–26.

106. Max Stanford (Muhammad Ahmad), "The Pan-African Party," in *Pan-Africanism,* ed. Robert Chrisman and Nathan Hare (Indianapolis and New York: Bobbs-Merrill, 1974), 168–74.

107. *National Black Political Agenda,* 6.

108. Johnson, "Black Assembly Voted at Parley," 1; William Greider, "Blacks Vote to Organize Political Arm at Gary Session," *Washington Post,* 13 March 1972, A1.

109. Amiri Baraka, "A Post Convention Strategy for Black People," unpublished position paper (1972), Amiri Baraka Collection, Moorland-Spingarn Research Center, Howard University, Washington, D.C.

110. Greider, "Blacks Vote to Organize," A8.

111. Johnson, "We Met Therefore We Won," 4.

112. Quoted in Robert Allen, *Black Awakening in Capitalist America: An Analytic History* (Trenton, NJ: Africa World Press, 1990 [orig. pub. 1969]), 139.

113. Paul Delaney, "House Caucus Lists 'Black Bill of Rights,'" *New York Times,* 2 June 1972, 22.

114. Amiri Baraka, "Black and Angry," *Newsweek,* 10 July 1972, 35.

115. Alex Poinsett, "Black Politics at the Crossroads," *Ebony* (1972), 38.

116. Smith, *We Have No Leaders,* 55.

117. Baraka, "Toward the Creation," 73–4.

118. "First Black Assembly Called Here," *Chicago Daily News,* 10 October 1972, 17; "Black Group Opens Sessions with Unity," *Washington Sunday Star,* 22 October 1972, A10.

119. Walters, "The New Black Political Culture," 4–17.

4. From Popular Anti-Imperialism to Sectarianism: The African Liberation Day Mobilizations and Radical Intellectuals

1. Cedric Robinson, "The African Diaspora and the Italo-Ethiopian Crisis," *Race & Class* 27, no. 2 (1986): 51–65; S. K. B. Asante, *Pan-African Protest: West Africa and the Italo Ethiopian Crisis, 1934–1941* (London: Longman, 1977); William R. Scott, "Black Nationalism and the Italo-Ethiopian Conflict, 1934–1936," *Journal of Negro History* 63 (1978): 118–34.

2. Brenda Gayle Plummer, *Rising Wind: Black Americans and U.S. Foreign Affairs, 1935–1960* (Chapel Hill: University of North Carolina Press, 1996); Penny Von Eschen, *Race Against Empire: Black Americans and Anticolonialism, 1937–1957* (Ithaca, NY: Cornell University Press, 1997).

3. Immanuel Maurice Wallerstein, *Africa: The Politics of Unity* (New York: Vintage, 1967); George Padmore, *Pan-Africanism or Communism* (New York: Doubleday, 1971).

4. Basil Davidson, *Let Freedom Come: Africa in Modern History* (Boston, MA: Little, Brown and Company, 1978), 341–71; Basil Davidson, *The Liberation of Guiné: Aspects of an African Revolution* (Baltimore, MD: Penguin, 1969); Bill Freund, *The Making of Contemporary Africa* (Bloomington, IN: Indiana University Press, 1984).

5. Quoted in Gerald Horne, *From the Barrel of a Gun: The United States and the War Against Zimbabwe, 1965–1980* (Chapel Hill, NC: University of North Carolina Press, 2001), 144; Andrew DeRoche, *Black, White and Chrome: The United States and Zimbabwe, 1953–1998* (Trenton, NJ: Africa World Press, 2000).

6. "UN Council Criticizes US on Rhodesian Chrome Issue," *Washington Post*, 29 February 1972, A17; Anthony A. Coker, "The Importation of Chrome from Rhodesia: A Case Study of Selected Aspects of US Foreign Policy toward Black Africa" (PhD diss., George Washington University, 1974).

7. Ann and Neva Seidman, *South Africa and U.S. Multinational Corporations* (Westport, CT: Lawrence Hill and Company, 1977), 92–93, 212–15.

8. Komozi Woodard, *A Nation within a Nation: Amiri Baraka (LeRoi Jones) and Black Power Politics* (Chapel Hill, NC: University of North Carolina Press, 1999), 173.

9. William H. Chafe, *Civilities and Civil Rights: Greensboro, North Carolina and the Black Struggle for Freedom* (New York: Oxford University Press, 1981); Aldon Morris, *The Origins of the Civil Rights Movement: Black Communities Organizing for Change* (New York: Free Press, 1984).

10. Howard Fuller, interview with the author, by telephone, 8 November 1999.

11. Fanon Ché Wilkins, "'In the Belly of the Beast': Black Power, Anti-Imperialism and the African Liberation Solidarity Movement, 1968–1975" (PhD diss., New York University Press, 2001), 123–34; "Report on the First Pan African Medical Program Collection," *The African World*, 6 February 1971, 4.

12. Owusu Sadaukai, "Inside Liberated Mozambique with the Frelimo Gueril-las, Part 1," *The African World*, 8 January 1972, 8; Owusu Sadaukai, "Inside Liberated Mozambique—An Ideology Put Into Action, Part 2," *The African World*, 22 January 1972, 8; Owusu Sadaukai, "Inside Liberated Mozambique—Attacked by the Por-tuguese, Part 4," *The African World*, 19 February 1972; Owusu Sadaukai, "Inside Lib-erated Mozambique—Helping on the Outside, Part 6," *The African World*, 18 March 1972, 8–9; see also Wilkins, "In the Belly of the Beast," 134–44.

13. Letter from Owusu Sadaukai, 17 February 1972, Ronald Walters Papers, Moorland-Spingarn Research Center, Howard University, Washington, D.C.

14. Roy Wilkins, "Whither 'Black Power'?" *Crisis* 73 (1966): 354; Roy Wilkins, "Integration," *Ebony* 25 (1970): 58; Roy Wilkins, "Black Nonsense," *Crisis* 78 (1971): 78; Roy Wilkins, "Black Neo Segregationists," *Crisis* 74 (1967): 439–40.

15. Marjorie Hyer, "Blacks Mobilize for African Liberation," *Washington Post*, 1 April 1972, B5.

16. Richard E. Prince, "12,000 Blacks March to Support Africa," *Washington Post*, 28 May 1972, A1, A4; Woodard, *A Nation within a Nation*, 176.

17. African Liberation Day Coordinating Committee, "African Peoples Statement of Indictment Against the Murderous State of Portugal," unpublished transcript, 1972.

18. African Liberation Day Coordinating Committee, "African Peoples State-ment of Indictment Against the Brutal/Racist/Oppressive State of South Africa," unpublished transcript, 1972.

19. African Liberation Day Coordinating Committee, "African Peoples' State-ment of Indictment against the Racist, Neo-Colonialist Government of the United States of America," unpublished transcript, 1972.

20. Black Workers Congress, "We Got the Same Enemy" promotional flyer for New Orleans African Liberation Day rally, 1972.

21. "Black Caucus Sues against Rhodesia Ore," *Washington Post*, 20 April 1972, A12.

22. *African Liberator*, 19 May 1972, 2.

23. Richard E. Price, "African Conference Asks Sanctions on White Rule," *Washington Post*, 27 May 1972, A26; Jake C. Miller, "Black Legislators in African American Relations, 1970–1975," *Journal of Black Studies* 10 (1979): 245–61.

24. Group Protests Rhodesia Trade," *Washington Post*, 18 March 1972, A11.

25. *African Liberator*, 19 May 1972, 5–6.

26. "Rising Black Support Greets Namibian Solidarity Day," *Muhammed Speaks*, 9 August 1972, 5.

27. Kalamu Ya Salaam, "Tell No Lies, Claim No Easy Victories," *Black World* 23, no. 12 (1974), 20.

28. Alice Bronner, "2d African Liberation Day Demonstrations Set May 26," *Washington Post*, 6 March 1973, C7; Alice Bronner, "Rallies Support Africans: Domination of Blacks by Whites Scored," *Washington Post*, 27 May 1973, B1.

29. Abdul Hakimu Ibn Alkalimat and Nelson Johnson, "Toward the Ideological Unity of the African Liberation Support Committee: A Response to Criticisms of the ALSC Statement of Principles adopted at Frogmore, South Carolina, June–July 1973," *Greensboro*, 1–3 February 1974; Abdul Alkalimat, *A Scientific Approach to Black Liberation: Which Road Against Racism and Imperialism for the Black Liberation Movement?* (Nashville, TN: Peoples College, 1974); Abdul Alkalimat and Bill Sales, "Lessons from ALSC," *City Sun*, 20 May 1987. For critical perspectives on the ideological shifts within and around the ALSC during the seventies, see the following that were published by in the Atlanta University Political Science Department's journal *Endarch*: Norman Harris, "A Recurring Malady: Baraka's Move to the 'Left,'" *Endarch* 1 (1974): 5–20; Adolph Reed, Jr. "Scientific Socialism: Notes on the New Afro-American Magic Marxism," *Endarch* 1 (1974): 21–39.

30. Amiri Baraka, "Some Questions about the Sixth Pan-African Congress," *Black Scholar* 6, no. 2 (1974): 42–46; James Turner, "Sixth Pan African Congress 1974: Historical Perspective," *Black World* (March 1974): 11–9; James Garrett, "The Sixth Pan African Congress: An Historical Sketch," *Black World* 26, no. 5 (1975): 4–20; C. L. R. James, "Sixth Pan African Congress: An Overview," *Black World* 23, no. 5 (March 1974): 20–25; Sixth Pan African Congress, "A Briefing Paper," *Black World* 23, no. 5 (March 1974): 5–9. For pro-nationalist interpretations of the events that transpired at 6PAC, see Ladun Anise, "The Tyranny of a Purist Ideology," *Black World* 24 (1975): 18–27; Opuku Agyeman, "The Supermarxists and Pan-Africanism," *Journal of Black Studies* 8 (1978): 489–510.

31. Paul Delaney, "Diggs to Resign as Unity Eludes Black Convention," *Washington Star News*, 15 March 1974, 1.

32. William Greider, "Deep Differences Cripple Black Unity," *Washington Post*, 18 March 1974.

33. Owusu Sadaukai, Letter to Amiri Baraka, c. 1973, Amiri Baraka Collection, Moorland-Spingarn Research Center, Howard University, Washington, D.C.

34. Bert J. Thomas, "Caribbean Black Power: From Slogan to Practical Politics," *Journal of Black Studies* 22, no. 3 (1992): 392–410; William R. Lux, "Black Power in the Caribbean," *Journal of Black Studies* 3, no. 2 (1972): 207–25.

35. Walter Rodney, *People's Power: No Dictator* (Guyana: Working People's Alliance Press, 1979); Rupert Lewis, *Walter Rodney's Intellectual and Political Thought* (Kingston: University of the West Indies Press with Wayne State University Press, 1998).

36. Thomas, "Caribbean Black Power," 402.

37. See Lewis, *Walter Rodney's Intellectual and Political Thought*; Walter Rodney, *How Europe Underdeveloped Africa* (Washington, D.C.: Howard University Press, 1974).

38. "The Black Scholar interviews: Walter Rodney," *Black Scholar* 6, no. 3 (1974): 39.

39. Ibid., 40.

40. Ibid., 40–41.

41. See Haki Madhubuti, "The Farrakhan Factor: The Questions that Will Not Go Away," in *Claiming Earth: Race, Rage, Rape, Redemption: Blacks Seeking A Culture of Enlightened Empowerment* (Chicago, IL: Third World Press, 1995); "BBB Interviews: Minister Abdul Farrakhan," *Black Books Bulletin* 6, no. 1 (1978): 42–45, 71.

42. James Hoard Smith, "Delegates get disturbed over snub to Farrakhan," *Muhammed Speaks*, 5 April 1974, 10, 14.

43. Quoted in Smith, "Delegates get disturbed," 14. In light of Farrakhan's exclusion, delegates from Arkansas, Colorado, Kansas, and other states drafted a resolution, which read in part: "Since this convention is structured to represent a cross-section of Black people, we feel that in all fairness and justice, it should be resolved that an invitation to present the views of the people they represent be extended to Minister Louis Farrakhan, the National Representative of the Nation of Islam, and Mrs. Beaulah Sanders, national chairlady of the National Welfare Rights Organization … otherwise, a large segment of our people will go unheard. And unless this convention addresses itself to all segments of the Black community, it cannot fulfill the aims and purposes set forth in its by-laws." Despite support from some delegates, this resolution was not selected by the resolutions committee for inclusion within the ten-item agenda finally ratified by the Little Rock Convention.

44. Amiri Baraka, "Why I Changed My Ideology: Black Nationalism and Socialist Revolution," *Black World* 24 (1975): 30–42; see Amiri Baraka, "The National Black Assembly and the Black Liberation Movement," *Black World* (March 1975) 23.

45. Baraka, "The National Black Assembly and the Black Liberation," 23; Baraka expanded this critique of black indigenous control to the international arena: "Certainly we must be enlightened by the neo-colonial development of the late Sixties and Seventies, when in state houses all over the world there are 'colored' collaborators with imperialism who trick their people into thinking they have achieved national independence, when all that has happened is that some new junior partners of world imperialism have been sworn in … The only thing that has changed is the 'complexion of Tyranny.' … A Black bureaucratic elite abounds—but no change for the masses." Amiri Baraka, "Nationalism, Pan-Africanism, Socialism: Toward Ideological Clarity," *Black World* (November 1974): 24–33, 84; Amiri Baraka, "Needed: A Revolutionary Strategy," *Black Scholar* 7 (1975): 42–45.

46. See Van Gosse, "Locating the Black Intellectual: An Interview with Harold Cruse," *Radical History Review* 71 (1998): 96–120; Harold Cruse, "The National Black Convention At Little Rock," *Black World* 23, no. 12 (1974): 10–17; Harold Cruse, "The National Black Convention at Little Rock, Part II," *Black World* (November 1974): 83–88.

47. Amiri Baraka, *The Autobiography of LeRoi Jones/Amiri Baraka* (New York: Freundlich Books, 1984), 120–23.

48. Amiri Baraka, "Black Nationalism: 1972," *Black Scholar* 4, no. 1 (1972): 23–29.

49. Ibid., 23.

50. Baraka, "Black Nationalism: 1972," 24.

51. By culturalism, I am referring to the hypostatization of culture and by exten-sion, the depoliticization of cultural practices. In his study of the movimento negro in Rio de Janeiro and Sao Paulo, Brazil, Michael George Hanchard defines culturalism as follows: "the equation of cultural practices with the material, expressive, artifactual elements of cultural production, and the neglect of normative and political aspects of the cultural process. Within culturalist politics, cultural practices operate as ends in themselves rather than as a means to more comprehensive, heterogeneous set of ethico-political activities." See Michael George Hanchard, *Orpheus and Power* (Princeton, NJ: Princeton University Press, 1994) 21.

52. Amiri Baraka, "The Congress of Afrikan People: A Position Paper," *Black Scholar* 6, no. 5 (1975): 2–15.

53. Baraka, "Why I Changed My Ideology," 30–31.

54. Phil Hutchings, "Report on the ALSC National Conference," *Black Scholar* 5, no. 10 (1974): 48–53.

55. Clayborne Carson, *In Struggle: SNCC and the Black Awakening of the 1960s* (Cambridge, MA: Harvard University Press, 1981), 269–70.

56. Julius Hobson, "Black Power: Right or Left," in *The Black Power Revolt: A Collection of Essays,* ed. Floyd Barbour (Boston, MA: Porter Sargent Press, 1968).

57. See Kathleen Cleaver and George Katsiaficas, eds., *Liberation, Imagination, and the Black Panther Party* (New York: Routledge, 2001); Charles Jones, ed., *The Black Panther Party (Reconsidered)* (Baltimore: Black Classic Press, 1998); Scott Brown, *Fighting for US: Maulana Karenga, the US Organization, and Black Cultural Nationalism* (New York: New York University Press, 2003).

58. Harold Cruse, *The Crisis of the Negro Intellectual* (New York: William Morrow, 1967); Robert Chrisman, "The Crisis of Harold Cruse," *Black Scholar* 1, no. 1 (1969); Robert Chrisman, "The Contradictions of Harold Cruse: Or Cruse's Blues, Take 2," *Black World* 20, no. 7 (1971); Ernest Kaiser, "The Crisis of the Negro Intellec-tual," *Freedomways* 9, no. 1 (1969).

59. Other Marxist and Nationalist polemics from this period include the follow-ing: Earl Ofari, "Marxism-Leninism: The Key to Black Liberation," *Black Scholar* 4, no. 1 (1972): 35–46; Tony Thomas, "Black Nationalism and Confused Marxists," *Black Scholar* 4, no. 1 (1972): 47–52; Maulana Ron Karenga, "Which Road: National-ism, Pan-Africanism, Socialism?" *Black Scholar* 6, no. 2 (1974): 21–74.

60. See Haki Madhubuti, "Enemy: From the White Left, White Right and In-Between," *Black World* 23, no. 12 (October 1974): 36–47; Haki Madhubuti, "The Latest Purge: The Attack on Black Nationalism and Pan-Afrikanism by the New Left, the Sons and Daughters of the Old Left," *Black Scholar* (September 1974): 43–56; Haki Madhubuti, "What is Being Done to Save the Black Race," *Black Books Bulletin* 2 (1974): 50.

61. Baraka, "The National Black Assembly and Black Liberation," 24.

62. Madhubuti, "Latest Purge," 43–44.

63. Ibid., 46.

64. Carlos Moore, *Were Marx and Engels White Racists? The Prolet-Aryan Out-look of Marx and Engels* (Chicago, IL: Institute of Positive Education, 1972).

65. Ronald Walters, "A Response to Haki Madhubuti," *Black Scholar* 6, no. 2 (October 1974): 47–49; Ronald Walters, "African American Nationalism: Toward a

Unifying Ideology," *Black World* 22 (1973): 9; See also Ronald W. Walters, "Marxism-Leninism and the Black Revolution: A Critical Essay," in *Black Separatism and Social Reality: Rhetoric and Reason,* ed. Raymond L. Hall (New York: Pergamon Press, 1977).

66. Kalamu Ya Salaam, "A Response to Haki Madhubuti," *Black Scholar* 6, no. 5 (1975): 40–43; Mary Ellison, "Kalamu Ya Salaam and the Black Blues Subversive Self," *Race & Class* 45, no. 1 (2003): 79–97.

67. Salaam, "A Response to Haki Madhubuti," 40–43.

68. Anise, "The Tyranny of a Purist Ideology," 18–27; S.E. Anderson, "A Response to Haki Madhubuti," *Black Scholar* 6, no. 2 (1974): 50–51; Alonzo 4X (Cannady), "A Response to Haki Madhubuti," *Black Scholar* 6, no. 2 (1974): 52–53.

69. Mark Smith, "A Response to Haki Madhubuti," *Black Scholar* 6, no. 5 (1975): 44–53.

70. Alonzo 4X, "A Response to Haki Madhubuti," 52.

71. Quoted in Ibid.

72. Madhubuti, "Latest Purge," 49–50.

73. Daryl Michael Scott, *Contempt and Pity: Social Policy and the Image of the Damaged Black Psyche 1880–1996* (Chapel Hill, NC: University of North Carolina Press, 1997).

74. Haki Madhubuti, *From Plan to Planet* (Detroit: Broadside, 1973), 69.

75. Doug Glasgow, *The Black Underclass: Poverty, Unemployment and Entrapment of Ghetto Youth* (San Francisco: Jossey-Bass Publishers, 1980); Ken Auletta, *The Underclass* (New York: Random House, 1982); William Julius Wilson, *The Truly Disadvantaged: The Inner City, the Underclass, and Public Policy* (Chicago, IL: University of Chicago Press, 1987); William Julius Wilson, *When Work Disappears: The World of the New Urban Poor* (New York: Random House, 1997); Nicholas Lemann, *The Promised Land: The Great Black Migration and How It Changed America* (New York: Alfred A. Knopf Inc., 1991); Charles Murray, *Losing Ground: American Social Policy, 1950–1980* (New York: Basic Books, 1984); Mickey Kaus, "The Work Ethic State," *The New Republic,* 7 July 1986: 22–33; Mickey Kaus, *The End of Equality* (New York: Basic Books, 1992); For critiques of underclass rhetoric of liberal and conservative thinkers, see Adolph Reed, Jr., "The Underclass as Myth and Symbol," in *Stirrings in the Jug: Black Politics in the Post-Segregation Era* (Minneapolis, MN: University of Minnesota Press, 1999), 179–96; Adolph Reed, Jr., "The Liberal Technocrat," *The Nation,* 2 February 1988; Herbert J. Gans, "Deconstructing the Underclass: The Term's Dangers as a Planning Concept," *Journal of the American Planning Association* 56, no. 3 (1990): 271–77; Ruth Conniff, "The Culture of Cruelty," *The Progressive* 56 (September 1992): 16–20; Carole Marks, "The Urban Underclass," *Annual Review of Sociology* 17 (1991): 445–66; Leslie Innis and Joe R. Feagin, "The Black 'Underclass' Ideology in Race Relations Analysis," *Social Justice* 16 (1989): 13–33.

76. See Anderson, "A Response to Haki Madhubuti," 51.

77. Cruse, *The Crisis of the Negro Intellectual*; James Boggs, *The American Revolution: Pages from a Negro Worker's Notebook* (New York: Monthly Review Press, 1963); James Boggs and Grace Lee Boggs, *Revolution and Evolution in the Twentieth Century* (New York: Monthly Review Press, 1974).

78. Smith, "A Response to Haki Madhubuti," 52.

79. Stanley Aronowitz, "Mass Culture and the Eclipse of Reason: Implications for Pedagogy," *College English* 38, no. 8 (1977): 768–74.

80. Although Mao's dictum came to be used as a means of enforcing the authority of charismatic, elite intellectuals within American black radical circles during the sixties and seventies, his original utterance was ostensibly more democratic. Although history would take a different turn, his initial assertion was that the power and authority of Communist party elites should always be in tune with and responsive to the objective conditions, experiences, and interests of working people. See Mao Tse-Tung, "Preface and Postscript to Rural Surveys," *The Selected Works of Mao Tse-Tung* 3 (1941): 13; Also, Mao Tse-Tung, *On Practice and Contradiction* (London and New York: Verso, 2007), 43–51.

81. Morris, *The Origins of the Civil Rights Movement*; Charles Payne, *I've Got the Light of Freedom: The Organizing Tradition and the Mississippi Freedom Struggle* (Berkeley, CA: University of California Press, 1995); Carson, *In Struggle*; Barbara Ransby, *Ella Baker and the Black Freedom Movement: A Radical Democratic Vision* (Chapel Hill, NC: University of North Carolina Press, 2003); Harold F. Smith, "Thoughts of Being Free Has Entered Many Minds: SNCC and the Process of Community Education, 1960–1966" (PhD diss., Harvard University, 2000); Myles Horton and Paulo Friere, *We Make the Road by Walking: Conversations on Education and Social Change* (Philadelphia, PA: Temple University Press, 1991); Myles Horton, *The Long Haul: An Autobiography* (New York: Teachers College Press, 1997).

82. Gwendolyn Patton, "Open Letter to Marxists," *Black Scholar* 6, no. 7 (1975): 50–52.

83. Patton, "Open Letter," 52.

84. Quoted in Salaam, "Tell No Lies," 30.

85. Ibid.

86. Ibid., 32–33.

87. Ibid., 33.

88. Salaam defines culture as "the concrete and historical manifestation (on a day-to-day basis supported and maintained through institutions and ideologies) of the productive forces (people, tools, and environment) of *a given race or nationality* at a given point in history." [emphasis mine] See Salaam, "A Response to Haki Madhubuti," 41.

89. Frances Cress Welsing, *The Isis (Yssis) Papers: The Keys to the Colors* (Chicago, IL: Third World Press, 1991); Frances Cress Welsing, "The Mother Fucker and the Original Mother, Fucker in the White Supremacy System and Culture," *Black Books Bulletin* 4, no. 3 (1976): 18–24; Frances Cress Welsing, "The Concept and the Color of God and Black Mental Health," *Black Books Bulletin* 7, no. 1 (1980): 27–29, 35.

90. Molefi Kete Asante, *The Afrocentric Idea* (Philadelphia, PA: Temple University Press, 1987); Molefi Kete Asante, "Afrocentricity, Race and Reason," *Race and Reason* 1, no. 1 (1994): 21; Molefi Kete Asante, *Kemet, Afrocentricity, and Knowledge* (Trenton, NJ: Africa World Press, 1990); Molefi Kete Asante, *Malcolm X as Cultural Hero and Other Afrocentric Essays* (Trenton, NJ: Africa World Press, 1993); Marimba Ani, *Yurugu: An African-Centered Critique of European Cultural Thought and Behavior* (Trenton, NJ: Africa World Press, 1994). For critiques of Afrocentricism, see Wilson Jeremiah Moses, *Afrotopia: the Roots of African American Popular History*

(New York: Cambridge University Press, 1998); Dean E. Robinson, *Black Nationalism in American Politics and Thought* (New York: Cambridge University Press, 2001).

91. Ofari, "Marxism-Leninism," 44.

92. Baraka, "The National Black Assembly and Black Liberation," 24.

93. Smith, "A Response to Haki Madhubuti," 46.

94. Baraka, "The National Black Assembly and Black Liberation," 25.

95. Kenneth Kusmer, "African Americans in the City Since World War II: From the Industrial to the Postindustrial era," *The New African American Urban History*, ed. Kenneth Goings and Raymond A. Mohl (Thousand Oaks, CA: Sage Publications, 1996), 328–29; Thomas Sugrue, *The Origins of the Urban Crisis: Race and Inequality in Postwar Detroit* (Princeton, NJ: Princeton University Press, 1996), 125–52; Barry Bluestone and Bennett Harrison, *The Deindustrialization of America: Plant Closings, Community Abandonment and the Dismantling of Basic Industry* (New York: Basic Books, 1982); Antonio Negri, *The Politics of Subversion: A Manifesto for the Twenty-First Century* (Malden, MA: Polity Press, 2005); Antonio Negri, "Archeology and Project: The Mass Worker and the Social Worker," in *Revolution Retrieved: Selected Writings on Marx, Keynes, Capitalist Crisis and New Social Subjects* (London: Red Notes, 1988); David Harvey, *The Condition of Postmodernity: An Inquiry into the Origins of Cultural Change* (Oxford: Blackwell Publishers, 1989).

96. Gérard Duménil and Dominique Lévy, "The Neoliberal (Counter) Revolution," in *Neoliberalism: A Critical Reader*, ed. Alfredo Saad-Filho and Deborah Johnston (London: Pluto Press, 2005), 9–19.

97. Ibid., 329.

98. Frantz Fanon, *Wretched of the Earth* (New York: Grove Press, 1963), 44–48, 59–62; Amilcar Cabral, *Revolution in Guinea: Selected Texts* (New York: Monthly Review Press, 1969); Basil Davidson, "On Revolutionary Nationalism: The Legacy of Cabral," *Race & Class* 27, no. 3 (1986): 21–45.

99. Manning Marable, *Blackwater: Historical Studies in Race, Class Consciousness and Revolution* (Dayton, Ohio: Black Praxis Press, 1981), 112; Madhubuti, *Claiming Earth*, 67–68.

5. Radical Departures: The National Black Political Assembly, the National Black Independent Political Party, and the Struggle for Alternatives

1. Curt Gentry, *The Last Days of the Great State of California* (New York: Ballantine, 1968).

2. Angela Y. Davis, *Angela Davis: An Autobiography* (New York: Bantam, 1974), 215–225.

3. Stephan Lesher, *George Wallace: American Populist* (Reading, MA: Addison-Wesley, 1994); Jody Carlson, *George Wallace and the Politics of Powerlessness: The Wallace Campaigns for the Presidency, 1964–1976* (New Brunswick: Transaction, 1981); Dan Carter, *From George Wallace to Newt Gingrich: Race in the Conservative Counterrevolution, 1963–1994* (Baton Rouge: Louisiana State University, 1996); Dan Carter, *The Politics of Rage: George Wallace, the Origins of the New Conservatism and the Transformation of American Politics* (Baton Rouge: Louisiana State University, 2000); Dan Carter, *George Wallace, Richard Nixon and the Transformation of American Politics* (Waco, TX: Markham Press Fund, 1992); Barry Goldwater, *The Conscience of a Conservative* (New York: Victor

Publishing, 1971); Rick Perlstein, *Before the Storm: Barry Goldwater and the Unmaking of the American Consensus* (New York: Hill and Wang, 2001).

4. Kathryn Flewellen, "The National Black Independent Political Party: Will History Repeat?" *Freedomways* 48, no. 1 (1981): 11.

5. Mashariki Kurudisha, memorandum to Ron Daniels (c. March 1979), 1.

6. Ibid., 2.

7. See Matthew Holden, *The Politics of the Black "Nation"* (New York: Chandler, 1973); Theophilus Herrington, "National Black Political Conventions and Black Politics, 1830–1976" (PhD diss., University of Illinois, 1977–1978); Robert C. Smith, *We Have No Leaders* (Albany: State University of New York, 1996), 123; Adolph Reed Jr., "Demobilization in the New Black Political Regime: Ideological Capitulation and Radical Failure in the Postsegregation Era," in *The Bubbling Cauldron: Race, Ethnicity and the Urban Crisis*, eds Michael Peter Smith and Joe R. Feagin (Minneapolis: University of Minnesota, 1995), 195.

8. National Black Political Convention, *National Black Political Agenda* (Washington, D.C.: National Black Political Convention, 1972).

9. Paulette Pierce, "Neglected Legacy: The Black Power Movement and Jesse Jackson's Presidential Campaigns," *Humanity and Society* 16, no. 1 (1992): 21–39.

10. "First Black Assembly Called Here," *Chicago Daily News*, October 10, 1972, 17; "Black Group Opens Session with Unity," *Washington Sunday Star*, October 22, 1972, A10.

11. Paul Delaney, "Black Assembly Seeks Wider Support," *New York Times*, October 23, 1972, 24.

12. "Building the Black Assembly: People Meet by Districts in N.C.," *African World*, September 30, 1972, 3.

13. Harold Cruse, "The Little Rock National Black Political Convention," *Black World* (October–November 1974): 10–17, 83–88; Harold 4X, James H. Smith and Minister George 4X, "Pan Africanists plus Arab Issue Agitate Elusive Unity at Second National Black Political Convention," *Muhammad Speaks*, April 5, 1974, 10–11.

14. Paul Delaney, "Diggs to Resign as Unity Eludes Black Convention," *Washington Star News*, March 15, 1974, 1.

15. Quoted in Harold 4X, James H. Smith and Minister George 4X, "Pan-Africanists plus Arab Issue Agitate Elusive Unity," 10.

16. Quoted in Norman Oliver, "Need for Independent Party Raised at National Black Political Convention," *The Militant*, March 29, 1974.

17. Barbara Campbell, "Little Rock Chosen for March Parley on Black Politics," *New York Times*, December 28, 1973, 55.

18. "Second Black Political Confab to be held in Little Rock," *Jet*, January 24, 1974, 7.

19. The following workshops were offered in the electoral politics tract: (1) *Campaign Organization*—Jeledi Majadi, CFUN; (2) *Voter Registration*—Ed Anderson, American Federation of State, County and Municipal Employees, and Julia Carson, Indiana; (3) *Campaign Finance*—Congressman John Conyers; (4) *Party Involvement*—Frank Cowan, National Democratic Party; (5) *Election Day Activities*, Mayor A.J. Cooper; (6) *Preliminary Planning*—Dr. Ronald Walters, Howard University; and (7) *Basic Campaign strategies*—Philip W. Carter, University of Pittsburgh.

20. Albert Green, interview with the author, March 12, 1999, New Orleans, Louisiana, 17; Yolanda Robinson, interview with the author, August 20, 1999, Columbus, Ohio.

21. "The Louisiana Black Assembly," *Black Agenda* (Spring 1980): 3–4, 6.

22. William E. Nelson, interview with the author, August 20, 1999, Columbus, Ohio.

23. "OBPA Sponsors Community Forum," Press Release, Columbus Chapter of the Ohio Black Political Assembly (April 1979).

24. Testimony of William E. Nelson Jr., Ohio Senate Judiciary Committee on Senate Bill 61 dealing with Police Use of Deadly Force, May 2, 1979, in possession of the author.

25. Nelson, interview with the author, 1999.

26. Talaamu Holiday, interview with the author, Brooklyn, New York, November 16, 1999: 20. Holiday's reflections on his work during the mid-seventies offer some insight into the level of intensity and commitment displayed by Assembly workers in their efforts to develop strong state and local organizations. A veteran of CFUN and CAP activism, Holiday had been intimately involved with Newark area radical activism since the late 1960s. He recalls the grueling work schedule that occupied a typical weekend as state chairperson: "I would leave on a Saturday morning at 5:30 am and I would drive from Newark to Atlantic City/Pleasantville area, which is in the southern most part of Jersey. And come back up and meet in Camden. Leave Camden, have a meeting in Trenton. Leave Trenton, meet in New Brunswick. Leave New Brunswick, meet in Elizabeth. Leave Elizabeth go to Jersey City. Leave Jersey City go to Patterson. Leave Patterson go to the Englewood-Teaneck area where we had organized folks for the National Black Political Convention. We had spread the word. We had four or five CAP cadres going on in New Jersey at one time. . . . We also did training through the Political School of Kawaida."

27. Reverend Albert McKnight, interview with the author, Opelousas, Louisiana, March 11, 1999, 7.

28. Quoted in Harold 4X, "Black Assembly Crumbling: 'Romantic Revolutionaries' Undermine National Unity," *Muhammed Speaks*, August 29, 1975, 5.

29. Boyd Lewis, "Muslims, Marxists Clash at Conference," *Atlanta Voice*, August 9, 1975, 1, 5.

30. Harold 4X, "Black Assembly Crumbling," 5.

31. John W. Lewis Jr., "Baraka May Be Ousted from Assembly Post," *Pittsburgh Courier*, February 15, 1975, 1, 31; "State Rep. Atkins Quits Black Assembly Post," *Jet*, February 25, 1975.

32. Hannah Atkins, interview with the author, by telephone, 8 November, 2000; Hannah Atkins, "Why I Resigned from the NBPA," *Black World* (October 1975): 44–46.

33. Lewis Jr., "Baraka May Be Ousted," 1.

34. Ron Daniels, "Some Reflections on the Ohio Black Political Assembly on the Occasion of its First Reunion," unpublished paper, September 17, 1988, in the author's possession.

35. Quoted in Atkins, "Why I Resigned from the NBPA," 45–46.

36. Amiri Baraka, "The National Black Assembly and the Black Liberation Movement," *Black World* (March 1975): 22–27.

37. "2 Line Struggle Heats Up National Black Assembly," *Unity and Struggle* (April 1975): 1, 6, 12.

38. Michael L. Culbert, "Black Press Complains Convention Disrespect," *Muhammed Speaks,* April 5, 1974, 10, 14.

39. Adolph Reed Jr., "The Allure of Malcolm X and the Changing Character of Black Politics," in *Stirrings in the Jug: Black Politics in the Post Segregation Era* (Minneapolis: University of Minnesota, 1999).

40. See Sara Evans, *Personal Politics: The Roots of Women's Liberation in the Civil Rights Movement and the New Left* (New York: Vintage, 1980), 87–88; In his best-selling book, *Soul on Ice,* Cleaver wrote: "I became a rapist. To refine my technique and modus operandi, I started out by practicing on black girls in the ghetto . . . and when I considered myself smooth enough, I crossed the tracks and sought out white prey. I did this consciously, deliberately, willfully, methodically. . . . Rape was an insurrectionary act. It delighted me that I was defying and trampling on the white man's law, on his system of values, and I was defiling his woman—and this point, I believe, was the most satisfying to me because I was very resentful over the histori-cal fact of how the white man has used the black woman. I felt I was getting revenge." See Eldridge Cleaver, *Soul on Ice* (New York: Dell, 1968), 14.

41. See Lee Rainwater and William L. Yancey, eds *The Moynihan Report and the Politics of Controversy* (Cambridge, MA: MIT, 1967), 3, 5–6.

42. For more regarding Daniel Patrick Moynihan's controversial study of the black family and its implications for both black public debate and American social policy, see *The Negro Family: A Case for National Action* (Washington, D.C.: Office of Policy Planning and Research, March 1965); Rainwater and Yancey, *The Moynihan Report*; Daryl Michael Scott, *Contempt and Pity: Social Policy and the Image of the Damaged Black Psyche, 1880–1996* (Chapel Hill: University of North Carolina, 1997); Alice O'Connor, *Poverty Knowledge: Social Science, Social Policy and the Poor in Twentieth-Century U.S. History* (Princeton: Princeton University, 2001), 203–210; Michael B. Katz, *The Undeserving Poor: From the War on Poverty to the War on Welfare* (New York: Pantheon, 1989).

43. Jerry Gafio Watts, *Amiri Baraka: The Politics and Art of a Black Intellectual* (New York: New York University Press, 2001), 291–324; Komozi Woodard, *A Nation within a Nation* (Chapel Hill: University of North Carolina, 1999), 49–90; Amiri Baraka, *Kawaida Studies: The New Nationalism* (Chicago: Third World, 1972).

44. Maulana Ron Karenga, "Marriage," no date, Amiri Baraka papers, Moorland-Spingarn Collection, Howard University, unprocessed; see Jerry Watts, "The Slave as Master: Black Nationalism, Kawaida and the Repression of Women," in *Amiri Baraka: The Politics and Art of a Black Intellectual* (New York: New York University Press, 2001); Jennifer Jordan, "Cultural Nationalism in the 1960s: Politics and Poetry," in *Race, Politics and Culture,* ed. Adolph Reed Jr. (New York: Greenwood, 1986).

45. Karenga, "Marriage," 7.

46. Woodard, *A Nation within a Nation,* 180–84.

47. Carol Mueller, "Ella Baker and the Origins of 'Participatory Democracy'," in *Women in the Civil Rights Movement: Trailblazers and Torchbearers, 1941–1965,* ed. Vicki L. Crawford, Jacqueline Anne Rouse and Barbara Woods (New York: Carlson, 1990); Sara Evans, *Personal Politics*; Belinda Robnett, *How Long? How Long? African American Women in the Struggle for Civil Rights* (New York: Oxford University, 1997).

48. Amiri Baraka, "Women's Concerns in the National Black Assembly," *National Black Political Assembly Newsletter* (November 1975): 7–8.

49. Mashariki Kurudisha, memo to "All Interested Black Women," 1975.

50. Ibid., 3–4.

51. "An Open Letter from Concerned NBA Members," September 29, 1975, Amiri Baraka Collection, Moorland-Spingarn Research Center, Howard University, Washington, D.C., unprocessed. This letter was signed by the following Assembly leaders: Ron Daniels; Riley Smith Jr., Chairperson, National Support Committee; Ralph Clarke, Ohio Black Assembly; George Hopkinson, Chairperson, Economic Conference; Jemadari Kazawa, Chairperson, Research and Strategy Committee; William A. Sanders Jr., Chairperson, D.C. Black Assembly; M. Henderson, Co-Chairperson, Convention Planning Committee; Mtangulizi Sanyika (formerly Hayward Henry), Chairperson, '76 Strategy Committee; Mashariki Kurudisha, Member, Executive Council; Lois DeBerry, State Representative, Tennessee Black Assembly; Reverend Albert McKnight, Chairperson, Louisiana Black Assembly; Bob Young, Chairperson, Massachusetts Black Assembly; John Warfield, Member of Executive Council; Wally Stewart, Chairperson, New York Black Assembly; James Heiglyer, Chairperson, Convention Planning Committee; and Imani Kazana, Chairperson, '76 Fund Raising Committee.

52. Vernon Jarrett, "Black Assembly Tries to Regroup," *Chicago Tribune*, November 19, 1975.

53. *National Black Political Assembly Newsletter* (November 1975), 1.

54. Mashariki Kurudisha, telephone interview with the author, January 20, 2000, 4.

55. "NBA: 'The Dayton Strategy' and the March of the Compradors," *Unity and Struggle* (November 1975): 1, 4–5; "Amiri Baraka Resigns as Secretary General of the National Black Assembly: CAP Calls for Intensification of Struggle inside the National Black Assembly," *Unity and Struggle* (November 1975): 12, 6–7.

56. "Amiri Baraka Resigns," 6.

57. Ronald Walters, "The New Black Political Culture," *Black World* (October 1972): 4–17.

58. When Cleaver returned to the United States from exile, he renounced his radical past and became a born-again Christian and vocal Cold Warrior. Owusu Sadaukai's transformation was less dramatic but nonetheless puzzling for some of his old comrades. He returned to using his birth name, Howard Fuller, obtained an education doctorate and channeled his desire to end racial inequality toward public education issues. During the early 1990s, Fuller served as superintendent for Milwaukee public schools. He pioneered Milwaukee's Parental Choice Program and led of the Black Alliance for Educational Options, Through these efforts, he arose as the foremost African American proponent of school vouchers. Touted by the New Right as a solution to urban inequality, this policy program allows parents in poorly performing districts to move their children to private or suburban schools. See Alex Willingham, "California Dreaming: Eldridge Cleaver's Epithet to the Activism of the Sixties," *Endarch* 1 (Winter 1976): 1–23.

59. "National Black Assembly Position on the 1976 National Elections," *Unity and Struggle* (July 1975).

60. "Ron Daniels Interview—The National Black Political Assembly: Its Position, Its Future," *Black World* 24, no. 12 (October 1975): 28–34.

61. Baxter Smith, "Black Convention Debates Electoral Action," *The Militant,* April 9, 1976.

62. Ronald V. Dellums, *Lying Down with the Lions: A Public Life from the Streets of Oakland to the Halls of Power* (Boston: Beacon, 2000).

63. Ron Daniels, "Some Reflections on the Ohio Black Political Assembly."

64. Thomas A. Johnson, "Black Political Convention Begins Petition Campaign," *New York Times,* March 21, 1976, 42.

65. Ron Daniels, "The National Black Political Assembly: Building Independent Black Politics in the 1980s," *Black Scholar* (March–April 1980): 32–42.

66. Ibid., 36–38.

67. Thomas A. Johnson, "Rep. Dellums Rejects Third Party Draft; Black Convention Still Plans to Name a Candidate," *New York Times,* March 22, 1976, 18; Peter Millius, "Dellums Hesitating on Bid by Black Party," *Washington Post,* March 20, 1976, A5; Peter Millius, "Rep. Dellums Declines Bid by 3d Party," *Washington Post,* March 21, 1976, A13; Peter Millius, "Dellums Declines 3d Party Bid," *Washington Post,* March 22, 1976, A2.

68. Millius, "Dellums Declines 3d Party Bid," A2.

69. Millius, "Dellums Hesitating," A5.

70. Millius, "Rep. Dellums Declines Bid," A13; Peter Millius, "Black Assembly Still a Force in Politics," *Washington Post,* March 23, 1976, A4; William Raspberry, "Candidates and Blacks," *Washington Post,* March 29, 1976, A19.

71. "Black Party Nominates Kirkpatrick," *Washington Post,* June 19, 1976, A5.

72. Lance Hill, *The Deacons for Defense: Armed Resistance and the Civil Rights Movement* (Chapel Hill: University of North Carolina, 2004).

73. Ronald W. Walters, "Black Presidential Politics in 1980: Bargaining or Begging?" *Black Scholar* (March–April 1980): 22–31; Ron Daniels, "Revitalizing Independent Black Politics: Towards a Strategy for 1980 and beyond," unpublished position paper, n.d.; Ron Daniels, "Towards a Structural Design for an Independent National Black Political Party," unpublished position paper, n.d., in the author's possession.

74. Herb Boyd, "Black Assembly Plans Conference," *Detroit Free Press,* March 4, 1979; Summary of NBPA Executive Council and State Chairpersons Meeting (March 1979), Yolanda Robinson, personal papers, Columbus, Ohio.

75. Harold Cruse, "The Black Political Process—Myth or Reality. A Theoretical Analysis," *Afro-American Communicator* 1, no.1 (1979): 1–13.

76. Quoted in Pierce, "Neglected Legacy," 35.

77. "Blacks to Form a Party," *Times-Picayune,* August 24, 1980, 1; Roger Wilkins, "Blacks Look outside Two Parties in Search of Influence," *Washington Star,* October 24, 1980.

78. Albert J. McKnight, interview with the author, 5.

79. Quoted in Manning Marable, "Toward a Black Political Party: Report on the New Orleans Black Political Convention," in *The National Black Political Party: An Important Step forward for Blacks and Other American Workers,* Nan Bailey, Malik Miah and Mac Warren (New York: Pathfinder, 1981).

80. Manning Marable, "Black Political Party Launched," press release, National Black Political Party (August 1980); "New Political Party Formed as Voice for Minorities," *New York Times*, August 25, 1980, A18. The resolution which gave birth to what would become NBIPP read as follows: "(1) The National Black Political Convention declares today, August 23, 1980 the creation of an Independent National Black Political Party, and we call upon all those organizations and concerned Black people within the Black Nation who share our fervent desire to build the Party to join with us in this endeavor; and, we hereby issue a mandate to the NBPA to spearhead that effort. (2) That the function of the Independent National Black Political Party is to advance a politics of social transformation and self-determination for the Black Nation and that the party will be a community-building, nation building party, primarily devoted to infrastructural, institutional and organizational development within the Black Community providing community services, engaging in community struggles, lobbying around private and public policy issues and electoral issues."

81. Ron Goldwyn, "Black Political Group Is Urging Vote, but Skip the President," *Philadelphia Bulletin*, September 7, 1980; Jovida Joylette, "Don't Vote for President, New Black Party Urges," *Philadelphia Tribune*, September 7, 1980; "Independent National Black Party Has Some Good Ideas," *Philadelphia Tribune*, September 12, 1980.

82. Isaiah Poole, "Swing to the Left," *Black Enterprise* (February 1981): 20; "1000 Meet to Found National Black Party and Plan Its Agenda," *New York Times*, November 23, 1980; Flewellen, "The National Black Independent Political Party"; Manning Marable, "NBIPP: A Short History, 1980–1981," unpublished paper, August 6, 1981.

83. Flewellen, "National Black Independent Political Party," 101; Marable, "NBIPP," 5–6; The precise fashion in which this survey was conducted is not clear—historian Manning Marable asserts that it was "informal" and neither "scientific nor all inclusive." Nonetheless, in postconvention reports and articles, organizers and party supporters cited the findings as a generally faithful representation of the meeting's demographic and ideological composition. Over 90% of the delegation was between the ages 18 and 40. Over 69% was college educated and worked in a professional career. With regard to partisanship, 67% said they identified with neither party. 78% self-identified as Pan-Africanists and/or Black Nationalists. Yet also among the delegates in sizable numbers were members of socialist and communist organizations, including the Democratic Socialist Organizing Committee, the New American Movement, the Socialist Worker's Party, Communist Worker's Party, the Communist Party USA and the Young Socialist Alliance. Regarding the convention's ideological diversity, Marable claims that there were three broad approaches concerning the issue of black economic development—(1) advocates of economic democracy as conceived by Tom Hayden and the California Campaign for Economic democracy; (2) advocates of Ujamaa or African Socialism which encouraged formation of black consumer and producer cooperatives and black land ownership; and (3) proponents of Marxism/Socialist revolution. In spite of these variations, he concludes the delegation was definitely anti-capitalist in character. Not surprisingly, 95% of those polled supported the statement that "America's economic system was not working on behalf of black people." The delegation also contained a considerable portion of newcomers to the independent black politics movement with 59% reporting that they had not attended a political convention of this type previously and only 5% having attended the 1972 Gary Convention.

84. National Black Independent Political Party Convention, Minutes (November 1980), 2. The Pennsylvania delegates defended their choice for the new party's title with the following reasoning: "national would explain the scope and attempt to build a national organization. Black because African's identify with that here. Independent to show our own independent party with no permanent friends. Political to speak to the level of discipline."

85. "The Purpose of the NPOC," *NBIP Party Line* 1, no. 1 (1981): 3.

86. For a compelling critique of the effort to bureaucratize gender equality within NBIPP and its limitations, see Paulette Pierce, "Boudoir Politics and the Birthing of the Nation: Sex, Marriage and Structural Deflection in the National Black Independent Political Party," in *Women Out of Place: The Gender of Agency and the Race of Nationality* (New York: Routledge, 1996).

87. Pierce, "Boudoir Politics," 227; NBIPP Promotional Brochure, c. 1981.

88. Pierce, "Boudoir Politics," 228.

89. Ibid., 228–229.

90. Flewellen, "The National Black Independent Political Party," 93–105.

91. Ka (Kathryn) Flewellen, interview with the author, March 23, 2000, Washington, D.C.

92. NBIPP Promotional Brochure, c. 1981.

93. Ibid.

94. Flewellen, "National Black Independent Political Party," 102.

95. Socialist Workers Party, "A Transitional Program for Black Liberation," in *Black Separatism and Social Reality: Rhetoric and Reason,* ed. Raymond Hall (New York: Pergamon, 1977), 101–108. This document was drafted by SWP cadre and adopted by the 23rd National Convention of the Socialist Workers Party in New York City, August 29–September 1, 1969.

96. Phil Hutchings, "Report on the ALSC National Conference," *Black Scholar* (July–August 1974): 48–53.

97. Mac Warren, "National Black Party: Emerging Leadership in the Struggle for Liberation," in *The National Black Political Party,* Nan Bailey, Malik Miah and Mac Warren, 7. The following statement by Mac Warren conveys the general approach to black liberation offered by SWP cadre: "We understood that the fight for Black liberation is a key component of the struggle for socialism in the U.S. We see the American socialist revolution as a combined revolution—workers as a class, fighting for socialism as well as Blacks fighting for socialism and liberation both as workers and as an oppressed nationality. That is, we see the fight for Black liberation bound up with the struggle by workers to take power in this country, to establish a workers government. This is our strategic goal."

98. Barbara Arnwine, Minutes of National Party Organizing Committee, April 11, 1981, 5.

99. Paulette Pierce, "Roots of the Rainbow Coalition," *Black Scholar* (March–April 1988): 2–16; Paulette Pierce, "Neglected Legacy," 21–39; Shiela Collins, *The Rainbow Challenge* (New York: Monthly Review, 1986).

100. Pierce, "Neglected Legacy," 31.

101. See Adolph Reed Jr., *The Jesse Jackson Phenomenon* (New Haven: Yale University, 1986); Robert C. Smith, *We Have No Leaders* (Albany: State University of New York, 1996).

102. Quoted in Pierce, "Neglected Legacy," 30.

103. Toni Morrison, "Clinton as the First Black President," *New Yorker* (October 1998).

Conclusion: The Ends of Black Politics

1. The State of Black America meetings organized by Tavis Smiley produced a best-selling book, *The Covenant with Black America*. This "national plan of action" is clearly descended from the black agenda-setting lineage beginning with the late 1960s Black Power conferences and it inherits their limitations. One problem with this approach, however, is the unquestioned assumption that African Americans represent a cohesive political body whose interests can and should be represented by Smiley and his cohort. In most cases, the policy proposals are reflective of the restraint, taste and idiosyncrasies of a particular stratum of moderate-to-liberal black politicos. The book consists of a series of essays on particular social issues, such as environmental justice, economic prosperity, healthcare and the "digital divide" among others, authored by various policy experts, civil rights leaders and intellectuals. See, Tavis Smiley, *The Covenant with Black America* (Chicago: Third World Press, 2006).

2. William Lucy, "Back to Gary," 34th Annual Convention of the Coalition of Black Trade Unionists; available at http://www.cbtu.org/2003website/2003home.html (accessed July 2, 2005); "Black Labor Calls for New 'Gary' Convention: National Gathering Planned on Broad Black Agenda," *The Black Commentator* available at http://www.blackcommentator.com/140/140_cover_cbtu_pf.html (accessed June 13, 2005).

3. Bill Cosby, "Dr. Bill Cosby Speaks at the 50th Anniversary Commemoration of the Brown v. Topeka Board of Education Supreme Court Decision, May 22, 2004," *Black Scholar* 34, no. 4 (Winter 2004): 2–5.

4. Bill Cosby, *Fatherhood* (New York: Berkley, 1987); Bill Cosby, *Love and Marriage* (New York: Bantam, 1990).

5. Cosby, "Dr. Bill Cosby Speaks," 3.

6. Ta-Nehisi Coates, "Mushmouth Reconsidered," *Village Voice,* July 13, 2004; Ta-Nehisi Coates, "Ebonics! Weird Names! $500 Shoes!" *Village Voice,* May26–June1, 2004; Jabari Asim, "Did Cosby Cross the Line?" *Washington Post,* May 24, 2004; Michael Eric Dyson, *Is Bill Cosby Right or Has the Black Middle Class Lost Its Mind?* (New York: Basic Civitas, 2005); David Kirkland, Jeffrey Robinson, Austin Jackson and Geneva Smitherman, "From 'The Lower Economic': Three Brothas and an Old School Womanist Respond to Dr. Bill Cosby," *Black Scholar* (Winter 2004): 10–15; John Woodford, "Bill Cosby, Education and the Lumpenizing of the Contemporary Black World," *Black Scholar* (Winter 2004): 21–26; Megan Garvey, "Cosby Takes a Stand in Compton," *Los Angeles Times,* October 20, 2005; Norman Kelley, "The Afro-Culture Wars: Bill Cosby vs. Michael Eric Dyson: Cultural Criticism as Pseudo-analysis, Pt. 1," *The Brooklyn Rail* (June 2005).

7. In late fall 2004, Cosby was summoned by Kilpatrick to lead an invitation-only "town hall" meeting to address Detroit's soaring murder rate. Rochelle Riley, "Cosby Bringing Tough Talk to Detroit," *Detroit Free Press* December 17, 2004, 1A, 13A; Johnnetta B. Cole, "On Speaking Truth to Ourselves and Doing Right by Our Children," *Black Scholar* (Winter 2004): 6–9.

8. Spinning his own Horatio Alger tale of inevitable mobility through hard work and determination, Obama celebrated the American Dream in his address to the 2004 DNC. Reflecting on his parents' humble origins—a Kenyan immigrant father and Midwestern white working-class mother—and his own personal triumphs over adversity, Obama concluded "in no other country on earth, is my story even possible." Although he acknowledged the hardships faced by American workers, Obama's speech elided class. According to Obama, "in a generous America you don't have to be rich to achieve your potential." Under such rhetoric, the place of the state recedes in importance as a guarantor of equality of opportunity. Evoking popular neoconservative themes of self-governance and personal responsibility, Obama claimed that, "The people I meet in small towns and big cities, in diners and office parks, they don't expect government to solve all their problems. They know they have to work hard to get ahead and they want to. Go into the collar counties around Chicago, and people will tell you they don't want their tax money wasted by a welfare agency or the Pentagon. Go into any inner city neighborhood, and folks will tell you that government alone can't teach kids to learn. They know that parents have to parent, that children can't achieve unless we raise their expectations and turn off the television sets and eradicate the slander that says a black youth with a book is acting white."

Here, Obama reiterated the popular Right-wing claim that anti-intellectualism among black youth is a driving factor behind scholastic underachievement. Obama elaborated on this claim and spoke approvingly of Cosby's crusade in an interview with celebrity talk show host, Oprah Winfrey. He asserted: "Bill Cosby got into trouble when he said some of these things, and he has a right to say things in ways that I'm not going to because he's an older man. But I completely agree with his underlying premise: We have to change attitudes. There's a strain of anti-intellectualism running in our community that we have to eliminate." See, "The O Interview: Oprah Talks to Barack Obama," O, The Oprah Magazine November 2004, 248–251, 288–292.

9. The historical significance of the 1995 Million Man March was comparable to Booker T. Washington's Atlanta Compromise speech delivered one hundred years earlier. Speaking to a majority white crowd at the 1895 Cotton States and International Exposition, Washington argued against agitation for full citizenship and helped to legitimate the emerging Jim Crow system. In a similar fashion, the Million Man March's emphasis on individual responsibility legitimated the New Right's and the New Democrat's converging assaults on the welfare state. Less than a year after the Million Man March, this broad movement against social liberalism reached its apotheosis with the enactment of the 1996 Personal Responsibility and Work Opportunity Act, which replaced Aid to Families with Dependent Children with a workfare system. For a sampling of key speeches and march propaganda, see, Kim Martin Sadler, ed. Atonement: The Millon Man March (New York: Pilgrim Press, 1996). For critical perspectives on notions of racial self-help and the black manhood rhetoric which undergirded the Million Man March, see, Angela Davis, "Black Nationalism: The Sixties and the Nineties," in The Angela Y. Davis Reader, ed. Joy James (Cambridge, US, and Oxford, UK: Blackwell, 1998); Willie Legette, "The Crisis of the Black Male: A New Ideology in Black Politics," and Preston H. Smith, "'Self Help,' Black Conservatives and the Reemergence of Black Privatism," in Without Justice for All: The New

Liberalism and Our Retreat from Racial Equality, ed. Adolph Reed Jr. (Boulder, CO: Westview, 1999); Nikol G.Alexander, "From Endangerment to Atonement: Reading Gender, Race and Nationalism in the Million Man March," Unpublished Doctoral Dissertation, Rutgers, 1999.

10. "Freedom Agenda (FA) of the Black Radical Congress (BRC) Ratified by the BRC National Council (NC) April 17, 1999, Baltimore, Maryland," *Black Scholar* 35, no. 1 (2005): 31–35.

11. Gerald Horne, "Black Radicals Unite," *Dollars & Sense* (September/October 1998), 219; Angela Ards, "The New Black Radicalism," *The Nation,* July 27, 1998, 19–23; Jennifer Hamer and Helen Neville, "Revolutionary Black Feminism: Toward a Theory of Unity and Liberation," *Black Scholar* 28, no. 3/4 (1998): 22–27; Sundiata Keita Cha-Jua, "the Black Radical Congress and the Reconstruction of the Black Freedom Movement,"*Black Scholar* 28, no. 3/4 (1998): 8–21.

12. Bill Fletcher Jr., "Can Black Radicalism Speak the Voice of Black Workers?" *Race & Class* 40 (1999): 1–14.

13. Ibid., 1–2.

14. Janet Reitman, "Ms. West Goes to Tokyo: A Louisiana Grandmother Battles Big Industry," *Life* 21 (1998): 98–106; Barbara L. Allen, *Uneasy Alchemy: Citizens and Experts in Louisiana's Chemical Corridor Disputes* (Cambridge: MIT press, 2003); Ziba Kashef, "Saving Our Backyard," *Essence* (September 1999): 160; Revathi I. Hines, "African Americans' Struggle for Environmental Justice and the Case of the Shintech Plant: Lessons Learned from a War Waged," *Journal of Black Studies* 31, no. 6 (2001): 777–789.

15. Reitman, "Ms. West Goes to Tokyo," 106.

Index

Cedric Johnson is associate professor of political science at Hobart and William Smith Colleges. His writing has appeared in *New Political Science, Monthly Review,* and *In These Times.*